DC 17

)

THE TORT OF CONVERSION

The legal and commercial importance of the tort of Conversion is difficult to overstate and yet there remains a sense that the principles of the tort are elusive. Most recently, this was illustrated by the difficulties posed for the House of Lords by the Conversion issue in *OBG v Allan* [2007] UKHL 21, on which it was closely divided.

Conversion, as we now recognise it, has a complex pedigree. Showing little regard for received taxonomies, it has elements which make lawyers think in terms of property, despite its eventful descent from actions in personam. Conversion is, therefore, something of a hybrid creature, which perhaps explains the paucity of scholarly analysis of the subject to date, property lawyers and tort lawyers each regarding it as the other's concern.

This book is the first comprehensive appraisal of the modern tort of Conversion. It offers a coherent and accessible rationalisation of the subject, supported by rigorous analysis of all aspects, from title to sue to the available remedies. The principal thesis of the work is that the development of Conversion has somewhat stagnated, and in consequence the tort has so far been unable to fulfil either its theoretical or its practical potential as a legal device. Whilst this is partly a result of historical factors, it is also a consequence of the fact that no systematic examination of the tort in England appears ever to have been carried out. The primary objectives of the book, therefore, are to provide such an analysis, to present Conversion as a useful and important tort, well suited to the demands of contemporary law and commerce, and to offer a principled framework for its future development.

The Tort of Conversion

Sarah Green

and

John Randall

·HART·
PUBLISHING

OXFORD AND PORTLAND, OREGON
2009

Published in North America (US and Canada) by
Hart Publishing
c/o International Specialized Book Services
920 NE 58th Avenue, Suite 300
Portland, OR 97213–3786
USA
Tel: +1 503 287 3093 or toll-free: (1) 800 944 6190
Fax: +1 503 280 8832
E-mail: orders@isbs.com
Website: http://www.isbs.com

Hart Publishing Ltd, 16C Worcester Place, Oxford, OX1 2JW
Telephone: +44 (0)1865 517530 Fax: +44 (0)1865 510710
E-mail: mail@hartpub.co.uk
Website: http://www.hartpub.co.uk

British Library Cataloguing in Publication Data
Data Available

ISBN: 978-1-84113-833-6

Typeset by Column Design Ltd, Reading
Printed and bound in Great Britain by
TJ International Ltd, Padstow, Cornwall

Foreword
by Lord Neuberger of Abbotsbury

The subject of this book is one which is fraught with paradoxes. Every lawyer, whether practitioner, academic or student, knows that the tort of conversion exists, but it is a subject about which very few of us know much, if anything. Conversion is also an issue which frequently requires to be considered in relation to a legal problem or dispute, but, despite the number of legal books that get published these days, it is not the subject of any modern or comprehensive treatment. Further, although it is a tort which has an important part to play in modern society, it has been developed by the judges over the centuries, and therefore it carries an enormous amount of historical baggage—both procedural and substantive. Conversion is also very much of an English law concept, but it has nonetheless been imported into other common law systems. Finally, although a lay person would consider a claim in conversion to be very much of a practical matter, it is hedged around with technicalities and limitations.

In these circumstances, the publication of an authoritative, practical, comprehensive and comprehensible book on the tort of conversion is both very welcome and a great challenge. It is very welcome from the viewpoint of lawyers, whether in the professions, researching and teaching, or studying and learning; indeed, it is very welcome in the public interest. But it is also a great challenge—to anyone embarking on the task of writing such a book. I am delighted to say that Sarah Green and John Randall have risen to the challenge, and have succeeded in producing a book which is thorough but readable, practical but rigorous, comprehensive but engaging, and detailed but well-structured. The authors have rightly cast their net widely, looking not merely at what English judges have said, but also referring to a number of important judgments from judges in other jurisdictions, such as the United States, Canada, and Australia, as well as citing Law Commission reports and learned articles. Further, while stating the law as it is laid down in the cases, the authors quite rightly give their own views as to how the judges (or, failing them, the legislature) should develop, and even change, the law.

Like any common law concept, in order to be properly understood, conversion has to be set in its historical and intellectual context. As reading chapter two demonstrates, the historical context spreads over a long period. The history of the tort, as set out in that chapter, is not only instructive and interesting, but it also provides a vignette of the course of the common law over the centuries. Chapter three discusses the tort in a way which, unusually and interestingly, enables the reader to perceive the difference between a common law system and a civil law system. The chapter additionally enables the reader to understand the tort of conversion in terms of its relationship with other torts, as well as setting out the fundamental components of the tort. The importance and meaning of that difficult concept, 'possession', is also rightly highlighted. Chapter three also helps explain why conversion is concerned with personal property, a theme taken up in chapter four.

Chapter four also contains an impressive explanation as to why there is a doctrine of relativity of title and how it works. The doctrine, which often seems to produce counter-intuitive results in individual cases, is of fundamental importance in a number of areas of law. Chapter five, which deals with the subject matter of conversion, explains the limitations of the reach of the tort, and contains vivid examples of the challenges which are presented to established legal principles by modern developments—whether technological, practical or moral. The discussion relating to digitized products demonstrates the challenges presented by technological change, and the challenge thrown up by a change of practical perception is highlighted by the discussion on intangible rights. And the earlier analysis of the law in relation to the human body contains interesting and challenging material which could be said to reflect technological, practical and moral developments.

The relationship between conversion and economic torts is yet another area which is intellectually demanding and important. The economic torts are probably less well known and less frequently encountered than conversion, although, like conversion, they have recently been attracting attention from academics and judges. In chapter six, the authors explain the law on this topic, and go on to suggest, with considerable force, how the law could—and indeed should—be developed to keep pace with modern commercial standards. The remedies section, chapter seven, discusses topics familiar to lawyers, such as remoteness and foreseeability, in a characteristically illuminating and interesting way.

To write a book which will be of as much interest and help to practical lawyers and judges as to academic lawyers and students is a real achievement. That is all the more true when, as here, the subject matter of the book is deceptively simple on its face, but turns out on examination to be technical and complex. Sarah Green, with her distinguished academic experience, and John Randall, with his justifiably formidable reputation at the Bar, have produced a book which reflects the strengths of both the academic legal world and the practical legal world, while avoiding the weaknesses of either. All lawyers, and their clients and students, have much to thank them for.

David Neuberger
House of Lords, May 2009

Preface

It became obvious to both of us that this was a book which needed to be written. In our respective realms of legal academe and practice, the absence of any extended analysis of the tort of Conversion was both notable and remarkable. It has been a highly rewarding subject to research and to analyse, and one which we hope will appeal more to others as a result of our efforts to present it as a useful and important action. The challenge, as we saw it, was to produce a book which would on the one hand inform and interest legal academics yet, on the other hand, provide a user-friendly, practical resource for busy practitioners. Though maintaining the balance between a scholarly work and a practitioner text has at times proved delicate, in our view we have managed to achieve our desired result. Along the way, this exercise has operated as a powerful practical demonstration of a point which many might acknowledge as a matter of theory, but is far too seldom put into practice: each of the two worlds can benefit enormously from the wisdom and experience of the other.

The final product owes much to the many people who have helped us with this project over the last two years. We acknowledge the contributions of many individuals, and thank them for their invaluable help. Amongst others, we would like to name: Guy Holborn, Catherine McArdle and their colleagues at Lincoln's Inn library, Kate Brookson-Morris, Tanya Corrigan, Caroline Covington and Paul Mora for their tireless research assistance; Andrew Bell, John Bell, Simon Deakin, James Lee, Rob Merkin, John Miller, John Murphy and Djakhongir Saidov, for their incisive comments on various draft chapters; George Applebey, Michael Bridge, Rob Cryer, PJ Denning, Robert Denning, Martin George and William Swadling for their assistance on the matters in which they are expert; and Jonathan Harris for suggesting that someone needed to undertake this project in the first place. We would both also like to express our gratitude to Richard Hart and Rachel Turner at Hart Publishing for their enthusiasm, encouragement and support throughout the writing of this book.

Responsibility for any lapses is, of course, entirely our own. We have endeavoured to state the law as at Easter, 2009.

Personal thanks from Sarah Green

First, thank you to John Randall for being a patient, efficient and good-humoured co-author, for being a fellow pedant, and for proving that, sometimes, two heads are better than one. I would also like to thank many of my colleagues; particularly Sharon Jones, John Baldwin, Claire McIvor, Joanne Thacker, Graham Gee and Kelly Chilton for helping to make Birmingham Law School such a congenial environment in which to write this book, and Jonathan Harris and Sonia Harris-Short for their ongoing advice and guidance, which I value a great deal. Thanks are also most definitely due to Rosie the Ridgeback, without whose hours of peaceful companionship, my work on this book would have been much more solitary, and much less serene, than it in fact was. I owe an enormous debt to my parents, Pat and Terry, for their belief in me and in whatever I choose to do; without them, I would never have been in a position to write this book. Finally, and most importantly, I would like to thank my husband, Alan Bogg, to whom my work on this book is dedicated; he is my counsel, my best friend and my soul mate.

Personal thanks from John Randall

I would first thank my co-author Sarah Green for accepting that an academic–practitioner collaboration could be made to work, for her willingness to put in the many extra hours required to achieve it, and for her good-natured tolerance of the long periods during which the demands of practice caused all input from me to dry up. I remain deeply grateful to Alistair Wyvill, now (though not, I trust, causally) of William Forster Chambers, Darwin NT, Marc Brown of St Philips Chambers here in Birmingham, and John Harris for their unstinting work and support in preparing *OBG Ltd v Allan* for the House of Lords, a Herculean task indeed (see Lord Nicholls at [139]). Working on that case did much to stimulate my interest in this subject, and brought me into contact with my co-author in the first place. I am greatly indebted to my parents Jean and Richard for their support and encouragement from my very beginning, to Peter Glazebrook for my grounding in the law, and to Brendan Edgeworth and many of my other occasional colleagues on the faculty at the University of New South Wales Law School in Sydney for nurturing my resumed involvement in university life after a quarter of a century 'treading the boards' at the bar. Last but by no means least, I thank my long-suffering wife Christine for extending me, with good grace, resigned tolerance of yet further hours spent in my study or in libraries preparing this work; I appreciate her love and support immensely.

Sarah Green   John Randall
University of Birmingham   St Philips Chambers

Birmingham, 2009

Table of Contents

Table of Contents

Table of Cases

Table of Statutes and Other Official Publications

1

Introduction

THIS BOOK IS long overdue. Conversion, and personal property in general, seem to be unpopular subjects for discussion. Perhaps consequently, there has to date been no in-depth analysis of the tort of Conversion in English law. Not only is there no immediately apparent reason why this should be so, but, more importantly, it has had adverse effects on the practical development of the tort: common to even the most detailed judicial examinations of Conversion is a sense that the principles of the tort are elusive, and the search for them hindered by the disparate nature of the sources in which they might be found. This point may be illustrated by contrasting the way in which Lord Hoffmann was able to deal with the economic torts issues in *OBG Ltd v Allan*[1] (where his Lordship acknowledged his indebtedness to the academic writings on the subject[2]), with the manner in which he had to approach the Conversion point therein, where the absence of comparable analyses was conspicuous.[3] It was clear to us, therefore, that there was a real need for a work which would facilitate a clear understanding of this, the 'forgotten tort'.[4] This book aims to provide such a resource, by examining the key elements of Conversion, and presenting them in a form which is both comprehensive and accessible.

It will become apparent to the reader that, throughout the text, we use the term 'assets' where one might expect to see more familiar legal terms. This is deliberate. The full reasons for this may be found in chapter five, but such an unorthodox linguistic approach merits a brief mention here. As our analysis in this book makes clear, the range of subject matter currently protected by Conversion is too limited. In part, this is a result of the common law's apparent reluctance to expand its conceptual boundaries in order to recognise that much of today's personal property is different in nature to that with which it has historically been familiar. The use of traditional legal terms, such as 'goods' or 'chattels', to refer to the subject matter which is protected by Conversion risks stifling or prejudging an open-minded inquiry as to what forms of property,

---

[1] *OBG Ltd and anor v Allan and ors*, and two other cases [2007] UKHL 21, [2008] 1 AC 1.
[2] ibid at [65].
[3] ibid at [95]–[107].
[4] WL Prosser, 'The Nature of Conversion' (1957) 42 *Cornell Law Quarterly* 168 at 168.

including intangible, or quasi-intangible,[5] property, are equally appropriate subjects of the tort. The term 'assets', on the other hand, is broader, and so more easily encompasses all forms of personal property.

Equally apparent to the reader will be our consistent capitalisation of 'Conversion', when we use that term as the name of the tort with which this book is concerned, whereas this does not happen when reference is made to any other action. This has been done to reflect the analytical focus of the work.

There are two further linguistic practices which merit some explanation. The first is the employment of the words 'incorporeal' and 'intangible', terms which feature particularly in chapter five. These adjectives are used interchangeably throughout the book since, for our purposes, there is no significant distinction between the concepts they represent. The second is the somewhat inevitable choice to be made between whether, and when, to use 'claimant' instead of 'plaintiff'. In our text, we have elected to use 'claimant' throughout the work, regardless of whether reference is being made to proceedings predating or postdating the Civil Procedure Rules , simply for the sake of consistency.

In the next chapter, we outline the history of Conversion's evolution to date, and explain why the tort takes the form it does today. Rather than just providing a background to the rest of the book's analysis, however, the story of how Conversion came to be what it is today is essential to an understanding of how its future development might best proceed. Of particular interest for the discussion which follows is the reason why Conversion came into being in the first place, and the facts that not only was it was predicated on a pleaders' fiction, but also that the subject of the fiction never was of any significance for the gist of the tort; this fiction is, unfortunately, still influencing the application of the tort today. Here we also explain the genesis of the Torts (Interference with Goods) Act 1977, which explanation demonstrates why it is, in our view, inappropriate to attribute undue weight to the scheme and provisions of this non-codifying statute when looking at the long-term development, and desirable future trajectory, of a tort which is quintessentially a creature of the common law.

Chapter three deals with the apparently facile, but substantively difficult, question of exactly what constitutes a Conversion. One of the objectives of this chapter is to provide a statement of the fundamental elements of a Conversion, sufficient to facilitate the identification of a Conversion on any given set of facts, even where such a situation has not previously been considered in the context of Conversion. A statement of three such elements, and an explanation of their role in the overall definition, is provided. This chapter explains how Conversion forms only one part of a set of wrongful interference torts, and why this limited remit accounts for what might otherwise be regarded as shortcomings of the tort. It also contains an analysis of the essential distinction between property rights

---

[5]   Such as digitized or 'dematerialized' assets, discussed under the heading Digitized Products in ch 5.

and possessory rights within the common law, and explains how such a distinction is of great significance for understanding precisely what a Conversion is. Included within this analysis are comparative elements, in order to demonstrate how Conversion measures up to alternative means of protecting personal property adopted in other legal systems; an evaluation which concludes that the common law approach does not suffer for its lack of a nominate vindicatory action.

We examine what constitutes the requisite title to sue in Conversion in chapter four. In some respects, the rules which determine this might at first glance appear to produce some surprising results, such as allowing a thief to sue a subsequent converter of the assets she had stolen, and not allowing some individuals with superior *proprietary* rights to sue in respect of assets to which someone else has superior *possessory* rights. The analysis in this chapter demonstrates how, rather than being anomalous or problematic effects of the tort, such functions are perfectly coherent given the role played by Conversion within the common law's provision for the protection of personal property. This chapter also examines the intrinsic value of possession, and considers the position of wrongdoers, parties to bailments and finders. The primary contention of the chapter is that Conversion is available to the individual with the superior *possessory* right in the asset concerned; it also explains why a contractual basis for such a right is sufficient, but an equitable basis is not.

Chapter five is concerned with the subject matter of Conversion. Essentially, it aims to provide a set of criteria to determine what can and cannot be subject to a Conversion. Its basic thesis is that these criteria are very simple; to be so subject, an asset must be something which is amenable to possession, and in which property rights can exist. In order effectively to distinguish between those assets which can be possessed and those which cannot, the chapter also outlines a set of meaningful indicia of possession, which should dispense with the need to rely on the crude and often unhelpful dichotomy between choses in action and choses in possession. Assets which meet the possession and property criteria are susceptible to Conversion; nothing more is required. There is, for example, no principled reason why the asset need be tangible, or visible to the naked eye. This chapter also makes the point that it is not only the physical characteristics of assets which should be determinative of whether they can be subject to Conversion, but the particular context of the relationship each has with its purported possessor. Money, for instance, will, in some circumstances, be susceptible to Conversion, such as where coins are held by a collector for their intrinsic worth, but not in others, such as where it has passed into currency. Money, body parts, digitized products, intangible property, information and copyright are all discussed in this chapter, in order to provide a reasonably comprehensive review of what is required for Conversion to remain a useful and effective tort in the contemporary commercial and social environment.

This is followed by a discussion of how Conversion fits alongside the economic torts. It is sometimes supposed that the latter group of actions is something of a substitute for Conversion where the assets concerned are intangible. The argument in this chapter is that this is not, and should not be, the case, since, for the reasons given therein, it is not appropriate for the economic torts to be the primary means of protecting property interests. Moreover, as the previous chapter will have shown, intangible assets are by no means necessarily excluded from the remit of Conversion. It is, therefore, neither appropriate nor necessary for the economic torts to be used to make up for the perceived deficiencies in the protection offered by Conversion: property torts and economic torts are not interchangeable.

In chapter seven we deal with the remedies available in Conversion. Since the subsumption of detinue within Conversion by the 1977 Act, these remedies are now potentially very broad, ranging from damages measured by the market value of the asset converted, to an order for delivery up of that asset. The fact that the latter alternative is, however, discretionary rather than automatic, raises questions about the sufficiency of the proprietary protection offered by Conversion. Modern case law in this area is surprisingly sparse, but we explore how the leading appellate case on remedies since the statute was passed, *IBL Ltd v Coussens*,[6] has its difficulties, and appears to raise more questions than it answers. Another issue which arises in this context is whether a more restrictive test for remoteness of damage should be applied in cases involving 'innocent' converters; those who do not knowingly infringe another's property interests when dealing with assets. Correlative to this is a discussion of the extent to which the calculation of Conversion damages should be influenced by the respective tortious and proprietary aspects of the action, and the possible implications of this for Conversion's strict liability standard.

The book ends with a brief concluding chapter, drawing together the main analytical themes of the work, identifying the principal areas in need of reconsideration, and making suggestions as to how best the tort of Conversion might now be developed. It also offers a suggested answer to the thorny question of how this hybrid action might best be classified for various purposes.

This is undoubtedly a joint work, and both authors accept responsibility for the whole. Whilst, however, every chapter has been a collaborative project, each of the principal chapters has a primary author: John Randall for chapters two, six and seven and Sarah Green for chapters three, four and five.

---

⁶ [1991] 2 All ER 133 (CA).

2

The History of Conversion

'The hand of history lies heavy upon the tort of conversion'[1]

Introduction and Context

GOING BACK TO the origins of the common law, in medieval times the law of torts (as we now know it) was notoriously dominated by the forms of action, and that of trespass focussed on invasive interferences with land, the person and corporeal assets.[2]

By about the middle of the fourteenth century the action of trespass on the case had become established.[3] Under it, a plea of some harm suffered by the claimant, and caused by some wrongful conduct of the defendant, could succeed without the way in which that harm had been brought about first having to be artificially re-stated so as (apparently) to fit into the straightjacket of one of the established forms of action. This enabled judges to award compensatory damages 'where harm had been caused in circumstances where the conduct of the authors of the harm had been sufficiently reprehensible to require the conclusion that they ought to be held responsible for the harm'.[4] Trespass *stricto sensu* remained a form of action 'used for a variety of different kinds of claim which had as their common element the fact that the damage was caused directly rather than indirectly'.[5]

Trespass on the case did not, of course, grow on an entirely unstructured basis, as is well illustrated by the manner in which, over the following 250 or so years, a raft of specific rules as to when and in what circumstances an action on the case for interference with corporeal assets would succeed was developed through

---

[1] WL Prosser, 'The Nature of Conversion' (1957) 42 *Cornell LQ* 168 at 169.
[2] DJ Ibbetson, *A Historical Introduction to the Law of Obligations* (Oxford, Oxford University Press, 1999) at 97.
[3] Though its origins go back earlier—see, eg, Bracton, *Treatise on the Law of England* at f 1b (AKR Kiralfy, *A Source Book of English Law* (London, Sweet & Maxwell, 1957) at 138).
[4] Per Lord Scott in *Revenue and Customs Commissioners v Total Network SL* [2008] UKHL 19, [2008] 1 AC 1174 at [56].
[5] Per Lord Hoffmann in *Wainwright and anor v Home Office* [2003] UKHL 53, [2004] 2 AC 406 at [8].

judicial precedent. This process was, however, progressive rather than simply ever more definitional, such that over this period there developed not only a bewildering array of sometimes arcane rules in respect of such actions, but also a new tort, trover, which gradually took over the legal territory thitherto occupied by a number of long established forms of action.

By the beginning of the seventeenth century the law of torts had three aspects: first trespass, dealing with invasive interferences; secondly a group of tolerably well defined 'nominate torts' (as they would later become known[6]), which had grown out of case, notably nuisance, trover and defamation; and thirdly an inherently unstructured collection of situations in which claimants had succeeded in persuading the courts that the defendants' causative conduct was sufficiently reprehensible that they ought to be held liable to pay compensatory damages.[7]

Yet of those nominate torts, the hand of history lay heaviest on trover, or as it became Conversion, such that even in the early twentieth century Sir John Salmond was driven to write, in a celebrated article in the *Law Quarterly Review*,[8] that

> the law of trover and conversion is a region still darkened with the mists of legal formalism, through which no man will find his way by the light of nature or any other guide save the old learning of writs and forms of action and the mysteries of pleading.[9]

Some 60 years later Lord Denning opined that 'we have in this century shaken off [the] trammels [of the old forms of action]'.[10] A consideration of the remainder of this work should enable readers to form their own view as to whether that opinion was, notwithstanding the great distinction of its author, somewhat premature. For in 1971 the Eighteenth Report of the Law Reform Committee[11] gave several examples of 'the extent to which the existing law perpetuates the old causes of action', and as recently as 2005 Peter Gibson LJ, giving the leading judgment in the Court of Appeal in *OBG Ltd v Allan*, said:

> In my judgment, as a matter of English law there can be no conversion of a chose in action. Historically that is obvious, the tort of conversion being derived from trover, which required averments of goods lost by their possessor and found by the defendant.[12]

---

[6]   The first text which referred to 'torts' in its title identified by Milsom is *The law of Actions on the Case for Torts and Wrongs* (London, R Gosling, 1720).

[7]   Ibbetson, *Historical Introduction* (1999) at 97.

[8]   JW Salmond, 'Observations on Trover and Conversion' (1905) 21 *Law Quarterly Review* 43. The famous opening passage is cited in the text to n 207.

[9]   ibid, at 43.

[10]   *Letang v Cooper* [1965] 1 QB 232 (CA) at 239C–D.

[11]   The 18th Report (Conversion and Detinue) of the Law Reform Committee (1971), Cmnd 4774 at para 5.

[12]   [2005] EWCA Civ 106, [2005] QB 762 (CA) at [56].

A full history of Conversion would be the history of numerous torts. It is well known that Conversion emerged as a development of trover. More precisely, as we shall see, a plea of 'Conversion' was from at least the mid-sixteenth century seen as an integral part of trover, and gradually came to be recognised as its whole substance. Behind trover, however, lay four old forms of action going back to the origins of our legal system.

The Medieval Ancestors of Conversion

The four forms of action in question were appeal of robbery or larceny, trespass de bonis asportatis, replevin and detinue. It is worth noting that whilst the first three were actions *ex delicto*; the nature of detinue, in its original form, was different, being an action based on an underlying bailment, and hence *ex contractu* (at least in a broad, non-technical sense[13]). We must deal with the first three but shortly, for there is much ground to cover. Those desirous of an analysis in greater depth should turn to Ames' seminal article in the *Harvard Law Review*,[14] from which the following passages draw heavily.

Pending the emergence of trespass on the case, the challenge for medieval lawyers was to characterise the facts underlying a proposed claim so as to fit one of the established forms of action, and the early cases in particular are to be understood in that context. Conversely, in the early days of trespass on the case, the challenge for lawyers was then to present such cases in such a manner as to avoid objection being taken founded on the double actionability rule discussed below.

Appeal of Robbery or Larceny

Appeal of robbery or larceny had its origins in days, prior to the Assize of Clarendon in 1166, when there was no public prosecution of crime, and hence proceedings against wrongdoers, whether their objective was punitive, compensatory or both, were a matter for private initiative. Such private actions were brought in the royal courts and known as appeals. In addition to compensatory

---

[13] Whether all bailments are to be analysed as strictly contractual in nature is at best highly questionable: see eg the contrary views of CHS Fifoot, *History & Sources of the Common Law* (London, Stevens & Sons, 1949) at 24–25, NE Palmer, *Bailment*, 2nd edn (London, Sweet & Maxwell, 1991) at 19–44, and A Bell, 'The Place of Bailment in the Modern Law of Obligations', ch 19 in NE Palmer and E McKendrick (eds), *Interests in Goods*, 2nd edn (London, LLP, 1998).

[14] JB Ames, 'The History of Trover' (1897) 11 *Harvard Law Review* 277 and 374. Ames viewed bailment as contractual in nature, as was conventional at the time.

appeals and punitory appeals, there were 'the recuperatory appeals of robbery or larceny, in which the appellor sought to recover the stolen chattels as well as to discover and punish the thief'.[15]

The ancient procedure depended on whether the thief was caught with the stolen asset by the victim and his accompanying pursuers, in a form of hot pursuit known as hue and cry. If he was, the procedure was summary indeed, with the thief being put to death and the asset restored to the victim. If not, the person found in possession was entitled to have the dispute resolved by a legal process, which depending on the circumstances could involve trial by battle, trial by jury (at the appellee's election), and the vouching to warranty of a third party from whom the appellee asserted that he had (lawfully) obtained the asset. The destination of the asset, not to mention the life or liberty of the parties, depended on the outcome. A plea of purchase at a fair or market would produce a split result: the appellee would be acquitted of theft, but the appellor, provided he could prove his former possession or loss, would recover the asset.

Particularly once the public prosecution of crime was established, and public confidence in the remedy of indictment grew, such appeals were an unattractive means of pursuing the recovery of one's assets. Ames identified a series of difficulties with it: the need for fresh pursuit of the thief; the need for the thief to have been captured by one of the pursuers (an asset recovered on a later arrest by a bailiff went to the King); the need for the asset to have been recovered from the possession of the thief; the need for the thief to have been 'convicted' (in modern parlance) at his trial (whichever form it took); and (prior to the fourteenth century, when the right of a thief who was taken on the pursuit in possession of the asset to trial by battle was ended) the risk of losing a trial by battle to a thief of greater strength or stamina than his victim.

As the concept of justice evolved, the need for a more effective civil remedy for the victims of theft was obvious.[16]

Trespass de bonis asportatis

Pollock explained the fundamental relationship between the remaining forms of action thus:

> The disturbed possessor had his action of trespass (in some special cases replevin); if at the time of the wrong done the person entitled to possess was not in actual legal possession, his remedy was detinue ... An owner who had neither possession nor the immediate right to possession could redress himself by a special action on the case, which did not acquire any technical name.[17]

---

[15]   ibid, at 278.

[16]   Although there is still reference to appeal of robbery as an available basis of claim in dicta of Rede CJ in *Anon* (1510) Keil 160 pl 2, 72 ER 334 Ct CP, JH Baker and SFC Milsom, *Sources of English Legal History* (London, Butterworths, 1986) at 528, Fifoot, *History & Sources* (1949) at 114.

[17]   F Pollock, *The Law of Torts*, 1st edn (London, Stevens & Sons, 1887) at 277.

Trespass de bonis asportatis was, as the name suggests, the physical taking of an asset from the actual or constructive possession of another, without legal justification. As Ames recounted,[18] records suggest that cases founded on trespass started to be brought in the mid-thirteenth century, and that thereafter this form of action quickly became popular. In order to establish jurisdiction in the King's Court, a plea that the defendant had acted *vi et armis* and *contra pacem regis* was included, but otherwise the count in trespass was similar to that in the corresponding appeal, subject to omitting the offer of battle and concluding with an allegation of loss (an *ad damnum* clause). By the statute 6 Ed I c8 (1278) those seeking writs of trespass had to swear on oath that the asset taken had a value of at least 40 shillings. The gist of the claimant's infringed right was that of possession, which he might have enjoyed either as owner or as bailee.[19] Exceptionally, however, a bailor at will was allowed to bring trespass,[20] 'doubtless by the fiction that the possession of a bailee at will was the possession of the bailor also'.[21] Trespass could only be brought against the person who had taken the asset, and not his subsequent grantee, for the wrong was the taking from the claimant's possession, which the latter had not committed.[22]

Trespass, in contrast to both detinue and appeal of robbery or larceny, was an action for damages only. The basic measure awarded was the value of the stolen asset, even where the claimant was merely a bailee, for as Hankford J explained, 'if a stranger takes beasts in my custody I shall have trespass against him and recover their value, because I am chargeable to my bailor who has the property'[23].

If, however, the asset in question had been returned, it became established, rejecting an early view to the contrary,[24] that the claimant could still recover damages in trespass without having to bring an action on the case, and that damages would be assessed taking into account the fact of the asset's return.[25]

---

[18]   Ames, History of Trover (*Harvard Law Review* 1897) at 282–83.

[19]   See further ch 4.

[20]   *Anon* YB T16 Ed II f 490 pl [14] Ct CP (1323) contains an unattributed suggestion that trespass would be available; see also *Anon* YB T48 Ed III f 20b pl 8 KB (1374)—'Cavendish CJKB said that … in this case, he who had the property could have a writ of Trespass, and the one who had the keeping could have another writ of Trespass. A serjeant said that this was true, but he who recovered first would oust the other from the action.' (as translated in the Commentary & Paraphrase in *An Index and Paraphrase of Printed Year Book Reports, 1268–1535* (ed DJ Seipp) at www.bu.edu/law/seipp/).

[21]   Ames (n 14) at 284.

[22]   *Anon* YB H21 Ed IV f 74b–75a pl 6 Ct CP (1482), Brooke's Abridg Pt II, Trespass f 298 pl 358.

[23]   Ames (n 14) at 285, citing *Thomas From' v Anon* YB M11 Hen IV f 23a–25a pl 46 Ct CP (1409).

[24]   *Anon* YB M21 Hen VI f 14b–15b pl 29 Ct CP (1442).

[25]   Adopting the view expressed by Paston J ibid: Ames (n 14) 285 at fn 6, *Chinery v Viall* (1860) 5 H & N 288 at 295, 157 ER 1192 at 1195. In this respect trespass therefore offered a more satisfactory remedy than detinue—see further at text to n 62 ff.

Replevin

Replevin can be understood as a subset of trespass de bonis asportatis, which covered the situation where the taking complained of was purportedly justified as a lawful levying of distress. There was some logic to giving it a separate status, if one bears in mind the underlying principle that:

> Every kind of intermeddling with anything which is the subject of property is a wrong unless it is either authorized by some person entitled to deal with the thing in that particular way, or justified by authority of law ... Broadly speaking, we touch the property of others at our peril, and honest mistake in acting for our own interest, or even an honest intention to act for the benefit of the true owner, will avail us nothing if we transgress.[26]

In replevin, the issue was almost inevitably whether the purported distress was lawful, and hence whether what would otherwise have been a trespass was justified by authority of law. Ames, in explaining the existence of a separate form of action, drew attention to the absence of any assertion of dominion, or even taking of legal possession, inherent in a levying of distress, on which the distrainee could found his complaint.[27]

> The Distrainor neither gains a general nor a special Property nor even the Possession in the Cattle or Things distrained: he cannot maintain Trover or Trespass ... it is not like a Pledge, for he has a Property for the Time[28]

A well-known doctrine which arose in cases of replevin was that of trespass *ab initio*, under which a defendant who first took possession of an asset by act of law, but later abused his legal authority (classically, by refusing their return after the sum distrained for was paid or tendered), was held to have been a trespasser *ab initio*.[29]

This tort, now regulated by the County Courts Act 1984, survives to the present day, notwithstanding the expectation of the Law Reform Committee in 1971 that the introduction of a statutory interim remedy for delivery up would pave the way for its abolition.[30]

---

[26] Pollock, *Torts* (1887) at 272.

[27] n 14, at 287 and 374.

[28] *R v Cotton* (1751) Parker 113 at 121–22, 145 ER 729 at 732 per Parker CB.

[29] YB P45 Ed III f 9a–b pl 13 Ct CP (1371) Wychyngham J, 2 Rolle Abridg 561, Trespass, pl 8.

[30] See County Courts Act 1984 ss 144 and Sched 1; 18th report of the LRC (1971) at paras 2 and 97; s 4, Torts (Interference with Goods) Act 1977 ('the 1977 Act'); *Clerk & Lindsell on Torts*, 19th edn (London, Sweet & Maxwell, 2006) at paras 17–142 to 17–143.

Detinue

Detinue sur bailment

As mentioned above, the origins of detinue were contractual, at least in a broad, non-technical sense.[31] Classically, the underlying agreement would be one under which an asset was delivered by the claimant to another with some provision for its redelivery, that is a bailment, although it could also be one for sale, under which delivery of the asset sold had not occurred. The gist of the action was a particular breach of contract, namely a failure or refusal of delivery up on the claimant's request.

The central nature of the request is well illustrated by cases in which limitation has been in issue. In *Wilkinson v Verity*[32] churchwardens sued an incumbent for certain parish silver, which he had taken from the church in 1859 for safe custody, to be restored when required, but later the same year had (without their knowledge) sold. Demand for its return was first made in 1870, and proceedings commenced upon the incumbent's non-compliance. Willes J, giving the judgment of the Court of Common Pleas, cited the well-known contract case of *Hochster v De La Tour*[33] as supporting the principle that a so-called 'anticipatory breach' of contract confers on the innocent party an election, but not an obligation, to treat that conduct as a violation and breach of the contract. Accordingly the churchwardens were entitled 'to wait until there is a breach of the bailee's duty in the ordinary course by refusal to deliver up on request',[34] and to rely on the failure to comply with the first request for redelivery made (in 1870) as founding their action in detinue which, accordingly, was not statute barred 'notwithstanding the previous unknown conversion ... by the defendant to his own use more than six years before action'.[35]

The Plea of devenerunt ad manus

One consequence of this contractual foundation for detinue sur bailment was that, in principle, only the original bailee (he who had given the express or implied promise to redeliver) could be sued by the bailor.[36] Ames explained how this reflected a rule of the old Teutonic law, which 'has maintained itself with

---

[31] Subject as per n 13.

[32] (1871) LR 6 CP 206. See also *Clayton v Le Roy* [1911] 2 KB 1031, especially at 1048 per Fletcher Moulton LJ (this case is discussed in S Douglas, 'The Abolition of Detinue' [2008] *Conveyancer and Property Lawyer* 30 at 34–35) and *Schwarzchild v Harrods Ltd* [2008] EWHC 521 (QB), (2008) 105 LSG 26.

[33] (1853) 2 E & B 678, 118 ER 922.

[34] (1871) LR 6 CP 206 at 210–11.

[35] ibid, at 209.

[36] See, eg, F Pollock and FW Maitland, *The History of English Law Vol 2*, 2nd edn (Cambridge, Cambridge University Press, 1898, reissued 1968) at 176.

great persistence in Germany and France'.[37] The absence of a remedy for the bailor against a sub-bailee or even a thief in possession of his asset was obviously unsatisfactory.

The first recognition of a cause of action in detinue against a defendant other than the original bailee came in cases where that bailee had died. In *Wagworth v Halyday*[38] the claimant pleaded a bailment to a person since deceased, and that after the death of the bailee the assets had come into the keeping of the defendant, without pleading how. Willoughby J asked the claimant's counsel how they had done so, adding that 'it is a mere formality and in no way against you, because the manner is not traversable'. Counsel then acknowledged that they had come to the defendant as executor. The defendant's application for an immediate judgment in her favour on that basis failed, though the case went for trial on her traverse that the assets ever came into her keeping, or that she detained them.[39] Such a plea that the claimant's assets had come into the defendant's hands, without being specific as to how, was known as a plea *devenerunt ad manus*,[40] or more fully *ad manus et possessionem defendentis devenerunt.*

The acceptability of such a plea was rapidly exploited in claims beyond those which followed the death of the original bailee. The first seeds of an idea which, as we shall see, achieved a profile out of all proportion to its (negligible) substantive significance, lasting for over 500 years, appear to have been sown by a dictum of Scrop CJKB in an early fourteenth-century claim for trespass in taking and mutilating a charter.[41] He is reported as having observed that 'if the defendant had found the charter in the road (en la voy) he would have his recovery against the defendant by the Praecipe quod reddat'.[42]

These early cases, taken together, support what is substantially Milsom's thesis that while a bare assertion of *devenerunt ad manus* sufficed for a claim in detinue against someone other than the original bailee, and some pleaders therefore limited themselves to that, a story generally followed, albeit that it was untraversable. One such story which proved convenient was that to which Scrop CJKB had given an early 'green light', that of loss and finding.[43]

---

[37]   Ames (n 14) at 377.

[38]   YB T29 Ed III f 38 pl [12] Ct CP (1355), Baker and Milsom, *Sources* (1986) at 267–69.

[39]   See also *Thornhill's Case* YB 17&18 Ed III (RS 510) (1344), Fifoot (n 13) at 41–42 (claim for a horse which had been bailed to the deceased); and *Salman v Wille* P11 Rich II (1388–89) Bellewe's Abridg 134–35 Detinue of Charters pl 3, Ames Fndn 5 YB Ser 283–88 (ed TFT Plucknett) (claim for a charter which had been bailed to the deceased).

[40]   The marginal annotation applied to the case of *Salman v Wille* (ibid) by Richard Bellewe in his *Abridgment* (London, R Robinson, 1585).

[41]   *Anon* YB H2 Ed III f 2 pl 5 (1328).

[42]   ibid, as translated in Seipp, *Index and Paraphrase* (Boston University website).

[43]   SFC Milsom, *Historical Foundations of the Common Law*, 2nd edn (London, Butterworths, 1981) at 273.

Detinue sur trover

From this point, the way was open for the development of detinue to cover cases where there had been no bailment in the first place. The acceptance of the plea of *devenerunt ad manus* had established that a defendant who had not undertaken any contractual commitment to return the subject asset to the claimant[44] could nevertheless be held liable in detinue, thereby freeing at least one limb of the tort from its contractual roots. There was still perceived to be a need to put forward some explanation of how the claimant's asset had come into the defendant's hands which did not involve an unlawful taking, because the latter was the province of trespass de bonis asportatis and replevin, and the rule against double remedies arising out of the same cause of action[45] held sway.[46] Loss and finding was convenient, had passed muster in the context of claims founded on the plea of *devenerunt ad manus*, and over time became standard.

Ames identified a case in 1370 as the first in which a loser is reported to have brought detinue against a finder. The count alleged that an ass had strayed onto the defendant's lordship, where it was taken as an estray, and one month later the claimant tendered reasonable satisfaction for its keep. The case went for trial on the adequacy of the satisfaction tendered.[47]

Some 20 years later a claim was brought against a husband and wife for detinue of a box of charters and muniments. The count alleged that they had found the box at Queenhithe in London, and refused a subsequent request for its delivery up. The count went uncriticised in that regard, though it failed on an unrelated technicality (namely that the wife should not have been joined).[48]

An important attraction of the plea of loss and finding was, as we saw in *Wagworth v Halyday* in the context of a plea of *devenerunt ad manus*, that it was viewed as unnecessary, and therefore was untraversable. A century later, in *Carles v Malpus*[49] the subject matter was again a box of charters. The count pleaded that it came to the defendant by finding ('*per inventionem*'). Prysot CJ affirmed the continuing importance of the request for delivery up in this branch of detinue, observing that 'by the finding itself he (defendant) commits no tort, but the tort begins by the detaining after he (defendant) has notice'.[50] Serjeant Littleton 'said

---

[44] *Aliter* where there was no holding by obligation.

[45] Meaning, at least in this context, a factual situation the existence of which entitles one person to obtain from the court a remedy against another person: per Diplock LJ in *Letang v Cooper* [1965] 1 QB 232 at 242G–43A.

[46] See AWB Simpson, 'The Introduction of the Action on Case for Conversion' (1959) 75 *LQR* 364 at 365.

[47] *Anon* YB P44 Ed III f 14a pl 30 (1370).

[48] *Anon* M13 Rich II, Bellewe's Abridg 135 Detinue of Charters pl 4 (1390–91), Ames Fndn 7 YB Ser 56–57 (ed TFT Plucknett).

[49] YB T33 Hen VI f 26b–27a pl 12 Ct CP (1455), Fifoot (n 13) at 42–43.

[50] ibid, as translated in Seipp (n 20). The making of a request remains significant to this day for the purposes of 'statutory conversion' under s 2(2) of the 1977 Act: see *Schwarzchild v Harrods Ltd* [2008] EWHC 521 (QB), (2008) 105 LSG 26, discussed in ch 3 under the heading An Exception to these Principles: Statutory Conversion.

privately[51] that this declaration *per inventionem* is a newfound Haliday: for the old declaration has always been in such case that the charters *ad manus et possessionem defendentis devenerunt* generally, without showing how'.[52] As Milsom cleverly divined,[53] the reference to a 'newfound Haliday' was probably an allusion to the case of *Wagworth v Halyday*. If, as seems likely, that is right, Littleton was justified in drawing the comparison, for what the plea of *ad manus devenerunt* in the earlier case had in common with the plea of finding in the later case was that both founded the desired[54] supposition that the asset had come into the defendant's hands lawfully, yet both were treated as untraversable.

In 1535, in a detinue case in the Court of Common Pleas, Fitzherbert J is reported as denying in terms that the allegation of finding was traversable even 'in some cases'.[55]

The position was well summarised by Salmond thus:

> in detinue ... this ... allegation as to losing and finding was in most cases a mere fiction; in any case it was immaterial and untraversable. Nor was it ever essential. The plaintiff might have alleged a bailment instead of a loss and finding ... Or a general allegation of *devenerunt ad manus defendentis* would have been good enough.[56]

The Shortcomings of Detinue sur trover

Despite considerable developments over time, detinue sur trover[57] remained a form of action which was unattractive for claimants in a number of respects.

The first disadvantage was procedural but fundamental. The defendant retained the right to elect for wager of law, the effect of which was to deprive a claimant of a determination of his claim on the merits. Under this ancient procedure the defendant could swear that he did not detain the subject asset, and then produce witnesses who would swear to his credibility.[58] It was 'a form of licensed perjury which made detinue singularly unattractive to an honest plaintiff

---

[51]   Though it seems not privately enough, for his observation made its way into the report!

[52]   As translated in Fifoot (n 13) at 42–43.

[53]   Milsom, *Historical Foundations* (1981) at 273.

[54]   To side-step the double remedies rule, given the existence of trespass as an available remedy in (at least most) cases where goods were taken unlawfully.

[55]   As Shelley J had postulated: *Anon* YB P27 Hen VIII f 13 pl 35 (1535), Baker and Milsom (n 16) at 272.

[56]   Salmond, Observations (*LQR* 1905) at 46, also JW Salmond, *The Law of Torts*, 1st edn (London, Stevens & Haynes, 1907) at 288.

[57]   Which, strictly, was simply one subset of the writ of detinue.

[58]   WS Holdsworth, *A History of English Law Vol 1*, 7th edn, AL Goodhart and HG Hanbury (eds) (London, Sweet & Maxwell, 1956) at 305–8. Fifoot (n 13) at 28–29 suggests that its availability in detinue was not, in practice, invariable.

suing a dishonest defendant'.[59] Though this was long recognised as a disadvantage,[60] somewhat remarkably it was not abolished until well into the nineteenth century.[61] Wager of law was not, however, available to those defending an action on the case.

Substantively, detinue did not cope well with a variety of relatively common situations, including where the subject asset was damaged, destroyed, or in some way transformed, or had simply passed out of the defendant's possession before action brought.

The basic position in detinue was that an order for restoration of the asset could be satisfied by compliance, regardless of the condition in which the asset was returned.[62] Therefore, if compensation for damage to the asset was sought, the claimant had to resort to a (separate) action on the case. An early example is afforded by *The Farrier's case* of 1372.[63] The owner of a horse injured by a farrier's nail, in consequence whereof he lost the profit from the horse for a long time, brought an action on the case for his loss flowing from the damage to the (returned) horse. The writ was held good.

The total destruction of bailed assets presented no difficulty in a claim for detinue sur bailment, for the defendant was in breach of his contractual obligation to deliver them up on demand, and the standard form of order (for the return of the assets or payment of their value) coped with the situation, by virtue of its second limb. However in a case against a defendant other than the original bailee, which therefore had to be brought in detinue sur trover, the defendant's possession of the subject assets at the time when the action was brought was a necessary element of the cause of action. Accordingly if the assets had already been destroyed by that time, even by the defendant, no remedy was available in detinue sur trover, for the position was in principle no different from that where the defendant had gone out of possession of the subject assets before action brought (considered below). Of course, if the act of destruction was itself a wrong actionable by the claimant, he could bring a claim (presumably in case) on that basis.

Greater complexities arose when the subject asset had undergone some form of transformation while out of the claimant's possession. Two cases which have attracted particular attention are *The Case of the Cloth of Gold* and *Calwodelegh v John (The Case of the Silver Cups)* 1479.[64] The former appears not to have been separately reported, and we are dependent on an extract from the Year Book

---

[59]   Prosser, Nature (*CLQ* 1957) at 169.

[60]   See, eg, W Blackstone, *Commentaries, Vol III Private Wrongs* (Oxford, Clarendon Press, 1768; Chicago, University of Chicago Press, 2001 facsimile reprint) at 151.

[61]   By s 13, Civil Procedure Act 1833 (3 and 4 Wm IV c42).

[62]   See, eg, *Calwodelegh v John (The Case of the Silver Cups)* YB H18 Ed IV f 23 pl 5 (1479), Baker and Milsom (n 16) at 526–28, Fifoot (n 13) at 113–14.

[63]   *Anon (The Farrier's case)* YB T46 Edw III f 19 pl 19 (1372), Baker and Milsom (n 16) at 341–42.

[64]   YB H18 Ed IV f 23a–b pl 5 Ct CP, Baker and Milsom (n 16) at 526–28, Fifoot (n 13) at 113–14. For an excellent discussion of both cases, see Simpson, Introduction (*LQR* 1959) at 372–74.

report of the latter, variously attributed to Choke J and Serjeant Catesby, for the following explanation of why there was held to be no remedy in detinue available in *The Case of the Cloth of Gold* (so that the action on the case was not barred by the rule against double actionability):

[A]nd also such an action (on the Case) was sued here lately (tarde), and the plaintiff counted that he bailed to defendant certain cloth (drapis) of gold (d'ore), and that he (defendant?) made clothes (vestements) of them, so it appeared to the Court that he (plaintiff) could not recover the same thing, the action (on the Case) was maintained[65]

The opposite result was reached in *Calwodelegh v John*. Two silver gilt cups were the subject of a sub-under-bailment to the defendant, who broke the same.[66] As in *The Case of the Cloth of Gold*, the claimant brought an action on the case. Here, however, Serjeant Tremayle's preliminary objection on behalf of the defendant, invoking the rule against double actionability, that the claimant 'could have a writ of detinue: for the property is not altered, and even though he cannot recover the very things he can still recover damages for them'[67] succeeded.[68] Thus in such a case the success or failure of a claim in detinue (or, conversely, on the case) was dependent on the claimant (or his lawyers) correctly predicting whether the court would view the transformation of the subject asset as sufficiently fundamental to destroy its identity and operate as a *specificatio*, that is to effect an alteration in the property therein.

In detinue sur trover,[69] a defendant was not liable if the subject asset had passed out of his possession before the action was commenced.[70] A report from 1535 records Fitzherbert J saying as much, and Shelley J agreeing.[71] This was confirmed in modern times by Donaldson J in *Alicia Hosiery v Brown Shipley & Co*.[72] A quantity of ladies' stockings of Italian manufacture, held in a warehouse under the constructive possession of Brown Shipley (as a pledgee to whom the warehouse owner had attorned title), were sold by the pledgor to the claimants. Brown Shipley then issued a delivery order to the warehouse owner requesting

---

[65]   As translated in Seipp (n 20).

[66]   According to Baker and Milsom (n 16) at 526 (drawing on CP 40/868 m 428), the broken silver was 'made … into various kinds of silver vessel'. On the face of things, this would have sufficed to effect a *specificatio*, destroying the claimant's property in the (former) silver cups. However the declaration in the case pleaded only that the cups were broken and converted to the defendant's use ('*fregit et in proprios usus ibidem convertit*')—AKR Kiralfy, *The Action on the Case* (London, Sweet & Maxwell, 1951) at 220, and the case was decided on that basis.

[67]   Baker and Milsom (n 16) at 526.

[68]   Choke J, dissenting, would have allowed the claimant an election between detinue and case, an approach which was to be vindicated in the early sixteenth century (see text to nn 134 and 135).

[69]   That is absent a contractual obligation owed to the claimant by the defendant arising out of a bailment.

[70]   In an action in trover sur bailment, where such a contractual obligation did exist, the result would be the opposite. For a modern analysis of why, based on the bailee being estopped from asserting his own wrong in losing possession of the bailed goods, see *General & Finance Facilities Ltd v Cooke Cars (Romford) Ltd* [1963] 1 WLR 644 (CA) at 649 per Diplock LJ.

[71]   *Anon* YB P27 Hen VIII f 13 pl 35, Baker and Milsom (n 16) at 272–73.

[72]   [1970] 1 QB 195.

their release to the claimants, but the warehouse owner did not release them, asserting a specific lien thereover in respect of monies disbursed on behalf of the vendor/pledgor which (in its view) were as yet unpaid.[73] The claimants' (first alternative) claim against Brown Shipley[74] in detinue failed. Donaldson J started his reasoning with the proposition that a 'claim in detinue lies at the suit of a person who has an immediate right to the possession of the goods against a person who is in possession of the goods and who, upon proper demand, fails or refuses to deliver them up without lawful excuse',[75] went on to hold that the delivery order (when it came to the warehouse owner's notice) brought Brown Shipley's constructive possession to an end, and therefore concluded that the action against Brown Shipley in detinue failed.[76]

Another noteworthy feature of detinue generally, and a shortcoming in the sense of a failure to live up to its superficial reputation, is that it did not offer a fully effective remedy *in rem*. The standard form of order (for the return of the asset or payment of its value) shows why. Pollock and Maitland[77] first quoted and then answered Bracton on this point:

'It would seem at first sight . . . that the action in which a movable is demanded should be as well *in rem* as *in personam* since a specific thing is demanded and the possessor is bound to restore that thing; but in truth it is merely *in personam*, for he from whom the thing is demanded is not absolutely bound to restore it, but is bound alternatively to restore it or its price; and this, whether the thing be forthcoming or no. And therefore if a man vindicates his movable chattel ... he must in his action define its price ...'. We may argue against him that the 'vindication' of a chattel, if it really be a vindication, if it be an assertion of ownership, is not the less an action *in rem* because the court will not go to all lengths to restore that chattel to its owner, but will do its best to give him what is of equal value.

Ibbetson[78] has expressed the view that the separation of detinue sur trover from detinue sur bailment 'provided an opportunity for English law to develop detinue as a straight-forward proprietary remedy for the recovery of chattels analogous to the Romans' *vindicatio*'. He sees the development of trover and Conversion out of the former as the manifestation of a failure to take up that opportunity. Detinue, however, was always far from a straightforward proprietary remedy.[79]

The underlying reason why English law would not normally go to all lengths to restore an asset to its owner was put thus by Blackstone:

---

[73] The sums disbursed were in respect of import duty and purchase tax. The warehouse owner viewed them as unpaid because it doubted whether a bill of exchange accepted by the vendor/pledgor would be honoured.

[74] Their claims against the warehouse owner had been settled before trial: [1970] 1 QB 195 at 195G–H.

[75] ibid, at 207B.

[76] ibid, at 207H–208A.

[77] *History* (1898) at 174–75.

[78] n 2, at 108.

[79] See further in ch 3, under the heading Relationship to *Vindicatio*.

For things personal are looked on by the law as of a nature so transitory and perishable, that is for the most part impossible either to ascertain their identity, or to restore them in the same condition as when they came to the hands of the wrongful possessor. And, since it is a maxim of the law that '*lex neminem cogit ad vana, seu impossibilia*,' it therefore contents itself in general with restoring, not the thing itself, but a pecuniary equivalent to the party injured; by giving him a satisfaction in damages.[80]

In a later passage Blackstone reverted to the question of sufficient identification specifically in the context of detinue, stating that in that action 'it is necessary to ascertain the thing detained, in such manner as that it may be specifically known and recovered', and citing the 'less degree of certainty requisite in describing the goods' as one of the 'considerable' advantages of trover over detinue.[81] Milsom put the point simply but clearly—'How can the plaintiff establish that this horse is indeed the one that he somehow lost?'[82]

Where movables were of a unique nature or of exceptional value, a specific remedy in equity compelling their delivery up could be sought from the Court of Chancery, but such applications were not common.[83] It was not until 1854 that the courts of common law gained jurisdiction to make such orders,[84] and the restrictive principle by which equity had limited the circumstances in which such a remedy was granted was still applied by them.[85] In the main the remedy was damages, and it has been argued that the measure of damages itself reflected the fact that detinue was a law of remedy, not rights, that is was truly tortious in nature.[86]

The Emergence of Trover

The first specifically pleaded allegation of trover (that is finding) which legal historians have identified came in the late fourteenth-century detinue case concerning a box of charters and muniments found at Queenhithe in London, which we have already mentioned above.[87] The count was, as recorded by Bellewe, '*que le baron et la femme troū les [charters] etc*'.[88] Understandably, given that his Abridgment was published almost 200 years later, at that point Bellewe added the marginal annotation 'Trouer'.

---

80   Blackstone, *Commentaries* (1768) at 146.
81   ibid, at 151–52.
82   n 43 at 272.
83   Pollock and Maitland (n 36) at 178 fn 1.
84   By s 78, Common Law Procedure Act 1854 (17 & 18 Vict c125)—see text to n 187 ff.
85   An example of the law following equity! See, eg, *Whiteley Ltd v Hilt* [1918] 2 KB 808, especially at 819 per Swinfen Eady J.
86   Douglas, Abolition (*Conv* 2008) at 42. As to the position with regard to remedies prior to the fourteenth century, see Fifoot (n 13) at 29.
87   Text to n 48.
88   *Anon* M13 Rich II, Bellewe's Abridg 135 Detinue of Charters pl 4 (1389). See also Ames Fndn 7 YB Ser 56–57 (ed TFT Plucknett).

The action of trover was, in its origin, an action of trespass on the case.[89] As its very name suggests, it undoubtedly developed out of detinue sur trover, of which the Queenhithe case was itself a very early example. Fifoot[90] takes the five allegations constituting a classic count of trover from Rastell's *Collection of Entries*,[91] recounting that they became common form (and were subsequently adopted by Coke as a precedent in his own *Book of Entries*[92]):

> The plaintiff alleged (1) that he was possessed of specified goods of a certain value 'as of his own proper goods', (2) that, being so possessed, he 'casually lost them out of his possession,' (3) that they afterwards 'came into the hands and possession of the defendant by finding,' (4) that the defendant, though often requested so to do, had failed to deliver them to the plaintiff, and (5) that he had converted them to his own use.[93]

1. Possessed of the Goods of his Own Property

As Fifoot observes,[94] the first allegation, though it may have been formulated and published by Rastell and subsequently adopted by Coke, contains an important ambiguity: was the claimant's case to depend on possession or ownership? As we shall see in a moment, cases in the seventeenth century demonstrate that, as with trespass, the answer was possession, including the 'special property' inherent in an immediate right to possession; and in the eighteenth century it was held that simple physical possession unaccompanied by any pre-existing right to possess sufficed, but (later) that a bare right of ownership unaccompanied by either possession or an immediate right to possession did not. Accordingly there is force in Fifoot's following analysis, explaining away the apparent import of the latter part of Rastell's first allegation:

> The development of pleading ... was not an analytical but a historical process, and its language was not to be subjected to the prim scrutiny of the jurist. Definition even to-day is perilous, and well into the nineteenth century 'property' might imply at discretion any one of the three conceptions of ownership, right to possess, or possession. A languid attempt at discrimination may be observed in the antithesis of the 'general' or 'absolute' property of the owner and the 'special' property of the bailee or other person with only a limited interest. But such epithets do not err upon the side of

---

[89] Blackstone (n 60) at 151.

[90] n 13, at 104.

[91] W Rastell, *Collection of Entries* (London, R Tottell, 1566) at Detinue of Charters f 204, Fifoot (n 13) at 43 and 104.

[92] E Coke, *Book of Entries* (London, Societie of Stationers, 1614) at f 38d, Fifoot (n 13) at 116.

[93] The fifth allegation was immediately followed by an allegation of having suffered loss and damage (see Fifoot (n 13) at 43).

[94] ibid, at 111.

precision, and it is not surprising that the task of determining the particular relation-ship between the plaintiff and the goods which would suffice for Trover was arduous and protracted.[95]

The adequacy of possession, without more, to found an action in trover was established in the late seventeenth century by *Wilbraham v Snow*[96] and *Arnold v Jefferson*[97], in both of which the court rejected the argument that, in contradis-tinction to trespass, liability in trover depended on the concept of property. The report of the former in Williams on Saunders is notable for the extensive annotations by, in particular, Serjeant Williams, well described by Pollock[98] as collecting 'All, or nearly all, the learning on the subject … (in a somewhat formless manner it must be allowed)'. A right to possession had already been held to suffice somewhat earlier, in *Ratcliff v Davies*.[99]

The well-known eighteenth century case of the chimney-sweep's boy who found a ring, *Armory v Delamirie*,[100] affords a striking illustration of the point. Though generally cited in modern times for its decision on quantification of damages, supporting the maxim *omnia praesumuntur contra spoliatorem*, for present purposes what is noteworthy is that the claimant's patently bare posses-sion was held to suffice for a claim against a wrongdoer (the goldsmith, sued as employer of his dishonest apprentice who took the stones from the ring).

At the end of that century came *Gordon v Harper*.[101] A Mr Biscoe had the exclusive right to possession of a mansion-house and its furniture, as the tenant of the claimant, for a term which had not expired. The defendant sheriff seized some of the furniture under a writ of *fieri facias*, and subsequently sold it. The plaintiff landlord sued in trover, relying on an earlier obiter dictum of Lord Kenyon CJ.[102] The same judge, with whom Ashurst, Grose and Lawrence JJ agreed, had to recant:

> What was said further by me in [*Ward v Macauley*], that trover was the proper remedy [in a case like the present], was an extra-judicial opinion, to which upon further consideration I cannot subscribe. The true question is whether, when a person has leased goods in a house to another for a certain time, whereby he parts with the right of

[95] ibid, at 111.

[96] (1669) 2 Wms Saund 47a, 85 ER 624. There the bare possession in question was that of a sheriff, who had taken the goods into his possession pursuant to a writ of *fieri facias*.

[97] (1697) 1 Ld Raym 275, 91 ER 1080; 2 Salk 654 pl 1, 91 ER 556. The bailee of a bond (the piece of paper), in respect of which the bailor continued to have the 'lien and right of action' vested in him, succeeded in an action for trover in respect of the bond. The defendant's argument that 'it was admitted, that the plaintiff might have had trespass, because that might be maintained upon the bare possession. But trover will not lie without property, therefore the plaintiff has mistaken his action' was rejected.

[98] Pollock (n 17) at 288 fn (d).

[99] (1611) Cro Jac 244, 79 ER 210, Fifoot (n 13) at 115 (and well summarised ibid, at 111).

[100] (1722) 1 Str 505, 93 ER 664, Baker and Milsom (n 16) at 547, Kiralfy, *Source Book* (1957) at 153, discussed more fully in ch 4, text to fns 10–11.

[101] (1796) 7 TR 9, 101 ER 828, Fifoot (n 13) at 124.

[102] In *Ward v Macauley* (1791) 4 TR 489 at 489 and 490, 100 ER 1135 at 1135.

possession during the term to the tenant and has only a reversionary interest, he can notwithstanding recover the value of the whole property pending the existence of the term in an action of trover. The very statement of the proposition affords an answer to it.[103]

Doubtless suitably chastened, on this occasion he declined to offer any obiter dicta as to what remedy the landlord did have in such a case 'not at present being called on to do so'![104] Grose J adverted to the standard form of pleading as exposing the fatal flaw in the claimant's case:

> The only question is whether trover will lie where the plaintiff had neither the actual possession of the goods taken at the time, nor the right of possession. The common form of pleading in such an action is decisive against him; for he declares that, being possessed, etc., he lost the goods; he is therefore bound to show either an actual or virtual possession. If he had a right to the possession, it is implied by law.[105]

2. Loss and 3. Finding

These pleas were, from the first emergence of trover, regarded as unnecessary and untraversable. This should come as no surprise given the history of the plea of *devenerunt ad manus*,[106] and then of the action of detinue sur trover which developed from it. In an action on the case for trover in the Queen's Bench in 1579 the above-mentioned detinue case from 1535[107] was cited, without contradiction on this point, for the proposition that the trover was not traversable.[108] Nevertheless the point was tested in the early seventeenth century, and the position confirmed.

In *Gumbleton v Grafton*, an action brought in case despite being brought by a bailor against his bailee, the second of two objections taken for the defendant was the absence of an allegation that the claimant lost the goods.[109] The action nevertheless succeeded. Similarly in *Kinaston v Moor*[110] it was said that in trover 'the losing is but a surmise and not material'.

---

[103]   (1796) 7 TR 9 at 11, 101 ER 828 at 829, Fifoot (n 13) at 124.

[104]   In this context, it is noteworthy that where a bailee recovers full damages in respect of the value of the subject goods from a wrongdoer, such recovery in itself thereafter precludes the bailor from pursuing a claim against the wrongdoer as a matter of common law (*The Winkfield* [1902] P 42 at 61 per Collins MR), and he must instead seek an account from his bailee in respect of his entitlement: 18th Report (n 11) at para 57, *Clerk & Lindsell on Torts* (2006) at para 17–115; see further in ch 4, text to fn 53 In the less usual situation where the bailor succeeds in so recovering, it is now established that the converse equally applies: *O'Sullivan and anor v Williams* [1992] 3 All ER 385 (CA).

[105]   (1796) 7 TR 9 at 12, 101 ER 828 at 829, Fifoot (n 13) at 125.

[106]   Especially *Wagworth v Halyday* (1355), discussed in text to n 38 ff.

[107]   See text to n 55.

[108]   *Anon* (1579) LI MS Misc 488 p64 (QB), Baker and Milsom (n 16) at 533.

[109]   As reported in (1600) Cro Eliz 781, 78 ER 1011, Baker and Milsom (n 16) at 530, especially fn 11.

[110]   (1626) Cro Car 89, 79 ER 678 (Ex Ch).

Nor was the plea of finding accorded any significance. In *Ratcliff v Davies*,[111] an action for trover and Conversion of a hatband set with pearls and diamonds, the court held that, where the defendant had converted assets by refusing to comply with a lawful demand for their delivery up, 'a trover and conversion well lies, although [the defendant] came unto them by a lawful delivery, and not by trover'. In *Isaack v Clark*[112] the defendant, on the jury's verdict, was not guilty of finding, because they found the goods to have been pledged, but this was brushed this aside by Coke CJ as immaterial.

By the mid-eighteenth century Lord Mansfield CJ was content openly to refer to the allegation of loss and finding as a fiction, coupling this with a reminder of the desired supposition which, as we have seen,[113] it served to support:

> In form it is a fiction ... The form supposes the defendant may have come lawfully by possession of the goods. This action [of trover] lies, and has been brought in many cases where, in truth, the defendant has got the possession lawfully.[114]

Again, we can turn to Salmond for his summation:

> [I]n trover, this ... allegation as to losing and finding was in most cases a mere fiction; in any case it was immaterial and untraversable ... The allegation of loss and finding was from the beginning merely a form of pleading imitated from the action of detinue.[115]

It is a curious irony that, of the pleader's five standard allegations, the one encapsulated in the name by which the tort became known for at least its first 300 years was one of two immaterial, non-traversable and 'notorious'[116] fictions.

4.   Delivery Up Requested but Refused

We have already seen that a failure to deliver up in response to a request was central to the cause of action in detinue.[117] This remained the position in trover. Thus in *Cooper v Chitty* Lord Mansfield CJ, distinguishing between trespass and trover, and analysing the position where a claimant chose to waive the illegality of an original taking in order to be able to sue in trover rather than trespass, observed that 'if the defendant delivers the thing upon demand, no damages can be recovered in this action [trover], for having taken it'.[118]

---

[111]   (1611) Cro Jac 244, 79 ER 210.

[112]   (1614) 2 Bulst 306 at 314, 80 ER 1143 at 1150; 1 Rolle Rep 59 at 60, 81 ER 326 at 327; Baker and Milsom (n 16) 541 at 545; Fifoot (n 13) 117 at 119.

[113]   See text to n 54.

[114]   *Cooper v Chitty* (1756) 1 Burr 20 at 31, 97 ER 166 at 172; 1 Keny 395 at 417, 96 ER 1033 at 1041; Baker and Milsom (n 16) 549 at 550. See also Blackstone (n 60) at 152.

[115]   Salmond, Observations (n 8) at 46; also Salmond, *Torts* (1907) at 288.

[116]   Ames (n 14) at 277.

[117]   See text to nn 32–35.

[118]   (1756) 1 Burr 20 at 31, 97 ER 166 at 172; 1 Keny 395 at 417, 96 ER 1033 at 1041; Baker and Milsom (n 16) 549 at 550.

That a refusal of delivery up on request could suffice to make out a Conversion (the fifth allegation, to which we shall come) was established in *Eason v Newman* 1596,[119] albeit with Popham CJ apparently dissenting. It did not, however, raise an irrebuttable presumption thereof; hence it was open to a defendant to seek to justify his withholding, in particular on the grounds that the obligation to deliver up was subject to an as yet unfulfilled condition precedent. Thus in 1591 a defendant was allowed to plead that the subject bag of money had come into his possession as a stakeholder to await a decision which had not yet been given.[120] Similarly in 1614 judgment was entered for a defendant who had taken a bag of money as a pledge to secure the redelivery of three butts of wine in the event that a judgment creditor did not accede to the pledgor's request to abandon a process of execution upon the same—the judgment creditor had not so agreed, and the redelivery of the wine was not established.[121]

5.   Conversion to Own Use (Causing Loss)

The earliest identified use of an allegation of 'Conversion' in a civil plea[122] for the loss of an asset is in *Calwodelegh v John* 1479,[123] a Common Pleas case where the count alleged that the defendant had converted the subject silver to his use (*'et eux convert a son œps'*). Baker and Milsom identify the case of *Wysse v Andrewe* 1531[124] as the first in the King's Bench rolls alleging Conversion against a finder. Within a further 15 years the allegation had become standard,[125] as part of the new form of trespass on the case which was trover. So, far from Conversion being a later development of trover, it was part of trover from its earliest days.

---

[119]   Baker and Milsom (n 16) at 537, drawing on HLS MS 110 fo 218v. For other reports of this case see Cro Eliz 495, 78 ER 745; Goulds 152, 75 ER 1059; Moo 460, 72 ER 695. See also *Ratcliff v Davies* (1611) Cro Jac 244, 79 ER 210, Fifoot (n 13) at 115.

[120]   *Anon* (1591) 1 Leon 247, 74 ER 226.

[121]   *Isaack v Clark* (1614) 2 Bulst 306, 80 ER 1143; 1 Rolle Rep 59, 81 ER 326; Baker and Milsom (n 16) at 541; Fifoot (n 13) at 117.

[122]   The like allegation formed part of the questioned felony debated six years earlier in *The Carrier's Case, Anon v Sheriff of London* YB P13 Edw IV f 9 pl 5 (1473), 64 Sel Soc (ed JH Baker) 30.

[123]   YB H18 Edw IV f 23a–b pl 5 Ct CP, Baker and Milsom (n 16) at 526, Fifoot (n 13) at 113; already discussed at text to n 66 ff.

[124]   Baker and Milsom (n 16) at 531, citing (1531) KB 27/1081 m78. See also 94 Sel Soc (ed JH Baker) at 252–53.

[125]   There is a limited number of cases over the intervening period to enable the development to be tracked closely. However Simpson (n 46) highlights several cases from this period in John Spelman's (manuscript) Reports (for which see now 93 and 94 Sel Soc (ed JH Baker)), which he discusses at 375–78.

A wrongful sale of an asset was soon recognised as sufficient to satisfy the requirement for a Conversion,[126] though an entirely innocent sale was only recognised as such some considerable time later.[127]

An allegation of Conversion was duly included in what Salmond referred to as 'the action in the modern form'[128] recorded as used in 1550,[129] where the count alleged '*in usum proprium convertit*'. Brooke duly applied the marginal annotation '*Converter in usum proprium*' to his note of the case.[130]

Conclusion

By the middle of the sixteenth century trover was a well recognised and distinct species of the action of trespass on the case, but nevertheless it was anything but a pedigree tort. Rather, it was a mongrel born of and developed by judicial pragmatism, which as we shall now see progressively expanded to take in the strains of trespass de bonis asportatis, detinue sur trover, and ultimately replevin, so as to become the common action for all cases of asportation, detention, misuse or destruction of assets.

The Hegemony of Trover

The obstacle standing in the way of trover's expansion was the rule against double actionability, which we have already come across—if one of the special writs was available, the old principle was that no action on the case would be permitted. Thus far, we have seen one situation in which the rule could be out-manoeuvred, namely where the identity of the subject asset had been fundamentally changed so as to amount to a *specificatio*, an alteration in its property.[131]

Over time there was a development in judicial thinking[132] which, although it stopped short of an outright abrogation of the rule, was sufficient to facilitate the expansion of trover. Rather than having to exclude the very existence of a claim under one of the special writs, claimants were set the lower task of having to

---

[126] *Anon* (1510) Keil 160 pl 2, 72 ER 334, Baker and Milsom (n 16) at 528, Fifoot (n 13) at 114 (sale by a bailee); *Vandrink v Archer* (1590) 1 Leon 221, 74 ER 203 (onward sale by innocent purchaser from vendor with no title); and *Wysse v Andrewe* (1531) Baker and Milsom (n 16) at 531, citing (1531) KB 27/1081 m78 (sale by a finder).

[127] See text to nn 173–74, and (later) under the side-heading Conversion in the Nineteenth Century, Affirmation of Strict Liability.

[128] Salmond, Observations (n 8) at 46, and Salmond, Torts (n 56) at 288.

[129] *Anon* 4 Edw VI, Brooke's Abridg Pt I, Accion sur le case f 8 pl 113.

[130] ibid—R Brooke, *Abridgement* (London, R Tottell, 1586).

[131] See text to nn 64 and 65, discussing inter alia *The Case of the Cloth of Gold*.

[132] Discussed by Simpson (n 46) at 374–80.

demonstrate that the substance of the cause of action relied on was different from that of the other writ. If it was, then they were permitted an election as to how to put their complaint.

The right of election took some time to become universally accepted. As we have seen, Choke J had dissented on the point in 1479.[133] Early in the sixteenth century Frowicke CJ stated in the Common Bench that a bailor whose assets had been lost for default of good custody 'shall have action of Detinue or action on [the] case at [his] pleasure',[134] and by 1510 'several of the justices' in the Court of Common Pleas expressed the view that a plaintiff bailor could proceed in case against a bailee who had sold the bailed assets even though he 'might have had an action in detinue if he wished'.[135] It seems that half a century later, however, again in Common Pleas, a claim brought in case failed on the ground that it was, in substance, in the nature of a detinue action.[136]

Trover takes the Ground of Trespass

As we have seen, trespass de bonis asportatis, incorporating the plea of *vi et armis* and *contra pacem regis*, was the action for the taking of assets from the actual or constructive possession of another. The original distinction from detinue sur bailment was clear enough; however, once first the plea *devenerunt ad manus* and then the action of detinue sur trover had become accepted, with the pleas of loss and finding immaterial and untraversable, there was no longer any substantial logic behind attaching importance to the manner by which the subject assets had come into the defendant's hands.

A series of decisions in the early seventeenth century definitively established the right of victims of a taking to elect between trespass and trover. In *Basset v Maynard* 1601[137] it was so decided in the Kings Bench. In 1604 the Court of Common Pleas, having been equally divided on the matter three years earlier,[138] followed suit in *Bishop v Viscountess Montague*, albeit by a bare majority.[139] The premise was that one could elect to qualify (that is in part waive) but not increase a tort, which in effect meant that by electing for trover when trespass was

---

[133] At n 68.

[134] *Orwell v Mortoft* YB M20 Hen VII f 8b–9b pl 18 (CB), Keil 76 at 77, 116 Sel Soc (ed JH Baker) 465 and 493 (Caryll) at 494, Baker and Milsom (n 16) at 406, Fifoot (n 13) at 351, Kiralfy, *Source Book* (n 3) at 150. There is some divergence between the sources as to the exact dating of this case; the better view appears to be 1505.

[135] *Anon* Keil 160 pl 2 (1510), 72 ER 334, Baker and Milsom (n 16) at 528, Fifoot (n 13) at 114. See also 94 Sel Soc (ed JH Baker) at *250*.

[136] *Mounteagle v Countess of Worcester* (1555) 2 Dyer 121, 73 ER 265, Baker and Milsom (n 16) at 531.

[137] 1 Rolle Abridg 105, Action sur Case, pl 5 (KB).

[138] *Bishop v Viscountess Montague* (1601) Cro Eliz 824 pl 1, 78 ER 1051 (Ct CP); Baker and Milsom (n 16) at 540; Fifoot (n 13) at 114.

[139] *Bishop v Viscountess Montague* (1604) Cro Jac 50 pl 21, 79 ER 42 (Ct CP); Baker and Milsom (n 16) at 541; Fifoot (n 13) at 115.

available a claimant was taken to waive the unlawfulness of the original taking. In 1610 a like decision was reached by the Exchequer Chamber in *Leveson v Kirk*.[140]

Salmond[141] drew attention to the implications for a claim pursued in trover of the same being founded on a taking which was unlawful in itself, that is a trespass. In such cases the unlawful taking suffced to make out a constructive Conversion—thus no refused request for delivery up (the fourth of the five allegations considered above) was required. He quotes Salkeld:

> Where the possession is lawful, the plaintiff must show a demand and a refusal to make a conversion. But if the possession was tortious, as if the defendant takes away the plaintiff's hat, there the very taking is a sufficient proof of the conversion.[142]

It should be noted that this principle, as stated, applies to trespasses which amount to a taking, and result in the defendant having possession of the subject asset. Hence it is not inconsistent with the principle mentioned below that minor interferences sufficient to constitute a technical trespass may not constitute a Conversion.

The consequences of making an election were examined by the Kings Bench in *Putt v Rawstorne* 1682,[143] a case which may have been argued twice.[144] The objection taken was that the claimant had previously brought an action for trespass *vi et armis* in respect of the same assets, and had failed. The Court concluded, Dolben J 'hesitante', that where the case was such that either trover or trespass would lie, then 'wheresoever the same evidence will maintain both the actions, then the recovery or judgment in one may be pleaded in bar of the other; but otherwise not'.

Williams on Saunders[145] notes Parke J's proposition in *Norman v Bell*[146] that whenever trespass for taking goods will lie, that is where they are taken wrong-fully, trover will also lie, but correctly observes that this

> requires some qualification; for a mere wrongful asportation of a chattel does not amount to a conversion, unless the taking or detention of the chattel is with intent to convert it to the taker's own use, or that of some third person, or unless the act done has the effect either of destroying or changing the quality of the chattel.

---

[140] (1610) 1 Rolle Abridg 105, Action sur Case, pl 10.
[141] Salmond, Observations (n 8) at 51–52.
[142] 3 Salk 365 pl 8, 91 ER 876.
[143] (1682) T Raym 472, 83 ER 246; 3 Mod 1, 87 ER 1; Baker and Milsom (n 16) at 546; Fifoot (n 13) at 120.
[144] Contrast the above reports with that at 2 Mod 318, 86 ER 1097.
[145] 2 Wms Saund, 6th edn E Vaughan Williams (ed) (London, W Benning & Co, 1845) at 47aa–bb.
[146] (1831) 2 B & Ad 190 at 192, 109 ER 1114 at 1115.

The well-known case of *Fouldes v Willoughby* is cited, and we will consider that in chapter three below.[147] The proposition was, however, of significantly greater antiquity.[148]

Trover takes the Ground of Detinue

We have already seen early examples, from the beginning of the sixteenth century, of judicial acceptance that a claimant might proceed in trover even though a claim in detinue would have been possible on the same facts.[149] At the end of that century Gawdy J is reported as having stated, in a case pleaded in trover, that 'although the plaintiff could have had an action of detinue for the goods ... nevertheless the withholding and refusing to deliver them is another wrong, properly to be punished by this action'.[150] The claim succeeded, finally vindicating Choke J's dissent in *Cadwodelegh v John*.[151]

Failure or refusal to comply with a request for delivery up came to be treated as evidence of a Conversion, notwithstanding that such always had been at the heart of the action in detinue;[152] the absence of judicial concern about this is amply reflected in the observation of Gawdy J just cited. We have seen that it was not, however, treated as conclusive evidence, and that justification of the withholding was permissible.[153] The language used was that of presumption,[154] and of a constructive Conversion.[155] Holt CJ would have gone further, taking the view that the failure or refusal itself amounted to an actual Conversion rather than mere evidence thereof.[156] As Salmond has summarised the position, however, 'This view did not prevail, although there was much conflict on the point'.[157]

We have seen that one of the circumstances which led to the emergence of detinue sur trover was where the original bailee had parted with possession before action.[158] Nevertheless, even where the parties to the case were the original

---

[147] At text to n 108 ff.

[148] See, eg, *Bushel v Miller* (1718) 1 Str 128, 93 ER 428, Fifoot (n 13) at 121 (misdating the case as 1731), discussed in ch 3, text to fn 93 ff.

[149] See text to nn 134–35.

[150] *Eason v Newman* (1596) Baker and Milsom (n 16) at 537, drawing on HLS MS 110 fo 218v. In the report at Goulds 152, 75 ER 1059 the same judge is recorded as having observed that such a claimant may pursue 'detinue or an Action upon the case at [his] pleasure'. For other reports of this case see n 119.

[151] For which, see n 68.

[152] See text to nn 32–35.

[153] See text to nn 120–21.

[154] *Chancellor of the University of Oxford v Bishop of Coventry and Litchfield* (1614) 10 Co Rep 53b at 56b, 77 ER 1006 at 1010; Blackstone (n 60) at 152.

[155] Per Abbot CJ in *Alexander v Southey* (1821) 5 B & Ald 247 at 248, 106 ER 1183.

[156] *Baldwin v Cole* (1704) 6 Mod 212, 87 ER 964; 1 Holt KB 707, 90 ER 1290.

[157] Salmond, Observations (n 8) at 48.

[158] See text to nn 38–40. Thus, eg, the decision in *Rilston v Holbeck* YB M12 Ed IV f 13 pl 9 (1472), Baker and Milsom (n 16) at 524 (a successful action on the case concerning a sub-under-bailment of various linen cloths; Bryan CJ dissented because the defendant was not the original bailee).

bailor and bailee, being the classic circumstance for an action in detinue sur bailment, trover was held available. An early example is afforded by *Warton v Ashepole* (1524). Warton alleged that he had delivered a horse to Ashepole to look after it and return it on request, and Ashepole undertook to do so in return for 40d. Warton further alleged that Ashepole had used the horse, and converted it to his own use. Ashepole was not permitted to traverse the undertaking (*assumpsit*) 'since it is immaterial. The cause of action is the delivery and the conversion to his own use'.[159]

Likewise in *Isaack v Clark* the first of five points for decision was 'May Case on a Trover and Conversion be brought on a Bailment?' This was answered in the affirmative: 'the judge is not to look at the bailment, if you can lay and well prove a conversion, which is the chief point of the action'.[160]

Simpson, considering the disadvantage of detinue where the subject assets were still available but in poorer condition, concluded that:

> What was required was some device of pleading which would enable him to sue his bailee in case and recover the whole value of the goods even though the damage to those goods was only partial ... The device ultimately adopted was this—the plaintiff did not complain of the damage caused by the defendant's misconduct *simpliciter*, or of misconduct in breach of an undertaking, but instead complained that the defendant's misconduct amounted to a total misappropriation of the goods bailed—a conversion to his own use—so that the damage which he suffered from the wrong was the whole value of the goods. This allegation ... proved extremely attractive to courts who were quite happy to supercede detinue if their consciences could be squared, and in the end case ... superceded detinue entirely.[161]

Cases such as *Warton v Ashepole* support Simpson's thesis, although it must be noted that this expansion of trover onto detinue's ground was not limited to cases where the point of allowing trover was to ensure that the claimant could obtain compensation for damage to bailed assets in the same action as their recovery. *Isaack v Clark*, for example, concerned a bag of money.

Residual Categories

For some time longer, replevin held out against trover's advance. The perceived difficulty was the same which had kept replevin distinct from trespass, in that there was room for drawing a theoretical distinction between what was inherent in taking assets for one's own use, and what was inherent in taking possession of assets under some (perceived) legal authority. In *Tinkler v Poole*,[162] however, Lord Mansfield brushed aside any such distinction, robustly asserting that 'A tortious

---

[159]   Baker and Milsom (n 16) at 529; (1524) Spelman f 4 pl 4, 93 Sel Soc (ed JH Baker) 4.
[160]   (1614) 2 Bulst 306 at 312, 80 ER 1143 at 1148; Baker and Milsom (n 16) at 541; Fifoot (n 13) at 117.
[161]   Simpson (n 46) at 370–71.
[162]   (1770) 5 Burr 2657, 98 ER 396.

taking is, in itself, a conversion'. A customs officer had seized and carried to the King's warehouse a parcel of herrings, for non-satisfaction of the salt duty. It was subsequently accepted that they were *not* seizable, but actionability in trover was disputed on the basis of two authorities then of some 50 years standing.[163] Lord Mansfield dismissed both of them as 'very loose notes'.

Despite the great expansion of trover, and the continued existence of the old forms of action for detinue and trespass (albeit much less used), Pollock observed that even with 'all their artificial extensions these forms of action did not completely suffice. There might still be circumstances in which a special action on the case was required.'[164] At least the principal example of this was the reversionary owner's right to sue in case for any permanent injury to his interest, for the rights of an owner who neither had nor was immediately entitled to possession did not fall within the compass of trover.

Conclusion

The triumph of trover was virtually, if not totally, complete. Trover became substantially concurrent with all the four ancient forms of actions, appeal of robbery or larceny, trespass, detinue and replevin. In particular, it was generally regarded as preferable to treat a detention as a Conversion and sue in trover rather than detinue, and trespass and Conversion became largely though not wholly interchangeable. Trover had become the common remedy in all cases of asportation or detention of assets or of their misuse or destruction by a defendant in possession.[165] As Ames put it:

> The career of trover in the field of torts is matched only by that of assumpsit, the other specialized form of action on the case, in the domain of contract.[166]

The Recognition of Conversion

We have already referred to the earliest identified usage of an allegation of 'Conversion' in 1479 (Common Pleas) and 1531 (King's Bench), and to its general adoption as part of a pleading of trover by the middle of the sixteenth century.[167]

---

[163] *Etriche v An Officer of the Revenue* (1720) Bunbury 67, 145 ER 597, and *Israel v Etheridge* (1721) Bunbury 80, 145 ER 602. Ames (n 14) at 385–86 pointed out that there were a number of authorities to like effect of yet greater antiquity: *Dee v Bacon* (1595) Cro Eliz 435, 78 ER 676 (QB); *Salter v Butler* (1602) Noy 46, 74 ER 1016 (KB); *Agars v Lisle* (1613) Hutt 10, 123 ER 1063 (Ct CP).

[164] Pollock (n 17) at 289, citing *Mears v London and South Western Railway Company* (1862) 11 CB (NS) 850, 142 ER 1029; see also at 277, cited at text to n 17. The tort of reversionary injury is discussed in ch 3, under the side-heading The Relationship between the Wrongful Interference Torts, Reversionary Injury.

[165] Ames (n 14) at 386; Pollock (n 17) at 279.

[166] Ames (n 14) at 386.

[167] See text to nn 123–30 and 91–93.

There was a potential ambiguity in the use of the term 'Conversion' in cases such as *Calwoledelgh v John*, for in that context it could linguistically be taken as a reference to a physical alteration of the subject asset which was being alleged to have brought about a *specificatio*.[168] In time, however, any such ambiguity was excluded, and its general meaning was recognised as being in the nature of a misappropriation, as the customary phrase 'converted to his own use' rather suggested.[169]

Generally a broad meaning of 'conversion to his own use' was accepted, and Pollock describes it as a phrase 'of which the scope has been greatly extended'.[170] However a mere non-feasance, such as negligently failing to look after the subject property, did not suffice.[171] Some act of positive misconduct was required. Further attempts at historical definition tend to prove circular, for in essence 'Conversion' became a convenient, composite term to describe dealings adverse to a claimant's rights in an asset sufficient to establish a claim for trover.

We have already demonstrated that proof of a failure or refusal to deliver up gave rise to a strong if not irrebuttable inference of a Conversion.[172] The concept of strict liability for unjustified intermeddling with assets belonging to another gradually emerged,[173] after 'considerable vacillation' at the end of the sixteenth century.[174] We shall see below that its decisive confirmation came in the nineteenth century.

It would be artificial to seek to identify a time at which trover became Conversion. We have seen that an allegation of 'Conversion' was a part of trover from its earliest days. Greater insight may be gained from noting that the composite title 'Trover and Conversion' was used to describe the tort in cases by the beginning of the seventeenth century,[175] by Blackstone in the second half of the eighteenth century,[176] and by Salmond in the early twentieth century.[177]

---

[168]   As to which see text to nn 64–68. The original meaning of 'Conversion' in this context is explored by Simpson (n 46).

[169]   See further in ch 3, under the heading Name.

[170]   Pollock (n 17) at 278.

[171]   *Walgrave v Ogden* (1590) 1 Leon 224, 74 ER 205 (CB); *Isaack v Clark* (1614) 2 Bulst 306, 80 ER 1143, 1 Rolle Rep 59, 81 ER 326, Baker and Milsom (n 16) at 541, Fifoot (n 13) at 117. Here an action on the case for negligence emerged as the generally appropriate remedy: see, eg, Ibbetson (n 2) at 164–68.

[172]   See text to nn 119–21.

[173]   *Gomersall v Medgate* (1610) Yelv 194, 80 ER 128 (an innocent technical error in the process of distraint); *Cooper v Chitty* (1756) 1 Burr 20 at 22, 97 ER 166 at 167, per Norton *arguendo*: 'A man may, without his own fault, be possessed of a horse which has been stolen: but nevertheless, he is answerable, *civiliter* to the true owner for it' (the case is also reported at 1 Keny 395, 96 ER 1033).

[174]   Baker and Milsom (n 16) at 537. The Court was equally divided in *Gallyard v Archer* (1589) LI MS Misc 791 f 113, Baker and Milsom at 535, and (if a different case—see Baker and Milsom at 535) in *Vandrink v Archer* (1590) 1 Leon 221, 74 ER 203.

[175]   *Ratcliff v Davies* (1611) Cro Jac 244, 79 ER 210, Fifoot (n 13) at 115; *Isaack v Clark* (1614) 2 Bulst. 306, 80 ER 1143, 1 Rolle Rep 59, 81 ER 326, Baker and Milsom (n 16) at 541–45, Fifoot 117–19.

[176]   n 60 at 151.

[177]   'Observations on Trover and Conversion' was the title of Salmond's celebrated article in the 1905 LQR (n 8). See also Salmond, Torts (n 56) at ch IX *passim*.

We have already commented on the irony inherent in this tort having become known as trover. Even when known by the composite name Trover and Conversion there was already no doubt as to which of the two eponymous allegations was the one which mattered. The position was recounted by Houghton J in *Isaack v Clark*:

> [M]any times in detinue or trover the bailment comes not in question, nor is material, if the conversion be actionable ... though the action is here brought for a trover and conversion, and no trover in the case because he had the goods by bailment, yet if there be a conversion the court shall judge upon this[178]

There can be no more definitive and succinct summation of the position than that of Lord Mansfield in *Cooper v Chitty*: 'the whole tort consists in the wrongful conversion'.[179] This dictum, however, echoed the statement of Coke *arguendo* in *Stransham's Case* (1588), almost two centuries earlier, that: 'the conversion ... is the substance of the action'.[180] Croke's marginal note to his report of *Gumbleton v Grafton* (1600) was to similar effect 'Conversion is the *gist* in an action of trover'.[181] Conversion had gained recognition as being the whole substance of trover.

Conversion in the Nineteenth Century

Statutory Reforms

As previously mentioned, it was not until 1833 that wager at law was formally abolished by statute.[182] Of greater practical importance, however, was the Common Law Procedure Act 1852,[183] which marked the beginning of the end of the forms of action.[184]

It was no longer necessary to mention any form or cause of action in a writ,[185] and by section 49 it was provided that:

---

[178] *Isaack v Clark* (1614) 2 Bulst. 306, 80 ER 1143, 1 Rolle Rep 59, 81 ER 326, Baker and Milsom (n 16) 541 at 542. For the converse proposition, that absent the element of conversion the claim would fail, see, eg, *Hartford v Jones* (1698) 1 Ld Raym 393, 91 ER 1161.

[179] (1756) 1 Burr 20 at 31, 97 ER 166 at 172; 1 Keny 395 at 417, 96 ER 1033 at 1041; Baker and Milsom (n 16) 549 at 550.

[180] Cro Eliz 98, 78 ER 356.

[181] Cro Eliz 781, 78 ER 1011. The reporter's note contrasted *Higgs v Holiday* (1600) Cro Eliz 746, 78 ER 978, in which the claimant's loss of possession of the subject money by his own action in, as his declaration pleaded, casually losing the same ('*casualiter perdidit*'), had as a matter of law (given the nature of money) caused him also to lose the property in the same; thus, no subsequent act of the defendant's could be characterised as a Conversion, and the action failed accordingly.

[182] s 13, Civil Procedure Act 1833 (3 and 4 Wm IV c42).

[183] 15 and 16 Vict c 76.

[184] Their formal abolition was effected by s 3, Judicature Act 1873 (36 and 37 Vict c 66).

[185] ibid, s 3.

> All Statements which need not be proved, such as ... the Statement of losing and finding ... in Actions for Goods or their Value; ... and all Statements of a like kind, shall be omitted.

It may be noted that the statutory text expressly acknowledged that, as we saw earlier in this chapter, the allegation of loss and finding was one which 'need not be proved'. Schedule B of the Act provided a new and much simplified statement of the cause of action, namely:

> That the Defendant converted to his own Use, or wrongfully deprived the Plaintiff of the Use and Possession of the Plaintiff's Goods; that is to say Iron, Hops, Household Furniture [or as the Case may be].

This, as Salmond put it, was 'the essence of the matter'.[186]

Two years later, the remedies available in detinue were expanded by the Common Law Procedure Act 1854.[187] The most fundamental point was that courts of common law were given the discretionary power to make orders for specific delivery up, something which thitherto could only be obtained, as an equitable remedy, in the court of Chancery. It is, however, worth noting the full text of section 78, for it gives an insight into the origins of what might be thought to be the slightly odd format of the statutory remedies now available under section 3 of the Torts (Interference with Goods) Act 1977, which we shall consider in chapter seven:

> The Court or a Judge shall have Power, if they or he see fit so to do, upon the Application of the Plaintiff in any Action for the Detention of any Chattel, to order that Execution shall issue for the Return of the Chattel detained, without giving the Defendant the Option of retaining such Chattel upon paying the Value assessed, and that if the said Chattel cannot be found, and unless the Court or a Judge should otherwise order, the Sheriff shall distrain the Defendant by all his Lands and Chattels in the said Sheriff's Bailiwick, till the Defendant render such Chattel, or at the Option of the Plaintiff, that he cause to be made of the Defendant's Goods the assessed Value of such Chattel; provided that the Plaintiff shall, either by the same or a separate Writ of Execution, be entitled to have made of the Defendant's Goods the Damages, Costs, and Interest in such Action.

The absence of jurisdiction in the courts of common law, prior to this enactment, to award an *in specie* remedy in respect of assets had not, however, been the only obstacle to the development of a wider system of such remedies for Conversion. There would in any event also have been a practical impediment, in that the common law had not enjoyed sufficient enforcement mechanisms realistically to support a system compelling the return of assets as a matter of course. The

---

[186]   Salmond, Observations (n 8), at 43.
[187]   17 and 18 Vict c 125.

performance of sheriffs in carrying out even the relatively limited duties in support of the courts which they did perform was, in practice, patchy.[188]

These nineteenth-century reforms have, nevertheless, been credited with sparking something of a revival in detinue, which had largely fallen into near desuetude in the face of the expanding utility and popularity of Conversion as a cause of action described earlier in this chapter.[189]

Another attraction of detinue, in comparison with many cases of Conversion,[190] was the beneficial effect, for the purposes of limitation, of the demand for delivery up being part of the cause of action. This was highlighted in 1871 by the decision in *Wilkinson v Verity*.[191]

Following the abolition of the forms of action Pollock,[192] and later Salmond,[193] both suggested that the name Conversion could be extended to cover the tort of reversionary injury. Nothing has become of this, which is probably no more than a reflection of the low profile of that relatively little used tort.

A New Legal Fiction—the Conversion of Choses in Action Evidenced by Converted Documents

In the mid-nineteenth century, and, somewhat ironically, just as statute was to remove from writs the old legal fiction of loss and finding, a new legal fiction began to be developed by the common law. Negotiable instruments and the like, when considered as tangible property, are no more than pieces of paper of negligible value. However as a pragmatic development of Conversion, recognising the need for an effective and straightforward legal remedy for their misappropriation, a new legal fiction as to their value was developed, just as the old fiction of loss and finding was being laid to rest.

An early example is afforded by *Alsager v Close*,[194] where an action was brought by assignees for trover in respect of a bill of exchange for £1,600. The assignor had deposited the same with the defendant as security for a bond, which was subsequently cancelled. The defendant, however, converted the bill by refusing a

---

[188] See JH Baker, *An Introduction to English Legal History*, 4th edn (London, Butterworths, 2002) at 64–67. Rightly or wrongly, the robust reputation of the Sheriff of Middlesex may suggest that this was less of a problem within his jurisdiction!

[189] See 18th Report (n 11) at para 7, and N Curwen, 'The remedy in conversion: confusing property and obligation', (2006) 26 *Legal Studies* 570 at 572.

[190] Although where an innocent defendant (eg a true finder) first converted the property by refusing a demand for delivery, the limitation position was the same as in detinue: see, eg, *Spackman v Foster* (1883) 11 QBD 99 (reversed as to whether the receipt of goods by way of pledge constitutes a conversion by s 11(2) of the 1977 Act).

[191] (1871) LR 6 CP 206, discussed in text to nn 32–35.

[192] Pollock (n 17) at 289.

[193] Salmond, Observations (n 8) at 54, as was noted in 18th Report (n 11) at para 34.

[194] (1842) 10 M & W 576, 152 ER 600.

demand for its return,[195] and by himself obtaining £800 against it. He was held liable, and since there had been a Conversion of the whole bill the proper measure of damages was £1,600, not just the lesser sum which the defendant had obtained against it, and even though £800 was still due on the bill.[196] In 1858, Wightman J sitting in Exchequer Chamber stated that 'trover for a bond is a well-known and common action',[197] which indicates that the recoverability of substantial damages in such an action was by then well established.

The fiction inherent in an award of substantial damages for Conversion of such a document—that although what in law has been converted is the piece of paper, it is valued as if what has been converted is the chose in action which it evidences—was not at the time expressly acknowledged as such.[198]

Affirmation of Strict Liability

The principle of strict liability for unjustified intermeddling with assets was assumed by the Court of King's Bench at the beginning of the nineteenth century in *M'Combie v Davies*.[199] A broker bought tobacco on behalf of the claimant, but then pledged it for his own benefit to the defendant, who was unaware of the claimant's interest. The defendant subsequently declined the claimant's request for delivery up, pending repayment of the sums he had advanced to the broker. Lord Ellenborough stated that:

> According to Lord Holt in *Baldwin v Cole*[200] the very assuming to oneself the property and right of disposing of another man's goods is a conversion: and certainly a man is guilty of a conversion who takes my property by assignment from another who has no authority to dispose of it; for what is that but assisting that other in carrying his wrongful act into effect.[201]

---

[195]   Subject to a technical issue as to who, as between assignor and assignee, was entitled to make the demand, which is of no consequence for present purposes.

[196]   Similarly, in *Watson v McLean* (1858) E B & E 75, 120 ER 435 the defendant was held liable in trover for the conversion of a life insurance policy, 'a specific chattel' (per Wightman J at 77, 436), and the damages assessed as the amount payable, and in fact received by the defendant from the underwriter, on the policy. See also *M'Leod v M'Ghie* (1841) 2 M & G 326, 133 ER 771 (trover in respect of a guarantee).

[197]   *Watson v McLean* (1858) E B & E 75 at 77, 120 ER 435 at 436.

[198]   As it later was by Scrutton LJ in *Lloyds Bank v The Chartered Bank of India, Australia and China* [1929] 1 KB 40 (CA) at 55, and more recently has been in terms—see *Smith v Lloyds TSB Group plc* [2001] QB 541 (CA) per Pill and Potter LJJ at 551B–C and 557G–H respectively, and *OBG Ltd v Allan* [2005] EWCA Civ 106, [2005] QB 762 per Mance LJ at [76] and [2007] UKHL 21, [2008] 1 AC 1 per Lord Nicholls at [227]–[229]; contrast 18th Report (n 11) at para 98, with which we would respectfully disagree on this point.

[199]   (1805) 6 East 538, 102 ER 1393.

[200]   (1704) 6 Mod 212, 87 ER 964; 1 Holt KB 707, 90 ER 1290. For the words of Holt CJ referred to, see in ch 3 under the heading The Gist of Conversion.

[201]   (1805) 6 East 538 at 540, 102 ER 1393 at 1394–95.

Its decisive affirmation, however, came in the leading case of *Hollins v Fowler*,[202] which we discuss in chapter three below.

The decision in favour of strict liability in *Hollins v Fowler* was then applied inter alia to hold an innocent bank liable for the Conversion of postal orders which it had presented for payment on behalf of the claimant society's secretary, unaware of his dishonesty, in *Fine Art Society v Union Bank of London*,[203] and to hold innocent auctioneers liable for the Conversion of household furniture they sold on a client's behalf at her private residence (there delivering it up to the purchasers in the ordinary course of their business), unaware that their client had previously executed a bill of sale thereover (in the claimants' favour), in *Consolidated Co v Curtis & Son*.[204]

The Common Law (Still) Presents Great Difficulties

Despite a number of improvements and clarifications during the nineteenth century, towards its end the exact nature and scope of Conversion was still regarded as obscure. In 1879 Baron Bramwell observed that 'I have frequently stated that I never did understand with precision what was a Conversion'.[205]

Sir Frederick Pollock considered that the common law presented 'great difficulties' in determining what amounted to a wrong to property, and who was the person wronged. The whole passage from his *Law of Torts*[206] merits quotation:

> It would seem that, apart from doubtful questions of title (which no system of law can wholly avoid), there ought not to be a great difficulty in determining what amounts to a wrong to property, and who is the person wronged. But in fact the common law does present great difficulties; and this because its remedies were bound, until a recent date, to medieval forms, and limited by medieval conceptions. The forms of action brought not Ownership but Possession to the front in accordance with a habit of thought which, strange as it may now seem to us, found the utmost difficulty in conceiving rights of property as having full existence or being capable of transfer and succession unless in close connexion with the physical control of something which could be passed from hand to hand, or at least a part of it delivered in the name of the whole. An owner in possession was protected against disturbance, but the rights of an owner out of possession were obscure and weak. To this day it continues so with regard to chattels. For many purposes the 'true owner' of goods is the person, and only the person, entitled to immediate possession. The term is a short and convenient one, and may be used without scruple, but on condition of being rightly understood. Regularly the common law protects ownership only through possessory rights and remedies. The reversion or reversionary interest of the freeholder or general owner out of possession is indeed well

---

[202]   *Hollins and ors v Fowler and ors* (1875) LR 7 HL 757, affg (1872) LR 7 QB 616 (Ex Ch).
[203]   (1886) LR 17 QBD 705.
[204]   [1892] 1 QB 495.
[205]   *Hiort and anor v The London and North-Western Railway Company* (1879) 4 Ex D 188 at 194.
[206]   (London, Stevens & Sons, 1887) at 275–76, unchanged at the end of the century—see 5th edn (1897) at 316–17.

known to our authorities, and by conveyancers it is regarded as a present estate or interest. But when it has to be defended in a court of common law, the forms of action treat it rather as the shadow cast before by a right to possess at a time still to come.

Conversion in the Twentieth Century

Obscurities Remain

Following the turn of the century, the perceived obscurities of the law of Conversion remained. No history of Conversion would be complete without quoting the famous opening words of Sir John Salmond's article *Observations on Trover and Conversion* in the *Law Quarterly Review* of 1905:

> Forms of action are dead, but their ghosts still haunt the precincts of the law. In their life they were powers of evil, and even in death they have not wholly ceased from troubling. In earlier days they filled the law with formalism and fiction, confusion and complexity, and though most of the mischief which they did has been buried with them, some portion of it remains inherent in the law of the present day. Thus if we open a book on the law of torts, howsoever modern and rationalized, we can still hear the echoes of the old controversies concerning the contents and boundaries of trespass and detinue and trover and case, and we are still called upon to observe distinctions and subtleties that have no substance or justification in them, but are nothing more than an evil inheritance from the days when forms of action and of pleading held the legal system in their clutches.[207]

Expansion of the New Legal Fiction

The legal fiction as to the Conversion of negotiable instruments which, as we have seen, had first been developed in the nineteenth century, was affirmed by a number of significant decisions in the early twentieth century, including *Morison v London County and Westminster Bank*,[208] *AL Underwood Ltd v Bank of Liverpool and Martins*[209] and *Lloyds Bank v The Chartered Bank of India, Australia and China*.[210]

In the first of those cases, Lord Reading CJ stated the rule thus:

> Damages for such conversion may be, and in my opinion are, in this case the face value of the instruments. The plaintiff is entitled to compensation for the loss he has sustained by reason of the conversion, and that loss is the equivalent of the amounts paid to the defendants by the National Provincial Bank and debited to the plaintiff's

---

[207]   n 8, at 43. Much of this article was to find its way into the chapter on Conversion, Detinue and Trespass to Goods in his *Law of Torts* (n 56).
[208]   [1914] 3 KB 356 (CA).
[209]   [1924] 1 KB 775 (CA).
[210]   [1929] 1 KB 40 (CA).

banking account. The defendants have wrongfully obtained money on valuable instruments of the plaintiff, and his banking account at the National Provincial Bank has been depleted to the amounts paid on the cheques. The plaintiff has lost the sums which the defendants have wrongfully received, and the plaintiff is therefore entitled to recover such sums as damages for the conversion. That such damages may be given for the conversion of a cheque or bill of exchange has been decided in many cases[211]

When it came to explaining the basis of the rule, however, it is noteworthy that Phillimore LJ was 'not altogether confident'.[212]

The defendant bank was the holder of the cheques ... and ... collected the proceeds in its own right ... Therefore, the defendant bank converted the cheques. That the damages for such conversion are (at any rate where the drawer has sufficient funds to his credit and the drawee bank is solvent) the face value of the cheques is established in a series of cases: ... so well established that it is not necessary to inquire into the principle which may underlie the authority. But the principle probably is that, though the plaintiff might at any moment destroy the cheques while they remained in his possession, they are potential instruments whereby the sums which they represent may be drawn from his bankers, and, if they get into other hands than his, he will be the loser to the extent of the sums which they represent. It may be also that any one who has obtained its value by presenting a cheque is estopped from asserting that it has only a nominal value.[213]

Although there are judicial statements suggesting that Conversion by this legal fiction is limited to negotiable instruments,[214] it has—albeit somewhat cautiously—been expanded beyond them. In particular, the Conversion of shares (in limited companies) is well recognised, and damages have been awarded for their value. In *Solloway v McLaughlin*[215] shares were sold without authority by a broker with whom the certificates had been deposited.[216] The claimant recovered the value of those shares in Conversion, less a credit for the value of certain shares which were returned.

In *Bavins Jnr & Sims v London & South Western Bank Ltd*[217] at least two members of the Court of Appeal suggested that the damages payable for Conversion of a document which was not a negotiable instrument, but mere documentary evidence of a chose in action (there, an acknowledgement of debt coupled with an informal instruction for payment to the debtor's bank), may nevertheless extend to the value of the chose in action.[218]

---

[211] [1914] 3 KB 356 at 365.

[212] Per Lord Hoffmann in *OBG Ltd v Allan* [2007] UKHL 21, [2008] 1 AC 1 at [104].

[213] [1914] 3 KB 356 at 379.

[214] eg per Mance LJ in *OBG Ltd v Allan* [2005] EWCA Civ 106, [2005] QB 762 at [76].

[215] *Solloway Mills & Co and ors v McLaughlin* [1938] AC 247 (PC) at 257–58 per Lord Atkin.

[216] We infer that the deposits of shares referred to in the report were effected by deliveries of the certificates.

[217] [1900] 1 QB 270 (CA).

[218] ibid, at 275 per AL Smith LJ, and (more tentatively) 276 per Collins LJ. Vaughan Williams LJ at 278 effectively reserved his view, whilst indicating some sympathy for a possible argument to like effect based on estoppel.

Although *Bavins* appears to mark the furthest point to which the fiction has been extended by an English court, *Clerk & Lindsell*[219] expresses the view that the exception would 'no doubt extend to tickets and tokens of various kinds evidencing valuable rights other than debts (eg travel tickets, credit cards, club membership cards), although assessment of damages may be more difficult'.[220]

As White J recognised in the 2006 Australian case of *Hoath v Connect Internet Services*,[221] quoting Balkin and Davis,[222] when considering the nature of this exception:

> This doctrine, which is certainly applicable to all negotiable instruments, makes substantial inroads on any possible rule, traceable to the former fiction of losing and finding, that conversion does not lie in respect of rights in intangible property.

Regrettably, the following year Lord Hoffmann, leading a bare majority of the House of Lords (on this point) in *OBG Ltd v Allan*, took a far more conservative view of the exception.

> [I]n cases in which the title to [a] debt was evidenced by a negotiable instrument, or even in some cases where it was not negotiable, the wrongful misappropriation of the document could cause actual loss to the true creditor, who might not be able to recover the debt. That left a gap in the law. The judges filled it by treating the misappropriation as a conversion of a chattel equal in value to the debt which it evidenced ... There do not appear to be any judicial statements offering a better explanation [than those of Phillimore LJ quoted above, and Scrutton LJ in *Lloyds Bank Limited v The Chartered Bank of India, Australia and China*[223]]. It is in my opinion an insecure base on which to erect a comprehensive system of strict liability for interference with choses in action.[224]

Financing of and Title to Motor Cars

The emergence after the Second World War of widespread popular ownership of motor cars, and of readily available consumer credit schemes to facilitate the same, gave rise to a considerable volume of litigation. This was perhaps a predictable consequence of the proliferation of relatively high value assets which were readily moveable, and hence ripe for misappropriation, and in which there were frequently multiple ownership interests. There were at least 25 reported cases in the High Court and above founded on the alleged Conversion of motor cars, many of which also involved finance agreements, in the 30 years preceding

---

219   n 30, at para 17–35, fn 54.
220   Citing 18th Report (n 11) at paras 90–91.
221   [2006] NSWSC 158, 69 IPR 62 at [125].
222   RP Balkin and JLR Davis, *Law of Torts* 3rd edn (Sydney, Butterworths, 2004) at 76.
223   [1929] 1 KB 40 at 55.
224   [2007] UKHL 21, [2008] 1 AC 1 at [104] and [106]. This question is considered further in ch 5, under the heading Intangible Property; see also ch 7 at text to nn 120–25.

the coming into force of the 1977 Act.[225] This was in addition to similar cases founded in the related torts of detinue[226] and trespass.[227]

The Report of the Law Reform Committee

In June 1967 the Law Reform Committee (which at the time co-existed with the recently created Law Commission) was invited to consider whether any changes in the law relating to Conversion and detinue, and to the recaption of chattels, were desirable; trespass to goods was subsequently added to its terms of reference. In September 1971, after a gestation period in excess of three years, its Eighteenth Report (Conversion and Detinue) was published as a Command Paper.[228]

The Committee identified two major features of the existing law worthy of attention, the continuing domination of the old causes of action and the extent to which concurrent remedies arose in detinue and Conversion, in trespass and Conversion, and to a lesser extent in Conversion, contract, quasi-contract and negligence.[229] It concluded that there was no advantage to retaining multiple sets of remedies and recommended the abolition of detinue and of trespass to goods,[230] with the retention of Conversion (under whatever name) 'as the main vehicle of English law for the protection of proprietary rights'.[231]

Its Report went on to identify and consider the possible courses of adopting an entirely new, self-contained statutory code centred on a single, statutory tort, and of retaining the common law in respect of Conversion, subject to renaming the tort and some statutory modifications. The Committee recognised that the

---

[225] *Robin & Rambler Coachers Ltd v Turner* [1947] 2 All ER 284 (KB), *Munro v Willmott* [1949] 1 KB 295, *R B Policies at Lloyd's v Butler* [1950] KB 76, *North Central Wagon and Finance Co Ltd v Graham* [1950] 2 KB 7 (CA), *Pearson v Rose & Young Ltd* [1951] 1 KB 275 (CA), *Du Jardin v Beadman Brothers Ltd* [1952] 2 QB 712, *Eisinger v General Accident Fire and Life Assurance Corporation Ltd* [1955] 1 WLR 869 (QB), *Central Newbury Car Auctions Ltd v Unity Finance Ltd and anor* [1957] 1 QB 371 (CA), *Ingram and ors v Little* [1961] 1 QB 31 (CA), *Moorgate Mercantile Co Ltd v Finch and Read* [1962] 1 QB 701 (CA), *Hollins v J Davy Ltd* [1963] 1 QB 844 , *Capital Finance Co Ltd v Bray* [1964] 1 WLR 323 (CA), *Newtons of Wembley Ltd v Williams* [1965] 1 QB 560 (CA), *Lloyds and Scottish Finance Ltd v Williamson and anor* [1965] 1 WLR 404 (CA), *Bowmaker (Commercial) Ltd v Day and ors* [1965] 1 WLR 1396 (QB), *Wickham Holdings Ltd v Brooke House Motors Ltd* [1967] 1 WLR 295 (CA), *Snook v London and West Riding Investments Ltd* [1967] 2 QB 786 (CA), *Belvoir Finance Co Ltd v Harold G Cole & Co Ltd* [1969] 1 WLR 1877 (QB), *Belvoir Finance Co Ltd v Stapleton* [1971] 1 QB 210 (CA), *Worcester Works Finance Ltd v Cooden Engineering Co Ltd* [1972] 1 QB 210 (CA), *Moorgate Mercantile Co Ltd v Twitchings* [1976] QB 225 (CA) and [1977] AC 890, *Stevenson v Beverley Bentinck Ltd* [1976] 1 WLR 483 (CA), *Bryanston Leasings v Principality Finance* [1977] RTR 45 (QB), *Union Transport Finance Ltd v British Car Auctions Ltd* [1978] 2 All ER 385 (CA), *R H Willis and Son (a firm) v British Car Auctions Ltd* [1978] 1 WLR 438 (CA).

[226] Notably *General & Finance Facilities Ltd v Cooke Cars (Romford) Ltd* [1963] 1 WLR 644 (CA).

[227] Notably *Wilson v Lombank Ltd* [1963] 1 WLR 1294 (QB).

[228] 18th Report (n 11).

[229] ibid, at para 5. See further the commentary thereon in G Samuel, 'Wrongful Interference with Goods' (1982) 31 *International & Comparative Law Quarterly* 357 at 358–59.

[230] 18th Report (n 11) at paras 10, 15, 24–25 and 128(1)–(2).

[231] ibid at para 15.

former course would require a much more substantial Bill, and be likely adversely to affect the legislative priority its recommendations would receive. The Report also saw advantage in some practical experience of the implementation of its individual recommendations being gained prior to any attempt at codification. It therefore came down in favour of the latter course.[232]

As to the subject matter of the proposed new tort, it suggested, without consideration of other possibilities or otherwise developing any reasons, a definition limiting the same to 'the existing subject-matter of conversion'. On that basis various types of asset, and notably choses in action including copyrights, patents and contractual rights, but not any tangible object which is evidence of a chose in action, were to be excluded from the definition.[233]

The Committee looked at the question of innocent converters, and in particular those no longer in possession of the subject asset. It noted that in French law liability for damages (as opposed to restitution of the asset, or its value—the equivalent of the Roman *vindicatio*) is dependent on fault, in the form of either bad faith or want of due care. Its reasons for rejecting a radical change in English law in favour of adopting the French model were both principled and pragmatic. As to the former, having noted that historically English law has protected proprietary rights not by a *vindicatio* but by an action *in personam*, classified as tortious, it continued that nevertheless trover and its derivative Conversion

> is and always has been primarily an action for the protection of ownership and it is because of this that questions as to the fault of the defendant are irrelevant, the principle adopted being that 'persons deal with the property in chattels or exercise acts of ownership over them at their peril.'[n][234]
>
> n *Hollins v Fowler* [1872] L.R. 7 Q.B. per Cleasby, B. at p. 639.

Its pragmatic reason was robust, but none the worse for that:

> It seems to us that, since the burden of proving bad faith or want of due care on the part of an intermediate vendor or handler is likely to be a difficult one, liability based on fault might well prove an encouragement to dishonesty and that this provides a strong practical ground for maintaining the English approach to the matter in preference to the French. In our view, for this reason alone, conversion should be retained as a remedy of strict liability but without prejudice to the consideration of any cases of particular hardship to which its rules may be found to give rise.[235]

The report contained a lengthy consideration of the long-established rule that a defendant otherwise liable in Conversion was not entitled to defend himself by alleging and proving that the true owner of the asset in question was a third party, also known as the rule of *jus tertii*.[236] Its again pragmatic conclusion, supported by six more specific and detailed proposals, was that this law

---

[232] ibid at paras 31–32 and 128(3)–(4).
[233] ibid, at para 29.
[234] ibid, at para 13.
[235] ibid, at para 14.
[236] ibid, at paras 51–78.

should be amended so as to secure, as far as practicable, that interested third parties have an opportunity to join in the action, that the defendant is not exposed to the risk of double liability and that the plaintiff's damages are measured in general by his real loss.[237]

There was also some consideration of recaption,[238] although the only conclusion drawn was that the law needed clarification, and that the steps taken by a person retaking his chattel by entry onto others' premises or the use of force should be judged by applying a standard of reasonableness.[239]

Overall, the Report received a lukewarm reception. It has been criticised for not 'examining in depth associated concepts such as bailment fault or indeed contract'.[240] One commentator suggested that it was 'not really satisfying because it lacks conceptual clarity', and concluded 'that in the absence of really concrete proposals, [it] has not done much more than to impress the seal of authority upon the criticisms that have long been made of this part of the law'.[241]

Legislation took some six years to follow, and when it did the Report's most far reaching proposal was not to be fully enacted (trespass to goods was not, after all, abolished). The Lord Chancellor's explanation for this, when moving the second reading of the Bill, was that the Act went a long way to meet the substance of the Committee's recommendation by providing for 'a substantial degree of common treatment for all the [surviving] torts ... including trespass', but that

> it would be difficult, indeed largely self-defeating, to attempt to unify in areas where the torts are, and must remain, distinct ... despite a valiant attempt by Parliamentary Counsel ... to follow the report more closely, it has proved impossible to put forward complete unification. This would have involved the conjuring tricks and contortions necessary to turn the tort of trespass to goods from a tort protecting a person's possession into a tort which protects his property, and the Committee themselves did foresee some of the difficulties which that would create.[242]

It seems that the Parliamentary draftsmen may have found force in Bentley's observation that some obviously very sensible proposals in the Report 'can perfectly well stand up without the doubtful support of the [proposed] new tort'.[243]

---

[237] ibid, at para 128(9).

[238] ibid, at paras 116–26.

[239] ibid, at para 128(21).

[240] Samuel, Wrongful Interference (*ICLQ* 1982) at 381; see also NE Palmer, 'The Application of the Torts (Interference with Goods) Act 1977 to Actions in Bailment' (1978) 41 *Modern Law Review* 629.

[241] DJ Bentley, 'A New-Found Haliday: The Eighteenth Report of the Law Reform Committee (Conversion and Detinue)' (1972) 35 *MLR* 170 at 173 and 175.

[242] Lord Elwyn-Jones LC, moving the second reading of the Bill, HL Vol 378 col 1061 (16 December 1976).

[243] Bentley, New-Found Haliday (*MLR* 1972) at 174.

Statutory Intervention

The 1977 Act, 'the first general venture by the Legislature into this ancient branch of the civil law',[244] commenced by making 'wrongful interference' or 'wrongful interference with goods' a defined term for the purposes of the Act, comprehending a number of different torts, namely (a) Conversion, (b) trespass to goods, (c) negligence so far as it results in damage to goods or an interest in goods, and (subject to the abolition of detinue) (d) any other tort so far as it results in damage to goods or to an interest in goods.[245] Contrary to the Committee's recommendation,[246] however, the Act did not create a new tort under either of those names, nor did it abolish or otherwise interfere with the separate identity of the torts listed within that definition. Accordingly, Conversion not only survived this enactment, but also, if by the skin of its teeth, retained its modern name, reflecting the central allegation which, as we have been seen, had by then been conventional for 400 years.

The Act abolished detinue,[247] but accompanied this by extending Conversion to cover the case where a bailee, in breach of his duty to the bailor, has allowed the subject assets to be lost or destroyed[248] (the Committee believed this to be the only case formerly a detinue but not also Conversion[249]), by extending the remedies available in Conversion and the other 'wrongful interference' torts against a person in possession or control of the subject goods[250] so as to include, in essence, the established remedies thitherto specific to detinue,[251] and by creating a specific interlocutory order 'for the delivery up of any goods which are or may become the subject matter of subsequent proceedings in the court, or as to which any question may arise in proceedings'.[252]

That apart, the Act 'neither replaces nor defines the other existing torts but refurbishes them in various ways'.[253] More prosaically, but nevertheless important to state, it was certainly not a codifying statute.

---

[244]   Lord Elwyn-Jones LC, moving the second reading of the Bill, HL Vol 378 col 1058 (16 December 1976).

[245]   s 1 ibid. The final words of s 1(d) catch the tort of reversionary injury, discussed in ch 3 at under the side-heading The Relationship between the Wrongful Interference Torts, Reversionary Injury.

[246]   18th Report (n 11) at paras 25, 27–28 and 128(2)(3).

[247]   s 2(1) of the 1977 Act.

[248]   s 2(2) ibid.

[249]   18th Report (n 11) at para 8.

[250]   As to the statutory definition thereof, see text to n 256.

[251]   s 3 of the 1977 Act, and compare s 78 Common Law Procedure Act 1854 (17 and 18 Vict c 125) quoted in the text following n 187. This addition of proprietary characteristics to the remedies available for Conversion was not without its difficulties, which we discuss in ch 7, text to fns 256–60.

[252]   s 4 of the 1977 Act.

[253]   JWA Thornely, 'New Torts for Old or Old Torts Refurbished?' [1977] *Cambridge Law Journal* 248, at 248.

There is little advantage in us rehearsing the details of the various statutory refurbishments to which Thornely referred,[254] but mention should be made of perhaps the most fundamental and best received of them, the reform of the position in relation to cases where there are or may be multiple claimants to the same assets. By section 7, any claimant who recovers more than he would have done had all potential claimants joined in one claim (where the relief 'shall be such as to avoid double liability of the wrongdoer'), is liable to account to the other potential claimants to such extent as will avoid double liability. Any claimant who ends up unjustly enriched is liable to reimburse the defendant wrongdoer to that extent.[255] Section 8 abolished the rule of *jus tertii*, and permits a defendant (subject to the requirements laid down by rules of court) to plead that another person has a better right than the claimant to all or any part of the claimant's alleged interest. Section 9 provides for the consolidation of concurrent claims in respect of the same goods.

The interpretation section[256] provided that in the Act, unless the context otherwise required, '"goods" includes all chattels personal other than things in action and money'. This provision did not purport to limit or otherwise affect the general law of Conversion, and, as Lord Nicholls has put it: 'Parliament cannot be taken to have intended to preclude the courts from developing the common law tort of conversion if that becomes necessary to achieve justice.'[257]

The most important cases since the Act came into force are, or at least include, the Court of Appeal decision in *IBL Ltd v Coussens* as to remedies,[258] and, since the turn of the century, the House of Lords decisions in *Kuwait Airways*[259] as to what constitutes a Conversion, and in *OBG Ltd v Allan*[260] as to what can be the subject of a Conversion.

Conclusions

> Conversion had distinct procedural advantages over [trespass and detinue] and rapidly extended its boundaries to cover much the same ground as they did. The contrivances used to achieve this desirable end led to many technicalities and controversies which continued to plague the law long after the reason for them had gone.[261]

The allegation of loss and finding has not only become recognised as a pleader's fiction, but, it should be appreciated, always was such. It pre-dated even the

---

[254] For which reference may be made to his article ibid, to V Sacks' Note on the Act in (1978) 41 *MLR* 713 and of course to the Act itself.

[255] See further in ch 4, under the side-heading What is Actual Possession?, Jus Tertii.

[256] s 14 of the 1977 Act.

[257] *OBG Ltd v Allan* [2007] UKHL 21, [2008] 1 AC 1 at [235].

[258] [1991] 2 All ER 133, discussed further in ch 7, especially text to nn 21–30 and 53–62.

[259] *Kuwait Airways Corpn v Iraqi Airways Co (Nos 4 and 5)* [2002] UKHL 19, [2002] 2 AC 886.

[260] [2007] UKHL 21, [2008] 1 AC 1.

[261] Baroness Hale in *OBG Ltd v Allan* [2007] UKHL 21, [2008] 1 AC 1 at [308].

emergence of trover as a distinct form of trespass on the case, having first been formulated to sidestep the absence of a bailment from the facts underlying claims being pursued in detinue. Even then it had no substantive relevance, but was merely a procedural convenience, adopted simply to give rise to a supposition that the defendant had first come by the asset lawfully.

Despite this, the conceptual development of the tort has been hindered by an apparent reluctance to dispense with the idea of a loss and finding, perhaps influenced by the encapsulation of that idea in the tort's former name, trover. For the common law to deny a remedy in Conversion in the twenty-first century on the basis that the subject matter of the claim could not have supported a plea of losing and finding,[262] would be every bit as absurd as to deny a remedy in trespass to goods on the basis that the circumstances would have precluded a conscientious plea of *vi et armis* and *contra pacem regis.*

A Conversion was an integral part of trover from its earliest days, and in time came to be recognised as its whole substance. As will be developed in chapter five, it is important that Conversion now be employed without its historical baggage, so that it can fulfil its role as an invaluable means of protecting interests in all types of valuable asset in a world where intangibles are frequently of great commercial importance.[263]

An appreciation of legal history should be a modern day lawyer's servant, not his master.

---

[262] See per Peter Gibson LJ in *OBG Ltd v Allan* [2005] EWCA Civ 106, [2005] QB 762 at [56], quoted in text to n 12.

[263] Even leaving aside intellectual property, in days when the contracted services of a Premier League footballer may command a 'transfer fee' in excess of £30 million, it will readily be appreciated that many intangible assets are of great commercial value. See further in ch 5 under the headings Intangible Property and The Importance of Effective Protection of Property Interests, and in ch 6 under the heading The Place of Contractual Rights and Other Intangible Property. On the facts of *OBG Ltd v Allan* [2005] EWCA Civ 106, [2005] QB 762 and [2007] UKHL 21, [2008] 1 AC 1 the trial judge, HHJ Maddocks, having carefully evaluated a considerable amount of detailed factual and expert evidence, found that the subject contractual rights had a realisable value of just under £2 million; that part of his judgment was not appealed.

3

What is a Conversion?

[I]t seems to me that, after all, no one can undertake to define what a Conversion is.[1]

I own that it is not always easy to say what does and what does not amount to a Conversion.[2]

T HE PROBLEM WITH Conversion is that few people understand with precision what it is. Consequently, it has developed something of a cabalistic reputation amongst even experienced lawyers. Previously, attempts to define the tort have taken the form of outlining the instances in which it might occur.[3] Whilst this goes some way to demonstrating the essence of the action of Conversion, it is somewhat retrospective in form, and does not, therefore, necessarily help to identify Conversion in situations yet to be considered, particularly where there is no perfect analogy available. This book, by contrast, aims to provide a working definition of Conversion; one which might be applied to any set of facts, whether or not they have yet presented themselves to a court.[4] Given the historical reluctance to provide such a definition, one might expect the tort to be either complicated or obscure. In fact, it is neither.

Name

It seems reasonable to suggest that some of the mystery surrounding Conversion owes its existence to a name which, in a contemporary setting, is not self-explanatory. Whilst, in the sixteenth century, when the pleading was so worded, the notion of 'converting' to one's own use something belonging to someone else would have been a concept familiar to laymen and lawyers alike,[5] it is not so today. Outside the law of torts (and the laws of rugby), the word 'Conversion' has come to describe a process by which something changes in nature, either

---

[1] Bramwell B in *Burroughes v Bayne* (1860) 5 H & N 296 at 308, 157 ER 1196 at 1200.
[2] Blackburn J in *Hollins v Fowler and ors* (1875) LR 7 HL 757 at 765.
[3] eg WL Prosser, *The Nature of Conversion* (1957) 42 *Cornell Law Quarterly* 168.
[4] It does so below, under the heading The Three Elements of Conversion.
[5] See SFC Milsom, *Historical Foundations of the Common Law*, 2nd edn (London, Butterworths, 1981) at 366 and ch 2, text to fn 159.

physically or spiritually, and 'converting' is no longer synonymous with appropriating or commandeering. In its 1971 report, the Law Reform Committee suggested that Conversion be replaced (at least in part) by a new tort, to be called 'wrongful interference with movables'.[6] Arguably, had this happened, it might have made the law in this area sound more accessible, even though the practical changes made by the resultant legislation have clarified little in substantive terms. The name change did not happen, however, and the legal creature that is Conversion not only survived the enactment of the Torts (Interference with Goods) Act 1977, but grew to become a tort with an even broader remit.

The relative obscurity of the tort's name, however, should not suggest that the idea of Conversion is itself cryptic. After all, lawyers are not strangers to the practice of dealing with concepts which are unhelpfully named.[7] Rather, what is necessary for the tort to become more accessible is that its substance be stated in its simplest terms, and that its common objectives be recognised.

Interests Protected

Simply stated, Conversion protects the current superior possessory interest in personal property. This point is, on occasion, obscured by the asking of ultimately unnecessary questions. For instance, one of the purported conceptual difficulties often associated with Conversion is the question of the exact nature of the interest it protects; that is, must the interest be proprietary, or will a contractual right to possession suffice?[8] Another difficulty relates to the interaction between property and possession, and the questions which arise because Conversion, a tort often supposed to protect property interests, will in some situations protect the interest of the possessor over a party with a superior property interest in the same asset.[9] There are more, but these are the most commonly cited 'oddities' which give the impression that Conversion is somehow an esoteric and complex concept. The point is that resolving these questions does not add anything to the understanding of precisely what a Conversion is. Questions such as these arise because the tort of Conversion does not make up the whole picture in terms of protecting personal property. Rather, it is one part of a set of torts, known collectively (if not particularly helpfully) as the wrongful interference torts. Together, these torts protect property interests in assets, and

---

[6]   The 18th Report (Conversion and Detinue) of the Law Reform Committee (1971), Cmnd 4774 at paras 27–30.

[7]   eg demurrage, rescous, the tort in *Wilkinson v Downton*.

[8]   See, eg, N Curwen, 'Title to Sue in Conversion' [2004] *Conveyancer and Property Lawyer* 308. This issue will be addressed more fully in ch 4 under the heading What Amounts to a Sufficient Proprietary Right?

[9]   As illustrated, eg, by the facts underlying *Gordon v Harper* (1796) 7 TR 9, 101 ER 828, CHS Fifoot, *History & Sources of the Common Law* (London, Stevens & Sons, 1949) at 124, for which see ch 2, text to fn 101ff.

Conversion plays a specific role within their sphere of protection: an awareness of this context is crucial to understanding precisely what a Conversion is.

The Relationship between the Wrongful Interference Torts

Trespass

There is some overlap in the coverage of trespass and Conversion. Trespass is concerned with direct and wrongful interference with possession, but it does not require there to be an element of appropriation, as does Conversion. To use Tettenborn's example

> if D takes P's bottle of wine and drinks it, he commits both. But they remain distinct. If D merely moves the bottle from one shelf to another, he commits trespass but not Conversion, since there is no appropriation.[10]

Essentially, as outlined below,[11] the two actions diverge at the point at which the defendant's interference crosses the line between acting in relation to another's assets and acting in relation to another's assets as if they were one's own.

Reversionary Injury

The tort of reversionary injury was developed to cover two instances previously outwith the common law's protection of personal property: the plight of the co-owner, whose assets have been converted by another co-owner, and the problems formerly faced by the owner out of possession.[12] Whilst co-owners can now sue other co-owners in Conversion generally,[13] reversionary injury is still a tort of considerable significance for the owner out of possession.

In protecting current superior possessory interests, Conversion is concerned with the loss to the person with the most immediate interest in an asset. Despite, therefore, the common confusion over whether it is a tortious or a proprietary claim, Conversion's substance strongly resemblance a tort, primarily because it looks straightaway to what one has lost, not to what one is owed.[14] Reversionary injury, on the other hand, another of the wrongful interference torts, is an action

---

[10]   *Clerk & Lindsell on Torts*, 19th edn (London, Sweet & Maxwell, 2006) at para 17–02.
[11]   See text to n 114 ff.
[12]   See *Clerk & Lindsell on Torts* (2006) at para 17–138.
[13]   S 10 of the Torts (Wrongful Interference with Goods) Act 1977 ('the 1977 Act').
[14]   'Loss' is used here in its broad sense, to cover that which a claimant loses simply by having his superior possessory right infringed; it is not limited to the narrow sense of 'loss' outlined by Lord Nicholls in *Kuwait Airways Corp v Iraqi Airways Co and anor (Nos 4 & 5)* [2002] UKHL 19, [2002] 2 AC 886 at [83]. See also R Stevens, *Torts and Rights* (Oxford, Oxford University Press, 2007) at 63–66, for the argument that 'loss' in its narrow sense is not the key to damages in Conversion.

for the reversioner (that is the party whose property interest in the asset is such that possession will revert to him when other possessory rights have expired) to recover for any damage caused to his property interest. Although, therefore, the reversioner might be the party with the superior *proprietary* interest in the asset, as long as somebody else is lawfully in possession of that asset, he is not the one who will suffer immediate loss as a result of a wrongful dispossession:

> The owner of a thing is not necessarily the person who at a given time has the whole power of use and disposal; very often there is no such person. We must look for the person having the residue of all such power when we have accounted for every detached and limited portion of it; and he will be the owner even if the immediate power of control and use is elsewhere.[15]

In *Tancred v Allgood*,[16] an action was brought against a sheriff for seizing goods from the possession of an execution debtor, and selling them so that they could not be followed. The claimant had the reversionary interest in those assets, which had been let to hire for a term, as yet unexpired, to the debtor from whom they had been seized. The reversioner could not succeed in her action because she had at that point sustained no actual damage: since the defendant had sold the assets as sheriff under a *fieri facias* and not in market overt, he had not thereby passed title in them so as to injure the claimant's interest.[17]

Perhaps the most intuitively difficult situation to accept, in terms of the operation of Conversion, is that of the term bailor who dispossesses his bailee before the expiration (or termination) of the agreed bailment term. Such a bailor, despite being what laymen and lawyers alike would regard as the 'owner' of the asset, would nonetheless be liable in Conversion. Although this is a factual situation which, prima facie, appears to highlight a potential incoherence within the common law's protection of personal property interests, it is actually a useful and graphic illustration of the purpose served by Conversion. Here, Conversion allows the bailee to recover against the bailor because the latter interfered with the former's possessory interests, and such an interference is regarded as a loss by the law of torts.[18] The bailor, on the other hand, has lost nothing; the only thing that he has to lose is his reversionary interest but this, on these facts, is clearly still intact.[19]

---

[15] F Pollock, *A First Book of Jurisprudence for Students of the Common Law* (London, Macmillan, 1896 (reprinted 1923)) at 179.

[16] (1859) 4 H & N 438, 157 ER 910.

[17] Although factually it seemed highly improbable that the assets would be recovered before the expiry of the term, legally, the claimant's title remained unimpaired and permanent injury to it had not necessarily arisen. See also *HSBC Rail (UK) Ltd v Network Rail Infrastructure Ltd* [2005] EWHC 403 (Comm), [2005] 2 Lloyd's Rep 343 discussed in text to nn 37–38 and *Mukibi v Bhavsar* [1967] EA 473.

[18] See Stevens, *Torts and Rights* (2007) at 66.

[19] Of course, he does not have the right to possession of his asset, but he did not 'lose' this; he voluntarily parted with it when he made the bailment agreement. See also *Brierly v Kendall* (1852) 17 QB 937, 117 ER 1540 for the application of the principle to a mortgagor in possession whose period of credit has not yet expired.

To alter the facts slightly, whilst retaining the element of apparent conceptual difficulty, consider the term bailee who has been dispossessed, this time by a third party. The term bailee, but not his bailor, may sue the dispossessor in Conversion.[20] This is because, once more, the term bailor in such a situation has, as yet, lost nothing; only possession has so far been interfered with and the term bailor would not have had that anyway. Should the third party do something which affects the bailor's reversionary interest, however, such as destroying the asset, permanently reducing its value or permanently absconding with it, then the term bailor may sue. His action, however, will not be for Conversion, but for the injury to his reversion. The existence of this separate tort explains and justifies the refusal of Conversion to grant recovery for anyone but the person with the most immediate (that is superior) right to possession. Were there to be no provision for the 'ultimate owner', there would be an unacceptable lacuna in the law, the existence of which would make the restrictions on recovery in Conversion appear remarkable. As it is, those restrictions are entirely justified: within the complex matrix of the common law's personal property rules, there needs to be something to protect possession, *independent* of any means of protecting superior proprietary rights. Otherwise, the concept of a possessory right, as distinct from any superior proprietary rights, would be redundant, with profound implications for commercial and economic efficacy.[21]

Bailment, for instance, is wholly dependent upon there being a distinct, legally enforced distinction between full ownership and lesser (but nonetheless practically valuable) proprietary rights. As Palmer points out:

> The essence of bailment is possession … The doctrine is confined to personal property and denotes a separation of the actual possession of goods from some ultimate or reversionary possessory right … the central theme of every standard bailment is the carving out, by the bailor, of a lesser interest than his own. That interest is possession, and without possession there can be no relationship of bailor and bailee. Conversely, a conveyance which simultaneously confers both possession and ownership upon the grantee cannot create a bailment; and an owner of goods cannot constitute himself their bailee at common law.[22]

In fact, the commercial world relies upon this means of allowing an 'owner' to divide up his property interests amongst other parties, in order to maximise the use and value of his assets.[23] Were Conversion to function according to a hierarchy of relative property rights which did not include possessory interests, possessors would always be liable to dispossession by those with superior title, despite the fact that this might in turn contravene any prior agreement made

---

[20]   *Gordon v Harper* (n 9).

[21]   See below under the heading The Importance of Possession.

[22]   NE Palmer, *Bailment*, 2nd edn (London, Sweet & Maxwell, 1991) at 2.

[23]   See J Gordley, *Foundations of Private Law: Property, Tort and Unjust Enrichment* (Oxford, Oxford University Press, 2008) at 61–65.

between the two parties concerned.[24] In short, were the law of torts not to protect purely possessory rights, it would effectively deny that there is any economic, social or legal value in possession in its own right. This is, of course, far from the truth, as Mattei has made clear:

> The protection of possession against ownership in the domain of movable property is one of the most important institutional evolutions that have guaranteed the development of efficient markets in Western societies ... the most important transactions relating to movables lie in their market transfer. Efficient legal institutions therefore are those which facilitate the transfer of movables. Such transfer is motivated by the protection of possession over title and ownership.[25]

The Importance of Possession

> In the very early law great importance was attached to possession by a man who said to the world: 'Keep off; this is mine.' The rudest people have some notion of ownership, but at the common law in medieval times the man in possession claiming to be the owner was the owner.[26]

Historically, possession was important in both practical and evidential terms. Practically, it was important because it was only really possessors who benefited from the assets in their possession. Evidentially, it was important because possession was the principal indicator of who had the property interest in the assets concerned: 'Because of its factual character, possession is as easy to prove as ownership is difficult.'[27] Furthermore, as far as the law was concerned, allowing individuals to interfere with another's possession at will would have been disastrous for public order and would have provided no incentive for possessors (often owners) to invest in, and to exploit, their assets for maximum economic gain. As Tony Weir has pointed out

> possession needs to be protected as a matter of public order. Expropriation may be unjust, but dispossession is unruly, so we must give a remedy to people whose

---

[24]   This is, therefore, in respectful disagreement with Tony Weir's assertion that 'trespass protects possession and Conversion protects ownership'. T Weir, *Tort Law* (Oxford, Oxford University Press, 2002) at 153.

[25]   U Mattei, *Basic Principles of Property Law: A Comparative, Legal and Economic Introduction* (Westport Connecticut, Greenwood Press, 2000) at 88.

[26]   HD Warren, *An Essay on Trover and Conversion* (Cambridge, Mass., Harvard Law Review Association, 1936) at 4.

[27]   B Nicholas, *An Introduction to Roman Law* (Oxford, Oxford University Press, 1962) at 109. As Honoré has put it, 'Possession, unless otherwise explained, is regarded as evidence of ownership and an earlier possession is regarded as better evidence of ownership than a later, independent possession.' See T Honoré, *Ownership* in AG Guest (ed) *Oxford Essays in Jurisprudence* (Oxford, Oxford University Press, 1961). See also Mattei, *Basic Principles* (2000) at 66–71 for an economic viewpoint on the protection of possession.

possession is invaded, sometimes even if it is invaded by the owner: as Sohm said, the justice of ownership yields to the order of possession.[28]

These concerns are still relevant today. There are, however, additional concerns in twenty-first century commerce. In a contemporary context, possession, as distinct from ownership, is an intrinsically valuable phenomenon.[29] Even where it is quite definitely (and quite deliberately) detached from full ownership, it is an interest which many individuals would litigate in order to protect. In fact, those same individuals would no doubt be astonished and outraged, should it be suggested to them that the law did not recognise theirs as an interest worthy of protection and, yet, this would be the case were Conversion not to protect possession over full ownership where the two conflict.

This gives us the answer to Tettenborn's question 'what is Conversion *for*?'[30] Conversion is for the protection of the superior *possessory* rights in assets and this objective is better pursued through the law of torts rather than through the law of property. Where Conversion is concerned, any proprietary rights beyond that of immediate possession are irrelevant; these only become relevant for the purposes of injury to the reversionary interest, which is, of course, a separate tort. Looking at Conversion only through a tort lawyer's eyes, this is obvious. Tort law, in its many forms, protects a range of interests: personal physical integrity, autonomy, integrity of property, reputation, economic loss, the right to certain contractual expectations, and the right to exercise exclusive possessory rights over one's property (real or personal). Whilst a strict property law approach to the situation might struggle to justify protecting a possessor's rights over those of an individual with a superior proprietary title, the law of torts faces no such conceptual difficulty.

The separation of property, possession and risk is a common and commercially convenient means of ensuring that assets are used and exchanged with maximum efficiency. Sometimes it is done in order to deal with the logistics of an arrangement, as with international sales contracts: where exchange is not instantaneous and assets need to be in transit for a period of time, it is in the interests of all concerned for there to be a clear delineation of rights and liabilities at each stage of the process.[31] In general, issues surrounding the separation of property and possession commonly arise in relation to sales. It is worth making clear at this point that selling assets to which another person has the superior possessory right is no Conversion, unless those assets are also delivered following the sale. Although it might seem surprising that a sale (which might appear to be the

---

[28]   Weir, *Tort* (2002) at 485.

[29]   See P Cane, *Tort Law and Economic Interests*, 2nd edn (Oxford, Oxford University Press, 1996) at 27.

[30]   Posed in 'Conversion, Tort and Restitution' in N Palmer and E McKendrick (eds) *Interests in Goods*, 2nd edn (London, LLP, 1998) at 825.

[31]   See MG Bridge, *The International Sale of Goods: Law and Practice*, 2nd edn (Oxford, Oxford University Press, 2007), ch 8 for a detailed explanation of this procedure and its implications.

ultimate exercise of rights over assets) is alone no Conversion, the reason for this was made clear in *Consolidated Company v Curtis & Son*:

> It is clear that there can be no Conversion by a mere bargain and sale without a transfer of possession. The act, unless in market overt, is merely void, and does not change the property or the possession: Lancashire Wagon Co. v. Fitzhugh[32], and per Brett, J., in Fowler v. Hollins.[33] A fortiori, mere intervention as broker or intermediary in a sale by others is not a Conversion. This is the case put by Bramwell, L.J., in Cochrane v. Rymill[34] of an introduction by an auctioneer of a purchaser to a vendor. But, unless Turner v. Hockey[35] decided the contrary, I should have thought it equally clear that a sale and delivery with intent to pass the property in chattels by a person who is not the true owner and has not got his authority is a Conversion.[36]

HSBC Rail (UK) Ltd v Network Rail Infrastructure Ltd[37] is a clear illustration of the practical importance of distinguishing between the current possessory interests and any reversionary interest which might exist. The claimant was the owner of railway rolling stock which had been leased to a train operating company and the defendant was the owner of the track infrastructure. Whilst the train operating company, under the terms of the lease, had possessory title, the rolling stock was involved in a collision alleged to have been caused by dangerous rails (which were the responsibility of the defendant). Two coaches were damaged beyond economic repair and those remaining had to undergo repairs. Under the terms of the lease between the train operating company and the claimants, the former had assumed all risk of loss, damage or destruction of the rolling stock. Pursuant to this, the insurers, on behalf of the train operating company (the possessors) paid the claimant (the owners) an agreed value for the written off coaches and reimbursed the possessors for the amount they had spent on the repairs of the remaining stock. The insurers then sought to recover the sums involved from the defendant, suing in the name of the claimant, and the question for the court was whether the claimant, having only a reversionary interest in the assets, was entitled to recover this money from the defendant. The Court found that it was not so entitled. The contractual relationship between the parties had expressly provided that such loss was to be at the train operating company's risk and not the claimant's.[38] As Collins MR pointed out in *The Winkfield*

---

[32]   (1861) 6 H & N 502, 158 ER 206.
[33]   (1872) LR 7 QB 616 (Ex Ch) at 627.
[34]   (1879) 40 LT (NS) 744 (CA).
[35]   (1887) 56 LJ (QB) 301.
[36]   [1892] 1 QB 495 per Collins J at 498. (Of course, the market overt exception to the rule of *nemo dat quod non habet* was abolished by the Sale of Goods (Amendment) Act 1994.)
[37]   [2005] EWHC 403 (Comm), [2005] 2 Lloyd's Rep 343.
[38]   The reason for the insurers' approach was that an action in the name of the train operating company would have been subject to a contractual limitation provision, putting a £5 million cap on damages recoverable. So, substantive reasons aside, it is unsurprising that the court refused to allow this inappropriate claim as a means of sidestepping such a provision. See also A Tettenborn, *Reversionary Damage to Chattels* [1994] *CLJ* 326.

as against a wrongdoer, possession is title. The chattel that has been converted or damaged is deemed to be the chattel of the possessor and of no other, and therefore its loss or deterioration is his loss, and to him, if he demands it, it must be recouped.[39]

A Peculiar Notion of Possession?

The common law concept of Conversion is perceived by those familiar with other legal systems as being an unusual means of protecting personal property interests. If this is the case, it may well be due, at least in part, to the fact that it is parasitic upon a correspondingly unusual notion of possession. Outside Anglo-American common law, the concept of possession is something of a different creature to the one described above. Scots law, for example, 'does not know the degrees of possession of English law'[40] and regards possession as an evidentiary fact rather than a substantive right:

> Unless and until possession becomes ownership it remains an inferior right, and this is so regardless of the fact that all the beneficial elements of ownership—use, fruits, and de facto control—may reside in the possessor.[41]

In Scots law, possession 'proper' is not a purely physical concept, but requires that the assets in question be held with the requisite state of mind in relation to them; that is, by someone who holds them as her own property.[42] Such possession proper does not, therefore, include bare de facto possession, a holding subject to the will of someone with a superior property right, or a holding which is the result only of a contractual right against the ultimate owner. 'Possession' is in this sense a term of art, with a far narrower meaning than the term has when used within the English common law. It is also important to note at this point that Scots law does not recognise the right to possess as being a property right and, as Lord Rodger pointed out sometime ago, 'Possession and the right to possession are not synonymous, the latter being a particular creation of the Common Law.'[43] In part, this is due to the fact that Scots law has inherited from Roman law an absolute right of ownership; a right which is, according to Carey Miller, 'the quintessential right' within the Scottish system of property law.[44] This means that such ownership right prevails over any claims not derived from it (including those of bona fide third party acquirers). It is, however, usually the attempt at

---

[39] [1902] P 42 at 60. Since s 8(1) of the 1977 Act abolished the rule against *jus tertii*, this principle now only applies insofar as no named third party is known to have a better possessory right. For a more detailed discussion, see ch 4 below under the side-heading What is Actual Possession?, Jus Tertii.

[40] DL Carey Miller, *Corporeal Moveables in Scots Law* 2nd edn (Edinburgh, W Green, 2005) at 18.

[41] ibid at 18.

[42] There is also a distinction made here between bona fide possession and mala fide possession, in which the former describes someone who has a genuine and reasonable belief that he is holding his own property and the latter someone who intends to hold as his own, but knows, or has reason to believe, that he does not. The latter does not give a good title to possession. See Carey Miller, *Corporeal Moveables* (2005) at 27 and 28.

[43] A Rodger, 'Spuilzie in the Modern World' [1970] *Scots Law Times (News)* 33.

[44] Carey Miller (n 40) at 11.

establishing this right that presents a claimant with his biggest challenge in Scots law; there is no formal system of registered title for movable property and so there is a rebuttable presumption that the present possessor is the owner. Whilst this once amounted to equating possession with ownership, it seems that, since the nineteenth century at least,[45] the rebuttable presumption approach has prevailed.

The civil law's conception of possession, however, is similar to the older Scots law notion. For instance, in French law

> article 2279 a. 1 of the Civil Code lays down a general rule for the protection of those who acquire possession in good faith: 'in the case of movable property, possession is equivalent to title.'[46]

In this context, possession has a different legal significance to that which it has within the common law. It is not something which is protected as a property right *eo ipso*, but is an evidentiary concept which goes to the question of ownership. Most notably for present purposes of comparison, civil law possession 'is always subject to the better right of the lawful owner and/or older possessor'.[47] The contrast with the common law approach outlined above is, therefore, striking:

> The civil law notion of possession is in essence conceptual, the normal sequel and shadow of ownership (of the relevant proprietary right). In common law, on the other hand, ownership and possession must each be seen as separate proprietary rights, at least when physical possession is separated from ownership, as in the case of bailment.[48]

Relationship to *Vindicatio*

> English law protects the possession of property by providing a remedy in tort; continental systems, deriving their inspiration from Roman law, protect the ownership of property with a fully-fledged proprietary remedy.[49]

A common objection to Conversion is that it is a poor substitute for a *vindicatio* action, which is essentially a proprietary action which enables a dispossessed individual to claim his asset *in specie* from the defendant. The common law lacks

---

[45]   See Lord Cockburn in *Anderson v Buchanan* (1848) 11 D 270 at 284.

[46]   Also known as the 'possession vaut titre' principle, which extends as far as third parties being able to rely on such possession as security. J Bell, S Boyron and S Whittaker, *Principles of French Law*, 2nd edn (Oxford, Oxford University Press, 2007) at 279. Note that this only applies to corporeal moveables.

[47]   JH Dalhiusen, *Dalhuisen on Transnational and Comparative Commercial, Financial and Trade Law*, 3rd edn (Oxford, Hart Publishing, 2007) 562 at fn 42.

[48]   ibid at 574.

[49]   CSP Harding and MS Rowell, 'Protection of Property versus Protection of Commercial Transactions in French and English Law' (1977) 26 *International & Commercial Law Quarterly* 354 at 355.

any such action, and this is regarded by some as a failing.[50] Far from being a compromise made to compensate for a common law deficiency, the law of torts' solution to the problem of dispossession is actually far more sophisticated than anything the law of property could easily achieve. The primary reason for this is that, by focussing on what one has lost rather than what one is owed, tort can provide protection for a wider range of parties than merely the 'ultimate' owner. What is more, the common law position is, in its entirety, closer to the Roman structure than unfavourable comparisons between Conversion and the *vindicatio* would suggest. The problem is that the *vindicatio* alone is not the most appropriate comparison to make with Conversion.

The *vindicatio* was an action concerned only with ownership, and so with the ultimate property rights in an asset. Conversion, as outlined above, is a different creature, to which ownership is not directly relevant, and, like the Roman possessory interdicts, is concerned only with possession. As the Roman maxim *nihil commune habet proprietas cum possessione* suggests, the two issues were regarded as discrete legal concepts, deserving distinct legal treatment. It is, therefore, inappropriate to compare the *vindicatio* directly with Conversion because the purpose served by the *vindicatio* is analogous to the aims and effects of the wrongful interference torts as a whole and, with its concern for ultimate ownership, certainly encompasses the objectives of the tort of reversionary injury. The tort of Conversion, on the other hand, bears more of a resemblance to the Roman possessory interdicts, and, as in the Roman system, makes up only part of the picture in terms of protecting personal property. Once more, this recognition that Conversion (and the possessory interdicts) make up only part of the law's protection for property is crucial for a proper understanding of the specific roles played by each action. As Nicholas has made clear,[51] the interrelationship between the possessory interdicts and the *vindicatio* led to some circuity, since, at some point, the ultimate owner was able to assert his title against someone who, despite having a lesser proprietary interest, had nonetheless succeeded under a possessory interdict: 'As Gaius puts it, the possessory interdict serves to determine which party shall be defendant in a *vindicatio*.'[52] Even so, this does not detract from the conceptual elegance of treating possession and ownership as distinct concepts;[53] a practice which the common law now imitates, not least to ensure that possessors have some form of protection against those who might have title, but no right to immediate possession.

---

[50] DJ Ibbetson, *A Historical Introduction to the Law of Obligations* (Oxford, Oxford University Press, 1999) at 108. See also ch 2, text to fn 78.

[51] Nicholas, *Roman Law* (1962) at 109.

[52] *ibid* at 109.

[53] Nicholas identifies a practical advantage to this conceptual separation in that it also guarded against the encouragement of self-help. This accords with the modern day objectives of Conversion because, as Tony Weir points out, 'possession needs to be protected as a matter of public order. Expropriation may be unjust, but dispossession is unruly', Weir, Tort (n 24) at 485.

As the common law's principal means of protecting personal property, Conversion could be regarded as being extraordinary in its lack of any automatic specific restitution for a dispossessed claimant. The Roman *vindicatio* itself was, however, not an action for which specific restitution was necessarily available; it was merely an order to pay the claimant the value of the asset if he failed to return it.[54] The courts' discretion, under section 3 of the 1977 Act,[55] to order specific restitution instead of the standard remedy of damages in certain situations, means that English law is able to provide a means of protection remarkably similar to that achieved by the *vindicatio*. In fact, since this discretion is likely to be exercised wherever damages would not be an adequate remedy, that is where the asset in question is unique, or where its subjective value to the claimant is not properly represented by its market value, the wrongful interference torts can provide for specific restitution where the *vindicatio* could not.

The civil law's means of dealing with dispossession resemble more closely the *vindicatio* than they do Conversion. Just as with Roman law, it is difficult to make a useful comparison here; there is no direct or meaningful comparison to be made where we are not comparing like systems with like. The principal difference between the approaches of Scots and civil law and those of the common law is that, in the latter, all interferences with personal property are dealt with through the law of torts whereas, in the former, this function is shared between tort (or delict) and property law, depending on the circumstances of the interference. Combine this point with the distinct notions of possession that exist between the different systems, and the fact that the common law does not have ownership as its 'quintessential right' in the way that the other systems do, and it becomes obvious why making a direct comparison between Conversion and nominate vindicatory actions is not a constructive exercise.

Scots law, for instance, has both a vindicatory action, known as restitution,[56] based on an owner claiming back an asset from someone who possesses it inconsistently with her rights, and spuilzie, a remedy for dispossession:

Spuilzie is the taking away of moveables without consent of the possessor or order of law, imposing an obligation to restore with all possible profits or to make reparation

---

[54]   The formula for a *vindicatio* actually reads: 'If it appears that the thing in question belongs to the plaintiff at civil law (*ex iure Quiritium*), then, unless at the direction of the judge the defendant restores the thing, let the judge condemn the defendant to pay the value of it to the plaintiff. If it does not so appear, let the judge absolve the defendant.' (as quoted in Nicholas (n 27) at 101, fn 1). Since the dispossessed party was allowed to make his own value assessment of the asset, the practical effect was often to compel the asset's return. Such a return remained, however, only a practical effect and not a legal direction.

[55]   Which applies to all the wrongful interference torts, not just to Conversion.

[56]   To be distinguished from the concept of restitution, as that concept is understood in the English common law.

therefor. The pursuer need only establish lawful right of possession or custody, not necessarily ownership, and the action lies against any custodier on the ground of unjustifiable dispossession.[57]

This possessory remedy looks remarkably like Conversion and is, in fact, very similar to the Roman possessory interdicts. In substance, however, Conversion is 'a tort which is rather different from spuilzie'.[58] In brief, spuilzie is a much narrower action than Conversion, in that it only applies to wrongful dispossessions in the sense of assets which have actively been taken from the possession of the claimant,[59] and can only be brought against immediate dispossessors and not from third party acquirers.[60] This is consistent with its being an action in delict. In Scots law, the (proprietary) vindicatory action covers any situations which fall outwith the ambit of spuilzie. This is similar to the situation in pure civil law systems in general, in which active fault-based dispossessions have a tortious remedy, *in addition* to there being a proprietary vindicatory action for any other situation in which an owner finds himself deprived of his assets.[61] In English law, there is no such proprietary action, although the differences between these approaches may well only be a question of formal classification; as Dalhuisen points out in his impressive comparative work:

> The special feature of the old possessory torts is that . . . (in civil law terms), they have a proprietary effect, as they allow the asset to be pursued in the hands of anyone with a lesser right to it.[62]

In fact, it appears that the only significant substantive difference between the common law approach to wrongful interference with assets in its entirety, and that of both Scots law and civil law systems, is the remedy provided in each case. Vindicatory actions entitle the successful claimant to his asset *in specie*, whereas such recovery is only a discretionary remedy under English law.[63] As discussed above, this discretionary approach should not usually be detrimental to a claimant, given the situations in which it is likely to be exercised, but it is true that 'This discretion naturally weakens the position of the dispossessed plaintiff and of any owner (if different) in the bankruptcy of the wrongful possessor'.[64]

---

[57]   DM Walker, *Principles of Scottish Private Law*, 4th edn (Oxford, Oxford University Press, 1988) at 676.

[58]   Rodger, 'Spuilzie' (*SLT*, 1970) at 35.

[59]   In *Brown v Hudelstone* (1625) Mor 11748, for instance, a claimant was denied spuilzie since the cow which he was claiming had not been taken violently from him. He was, however, allowed restitution of the cow, on the basis of his ownership of it.

[60]   See Carey Miller (n 40) at 282 and particularly fn 72.

[61]   See eg, Dalhuisen, *Dalhuisen* (2007) at 580–82 and Bell et al, *Principles* (2007) at 414–17 for the position in France; and see §823 1 BGB and §985 BGB and BS Markesinis and H Hunberath, *The German Law of Torts: a Comparative Treatise*, 4th edn (Oxford, Hart Publishing, 2002) at 49–52 for the separate German provisions on these matters.

[62]   Dalhuisen (n 47) at 577.

[63]   See ch 7 generally, and under the heading Other Remedies for a detailed discussion of the remedies for Conversion.

[64]   Dalhuisen (n 47) at 577.

Consequently, this may well be one aspect of Conversion which might benefit from reconsideration, so as to ensure that the common law maintains a robust and comprehensive system of protection for personal property interests.[65]

The Gist of Conversion

> The very denial of goods to him that has a right to demand them, is an actual Conversion, and not only evidence of it, as has been holden; for what is a Conversion but an assuming to one's self the property and right of disposing of another's goods.[66]

This is probably the simplest, and yet also the most crucial, point to make about Conversion; the claimant in a Conversion action is suing because his superior possessory interest has been infringed. Nothing more is required.[67] There need be no loss *consequent* upon the defendant's interference with his interest, nor need there be any corresponding gain to the defendant.[68] Significantly, there is also no problem in a claimant's loss being classified as 'purely economic'; something which would cause difficulties were the action to have been brought under a tort such as negligence.

In *OBG Ltd v Allan*,[69] however, Lord Hoffmann suggested that pure economic loss should not be recoverable in Conversion, a strict liability tort, particularly since it is not easily recoverable even under a negligence standard. With the greatest of respect, however, it is not the liability standard of a tort which should determine what a claimant can recover, but the nature of the interest which that tort seeks to protect. Negligence protects the right of one individual not to suffer loss as a result of the careless actions of others. One of the reasons for allowing only very limited claims for pure economic loss in negligence[70] is to avoid the possibility of exposing a defendant to indeterminate liability; that is, 'liability in an indeterminate amount, for an indeterminate time, to an indeterminate class'.[71] Since Conversion protects an individual's right not to have his possessory rights infringed, the indeterminacy issue is not relevant since, in terms of dealing with any one asset, there is always going to be only a limited number of parties (those with a sufficient possessory interest) to whom the defendant will have to answer.[72]

---

[65] See ch 8, text to fn 10 ff.

[66] Holt CJ in *Baldwin v Cole* (1704) 6 Mod Rep 212, 87 ER 964.

[67] See further under the heading The Three Elements of Conversion, below.

[68] Although both of these outcomes can be of additional significance to a claimant—see ch 7 under the side-heading The Measure of Damages for Conversion, (g) Consequential Loss.

[69] [2007] UKHL 21, [2008] 1 AC 1 at [99].

[70] For the significant exception, see *Hedley Byrne & Co Ltd v Heller & Partners Ltd* [1964] AC 465. See also, for further discussion of the policy reasons underlying the issue, P Benson, 'The Basis for Excluding Liability for Economic Loss in Tort Law' in D Owen, (ed) *Philosophical Foundations of Tort Law* (Oxford, Oxford University Press,1995).

[71] *Ultramares Corp v Touche* 255 NY 170 (NY Ct Apps 1931) at 179 per Cardozo CJ.

[72] For a more detail discussion of this, see ch 4 under the heading Relativity of Title.

In his (certain to be) influential book, *Torts and Rights*, Robert Stevens asserts that 'The law of torts is concerned with the secondary obligations generated by the infringement of primary rights. The infringement of rights, not the infliction of loss, is the gist of the law of torts.' He refers to this as his 'rights model'.[73] Stevens' view on the common law's general refusal to recognise economic loss as a form of actionable damage is that 'There is no "exclusionary rule" for economic loss. The common law's starting position is that the infliction of economic loss does not per se infringe any right of the claimant.'[74] Stevens' argument is based on the need for the claimant to have had a right, good against the whole world, infringed by the defendant. In property torts, however, this by definition occurs when a claimant's superior possessory right is infringed by the defendant's interference with his asset. In short, and despite Lord Hoffmann's dictum in *OBG Ltd v Allan*, it is neither necessary nor helpful to talk in terms of economic loss as a distinct or problematic issue in the context of Conversion. Were it otherwise, it is difficult to see how the infringement of property rights could properly be compensated for in many (particularly commercial) situations, where the loss suffered is bound to be economic in nature.[75]

The other reason sometimes given where recovery for pure economic loss is not permitted is that the infliction of economic loss can be constructive, in terms of promoting healthy competition, in a capitalist economy. This argument can easily be countered in the context of Conversion: whilst the (actual or threatened) infliction of economic loss through competitive commercial enterprises is something which will often prove socially beneficial for the law to encourage, the same cannot be said for the infliction of the same loss through direct infringement of someone else's possessory rights. As discussed in more detail in chapter five, the contrary is true, and failing to protect possessory and proprietary interests in assets will be socially and economically disadvantageous as it will discourage owners and possessors from investing in those assets, or employing them in their most efficient uses.[76]

Conversion in the Context of the Property Torts

Whilst it is generally not regarded as easy to give any comprehensive definition of Conversion, this is not something which is exceptional within the law of torts. Although Prosser noted half a century ago that 'Conversion is unique amongst torts [in] that its existence may depend upon the degree of the damages',[77] this is, with respect, not strictly accurate. Nuisance is also a tort whose existence depends

---

[73] Stevens (n 14) at 2 (footnotes omitted).
[74] ibid at 21.
[75] In order to see how recovery for pure economic loss is not problematic for torts other than negligence, one need only consider, eg, nuisance and the economic torts.
[76] See Mattei (n 25), ch 3 and p 88.
[77] Prosser, Nature (*CLQ*, 1957) at 184 (an excellent and illuminating article in all other respects).

upon the extent of the defendant's interference with the property[78] of which the claimant has exclusive possession. It would be reasonable to argue that this context-dependent standard is a natural characteristic of property torts: since there are an inordinate number of different types of property and of different uses of that property, it is impossible to say in advance what will amount to actionable interference on any given set of facts. In relation to nuisance, there appear to be fewer judicial and academic statements of unease than in relation to Conversion, despite the striking (and unsurprising) parallels between the two actions.[79] Prosser goes on to make the following point in relation to Conversion:

> There is … no one factor which is controlling in all cases, although any one of them may be sufficient in a particular case. Conduct which is sufficiently aggravated to constitute a major defiance and infringement of the plaintiff's right, such as the deliberate theft of the chattel, may be sufficient in itself for a conversion, even though the plaintiff promptly recovers the goods and suffers no actual harm. Conduct which is relatively innocent, or trivial, becomes a conversion only if the consequences are a major interference with the plaintiff's interests.[80]

Arguably, however, similar principles apply in the tort of private nuisance:

> [I]n private nuisance … the conduct of the defendant which results in the nuisance is, of itself, not necessarily or usually unlawful. A private nuisance may be and usually is caused by a person doing, on his own land, something which he is lawfully entitled to do. His conduct only becomes a nuisance when the consequences of his act are not confined to his own land but extend to the land of his neighbour[81]

In many ways, nuisance is to real property what Conversion is to personal property. Of course, there are differences between the two torts, which exist as natural consequences of the logistical differences between real and personal property. The first significant difference stems from Conversion's descent from trespass de bonis asportatis,[82] something which could never apply to real property, since it cannot be carried off in the way that many forms of personal property can. The fact that real property is immovable also means that there is some inevitability in terms of occupiers of land interfering with their neighbours' proprietary interests, something which does not occur in the context of personal

---

[78]   Although nuisance is of course concerned with real property.

[79]   Although it is very interesting to note that FH Newark, in his landmark article 'The Boundaries of Nuisance' (1949) 65 *Law Quarterly Review* 480 at 480 remarked 'When dealing with a subject such as trespass or conversion or deceit one is conscious of knowing the limits of one's sphere of operations; and even in those cases where the limits are a little hazy there is no danger of confusing one tort with another. But in nuisance it is very different: the subject as commonly taught comprises a mass of material which proves so intractable to definition and analysis that it immediately betrays its mongrel origins.'

[80]   ibid.

[81]   Clerk & Lindsell (n 10) at para 20–06.

[82]   See ch 2 under the side-heading 'The Medieval Ancestors of Conversion, Trespass de bonis asportatis.

property.[83] This, in turn, perhaps explains another potential distinction between Conversion and nuisance; the fact that, certainly in more recent times, the strictness of liability in nuisance has been tempered somewhat by a judicial concession to an element of foreseeability,[84] although foreseeability in this sense forms part of the reasonableness equation, rather than being a freestanding requirement. As Lord Cooke of Thorndon explained in *Delaware Mansions Ltd v Westminster City Council*:

> I think that the answer to the issue falls to be found by applying the concepts of reasonableness between neighbours (real or figurative) and reasonable foreseeability which underlie much modern tort law and, more particularly, the law of nuisance. The great cases in nuisance decided in our time have these concepts at their heart.[85]

Since owners of real property, through the very act of exercising their rights, are likely to interfere to some extent with rights over neighbouring property, adding the requirement of foreseeability to the reasonableness criteria achieves some balance between the competing interests of real property owners. Since most personal property assets are to some extent portable, however, and not affixed to the personal property of others, this element of inevitable interference is absent. This explains why foreseeability does not form part of the tort of Conversion, and why the strictness of the liability remains undiluted; dealing with another's assets inconsistently with his rights over them generally requires some form of intentional act and is unlikely directly to result from the use of one's own assets. Therefore, there is not necessarily in the context of personal property a need to balance competing proprietary interests. The message, as expressed by Diplock LJ (as he then was), remains

> At common law one's duty to one's neighbour who is the owner, or entitled to possession, of any goods is to refrain from doing any voluntary act in relation to his goods which is a usurpation of his proprietary or possessory rights in them. Subject to some exceptions it matters not that the doer of the act of usurpation did not know, and could not by the exercise of any reasonable care have known of his neighbour's interest in the goods. This duty is absolute; he acts at his peril.[86]

This practical difference aside, however, there would appear to be no other compelling reason for Conversion to be regarded as any more of a complex concept than nuisance. That it is, however, might be a result of the law of personal property in general having become unpopular, and consequently rarely taught, in many law schools. As Birks has pointed out:

---

[83] See Mattei (n 25) at 69, text to fn 66.

[84] In *Cambridge Water Co v Eastern Counties Leather plc* [1994] 2 AC 264 at p 301D, Lord Goff (with whom all four other judges agreed) held that Lord Reid's opinion in *The Wagon Mound* (No 2) [1967] 1 AC 617 'settled the law to the effect that foreseeability of harm is indeed a prerequisite of the recovery of damages in private nuisance'.

[85] [2001] UKHL 55, [2002] 1 AC 321 at [29].

[86] *Marfani & Co Ltd v Midland Bank Ltd* [1968] 1 WLR 956 (CA) at 970H-971B.

This neglect is making personal property more difficult. Cases still need to be decided, but there is no secure foundation on which to build. Every area of the law nowadays needs its academic community. And that community in turn needs a certain critical mass, notably lacking here. Even simple matters begin to seem obscure.[87]

Indeed they do, as Conversion itself demonstrates. For instance, lawyers seem to be confident that they will know a nuisance when they see one, but less so a Conversion. The establishment of an actionable private nuisance, as Lord Cooke suggests above, depends on the court's finding that the defendant's actions constituted an unreasonable interference with the claimant's rights. This fits well with the idea of its being a property tort. Property torts are often referred to as intentional torts, but this is not accurate.[88] There is, in neither Conversion nor nuisance, any requirement that the defendant intended to interfere with the claimant's interests.[89] In affording primacy to the protection of property interests, property torts look not to the conduct of the defendant, but to its effect on the claimant.

On closer inspection, Conversion and nuisance have much substance in common. There are, for instance, some striking similarities between judicial approaches to establishing whether a given interference is sufficient for the respective causes of action to be established.

Nature of the Interference

This is arguably a policy based consideration, and involves the court asking whether the type of interference about which the claimant is complaining is *capable* of constituting a private nuisance. At its root is the notion that the nuisance inquiry is essentially an exercise in *balancing* the interests of neighbouring landowners, so that they might get the best use of their own land without interfering with that of their neighbours. The obvious authority to use for this proposition is *Southwark LBC v Mills*.[90] In this case, the claimants were tenants of the local authority, housed in flats which were not purpose-built and in which the soundproofing was very poor. The claimants could hear every aspect of their neighbours' day to day lives which, they contended, unreasonably interfered with the use and enjoyment of their property, despite the fact that the neighbours were not behaving unreasonably in creating such noise as they did. Expressing sympathy for the plight of the claimants, the House of Lords found nevertheless for the defendants and held that the daily activities of life cannot amount to an

---

[87]   P Birks, 'Personal Property: Proprietary Rights and Remedies' (2000) 11 *Kings College Law Journal* 1 at 2.

[88]   P Cane, 'Causing Conversion' (2002) 118 *LQR* 544 at 544.

[89]   This is characteristic of the property torts generally, since, eg, where trespass to land is concerned, liability lies for simply entering another's land, even if the defendant genuinely believed the land to belong to her: *Basely v Clarkson* (1682) 3 Lev 37, 83 ER 565.

[90]   *sub nom Southwark LBC v Tanner and ors* and another case [2001] 1 AC 1.

interference capable of constituting an actionable private nuisance. The House held that the neighbours' activities met both of the criteria outlined by Bramwell B in *Bamford v Turnley*[91] in order to avoid liability, namely that such acts

> must (i) 'be necessary for the common and ordinary use and occupation of land and houses' and (ii) must be 'conveniently done', that is to say done with proper consideration for the interests of neighbouring occupiers. Where these two conditions are satisfied, no action will lie for that substantial interference with the use and enjoyment of his neighbour's land that would otherwise have been an actionable nuisance.[92]

A similar limitation applies also in the context of Conversion: where a defendant acts towards a claimant's assets in such a way as is necessary in order practically to use or to access his own assets, this will not amount to a Conversion even if the result of it is effectively to deprive the claimant of those assets. In *Bushel v Miller*,[93] the claimant and defendant were porters on the Custom-House quay and, as such, had the use of a hut for the storage of parcels which were waiting to be loaded on board ship. The claimant had placed goods belonging to a third party in the hut in such a way as to prevent the defendant from getting to his own storage chest without removing them. The defendant subsequently removed them, in order to get access to his own goods, and placed them a yard away from their original position. The defendant then left without replacing the goods in their original position, and those goods were later lost. The claimant paid the third party the value of the lost goods and sued the defendant in Conversion. The action failed, however, because the court found that the defendant's actions in removing the goods had not been wrongful, since they were necessary for him to be able to access his own personal property, and that he only acted reasonably in what he did.[94] Of course, the nature of the defendant's action may be coloured, if not determined, by the intention and purpose with which he acts.[95]

Degree and Extent of the Interference

This consideration is another element of the balancing exercise referred to above. As far as nuisance is concerned, the degree to which the activity at issue interferes with the claimant's property interest will be influential in the court's deciding whether it amounts to an unreasonable interference. This is illustrated in *Vanderpant v Mayfair Hotel Co Ltd*,[96] in which the defendant company ran a hotel next door to the claimant's private residence. The claimant argued that the

---

[91] (1860) 3 B & S 66 at 83–84, 122 ER 27 at 33.

[92] [2001] 1 AC 1 at 21A–B per Lord Millett.

[93] 1 Strange 128, 93 ER 428.

[94] The court also found that the failure to replace the goods might have amounted a trespass, but was definitely not a Conversion.

[95] See under the side-heading The Requisite Conduct of the Defendant, Intention, below, for more on the intention and purpose of the defendant.

[96] [1930] 1 Ch 138.

(inevitable) noise and activity associated with the operation of a large hotel unreasonably interfered with his enjoyment of his property. His application for an injunction was allowed to a certain extent, in that it was granted against the hotel kitchen in general terms, and against the coming and going of staff and deliveries between 10 pm and 8 am. In his judgment, Luxmoore J made it clear that these were the only elements of the hotel's operations which, in terms of their duration and extent, constituted an unreasonable interference with the claimant's enjoyment of his property: the night-time deliveries because they prevented the residents of the claimant's property from sleeping, and the noise of the kitchen because, accommodating 70 staff, being heavily in use several times a day and being situated right next to the claimant's house, it created a greater interference than a reasonable neighbour could be expected to endure. It was the extent of these disturbances which set them apart from the hotel's other activities in terms of their effect on the claimant.

In the context of personal property and Conversion, a similar question of degree and extent determines whether the interference in question is sufficient to constitute an assumption by the defendant of the superior possessory right over the asset for himself. It is important to note, however, that the use of the term 'sufficient' in this context does not have a one-dimensional meaning. There is no requirement, as there is in the case of theft, for the defendant permanently to have deprived the claimant of the assets in question. As Lord Ackner pointed out in *The Playa Larga*, 'it is well established that even a temporary deprivation of possession amounts to Conversion'.[97] Sufficiency, in the context of Conversion, does not necessarily refer to the temporal aspect of the interference, but to its qualitative extent; the important question is whether it operated so as effectively to transfer the superior possessory interest in the asset from the original possessor to the interferer.[98] In *Hiort v London & North Western Railway Co*,[99] the defendants, who warehoused corn to the claimants' order, wrongly delivered it to an agent of the claimants. Subsequently, the claimants sold that corn to a third party, and a delivery order for the same was endorsed to the claimant's agent, who passed it on to the defendants. When the third party purchaser failed to pay for the corn, the claimants sued the defendants for, inter alia, converting their corn by delivering it to their agent without their permission. In the end, of course, this Conversion made no difference to the ultimate outcome because, even had the defendants not delivered the corn to the agent, but delivered to the third party purchaser against the order, the claimants would still have suffered the same loss. Nonetheless, according to Thesiger LJ

---

[97]   *Empresa Exportadora de Azucar v Industria Azucarera Nacional SA, (The Playa Larga and The Marble Islands)* [1983] 2 Lloyd's Rep 171 at 181.

[98]   See Prosser (n 3) at 174.

[99]   *Hiort and anor v The London and North-Western Railway Company* (1879) 4 Ex D 188.

there was sufficient damage in the eyes of the law to enable the plaintiffs to sue, for this reason, that they were for some days deprived of the control of their goods, to which they were entitled by their contract with the defendants, and the law presumes a damage in respect of that unlawful act.[100]

Despite the fact that the claimants in *Hiort v LNWR* were awarded only nominal damages, to recognise the fact that they would ultimately have suffered the same loss, with or without the wrongful delivery, the point remains that the defendant's actions, in delivering the corn and so assuming the claimants' rights over it, had constituted a Conversion. *Hiort v LNWR* demonstrates that this is sufficient for a successful claim, whether any additional damage occurs as a consequence or not.

The fact that Conversion and nuisance have these significant elements in common, and that the latter tort is generally regarded as a far more accessible concept than the former, suggests that Conversion is not in substance the esoteric concept that it is often made out to be. It also seems reasonable to argue that some application of the considerations used to establish nuisance might well aid the courts in identifying whether, on a given set of facts, a Conversion exists. It is both intuitively appealing and practically beneficial to recognise that these property torts are closely conceptually related, and that an understanding of one can contribute to an understanding of the other.

The Requisite Conduct of the Defendant

Actions of the Defendant: Use and Possession

In order to be liable in Conversion, a defendant does not have to be in possession of the claimant's assets at the time of the claim. In fact, he can be liable in Conversion even though he never was in possession of them. According to *Salmond on Torts* 'there may be a Conversion even though the defendant has never been in physical possession of the goods, if his act has amounted to an absolute denial and repudiation of the plaintiff's rights'.[101]

The point was revisited in *Douglas Valley Finance Co Ltd v S Hughes (Hirers) Ltd*.[102] The assets which were the subject of this action included two lorries which were designed for the purpose of road haulage. Appurtenant to these lorries, however, were special licences, of which only a finite number were issued; these were the main concern of the claimants in this action. The licences in question

---

[100]   ibid at 198.

[101]   JW Salmond, *The Law of Torts*, 7th edn (London, Sweet & Maxwell, 1927) at 394, which was cited with apparent approval by Scrutton LJ *arguendo* in *Oakley v Lyster* [1931] 1 KB 148 (CA) at 150 (and appears unchanged in the current edition—see RVF Heuston and RA Buckley, *Salmond and Heuston on Torts*, 21st edn (London, Sweet & Maxwell, 1996) at 103).

[102]   [1969] 1 QB 738.

were necessary in order for the lorries to be used for their sole commercial purpose, namely carrying goods by road. The special licences also applied only to the vehicle to which they were attached, unless, on a successful application by the holder to the licensing authority, they were transferred to another specified vehicle. In such an event, the original vehicle was removed from the licence. Essentially, this meant that vehicles bearing these special and limited edition licences were worth significantly more than they would have been without them. The claimants were a finance company who had let out the lorries, bearing their licences, to a third party on hire purchase terms. The defendants were purchasers of those lorries and licences from the hirer. As a result of a series of machinations by the defendant, by the time that the claimants came to repossess their lorries, on the hirer's default, only the lorries themselves were available to the claimants, having been severed from their valuable licences.

The defendants, however, argued that, since they were never in possession of either the lorries or the special licences, they could not be liable in Conversion because the tort requires adverse possession. Nonetheless, in deciding in favour of the claimants, McNair J said

> it seems to me to be clear beyond any controversy that the defendants were guilty of such a wrongful assumption of ownership, coupled with acts as owner, as to constitute the tort of Conversion, whether or not the defendants had at any time actual or constructive possession of the lorries.[103]

The gist of Conversion is that the claimant has lost the ability fully to exercise his superior possessory rights over his assets and the defendant has assumed such rights; that is all that is necessary for liability in Conversion.[104] Although the original use of the word 'Conversion' was to denote an action whereby an individual had taken an asset belonging to another and 'converted' it to his own use, a defendant need not have actually done this in order to be liable for the tort; he will be liable whether he assumed possessory rights over the assets concerned in order to use them for himself, to transfer to another, or to do nothing with them at all. The material element of his action is that it deprives the rightful possessor of his rights over the assets in question and involves an assumption by the defendant of the claimant's possessory rights. A defendant will not be liable, however, if his acts in relation to the assets are 'purely ministerial', such as those of a broker or someone acting only as a passive intermediary between the parties.[105] The acts of auctioneers, on the other hand are generally deemed to be more than purely ministerial if they have possession or constructive possession of the assets

---

[103] In coming to his conclusion on this point, he applied *Lancashire & Yorkshire Railway v MacNicoll* (1918) 88 LJ (KB) 601, *Van Oppen & Co Ltd v Tredegars Ltd* (1921) 37 TLR 504 (KB) and *Oakley v Lyster* [1931] 1 KB 148 (CA). His Lordship made a second point herein, saying that, even if it were necessary to establish possession on behalf of the defendants, constructive possession would suffice. For a detailed discussion of this, see ch 4 under the heading Legal Possession.

[104] See under the heading The Gist of Conversion, above.

[105] *Re Samuel (No 2)* [1945] Ch 408 (CA).

in question and act so as to transfer that possession to a third party.[106] The material behavioural element in such cases would seem to be the defendant's active involvement in delivering the assets from one party to another, and thereby interfering with another's right to possession of those assets.[107]

Intention

Conversion is a tort of strict liability.[108] The intention of the defendant *in relation to the claimant* is, therefore, of no significance.[109] That is to say that, should a defendant have exercised full possessory rights over an asset, honestly and reasonably believing himself to be the one legally entitled to do so, he will still be liable in Conversion, should someone else turn out to have the current superior possessory right in that asset. Conversion presents, therefore, as a classic tort of strict liability. Nevertheless, although the defendant's intention is not a necessary element of the tort, it will often indicate something material about the defendant's interference.

Fouldes v Willoughby[110] is instructive here. In this, possibly one of the best known Conversion cases, the claimant was attempting to travel, with his horses, on the Birkenhead to Liverpool ferry. The defendant, the proprietor of the ferry, did not want to carry the claimant as a passenger and so, with the intention of encouraging the claimant to disembark, he removed the claimant's horses from the ferry and returned them to the shore. The claimant still refused to leave the ferry and continued on his journey to Liverpool, leaving the horses on the quayside.[111] The fact that the defendant ferryman removed the claimant's horses from his ferry *in order to induce the claimant also to leave* is a material consideration, in that it demonstrates that the defendant was at all times behaving towards the horses in a way which recognised that they were *someone else's* assets rather than behaving as if they were his own:

---

[106] See *RH Willis & Son v British Car Auctions Ltd* [1978] 1 WLR 438 (CA) for the liability of auctioneers, but see F Meisel, 'Return is No Conversion' [2004] *Conv* 145 and *Marcq v Christie Manson & Woods Ltd (t/a Christie's)* [2003] EWCA Civ 731, [2004] QB 286 for the proposition that merely returning a (previously stolen) asset unsold to a principal does not amount to a Conversion of it.

[107] See *Penfolds Wines Pty Ltd v Elliott* [1946] HCA 46, 74 CLR 204.

[108] *MCC Proceeds Inc v Lehman Bros International (Europe)* [1998] 4 All ER 675 (CA), at 685j per Mummery LJ. There are, however, a number of exceptions to this: see Clerk & Lindsell (n 10) at paras 17–70 to 17–76.

[109] To the cause of action itself. It might be relevant to 'the sporadically available defence of *bona fide* purchase to say that the title of the claimant was destroyed *vis-à-vis* him by his act of purchase'. W Swadling, 'Unjust Delivery' in A Burrows and A Rodger (eds), *Mapping the Law: Essays in Honour of Peter Birks* (Oxford, Oxford University Press, 2006) at 287.

[110] (1841) 8 M & W 540, 151 ER 1153.

[111] As it happens, what occurred thereafter would, had it been relevant to the case as presented to the court, have complicated matters somewhat, since the horses, abandoned on the turnpike, later turned up at the defendant's brother's inn.

> It is a proposition familiar to all lawyers, that a simple asportation of a chattel, without any intention of making any further use of it, although it may be a sufficient foundation for an action of trespass, is not sufficient to establish a Conversion.[112]

Had there been an accomplice of the defendant waiting at the shore, however, and had he removed the horses with the intention of having them taken off to the defendant's own stables, the same action would have sufficed to be a Conversion of the assets: there would have been the requisite evidence of the defendant treating the goods as if they were his own. So, whilst a defendant does not need to intend to convert an asset in order to do so, intention is by no means always irrelevant to the ultimate classification of his behaviour. The intentions of the defendant may be relevant insofar as they affect the distinction between the defendant doing something to another's asset and his behaving towards an asset as if it were his own; in other words, they apply only to the *nature* of his action, and not the *consequences* of it.[113] It matters why the ferry owner removed the horses to the quay, not because of the effect this had on the claimant, but because it tells us what the defendant was doing. It is irrelevant whether the defendant's intention was to deal with assets belonging to someone else (that is, whether he knew that someone else had the superior possessory interest in the assets with which he was dealing); all that matters is that he intended to deal with those particular assets as if they were his own. Only to this extent is intention relevant to the strict liability tort of Conversion.

Fouldes v Willoughby has been subjected to trenchant criticism by Salmond.[114] One objection is that the case makes an unnecessary distinction between trespass and trover in cases of tortious asportation; another is that it suggests that every Conversion involves a denial of the claimant's title. According to Salmond, the latter point is inconsistent with later decisions such as *Hiort v Bott*, in which the defendant was held liable in Conversion, despite the fact that he dealt with the assets concerned for the specific purpose of returning them to their rightful possessor.[115] With respect, however, neither of these objections succeeds in detracting from the worth of *Fouldes*. First, there is a clear need to be able to distinguish between Conversion and trespass so as to establish when the claimant will be able to recover the full measure of Conversion damages,[116] and when he will be limited to the value of his loss. Secondly, *Fouldes* is not inconsistent with

---

[112]   *Fouldes v Willoughby* (1841) 8 M & W 540 at 544–45, 151 ER 1153 at 1155 per Abinger CB.

[113]   Although see the diverging views of J Faust Jr, 'Distinction between Conversion and Trespass to Chattels' (1958) 37 *Oregon Law Review* 256 at 260 and Prosser (n 3) at 172.

[114]   JW Salmond, 'Observations on Trover and Conversion' (1905) 21 *LQR* 43.

[115]   In *Hiort v Bott* (1874) LR 9 Ex 86, the defendant had some barley delivered to him by mistake. The defendant then indorsed the delivery order for the barley to a third party, who usually acted as a broker, telling him about the mistake and intending that the barley would thereby be returned to the seller. The third party subsequently absconded with the barley and the defendant was successfully sued in trover by its suppliers.

[116]   The standard measure of which is the full market value of the assets—see ch 7, under the side-heading The Measure of Damages for Conversion, (a) The Basic Rule.

Hiort v Bott because, as outlined above, the defendant's intention as to the *consequences* of his dealing is irrelevant, as long as he intended to deal with those assets in a way which is inconsistent with the superior possessory right of another party. In *Hiort v Bott*, the defendant consigned the assets over to a third party, enabling him to abscond with them. The nature of this act is totally different to the nature of the defendant's act in *Fouldes*, since removing someone's property from your own is not necessarily inconsistent with another's superior possessory right to that property, whereas assigning the property rights in another's assets to a third party is, surely, the paradigm case of acting inconsistently with that other's proprietary interests. Despite Salmond's criticism of *Fouldes*, therefore, it remains, in our view, an elemental case on Conversion.

The defendant's intention has been held to be more relevant in one type of case than it is in another. In *Sanderson v Marsden & Jones*, Bankes LJ said:

> [I]n considering whether a person has been guilty of conversion there are two classes of acts which you may have to consider: the one is a class of act from which an intention on the part of the person committing the act may be inferred that he deliberately intended to do something the effect of which would be to deprive the owner of what is sometimes spoken of as the dominion over a particular chattel and in other cases the title to or ownership of the chattel. That is one class of acts, and with reference to that class of acts the intention of the person doing the act is most material. There is another class of act in which the act itself may be of such a character as, without any intention on the part of the person doing the act, to deprive the owner of both possession and ownership, as for instance where the effect of the particular act may be the destruction of the chattel.[117]

A similar dichotomy had been identified nearly half a century earlier by Blackburn J in *Hollins v Fowler*:

> There are some acts which from their nature are necessarily a conversion, whether there was notice of the Plaintiff's title or not. There are others which if done in a *bonâ fide* ignorance of the Plaintiff's title are excused, though if done in disregard of a title of which there was notice they would be a conversion. And this, I think, is borne out by the decided cases.[118]

This is basically an evidentiary issue and addresses the problem of how to deal with cases which lie on the boundary between trespass and Conversion. As *Fouldes*, *Hollins* and *Sanderson* all illustrate, intention can be a helpful evidentiary tool.

A judicial pronouncement apt to cause confusion in respect of intention, however, is that of Lord Nicholls in *Kuwait Airways*.[119] There, His Lordship asserted that, in order to amount to a Conversion, conduct must be 'deliberate,

---

[117] (1922) 10 Ll L Rep 467 (CA) at 470.
[118] (1875) LR 7 HL 757 at 766.
[119] n 14.

not accidental'.[120] As highlighted by Peter Cane,[121] the use of the word 'deliberate' in this context is potentially confusing. Cane explains that there is an important distinction to be made here between conduct which is voluntary and that which is deliberate. It is voluntary conduct which is a requirement of the tort of Conversion. Such conduct need not be deliberate in the sense that the actor was aware of what its consequences would be; only in the sense that the actor had control over the commission of the act itself: 'The fundamental point is that conversion consists of conduct inconsistent with the owner's rights regardless of the intention with which it is done.'[122]

According to Lord Porter in *Caxton Publishing Co Ltd v Sutherland Publishing Co Ltd*:

> Conversion was defined by Atkin J, as he then was, in Lancashire & Yorkshire Railway Co. v MacNicoll. 'Dealing', he said, 'with goods in a manner inconsistent with the right of the true owner amounts to a conversion, provided that it is also established that there is also an intention on the part of the defendant in so doing to deny the owner's right or to assert a right which is inconsistent with the owner's right.' This definition was approved by Scrutton LJ in Oakley v Lyster. Atkin J goes on to point out that, where the act done is necessarily a denial of the owner's right or an assertion of a right inconsistent therewith, intention does not matter. Another way of reaching the same conclusion would be to say that conversion consists in an act intentionally done inconsistent with the owner's right, though the doer may not know of or intend to challenge the property or possession of the true owner.[123]

Innocent Converters

What this means, of course, is that an individual may be held liable in Conversion, even though he is 'innocent' in moral terms, not having realised that his action, intentional in itself, was inconsistent with anyone else's possessory rights. That such 'innocence' is no excuse for behaviour which amounts to a Conversion was made very clear by the House of Lords in *Hollins v Fowler*.[124] In that case, the defendant cotton brokers had purchased bales of cotton from a third party, who had (unbeknownst to the brokers) obtained the bales fraudulently from the claimants. In taking delivery of the cotton, and transferring it to a customer of theirs, the defendants, despite having earned only commission on the transaction, remained liable to the claimants in Conversion. Some justification for such a position was offered by Lord O'Hagan, when he said of the defendants:

> They are innocent of any actual wrongdoing, but those with whom they are in conflict are as innocent as they, and we can only regard the liability attached to them by the law,

---

[120]   ibid at [39].

[121]   Cane, Conversion (*LQR*, 2002) at 544.

[122]   ibid at 547.

[123]   [1939] AC 178 at 201.

[124]   (1875) LR 7 HL 757. For a more recent consideration of the issue, see *Wilson v Robertsons (London) Ltd* [2006] EWCA Civ 1088.

without being affected in our judgment by its unpleasant consequences. They appear to me to have been guilty of a conversion in dealing with the Plaintiffs' property, and disposing of it to other persons, without any right or authority to do so.[125]

This highlights the inherent difficulty in the law's attempts to protect personal property. Whilst there is not, as noted above, any need to balance the competing interests of neighbouring property interests, as there is in nuisance,[126] there is a need to balance the competing interests of integrity of personal property with the security of commercial transactions. In holding 'innocent' converters liable, the law as it stands favours the protection of property interests and, consequently, puts the onus on those dealing with assets to ensure their actions are not inconsistent with another's rights, rather than requiring possessors actively to exclude others from their assets. This hard line against 'innocent' converters is fortified by the fact that contributory negligence is irrelevant to a claim in Conversion.[127]

This issue of defendants found liable in Conversion, despite the absence of moral wrongdoing, manifests itself in two forms. The first, and less contentious, form is that of the innocent acquirer of assets; the second is that of the innocent handler. The material difference between the two is that the former label is used to describe someone currently in possession of the assets which are the subject matter of the action, whereas the latter refers to one whom no longer possesses the assets or, in some cases, has never possessed them. The reason for the intuitive difficulties generated by this issue is that no-fault liability is generally ill at ease within the law of torts, and the real source of the problem is that it throws into stark relief the conceptual boundaries between the tortious and the proprietary elements of Conversion. The innocent acquirer, despite his lack of wrongdoing, is nevertheless in possession of something which, in the absence of any rightful claim, he must return to the party entitled to it. Were Conversion a purely proprietary concept, this would be a straightforward and unproblematic solution; the true owner must recover his asset, or its market value. This is because 'property is concerned with what people have and tort with what people do'.[128] In civil law systems, where, as outlined above, the proprietary action is separated from the tort action, there is no such perceived difficulty because there is nothing intuitively difficult about allowing someone who has been dispossessed to pursue even an innocent dispossessor through the law of property.

The law of torts, on the other hand, because it generally takes account of the nature of the defendant's actions, finds itself faced with something of a potential anomaly in that it must protect a claimant's proprietary interest despite the apparently unobjectionable conduct of the defendant. This issue is, however, disposed of by considering the broader aims of the law of torts; a defendant's

---

[125]   (1875) LR 7 HL 757 at 798.
[126]   See text to n 83 ff.
[127]   s 11(1) of the 1977 Act.
[128]   Weir (n 24) at 154.

actions are only relevant in terms of their connection to a claimant's loss and, where innocent acquirers are concerned, the acquirer's actions, although not bad, are wrongful, and they cause the claimant to lose the ability to exercise his superior possessory right over the assets in question.[129] Since this loss of ability fully to exercise one's possessory rights over one's assets is, as outlined above, the gist of Conversion, it is clear why the acquirer's state of mind is of no relevance.

The position is harder to justify in terms of the innocent handler, who no longer possesses the assets in question or who might never have possessed them, and this is an issue that has troubled judges, academics and policy makers alike.[130] Here, the tortious element of Conversion takes precedence. Once more, the gist of the tort is significant in that it indicates that what the claimants have lost is their ability fully to exercise their superior possessory rights over their assets as a result of a wrongful interference by the defendant. Consider the counterfactual situation: were claimants not able to sue anyone who had innocently caused them to lose their ability to exercise their superior possessory rights, but only to sue those who had done so with full knowledge and intent, or those who were still in possession of the assets in question, this would have the effect of transferring the risk of loss from those who interfere with someone else's rights (albeit without moral blame) to those who have lost a right to which they are entitled (and may well also be without moral culpability). As the Law Reform Committee stated in its Eighteenth Report:

> The action of conversion has long been established in English law as a vehicle for the protection of proprietary rights.[131] Unlike Roman law, English law achieves this purpose by means of an action in personam for damages which, when trover (from which conversion is derived) first appeared in the 15th century, was classified as tortious.[132] But, although so classified, it is and always has been primarily an action for the protection of ownership and it is because of this that questions as to the fault of the defendant are irrelevant, the principle adopted being that 'persons deal with the property in chattels or exercise acts of ownership over them at their peril.'[133] It seems to us that there are sound practical reasons for retaining this principle and that to depart from it would be inconsistent with the view taken by this committee in its 12th Report

[129]   See S Green, 'To Have and to Hold? Conversion and Intangible Property', (2008) 71 *Modern Law Review* 114 at 114.

[130]   See, in particular, Lord Nicholls in *Kuwait Airways* (n 14), Lords Brown and Hoffmann in *OBG Ltd v Allan* (n 69), Weir (n 24) at 483 and 18th Report of the LRC (1971) at para 10.

[131]   This proposition and the references below to 'protection of ownership' rest on the authority of, among others, Holdsworth and Maitland, and, because possession is taken to be a full title, are in no way inconsistent with the rule that a plaintiff, in order to sue in conversion, must be able to rely either on actual possession or an immediate right to it. The proposition is, however, subject to the qualification that Conversion has not hitherto been available to a reversionary owner with no right to immediate possession.

[132]   On the reasoning that, since the thing itself could not be recovered, it was not proprietary and must therefore be based either on contract or on tort, and, since it lay against persons other than bailees, it could not be contractual.

[133]   *Hollins v Fowler* (1872) LR 7 QB 616 (Ex Ch) per Cleasby B at 639.

as to the balance to be struck between sanctity of property on the one hand and, on the other, the commercial advantages to be derived from facilitating transfer of title.[134]

In other words, the sanctity of property takes precedence. Not only is this congruent with the common law's long-established practice of according such precedence to original property rights,[135] but it makes logistical sense. The practical effect of putting the risk of loss on the potential interferer, rather than on the possessor, is that the law also puts on to the potential interferer the onus of investigating title to the assets in question. The potential interferer is in a far better position to do this in relation to a specific asset, or set of assets, with which he knows he intends to deal, than is the possessor to protect his assets from every potential interferer, of which there might be an indeterminate number.[136] As Cane makes clear 'in English law, the law of tort plays a major role in protecting property interests. Introducing fault elements into the tort may undermine that function'.[137] Of course, an alternative would be to find some sort of middle ground, similar to that taken in spuilzie. In that action, intermediate possessors without fault are held liable only if, and to the extent, that they are unjustly enriched by the transaction.[138] This, however, whilst undoubtedly imposing less of a hardship on the innocent intermediate converter, and resembling more closely a purely vindicatory action (which bases the liability of such a party on fault or unjust enrichment), still detracts from the protection afforded to the party with the superior possessory interest. In our view, such property interests are more deserving of protection than is the freedom of individuals in general to deal with personal property (to whomsoever it may belong) with impunity.[139]

The one situation in which this explanation appears less convincing is where the party with the superior possessory right is negligent in allowing his property to be converted. Take, for example, the train passenger who leaves his laptop

---

[134]   18th Report (n 6) at para 13.

[135]   To be contrasted with the civil law tendency to favour the good faith acquirer: see Bell et al (n 46) at 279–80 and, for a more detailed comparative analysis of the two systems, see Harding & Rowell, Protection (*ICLQ* 1977). In Scots law, however, the only protection available to a good faith enquirer is that which results from the rebuttable presumption that the possessor is the owner: see Carey Miller (n 40) at 251.

[136]   Although in some cases, it must be conceded, a defendant may still be liable, despite his best efforts at such investigations. Examples of this may be found in the cases where hire purchase companies have not registered their interests in assets and yet still succeed against defendants who checked such registers before dealing with those assets. See *Moorgate Mercantile Co Ltd v Twitchings* [1977] AC 890 and *Industrial & Corporate Finance Ltd v Wyder Group Ltd* (2008) 152 SJLB 31, Lawtel AC0118437.

[137]   Cane, LQR (n 88) at 550. See also Mattei (n 25) at 88, and A Ogus, *Costs and Cautionary Tales: Economic Insights for the Law* (Oxford, Hart Publishing, 2006) at 43 for the economic efficiency arguments in favour of protecting possessors.

[138]   *HarperCollins Publishers Ltd v Stewart Young* [2007] CSOH 65 and A Steven, 'By the book: enrichment by interference' (2007) 11 *Edinburgh Law Review* 411.

[139]   It must be conceded that, without a system of registration comparable to that which exists for land, it is true that it is often difficult effectively to investigate title to personal property. Nevertheless, it is not immediately clear why this risk should fall on the party with the superior possessory right rather than on the interferer.

unattended on a bench whilst he goes to buy his ticket. Whilst few would find anything objectionable about his retaining his right to sue whoever took this opportunity to interfere with his possessory rights, it is not so easy to accept that he should also retain the right to sue any subsequent innocent purchasers from the original converter. According to section 11(1) of 1977 Act, contributory negligence is no defence to an action founded on Conversion.[140] This leaves our innocent purchaser, in the example given above, in the situation where he will be liable to its negligent former possessor, with little hope of recovering anything from his seller, who is hardly likely to have left himself in a position to be found.

The reasoning behind this statutory position was, however, made very clear in the Law Reform Committee's Eighteenth Report (Conversion and Detinue).[141] First, it pointed out that the Law Reform (Contributory Negligence) Act 1945

> was passed with the object of dealing with those cases in which, before 1945, contributory negligence was a complete defence: if, therefore, contributory negligence was not previously a defence to an action of conversion, the Act does not apply to that tort.[142]

Of course, the 1977 Act could still have decreed that the partial defence should apply, but the Law Reform Committee did not favour recommending such a course of action. In part, this was because it agreed with the recommendations made in its Twelfth Report (Transfer of Title to Chattels)[143] in which it rejected any apportionment of liability as between a claimant and defendant, whether that defendant be an innocent handler or an innocent acquirer. These recommendations were made on the basis that apportionment would detract from the clarity and certainty which is so important in this field of law; that the wide judicial discretion which would result would not be appropriate where the transfer of property is concerned; that the practical and procedural difficulties of deciding such cases would be excessive (particularly where the assets had passed through several hands); and that, consequently, the cost of litigation would increase. The other reason given in the Eighteenth Report for not advocating contributory negligence as a defence to Conversion was that

> much judicial time would be occupied, to little advantage, in considering what particular precautions are required from householders against burglars, or from an ordinary citizen against pickpockets, or from a store proprietor against shoplifters.[144]

---

[140]   S 47, Banking Act 1979, under which contributory negligence by the drawer remains a partial defence to an action against a bank for Conversion of a cheque affords a statutory exception. See further ch 7 under the heading Contributory Negligence.

[141]   n 6.

[142]   ibid at para 80.

[143]   The 12th Report (Transfer of Title to Chattels) of the Law Reform Committee (1966), Cmnd 2958 at paras 8–12.

[144]   18th Report (n 6) at para 81.

The Three Elements of Conversion

Having examined the principles underlying Conversion, we suggest that it is possible to identify three elements which comprise the tort. They are, in essence:

1. A claimant who has the superior possessory right;
2. A deprivation of the claimant's full benefit of that right; and
3. An assumption by the defendant of that right.

1. A Claimant who has the Superior Possessory Right

The first element of Conversion is that, at the time of the Conversion, the claimant had the superior possessory right in the asset concerned. Such rights comprise the ability to recover it, reclaim it, or take action after the commission of a trespass in relation to it. As outlined above, the superior possessory right must be carefully distinguished from ownership, as, although they may be concurrent in any given case, this is not necessarily so. In favouring the superior possessory right over the ultimate proprietary interest in assets, Conversion stands apart from the separate tort of reversionary injury, which lies for a true owner, out of possession, whose reversionary interest has been permanently damaged. The need for the claimant's superior possessory right to exist at the time of the Conversion was made clear in both *Smith (Administrator of Cosslett (Contractors) Ltd) v Bridgend CBC*[145] and *The Future Express*.[146] This principle is dealt with in much greater detail in the following chapter.

2. A Deprivation of the Claimant's Full Benefit of that Right

The defendant's act must have deprived the claimant of the full benefit of that right, such that he is unable to exercise that right in its full spectrum. The most instructive way of illustrating this element is to look to those cases which have presented factual situations which lie near the margins of Conversion. After all, the cases involving, for instance, the sale by a hire-purchaser of a car on which he has not yet completed the payments, feature a clear Conversion,[147] and, as such, tell us nothing particularly instructive about the parameters of the tort.

On the other hand, the cases of *Fouldes v Willoughby*[148] and *Hiort v Bott*[149] provide examples of acts which lie at the margins of the tort, thereby enabling us to see where those margins fall. The actions of the defendant in *Fouldes*[150] were

---

[145] [2001] UKHL 58, [2002] 1 AC 336.
[146] [1993] 2 Lloyd's Rep 542 (CA).
[147] See, eg, *RH Willis & Son v British Car Auctions Ltd* [1978] 1 WLR 438 (CA) and *Wickham Holdings Ltd v Brooke House Motors Ltd* [1967] 1 WLR 295 (CA).
[148] n 110.
[149] n 115
[150] Discussed in more detail at text to n 110 ff.

held not to amount to a Conversion because the defendant did not prevent the claimant from exercising his full possessory rights over his assets.[151] On the contrary, the defendant ferryman was *inviting* the claimant to exercise such powers by encouraging him to leave the ferry to reclaim them:

> In the present case, therefore, the simple removal of these horses by the defendant, for a purpose wholly unconnected with any the least denial of the right of the plaintiff to the possession and enjoyment of them, is no conversion of the horses[152]

Whilst no doubt amounting to a trespass, in infringing the claimant's possessory rights, the defendant's actions did not operate so as to render the claimant unable to exercise any of those rights, such as the right immediately to reclaim the horses.

In contrast, as we have pointed out above,[153] the actions of the defendant in *Hiort v Bott* in consigning the claimant's assets to a third party, thereby enabling him to abscond with them, did so operate.

3.   An Assumption by the Defendant of that Right

More fully stated, by his action the defendant must have assumed, in whole or in part, those possessory rights which rightfully belong to the claimant; as long as he did so at some point, it does not matter whether he is still exercising those rights at the time the action is brought, or for howsoever short a time he did so; neither does it matter whether he took physical possession of the assets at any point; what is important is whether he purported to exercise possessory rights over the assets.[154] Whilst, in terms of Conversion, this has been made explicit relatively recently,[155] it is, as the cases below demonstrate, now a firmly established characteristic of the tort.

In *Van Oppen v Tredegars*,[156] the claimants were carriers who delivered some assets to a firm by mistake. The managing director of the defendant firm tried to claim them as the defendant's property, and purported to sell them to the firm to whom they had been delivered by mistake. Despite the fact that the defendant

---

[151] See also *Club Cruise Entertainment and Travelling Services Europe BV v The Department for Transport* [2008] EWHC 2794 (Comm), [2009] 1 Lloyd's Rep 201 at [51].

[152] ibid at 547.

[153] At n 115. See also *Fairfax Gerrard Holdings Ltd and ors v Capital Bank plc* [2006] EWHC 3439 (Comm), [2007] 1 Lloyd's Rep 171 (reversed on other grounds at [2007] EWCA Civ 1226, [2008] 1 Lloyd's Rep 297) for an example of how a Conversion might occur in a modern commercial context (granting of a finance lease over a printing machine).

[154] See *Kuwait Airways* [2002] UKHL 19, [2002] 2 AC 886 at [39]–[42].

[155] See per Greer LJ in *Oakley v Lyster* [1931] 1 KB 148 (CA) at 154, where, in stating this third principle to be true of a modern Conversion, he said 'Whether a century or two centuries ago that action would have been called trover or an action on the case is quite immaterial', and, in the same case, Scrutton LJ declared that, in finding a Conversion despite the defendant's not having had possession of the assets, 'I think we are carrying out the modern duty of the Court to do justice irrespective of the form of the writ' (also at 154).

[156] (1921) 37 TLR 504 (KB).

firm never physically dealt with the assets in question, it was held liable in Conversion on the grounds that its actions had, nevertheless, interfered with the claimants' superior possessory rights in those assets.

Furthermore, in the case of *Oakley v Lyster*,[157] the claimant had arranged with the tenant of a farm to rent from him some land on which to store hard core and tar macadam, of which the claimant was the owner. Some time later, the defendant purchased the freehold of the farm and started moving some of the hard core. When the claimant heard about this, and contacted the defendant about it, he received a letter from the defendant's solicitors, stating that the defendant had bought the land and everything on it and that, should the claimant attempt to remove the hard core, he would be trespassing upon the defendant's land. The claimant sued in Conversion in respect of the removal of some of the material belonging to him, and for the prevention of his access to it. According to Scrutton LJ, counsel for the defence

> argued that there can be no conversion if the defendant is not in possession of the thing alleged to have been converted, and he cited in support of that proposition England v Cowley,[158] but in that case I find Kelly CB saying this 'Apart from mere dicta, no case, so far as I am aware, can be found where a man not in possession of the property has been held liable in trover unless he has absolutely denied the plaintiff's right.'[159] In this case, the appellant has denied the respondent's right to remove the hard core, which he says is his own, and he backed that opinion by acts—namely, by using some of the stuff himself and by stopping the respondent and his purchaser from removing it. That brings the case within the definition of conversion given by Kelly CB and by Atkin J in the cases I have referred to.[160]

Here it is clear how trespass and Conversion diverge; a trespass being an interference *with another's asset* and a Conversion being the treatment of that asset as one's own, (or 'treating "teum" as "meum"'[161]). The distinction lies, in other words, in whether the defendant interferes with another's possessory rights, or whether he assumes those rights for himself:

> There might, perhaps, in such a case be ground for maintaining an action of trespass, because the defendant may have had no right to meddle with the horses at all: but it is

---

[157]   [1931] 1 KB 148 (CA).

[158]   (1873) LR 8 Ex 126.

[159]   ibid at 131.

[160]   His Lordship had earlier referred to Atkin J's judgment in *Lancashire & Yorkshire Rly Co v MacNicoll* (1918) 88 LJ (KB) 601 at 605.

[161]   The 8th Report (Theft and Related Offences) of the Criminal Law Revision Committee (1966), Cmnd 2977 at para 33. See also Val D Ricks, 'The Conversion of Intangible Property: Bursting the Ancient Trover Bottle with New Wine' (1991) 4 *Brigham Young University Law Review* 1681, text to fn 38: 'The essence of dominion in conversion seems to be a right to use of the chattel at all times and in all places.'

clear that he did not do so for the purposes of taking them away from the plaintiff, or of exercising any right over them, either for himself of for any other person.[162]

An Exception to these Principles: Statutory Conversion

Under section 2(2) of the 1977 Act, something which was at common law only actionable in detinue is now a Conversion. The tort called 'detinue', or at least, the name 'detinue', was summarily abolished by section 2(1). The statutory tort now known as a Conversion covers situations where a bailee has allowed the goods bailed to him to become lost or destroyed in breach of his duty to his bailor. Arguably, detinue was not *in substance* abolished by the 1977 Act at all, but merely has now to be referred to under a new name.[163] This means that, despite being called a Conversion, the substantive features of detinue remain, and the requirements for this statutory Conversion differ somewhat from those outlined above (all of which are principles derived from the common law tort).

The difference is, however, very simple: what is required for this statutory Conversion to exist is that there be both a demand for the assets so lost or destroyed, to be returned, and an unequivocal refusal.[164] A recent application of this rule can be seen in *Schwarzschild v Harrods Ltd*.[165] The appellant in that case was concerned to establish that there had *not* been a cause of action for statutory Conversion at the time at which the defendant contended there was, in order that her claim would not be time-barred. Some jewellery belonging to the appellant had been stored by the defendant in a safety deposit box but, after the payments had fallen into arrears, the defendant had removed the contents of the claimant's box and lost the same by mixing them with the contents of other boxes, whose payments were similarly in arrears. On behalf of the claimant, a private detective wrote to the defendant, requesting the return of the jewellery, to which the defendant made no reply. The parties then had a meeting, but nothing further was done for another eight years, at which point the appellant brought the action for statutory Conversion. In allowing her appeal against summary judgment in the respondent's favour (made on the basis that her claim was time-barred), Eady J held, on the authority of *Clayton v LeRoy*,[166] that there had been no cause of

---

[162] *Fouldes v Willoughby* (1841) 8 M & W 540 at 546, 151 ER 1153 at 1155–56 per Lord Abinger CB. See also *Club Cruise Entertainment and Travelling Services Europe BV v The Department for Transport* [2008] EWHC 2794 (Comm), [2009] 1 Lloyd's Rep 201 at [53]–[54].

[163] See S Douglas, 'The Abolition of Detinue' [2008] *Conv* 30 for a detailed analysis of this point, concluding ultimately that detinue has been comprehensively subsumed within the new expanded tort of Conversion.

[164] *Clayton v LeRoy* [1911] 2 KB 1031 (CA).

[165] [2008] EWHC 521 (QB), (2008) 105 LSG 26.

[166] [1911] 2 KB 1031 CA.

action eight years earlier since, although the letter had been a demand (and an equivocal one at that),[167] the respondent's lack of response did not constitute an unequivocal refusal.[168]

Consequently, where an act is a Conversion only by reason of this particular statutory provision, this requirement needs to be added to those principles outlined above.[169]

---

[167] [2008] EWHC 521 (QB), (2008) 105 LSG 26 at [30].

[168] Although the Judge did acknowledge that, in certain rare circumstances, such behaviour might amount to an unequivocal refusal: ibid at [22].

[169] See Clerk & Lindsell (n 10) at para 17–03: it does not matter if the bailee is no longer in possession of the goods, and that this is the reason for the unequivocal refusal, since a bailee cannot invoke his own wrong in order to evade his liability to his bailor.

4

Title to Sue

IDENTIFYING WHO HAS title to sue in Conversion is not always easy, particularly where there are several parties involved, each with a different type of proprietary interest. This chapter aims to clarify the issue by outlining the requisite elements of such title, and, where necessary, justifying the existence of those elements in terms of the system of relative title within the common law.

The Nature of the Problem

> There is uncertainty and confusion in modern attempts to understand the nature of a claimant's interest in goods sufficient to sue in conversion.[1]

The primary reason for this is that these 'modern attempts' confuse lay and legal concepts. Understanding the requisite title to sue in Conversion is straightforward as long as the concept of 'ownership' is not allowed to confuse matters. 'Ownership' is a term ill at ease in the common law; historically there was no such thing, and modern use of the term is inconsistent and often unhelpful in a legal context. In a system where title to property is relative, there is no room for the concept to which non-lawyers would refer as 'ownership' and, even in its lay usage, the word is used to describe various, and very different, relationships between persons and things. The layman's idea of ownership essentially amounts to an absolute entitlement to an asset; being the 'owner' of an asset means that one has the right to decide what happens to that asset, how it is used and by whom, to whom it can be transferred temporarily and for how long, to whom it can be transferred permanently and on what conditions, the right to take action against one who appropriates that asset without permission, and the right to reclaim that asset, should the action be successful. The lawyer knows that this concept does not exist as such in the common law. This is largely, however, because it is not needed. Arguably, 'ownership' is an important label to those who regard it as applicable to them, because it signifies that the relationship they have

---

[1] N Curwen, 'Title to Sue in Conversion' [2004] *Conveyancer and Property Lawyer* 308 at 308.

with the asset in question attracts some form of legal protection. Several individuals can, however, each have different relationships concurrently with the same asset. Each of these can be sufficiently protected without any reference made to a concept such as 'ownership'.

According to Swadling

> it is title and not ownership which English law protects. Despite what the layman might think, there is no concept of ownership in English law. The proof of that proposition lies in the fact that English law provides no form of protection to anyone we might wish to describe as the 'owner' of goods greater than that provided to someone who simply finds them in the street.[2]

Honoré offers a provisional definition of ownership as being 'the greatest possible interest in a thing which a mature system of law recognizes'.[3] Sir Frederick Pollock asserted that ownership is 'the entirety of the powers of use and disposal allowed by law'.[4] In substance, there is no disagreement. Their common assertion is that 'ownership', *as the notion is colloquially understood*, does not exist: there is in English law no absolute and inviolable entitlement to assets. Whether one chooses to label the greatest possible interest in a thing as ownership or not is really only a question of semantics, and does not affect the fact that common law title to assets is nothing more than a practical and relative concept.[5] As has been established in the previous chapter, 'ownership', in the sense of the residuary proprietary right in an asset, is of less significance to Conversion than the concept of possession. Only if the party with the residuary proprietary interest in an asset also has the superior possessory right will she be able to sue in Conversion. The residuary proprietary right *eo ipso* is of more direct relevance to the tort of reversionary injury than it is to Conversion.

Another term often used to describe the relationship between a person and an asset is 'dominion'.[6] Such a term is technically unhelpful and historically inaccurate. As outlined above, Conversion is available to the party with the superior possessory interest in the asset concerned, whether or not he is the asset's ultimate owner. The term 'dominion', on the other hand, certainly according to the Roman law from which it is borrowed, ought not to extend to one who has the superior possessory interest and no more:

---

[2] W Swadling, 'Unjust Delivery' in A Burrows and A Rodger, *Mapping the Law: Essays in Honour of Peter Birks* (Oxford, Oxford University Press, 2006) at 281.

[3] T Honoré, 'Ownership' in AG Guest (ed), *Oxford Essays in Jurisprudence* (Oxford, Oxford University Press, 1961) at 108.

[4] F Pollock, *A First Book of Jurisprudence for Students of the Common Law* (London, Macmillan, 1923) at 179.

[5] See J Gordley, *Foundations of Private Law: Property, Tort and Unjust Enrichment* (Oxford, Oxford University Press, 2008) and U Mattei, *Basic Principles of Property Law: A Comparative Legal and Economic Introduction* (Westport Connecticut, Greenwood Press, 2000) at 77 for a discussion as to the historical pedigree of this principle.

[6] See inter alia *Clerk & Lindsell on Torts*, 19th edn (London, Sweet & Maxwell, 2006) at para 17–09.

> The underlying idea of *dominium* is akin to that of feudal lordship . . . In general, the
> term *dominus* is not applied by jurists to any person but the holder of the *dominium ex
> iure Quiritium*, the ultimate right.[7]

'*Dominium*' has more in common with ideas of 'ownership' than with possession,
and the distinction between ownership and possession has been concisely and
elegantly made by Weir:

> The distinction is basically simple: ownership is a legal right, possession a physical fact.
> The owner is entitled to a thing, whether he has it or not; the possessor has it, whether
> he is entitled to it or not. Proudhon, the revolutionary, put the point in a neat but nasty
> way: the husband owns, the lover possesses.[8]

In order to avoid any unnecessary confusion, and to ensure that the notion of
ownership remains dissociated from the concept of Conversion, it is better to
avoid the use of the word '*dominium*' and to stick to the technically accurate term
'superior possessory right'.

Essential to a proper understanding of the requisite title to sue in Conversion is
a corresponding understanding of the relativity of title within the common law.
The whole process is made much easier by abandoning any notion of a binary
relationship between owners and non-owners, and substituting for it the idea of a
spectrum of property interests, all of which can concurrently be held by different
parties in relation to the same asset. Once one thinks in these terms, Conversion
(and, indeed, the whole of personal property law) becomes a much less daunting
concept. This characteristic of the common law sets it apart from other legal
systems, particularly those based on Roman law, in which there is an absolute
concept of ownership. Within such systems, the tort of Conversion would make
little sense; within the common law, with its recognition of relative titles, it is an
entirely appropriate means of protecting personal property interests.

The rules about title to sue in Conversion provide some of the more controversial aspects of the tort. It could, after all, be regarded as intuitively difficult to
accept that a thief may sue someone who appropriates from him the asset he
appropriated from its erstwhile possessor, or that a claimant may sue someone
who no longer has the asset in question (or, in fact, never did have it). Rather
than being anomalous or problematic features of this area of the law, however,
these rules are not only perfectly consistent with the legal framework of personal
property protection, but *necessary* to ensure that that protection is both effective
and comprehensive. It is, for reasons which will be explained in this chapter,
entirely correct that a thief should in principle be able to sue someone who has
converted an asset previously in her possession, and that a term bailee should be
able to recover in Conversion from a bailor who retakes the bailed asset before

---

[7]   W Buckland, *Elementary Principles of the Roman Private Law* (Cambridge, Cambridge University Press, 1912) at 64–65.

[8]   T Weir, *A Casebook on Tort*, 10th edn (London, Sweet & Maxwell, 2004) at 484.

the expiration of the agreed term. Such rules are a natural consequence of the common law's approach to personal property.

Relativity of Title

> It must never be forgotten that titles are relative. If I have a right to possession of a book, it does not thereby follow that my title is the strongest there is, for I may have only found it in the street. But though my right to possession may not be as strong as that of the loser of the book, it does not follow that I have no title at all.[9]

This well-established common law principle is illustrated by *Armory v Delamirie*,[10] in which the claimant, having found a ring whilst sweeping a chimney, took it to the defendant for valuation. When the defendant returned only the empty socket, the claimant sued him successfully for Conversion of the jewel. In finding the jewel, the claimant chimney-sweep's boy acquired a title to it which, whilst not good against the whole world, was certainly good against the defendant goldsmith. In fact, the claimant's title to the jewel was good against everyone except those with a superior title to it, which on such facts would usually be the individual who had lost it and, should the asset have been the subject of a bailment at the time of its loss, its bailor as well.[11]

Were this not the case, and the finder in such a situation were to be denied title to the asset found, there would remain only the title in the loser (and/or his bailor), and the asset would continue to be possessed by persons with no legal interest in it. In such a situation, unless those with title happened to come across the asset in the hands of a subsequent acquirer (which in some cases would require an enormous coincidence), title and actual possession would never again be reunited. This result would be not only bizarre in theory, in that every subsequent possessor would be a wrongful possessor, but also unworkable in practice. Unlike realty, title to personalty is not registered and there would, therefore, in most cases, be no way of knowing whether someone was wrongfully in possession of an asset or had any form of title to it. If individuals did not have to presume (correctly) that others have title to the assets in their possession, the security of everyone's possessions would be dramatically reduced.[12] There is, therefore, a very good reason for the common law's early recognition of the need for, and the longevity of, the principle that possession is the root of title and that a possessor therefore has good title as against a subsequent wrongdoer.[13] Over

---

[9] Swadling, Unjust Delivery (*Mapping* 2006) at 281.

[10] (1722) 1 Str 505, 93 ER 644, JH Baker and SFC Milsom, *Sources of English Legal History* (London, Butterworths, 1986) at 547, AKR Kiralfy, *A Source Book of English Law* (London, Sweet & Maxwell, 1957) at 153.

[11] The superior possessory right might also have been deemed to lie in the owner or occupier of the premises on which it was found. See under the heading Finders, below.

[12] See Mattei, *Basic Principles* (2000) at 88.

[13] For more on this, see also text to nn 15–16 and 21, below.

150 years ago, for instance, Lord Campbell CJ declared: 'I think it most reasonable law, and essential for the interests of society, that peaceable possession should not be disturbed by wrongdoers'.[14]

Why the Common Law Protects the Possession of Wrongdoers

A major intuitive difficulty which could be said to arise in relation to the rules regarding title to sue in Conversion is the way in which the possession of wrongdoers is protected. It is not only non-lawyers who baulk at the idea of a thief being entitled to recover in respect of something which she has stolen from another. Such unease is, however, misplaced. Whilst it is true that wrongdoers are protected, such protection only exists against subsequent wrongdoers and does not, for example, allow them to sue any party with a superior possessory title.[15] Were the law to be otherwise, it would *effectively* protect subsequent wrongdoers by granting them immunity from legal action in respect of their wrongful acts. As Heck points out, in relation to Conversion, the 'protected legal good is the organisational value of possession'.[16] This organisational value is essential for a society in which peaceful possession and progressive commerce can both flourish.

In policy terms, however, such a position can sometimes produce results which appear morally unattractive, as the cases of *Costello v Chief Constable of Derbyshire Constabulary*[17] and *Gough & anor v Chief Constable of West Midlands Police*[18] demonstrate. In *Costello,* the police seized a car from the claimant on the suspicion that it had been stolen. Such a seizure was lawful under section 19 of the Police and Criminal Evidence Act 1984. When, however, no criminal proceedings were brought against the claimant, the police refused to return the car to him. Whilst the judge at first instance found in favour of the police, the Court of Appeal reversed this decision and ordered that the car be returned to the claimant. The judgment of Lightman J contains the following explanation:

> The fact of possession of a chattel of itself gives to the possessor possessory title and the possessor is entitled to rely on such title without reference to the circumstances in which such possession was obtained: his entitlement to do so is not prejudiced by the fact that he obtained such possession unlawfully or under an illegal transaction. His

---

[14] *Jeffries v The Great Western Railway Company* (1856) 5 E & B 802 at 805, 119 ER 680 at 681.

[15] See *National Employers' Mutual General Insurance Association Ltd v Jones* [1990] 1AC 24 where, although, since the defendant's title was acquired from a thief, he did not have superior title to the original possessor, there was no suggestion that he had no title at all. See also J Tarrant, 'Property Rights to Stolen Money, (2005) 32 *University of Western Australia Law Review* 234 at 240.

[16] P Heck, *Grundriss* para 3 at 13, as cited in Gordley, *Foundations* (2008) at 57, fn 64.

[17] [2001] EWCA Civ 381, [2001] 1 WLR 1437. See also *Webb v Chief Constable of Merseyside Police* [2000] QB 427 (CA).

[18] [2004] EWCA Civ 206, [2004] Po LR 164.

claim can only be defeated by proof of a title superior to his possessory title ... The statutory power of the police conferred by section 19 of the 1984 Act to seize goods and by section 22 of the 1984 Act to retain them so long as is necessary in all the circumstances places in suspension or temporarily divests all existing rights to possession over the period of the detention, but does not otherwise affect those rights or vest in the police any permanent entitlement to retain the property in the police.[19]

The Court of Appeal in *Gough*, bound by *Costello*, reached a similar result in relation to car parts seized from the claimants on suspicion of their having been taken from stolen vehicles. In ordering the police to return the car parts, Park J explained that 'if the police do not have a continuing statutory power or right to retain the property, the former possessor's right of possession is superior to theirs'.[20]

The intuitive difficulty of these cases is no doubt increased many times by the fact that the police were made to return assets to suspected criminals. There is, however, no real alternative to this way of deciding the issue; at least not if the law in its broader context is to maintain its integrity. Without any continuing statutory authority to retain assets taken from someone in actual possession of them, the police are themselves wrongdoers according to the law and, as between wrongdoers, the law gives preference to the first in time.[21] There would seem to be little justification in this context for treating wrongful acts of police officers differently to the wrongful acts of private individuals. It might, of course, be argued that public policy should militate against such a result but this is countered by the point that the claimants in neither *Costello* nor *Gough* were convicted, nor even tried, for the offences of which they were suspected. Since, therefore, the assets were not legally recognised as being the proceeds of criminal activity, it is difficult to see how public policy arguments could be invoked on the basis of suspicion alone (however well founded).

More prosaic, but equally important, is the fact that the conclusions reached in both of these cases were predicated on the relativity of the titles involved. Had the police been able to identify a party with a superior possessory right (someone from whom the car parts in *Gough* were stolen, for example), the assets would have been returned to him without question, rather than to the suspected thief.[22] Moreover, in reality, the problem is unlikely to be troublesome in many instances, since the majority of wrongdoers are unlikely to bring such actions and, even when they do, there are other means open to a court of ensuring that true wrongdoers do not retain the profits of their crimes.[23] There is, therefore, little

---

[19]   [2001] EWCA Civ 381, [2001] 1 WLR 1437 at [14].
[20]   [2004] EWCA Civ 206, [2004] PoLR 164 at [15].
[21]   See G Battersby, 'Acquiring Title by Theft' (2002) 65 *Modern Law Review* 603.
[22]   s 8(1), The Torts (Interference with Goods) Act 1977 ('the 1977 Act').
[23]   Such as s 28, Theft Act 1968 and the Proceeds of Crime Act 2002. See *Clerk & Lindsell on Torts* (2006) at para 17–47.

justification for manipulating the common law rules on possessory entitlement in order to avoid unattractive results in occasional cases.

Legal Possession

Possession means a different thing to lawyers than it does to everyone else. The essence of legal possession, also referred to as constructive possession or the right to immediate possession, lies in the element of control exercised over an asset.[24] More specifically, it is the cognitive element of control which is of the greatest relevance to legal possession, as opposed to the manual control which character-ises actual possession.[25] This means that, in order for someone to have legal possession of an asset, it need not physically be in her hands, nor need her control be capable of being observed; legal possession is rights-based, not facts-based. Cognitive control amounts essentially to having the ultimate right to determine how an asset is to be used and treated, and in whose actual possession it should be at any given time (the 'ultimate' nature of this right is important because, of course, actual possessors have the ability to do the same, but not as against the individual with legal possession):

> The plaintiff must have the possession at the time of the act complained of, or, at least, he must have the right against the possessor at the time of that act to require the possession forthwith to be surrendered upon demand. True, [the claimant] need not have a right to immediate possession against the world, but he does not have a right to the immediate possession *at a given moment* unless he has such right *against the person who is the possessor at that moment.* He must be that close to the possession; he must have possession or 'virtual possession'.[26]

Depending on the exact derivation of this right to immediate possession, such control might not amount, however, to the ultimate ability to determine the economic fate of the asset and, in certain cases, where legal possession has been separated from the ultimate proprietary right, such control will be constrained by the nature of the agreement from which the right to immediate possession derives.

If, for instance, a dealer supplies a car to a customer on hire purchase, that customer will have as much cognitive control over the car as allowed by the specific agreement between him and the dealer. Any attempts to sell or otherwise dispose of the car are likely to bring that agreement to an end automatically, with

---

[24] Since 'the right to immediate possession' is the phrase most commonly associated with title to sue in Conversion, we will adopt that label herein. Substantively, it is synonymous with both legal possession and constructive possession.

[25] For a more detailed discussion of the difference between the manual and the cognitive elements of possession, see ch 5.

[26] HD Warren, *An Essay on Trover and Conversion* (Cambridge, Mass., Harvard Law Review Association, 1936) at 25.

the result that the right to immediate possession will re-vest in the supplier.[27] Within the terms of the specific agreement, however, the hirer has cognitive control over the car for the duration of the period, which means that he has the right to immediate possession and, consequently, the title to sue in Conversion. This means that he may do anything he wishes to the car, as long as it does not affect the hire purchase company's interest in it, or breach any terms of the hire agreement. He may, for example, give permission for another party to take actual possession of the car[28] and, should someone take such possession without his permission during this time, only he and not the hire purchase company has title to sue.[29]

Bridge has suggested that where, under the terms of the particular bailment or at common law, a bailor retains the immediate right to terminate the bailment, that bailor also retains the right to immediate possession of the bailed asset.[30] Bridge offered this assertion as a means of explaining why the bailor's right to terminate the bailment can be extended by the terms of an agreement to cover any breach by the hirer, when it is now an established tenet of the law of contract that repudiatory breaches do not, without more, terminate a contract.[31] Professor Palmer, on the other hand, takes the view that bailments are *sui generis* and not subject to the general contractual position.[32] With respect, it is submitted that the latter is the better view: whether the bailor retains the right to terminate the bailment under common law rules or under the terms of his agreement with the bailee, his ability to exercise this right will *only* become effective on the occurrence of certain events. Until such an event occurs, therefore, the bailor has no right to terminate the agreement and, consequently, no right to immediate possession of the asset.[33]

---

[27] See *Jelks v Hayward* [1905] 2 KB 460, *North Central Wagon & Finance Co Ltd v Graham* [1950] 2 KB 7 (CA), *Union Transport Finance Ltd v British Car Auctions Ltd* [1978] 2 All ER 385 (CA), *Moorgate Mercantile Co Ltd v Finch & Read* [1962] 1 QB 701 (CA), (but *cf Reliance Car Facilities v Roding Motors* [1952] 2 QB 844 (CA)), *Fenn v Bittleston* (1851) 7 Ex 152, 155 ER 895 *Farrant v Thompson* (1822) 5 B & Ald 826, 106 ER 139 (these latter cases being instances of bailment without the hire purchase dimension); such cases must, however, now be considered in the light of s 87, Consumer Credit Act 1974.

[28] But see *Chapman v Robinson* (1969) 71 WWR 515 and *Queens Sales and Service Ltd v Smith* (1963) 48 MPR 364 (NS Sup Ct) for the identification and effect of restricted permissions, and NE Palmer, *Bailment*, 2nd edn (London, Sweet & Maxwell, 1991) at 211 and 670–74.

[29] For the classification of the rights granted to a hirer under such an arrangement, see the judgment of Robert Walker LJ in *On Demand Information plc (In Administrative Receivership) v Michael Gerson (Finance) plc* [2001] 1 WLR 155 (CA) at 170F–171B (the decision was reversed by the House of Lords on unrelated grounds at [2002] UKHL 13, [2003] 1 AC 368), citing with approval Warrington LJ in *Whiteley Ltd v Hilt* [1918] 2 KB 808 (CA) at 819–20.

[30] M Bridge, *Personal Property Law*, 3rd edn (Oxford, Oxford University Press, 2002) at 70–71.

[31] *Photo Production Ltd v Securicor Transport Ltd* [1980] AC 827.

[32] See Palmer, *Bailment* (1991) at 60.

[33] See also *Manders v Williams* (1849) 4 Ex 339, 154 ER 1242 for the revesting of the right to immediate possession in the bailor on the occurrence of a predetermined event and *Donald v Suckling* (1866) LR 1 QB 585, which demonstrates the significance of that predetermined event.

Legal possession, whilst not in itself amounting to the superior *proprietary* right, does constitute the superior *possessory* right to a given asset and is, therefore, the interest which determines which party has title to sue in Conversion. Care must be taken to distinguish this interest both from the superior proprietary right in an asset and from actual possession, discussed below. That is not to suggest, however, that the three concepts are mutually exclusive; sometimes two, and sometimes all three, will reside in one individual. Their characteristics must, however, be clearly defined because this will not always be so.

What Is Actual Possession?

Actual possession is possession which is determined by the facts of a given situation. It amounts to manual (as opposed to cognitive) control over an asset and the right to use that asset at least temporarily, where 'temporarily' refers to the period of time up to the point at which the individual with the right to immediate possession exercises that right. Whilst such a taking of possession might well be an event which never happens, the right of user in the individual who has (only) actual possession is necessarily temporary in nature, since it is determinable at the will of another. Despite the fact that it is temporary, however, the actual possessor nevertheless has a right worth having. This is partly because of the obvious benefits associated with having the use of such an asset, and partly because it is a right which can amount to legal possession. As against someone else with legal possession, all that the actual possessor has is her bare factual possession. As against everyone else, however, the bare possessor does have legal possession, that is the right to immediate possession:

> A possessor may be a mere wrongdoer against the true owner, and a wrongdoer for the very reason that he has got possession; while yet his possession is not only legal but, as against all third persons not claiming under the true owner, fully protected by law.[34]

One individual, therefore, can have two types of possession over the same asset. This is a necessary phenomenon in a system of relative title, and means that some individuals assume a Janus-like status: looking 'down' towards those with lesser title, they are legal possessors whilst, when looking 'up' to those with superior title, they are only actual possessors.[35] Title to sue depends, therefore, both on one's position in the relative title chain and on that of the party one intends to sue. Stated in general terms, this brings us once more to the assertion that title to sue in Conversion attaches to the superior possessory right in the asset.

---

[34]   F Pollock and RS Wright, *An Essay on Possession in the Common Law* (Oxford, Clarendon Press, 1888) at 11.

[35]   'Defined in this way, possession is a relative ownership, ownership as against everyone but the true owner.'—Gordley (n 5) at 59; see also Mattei (n 5) at 302.

Jus Tertii

Since 'superior' is a comparative term, however, this statement requires further analysis. Before 1977, 'superior' in this context meant the better title as between the claimant and the defendant.[36] Since the 1977 Act, however, it now means as between the claimant, the defendant and any *named* third party joined by the defendant under the *jus tertii* defence. Under section 8(1) of the 1977 Act, a defendant may name a third party believed to have better title than the claimant, and all known competing claims will then be determined at once. In fact, as a result of Civil Procedure Rules 19.5A, this is, in practice, a mandatory course of action, since

> a claimant in a claim for wrongful interference with goods must, in the particulars of the claim, state the name and address of every person who, to his knowledge, has or claims an interest in the goods and who is not a party to the claim.[37]

This simultaneous title resolution is as practically efficient as it is conceptually tidy, and the abolition of the common law *jus tertii* rule is welcome. It also, to some extent, reduces the significance of the distinction between actual possession and the right to immediate possession, where the two do not reside in the same party.[38]

The problems caused by the former common law rule are set out in detail in the Law Reform Committee's Eighteenth Report,[39] but the principal concern is that a system which does not allow the *jus tertii* defence to be raised does not in fact protect relative title, but affords excessive protection to the title of the first person to sue the defendant. This is because, without being free to raise the *jus tertii*, a defendant may relinquish an asset or its value to a claimant who is relying on possession, and yet remain liable to anyone with a superior title, without any apparent means of recovery against that first claimant.[40] A defendant might, therefore, be liable twice over for the same Conversion. The effect of section 8(1), on the other hand, is that, where necessary, the relative titles of various parties can be recognised at once, without the need for either multiplicity of actions or double liability. One effect of the abolition of the rule against pleading the *jus*

---

[36] For a particularly graphic illustration of the operation of the common law rule, see *Wilson v Lombank Ltd* [1963] 1 WLR 1294 (QB). The rule applied other than in the following circumstances: where the defendant acted with the authority of the party with superior title; where the defendant defends the action in the name of the party with superior title; where neither the claimant nor anyone through whom he claimed ever had a possessory right in the goods; and where the claimant's possessory right had been either given up by the claimant or removed by operation of law. See Clerk & Lindsell (n 6) at para 17–77 and the 18th Report (Conversion and Detinue) of the Law Reform Committee (1971), Cmnd 4774 at para 51.

[37] CPR 19.5A (1). See also 19.5A (2)–(4) for further practical provisions.

[38] See Clerk & Lindsell (n 6) at para 17–107.

[39] In particular, paras 51–78.

[40] At para 52, the report suggests that the defendant will not even have any claim in unjust enrichment against the claimant in possession.

tertii is that, in this limited context, the common law bears something of a resemblance to the civil law in its nod towards the recognition of absolute, as opposed to relative title.[41]

Why Actual Possession Can Be Sufficient

Actual possession is of great importance to the establishment, creation or transfer of title to assets. If relative title to assets did not follow actual possession, this would suggest that title could only be transferred through a consensual act or concession on the part of an individual with a current possessory right. Where this permission is not forthcoming, either because the current possessor has no reason to think the asset is going to leave her control or because she has no choice about the matter, that asset is bound never again to be the subject of any lawful possessory relationship. As indicated above,[42] this would hardly be a workable system in practice. As it is, however, there are three principal ways in which possession may be transferred from one individual to another: the first is by the operation of law, the second is by consensual delivery by the current possessor and the third is by a taking from the previous possessor without or irrespective of his consent.[43] Each of these will give the possessor a title to the assets concerned, which, whilst it might not be the ultimate title in existence, will nonetheless be a legally recognised right.

Another reason actual possession receives some degree of legal protection is that it constitutes something of value in itself. Regardless of whether or not actual possession is legally protected, it is worth having because, for the time being at least, the individual in factual possession has the exclusive use and control of the asset, along with any incidental benefits, such as the status implications it might have, or any income which it generates. What is more, although these benefits might be only temporary and might have to be restored at some point to someone with a superior title, there is also a chance that they might not. In other words, an individual in actual possession of an asset has the chance of keeping it, thereby retaining title and the benefits associated with it. Such a possibility constitutes something of value, worthy of legal protection.

Of course, benefits are not the only incidents of possession; there are burdens too. Someone in actual possession of an asset has to maintain it, store it, guard it against others, perhaps insure it and so forth. The nature and extent of these duties will obviously depend upon the type of asset itself and, whilst they might sometimes be onerous, they will, at other times, be negligible. Nevertheless, it is clear that the protection of such possession is important, since it gives such

---

[41] See JH Dalhuisen, *Dalhuisen on Transnational and Comparative Commercial, Financial and Trade Law*, 3rd edn (Oxford, Hart Publishing, 2007) at 569, fn 52 and 579, fn 76.

[42] See text following n 11.

[43] Pollock and Wright, *Possession* (1888) at 56.

'chance' possessors an incentive to discharge these burdens.[44] An example of why such 'downwards-looking' possession gives good title to sue in Conversion is provided by the famous case of *Wilbraham v Snow*.[45] In that case, the claimant was a sheriff who had seized assets under a writ of *fieri facias*.[46] When the defendant then removed these goods before they were sold, and converted them to his own use, the sheriff was allowed to bring trover. In his note on the case, Serjeant Williams explained the court's decision to allow the claimant to sue on the grounds that 'he is answerable to the plaintiff [the plaintiff in the action in which the writ was issued] to the value of the goods taken under the writ of *fieri facias*'.[47] In other words, where a possessor has potential liability to someone with a superior possessory title to an asset, it makes sense for him to be able to recover in respect of any interference with that asset, so that he could then have no complaint if himself pursued. So, whilst actual possession brings with it benefits, it also carries responsibilities to which the law needs to give effect and recognition.

The final point is largely logistical, but no less significant for that. The party in actual possession (as opposed to the party with superior proprietary right who is not currently in actual possession) is also likely to be in a better position to pursue an action against a wrongdoer, in that he will probably have a greater awareness of the facts of the situation and, indeed, is more likely to know that a Conversion has taken place at all. This logistical consideration is also applicable to bailments.

Bailment

As identified in the previous chapter, the relative positions of the bailor and his bailee in the context of a term bailment present one of the most intuitively difficult aspects of the tort of Conversion. Following *Gordon v Harper*,[48] a term bailor does not have title to sue third parties in Conversion during the term of the bailment; this title vests only in his bailee.[49] What is more, as was established in

---

[44] See Gordley (n 5) at 61–65 and Mattei (n 5) at 332 for the argument that protecting possessors who are not owners promotes the protection of property, since a single protected possessor is more likely to care for assets to which she has some title than if she did not have this recognition. It also means that the individual with the ultimate proprietary right will have only one party to pursue when she returns to possession, should the asset have been damaged or reduced in value in any way.

[45] (1669) 2 Wms Saund 47a, 85 ER 624.

[46] A writ of execution issued after a judgment for debt or damages.

[47] 2 Williams on Saunders, 6th edn, E Vaughan Williams (ed) (London, W Benning & Co, 1845) 47a at 47a, fn 1, 85 ER 624 at 625. As to the position of a sheriff who has seized goods under a writ of *fi fa*, see *Halsbury's Laws of England*, 4th edn Vol 17(1) 2002 reissue, especially at paras 132 and 166.

[48] (1796) 7 TR 9, 101 ER 828.

[49] The bailor has only a possible action in the tort of reversionary injury, and then only if his reversionary interest has been damaged. See *Tancred v Allgood* (1859) 4 H & N 438, 157 ER 910.

Brierly v Kendall,[50] should a term bailor dispossess his bailee before the expiration of the term, he himself may be sued by the bailee.[51] Since this is a situation which throws into sharp relief the essence of the tort of Conversion, it has already been dealt with in the previous chapter. Suffice it to point out here that, rather than being anomalous, this position is a perfectly consistent, if not defining, aspect of Conversion, in that it confirms that it is a tort to which the superior *possessory* interest in an asset is of the utmost significance.

Another point of significance with regard to bailment and title to sue in Conversion is the position of third party defendants. Where, for instance, a bailor has been able to recover in respect of loss or damage to a bailed asset caused by a third party, the bailee cannot then recover in respect of the same loss or damage, but must look to his bailor for satisfaction.[52] The same principle applies in reverse; if a bailee has recovered, he must account to his bailor for anything exceeding his interest in the asset.[53] Since the 1977 Act, a claimant is required to name any other party with an interest in the assets which are the subject matter of the action.[54] This obviously gives the defendant the opportunity to have the relevant interests in those assets determined at once, thereby avoiding double liability.[55]

It is also worth noting that a transferee of a bailor is entitled to sue a bailee who has wrongfully interfered with his interest in the bailed assets even though the bailee has not attorned to him, on the basis that the bailee in such a situation has no superior title to the bailor.[56] In fact, it appears to be the case that a bailor can sue a bailee in Conversion, regardless of whether or not the bailee was aware of the actual identity of his true bailor.[57]

Finders

Where finders are concerned, the rules about title to sue are fairly straightforward; the finder, like any actual possessor, has good title against all except those with a superior possessory right. The only instances in which complications really arise are those in which it is difficult to ascertain which of two or more

---

[50]   (1852) 17 QB 937, 117 ER 1540.

[51]   See also *Massey v Sladen* (1868) LR 4 Ex 13 for the principle as applicable to mortgagees.

[52]   *O'Sullivan and anor v Williams* [1992] 3 All ER 385 (CA).

[53]   *The Winkfield* [1902] P 42 (CA) at 55 per Collins MR; this applies equally to gratuitous bailees. See also *Nicolls v Bastard* (1835) 2 CrM & R 659, 150 ER 279, *Rooth v Wilson* (1817) 1 B & Ald 59, 106 ER 22 and *Swire v Leach* (1865) 18 CB (NS) 479, 141 ER 531. The principle can be traced back to at least the early fifteenth century, see ch 2, text to fn 23.

[54]   s 8(2)(b), and CPR 19.5A(1), for which see text to n 37.

[55]   s 7(2) ibid.

[56]   See *Batut v Hartley* (1872) 26 LT 968 and NE Palmer, 'The Vindication of Commercial Security over Commodities: Equitable Pledges and Conversion' [1986] *Lloyd's Maritime and Commercial Law Quarterly* 218 at 226.

[57]   See Palmer, Bailment (n 28) at 112–22.

parties has possession following the finding. This may occur as between employers and employees, and between finders of assets and the occupiers of land on which they are found. In none of the cases, however, has the factual position been especially complicated. *Waverley Borough Council v Fletcher*[58] was concerned with the distinction between objects found in, or attached to the land, and those found upon it. The defendant had found, with the use of a metal detector, an antique brooch nine inches below the surface of the claimant's land, and the question for the court was whether the latter had the title to sue in respect of the find. In pointing out that the 'English law of ownership and possession, unlike that of Roman Law, is not a system of absolute entitlement but of priority of entitlement',[59] the court found in favour of the claimant council. *Waverley* made the point that, where objects are found in, or attached to, land, the occupier will have a better right to them[60] but, where the object in question is found upon the land, the occupier will have a better right only if he has manifestly exercised an intention to control the object.

This notion of control goes to the core of the issue. As Eveleigh LJ made clear in *Parker v British Airways Board,* the 'firmer the control, the less will be the need to demonstrate independently the animus possidendi'.[61] In that case, the claimant had found a gold bracelet whilst waiting in a passenger lounge which was occupied by the defendant. The claimant had handed the bracelet to one of the defendant's employees and asked that it be returned to him if the individual who had lost it did not come forward. When no-one claimed the bracelet, however, the defendant sold it and retained the proceeds. The court allowed the claimant to recover in respect of the defendant's actions, based on the finding that the defendant had not in this case shown the requisite manifest intention to control the bracelet before it was found. This is important, since this is the means by which occupiers of land 'trump' the interests of finders; in appropriate cases, their control is deemed to pre-date the finder's control and so give them the superior possessory right on the basis of a prior entitlement. This is what was lacking on the part of British Airways.

The Court of Appeal in *Parker* made it admirably clear that such questions about entitlement would always need to be settled on the facts of a given case. Examples were given of a bank strong room and a private house, both of which are subject to degrees of control which give rise to a presumption that the occupier has a manifest intention to control the contents sufficient to give priority over a finder.[62] One of the material considerations here is that of exclusivity; a bank manager and a householder generally intend to exclude

---

[58] [1996] QB 334 (CA).

[59] Auld LJ at 345C–D.

[60] See also *City of London Corporation and ors v Appleyard and anor* [1963] 1 WLR 982 (QB) and *Grafstein v Holme & Freeman* (1958) 12 DLR (2d) 727.

[61] [1982] QB 1004 (CA) at 1020D.

[62] ibid per Donaldson LJ at 1019B–D. See also *Hibbert v McKiernan* [1948] 2 KB 142 (DC).

members of the public from their premises, other than under specific consensual arrangements. The same cannot be said for an airport passenger lounge.[63]

Intention is also relevant to another type of finder; he to whom an asset is mistakenly transferred.[64] *Merry v Green*,[65] *Cartwright v Green*[66] and *Thomas v Greenslade*[67] are all examples of this. The first two cases both concern defendants who found money in furniture which came into their possession (in *Merry* because he purchased a secretary, and in *Cartwright* because he took custody of a bureau in order to effect repairs). The third case involved the sale by the claimants of old iron boxes, apparently containing nuts and bolts, but in fact also containing a substantial number of National Savings certificates. In none of the cases were the transferors aware that the money or the certificates had been contained in the objects of the transfer, and so the question arose whether title in them had passed, or whether the claimants still had the legal capacity to sue in respect of them. In all three cases, the claimants were held entitled to sue on the basis that legal possession could not be transferred in the absence of the intention to do so. Essentially, although the defendants in each of these cases had actual possession of the assets concerned, there was no transfer of cognitive possession, leaving the transferors with the superior possessory right. This is somewhat similar to the position in Scots law where, so long as the erstwhile possessor has *animus possidendi*, he remains in constructive possession of the asset, meaning that any finder who has not taken reasonable steps to ascertain the identity of the true possessor will be liable in spuilzie.[68]

The Significance of Legal Possession

Whilst the bare fact of possession is the root of title, in that it provides prima facie evidence of the right to sue in Conversion, it is not necessarily conclusive of the issue. In the hierarchy of titles to assets, bare possession yields to the right to immediate possession. The reason for this is perhaps too obvious to state, and yet too important to assume: the right to immediate possession is based on right rather than on fact. Whilst it is important to protect actual possession, for the reasons outlined above, it is also important, for much the same reasons, not to protect actual possession above legal possession, for, if the ultimate legal right in

---

[63] Although the lounge in question was exclusive to the extent that its use was limited to passengers with specific classes of tickets, this did not give it the requisite exclusivity to generate the presumption that the British Airways Board intended to exercise control over all its contents. For an economic evaluation of this decision, see A Ogus, *Costs and Cautionary Tales: Economic Insights for the Law*, (Oxford, Hart Publishing, 2006) at 43. See also *White v Alton-Lewis Ltd* (1974) 49 DLR (3d) 189.

[64] For a full discussion of the wider implications of this factual situation, see W Swadling's excellent essay, Unjust Delivery (n 2).

[65] (1841) 7 M & W 623, 151 ER 916.

[66] (1803) 8 Ves 405, 32 ER 412.

[67] *The Times* 6 November 1954.

[68] See DM Walker, *Delict*, 2nd edn, (Edinburgh, W Green, 1981) at 1008.

an asset could be acquired simply by taking actual possession of it, security of possession would become a particularly elusive concept.

Moreover, the protection of the right to immediate possession, rather than any other form of proprietary right, tends to reflect the commercial objectives of a situation. Take, for instance, the case of *Lord v Price*,[69] in which the claimant had purchased some cotton from a vendor in whose actual possession the cotton remained, subject to a lien for the claimant's unpaid purchase money. When the cotton was removed from the vendor's possession by the defendant, the claimant attempted to sue him in Conversion, but was unsuccessful because of his lack of title to sue. The court found that, although the property in the cotton had passed to the claimant under the sale, the vendor's lien deprived him of the right to immediate possession, which remained in the vendor. Were the court to have decided the matter otherwise, and allowed the claimant to sue on these facts, the vendor would have lost his lien and the action in Conversion would have countermanded the economic realities of the situation. This is another situation in which the result might, on first impression, look a little surprising: that someone can have the property in an asset and yet still be denied the title to sue in Conversion in respect of it. On closer inspection, however, the reason for the position is clear, and provides yet another illustration of the fact that Conversion is concerned with possessory rights over and above proprietary rights. This statement, however, begs a new question: if possession is Conversion's main concern, to what extent is a proprietary right required?

What Amounts to a Sufficient Proprietary Right?

There has been some contention, both judicial and academic, about exactly what constitutes a sufficient proprietary right to establish a title to sue in Conversion. The simplicity of the resolution has, however, been unnecessarily complicated by tangential questions. One such question is whether the claimant's right to possession needs to be proprietary, or whether a contractual right will suffice.[70] One attempt to answer this question contains the following passage:

> The old vocabulary that referred to 'property' in goods, with even more esoteric qualifications such as 'general property' and 'special property,' is largely to blame for

---

[69] (1874) LR 9 Ex 54. See also *Milgate v Kebble* (1841) 3 Man & G 100, 133 ER 1073.

[70] See Curwen, Title (*Conv*, 2004) and Clerk & Lindsell (n 6) at para 17–88. It is also worth pointing out at this stage that the two things are not necessarily mutually exclusive: see, eg, Robert Walker LJ in *On Demand plc v Michael Gerson plc* [2001] 1 WLR 155 at 171B (see also at n 29) and R Cunnington, 'Contract Rights as Property Rights' in A Robertson (ed) *The Law of Obligations: Connections and Boundaries* (London, UCL Press, 2004).

modern uncertainty about the nature of the interest protected by conversion. The cases traditionally held that this right to possession had to be based upon, or arise out of, 'property' in the goods[71]

This is true.[72] As mentioned above, however, the use of the term 'property' is not a helpful one in the context of Conversion: whilst the concept of 'property' in assets is not irrelevant to the tort, it is a term which, if not used accurately, or at least consistently, is bound to confuse more than it clarifies. It is far better to stick to the idea of possession, since, as Goode points out, Conversion 'is possessory, not proprietary in character'.[73] Once this has been recognised, it becomes clear that to ask whether a right must be contractual or proprietary in nature is to ask the wrong question: all that needs to be established is which party has the superior right to possession, regardless of its origins.

According to *Clerk & Lindsell*, 'it seems that the immediate right to possession on which the owner relies must be a proprietary right; a mere contractual right will not do'.[74] The presence of this assertion in the nineteenth edition is somewhat surprising, given that the sixteenth edition, having referred to the dictum of Ashurst J in *Gordon v Harper* 'I have always understood the rule of law to be that, in order to maintain trover, the plaintiff must have a right of property in the thing and a right of possession, and that unless both these rights concur the action will not lie,'[75] went on to comment that the statement

> is apt to mislead unless the right of property is understood in any extended sense. The old forms of pleading adopted this extended sense. 'Any person having a right to the possession of goods may bring trover in respect of the conversion of them, and allege them to be his property.'"[76]
>
> n *Rogers v Kennay* (1846) 9 QB 592, 596 per Patteson J.

We would suggest, with respect, that the position adopted in the earlier edition is to be preferred for its greater clarity and consistency with the authorities on the point.

The assertion in the nineteenth edition is apparently based on the Court of Appeal decision in *Jarvis v Williams*.[77] In that case, the claimant had sold some bathroom fittings to a buyer who requested that they be delivered to the defendant. Later, the claimant agreed with the buyer (who had still not paid the purchase price) that he would collect the goods and take them back. When, however, the claimant arrived at the defendant's premises to collect the goods, the

---

[71]   See Curwen (n 1) at 309.
[72]   Although, in his interesting and thought-provoking article, Curwen goes on to use both 'property' and 'ownership' in confusing ways.
[73]   RM Goode, 'The Right to Trace and Its Impact on Commercial Transactions—I' (1976) 92 *Law Quarterly Review* 360 at 364.
[74]   Clerk & Lindsell (n 6) at para 17–59.
[75]   n 48.
[76]   *Clerk & Lindsell on Torts*, 16th edn (London, Sweet & Maxwell, 1989) at para 22–44.
[77]   [1955] 1 WLR 71 (CA).

defendant (to whom the buyer also owed money) refused to hand them over. The principal issue was, therefore, whether the claimant had title to sue the defendant (rather than the party with whom he had a contract) in detinue (then still an available action in its own right, since the case predated the 1977 Act).

The Court of Appeal's judgment hinged on the question of when property in the goods had passed. The defendant's appeal against the finding of detinue at first instance was allowed, on the basis that property in the goods had passed to the buyer under the original contract of sale, and did not revest as a result of the subsequent contractual arrangement for re-collection; thus, the claimant had no 'property interest' in the goods sufficient to sue the defendant in detinue. From this, the conclusion has sometimes been drawn that 'a mere contractual right to delivery could not amount to an immediate right to possession sufficient to found conversion'.[78] This is, however, an unfortunate interpretation of the decision (albeit one that was understandable in the light of the language used therein). The correct explanation of the result in *Jarvis v Williams* is that the claimant vendor had no proprietary right on which to base a possessory right, nor did his contractual right as against the buyer to collect the assets give him a right to possession. This (but not its subsequent interpretation) is both correct and congruent with the law on Conversion.

Were its interpretation to stand, and a contractual right to delivery never to be sufficient for title to sue in Conversion, it would be difficult to explain the reasoning and result in cases such as *Indian Herbs v Hadley & Ottoway*[79] and *International Factors Ltd v Rodriguez*,[80] in which claimants were successful in their Conversion (or detinue) actions despite not having 'property' in the assets concerned. The real reason for the inability of the claimant to recover in *Jarvis* was simply that he did not have the superior possessory right in the assets concerned because the buyer retained the property in the assets (to which the right to immediate possession can attach) and the defendant had actual possession of the assets. On the facts of the case, the claimant had nothing from which to derive a possessory right superior to either of these two interests.

In *Indian Herbs*, the claimants were buyers of herbal animal feed from one of the defendants, which they stored with another two of the defendants. The sale agreement contained a reservation of title clause, asserting that property in the feed was not to pass until the purchase price had been paid. Subsequently, the defendant vendors removed the feed from those defendants who were storing it, without the consent of the claimants. Some of the feed they removed had been paid for and some had not, but the unpaid element of the price had not yet

---

[78] A Tettenborn, 'Trust Property and Conversion: An Equitable Confusion' [1996] *Cambridge Law Journal* 36 at 37. See also Clerk & Lindsell (n 6) at para 17–59 and *International Factors Ltd v Rodriguez* [1979] QB 351 (CA), per Sir David Cairns at 357.

[79] *Indian Herbs (UK) Ltd v Hadley & Ottoway Ltd and ors* [1999] EWCA Civ 627, www.bailii.org/ew/cases/EWCA/Civ/1999/627.html.

[80] [1979] QB 351.

become due. The relevant questions were, therefore, whether the claimants could sue the vendors in Conversion, and whether the vendors had the right to repossess the feed. In the Court of Appeal, Mummery LJ said:

> The crucial point is not the ownership of the products, but what right there is to repossess the products or goods. It is clear from the terms of the retention of title clause that, whatever the position about ownership, there was only a right to repossess goods which had been supplied if payment had not been made 'in the due period'. The judge held that the third defendant's right to repossess the goods only arose when the plaintiff was in default of its payment obligation. It was not in default if either it had made payment or payment had not been made because it was not yet due at the date of the purported exercise of the right to take possession under the retention of title clause … The judge also considered submissions that, even if the clause did apply, the defendants were entitled to repossess the goods. The judge held that the defendants were not entitled to interfere with the plaintiff's right to immediate possession of these goods.[81]

Whereas in *Jarvis v Williams* the claimant vendor had no property interest on which to found a possessory right, in *Indian Herbs* the claimant buyers did have a (contractual) right to immediate possession. Whilst they had neither the superior proprietary right in, nor actual possession of, the animal feed, their rights under their contract of purchase (in contrast to the position in *Jarvis*) gave them a right to possession. The point, then, is not that contractual rights are never a sufficient basis for title to sue in Conversion, but that they are only sufficient if they are contractual rights *to possession.*

The facts of *International Factors* are well known: the claimants were debt factors, to whom a company had assigned its book debts. The agreement between them provided that, were the company to receive a cheque from any of the debtors in respect of the assigned debts, it should immediately be handed it over to the claimants. The director of the company, which was at this time in financial difficulty, wrongfully diverted such a cheque into the company's own bank account, an action for which the claimants sued him in Conversion. Their action was successful, although the precise reason behind this decision was not easy to discern. Nearly a decade later, however, the Court of Appeal in *MCC Proceeds v Lehman Bros*[82] explained the decision on the basis that the claimant in *International Factors* had title to sue founded on a contractual right to possession,[83] which derived from the factoring agreement.

Looked at in this way, it would seem to be a simple matter, but this area of the law has been complicated by two factors; first, Sir David Cairns' reference in his judgment in *International Factors* (deemed by all three members of the Court of

---

[81] n 79, under the heading The Judgment.

[82] *MCC Proceeds Inc v Lehman Bros International (Europe)* [1998] 4 All ER 675 (CA).

[83] ibid at 690d–j, and 698a and e–f. See Curwen (n 1) for a trenchant criticism of this interpretation of *International Factors*. With respect, however, this is the only feasible interpretation remaining, since Curwen also (correctly) criticises the alternative interpretation, which is that the claimants in *International Factors* had title to sue on the basis of their equitable interest in the cheques (for a full discussion of which see under the heading Equitable Rights and Conversion, below).

Appeal in *MCC Proceeds* to have been obiter)[84] to the claimants' equitable interest in the cheques as being material to their title to sue in Conversion and, secondly, the subsequent identification of the distinction between contractual and proprietary rights as being relevant to the same issue.[85] The only question the court answered was which party had the superior possessory interest in the cheques at the time of the Conversion. The court's decision in the claimant factors' favour fits perfectly well with the tenets of Conversion. Indeed, there was no other justifiable explanation for the decision, since it is clear that the claimants' equitable interest in the cheques was not sufficient to give them title to sue in Conversion. The true position had in fact already been clearly stated in Goode's 1976 article, where he stated (of detinue, as it still was at the time)

> detinue is often mistakenly conceived as a remedy exclusively designed to enforce an existing real right. See, for example, Salmond on the Law of Torts (16th ed,), p.114, 'The plaintiff must show that he has a right to the immediate possession of the chattel at the time of the commencement of the action, *arising out of an absolute or special property in it.*' There is no warrant for the qualification introduced by the words I have italicised. The question is not whether the plaintiff has an existing real right but whether (if not himself divested of possession by the defendant) he has the best right to possess. Even a contractual right suffices for this purpose.[86]

In support of his opposing argument, that title to sue in Conversion must have a proprietary, as opposed to a contractual basis, Curwen refers to the cases of *Addison v Round*,[87] *Nyberg v Handelaar*,[88] and *Singh v Ali*.[89] A closer analysis of these decisions, however, demonstrates how contractual and proprietary rights are not necessarily mutually exclusive and, consequently, how none of the judgments excludes the possibility of a contractual right sufficing to give a claimant title to sue in Conversion.

In *Addison v Round*, the defendant was a surveyor of highways who had agreed, on leaving office, to deliver up his books in return for a sum due to him from the parish. Following the payment of the sum due to him, he failed to deliver the books and the churchwardens and officers of the parish for that year demanded them of him. When he still failed to return them, the officers of subsequent years made the same demands until, two years later, the then officers of the parish became the claimants in the action before the court. The court held that such officers were not entitled to sue in trover. Its reasoning for this is varied, but appears to owe more to a sense that trover was not the appropriate means of

---

[84] ibid at 690d and j, 698g and 700e; they were also difficult to reconcile with the later decision of the House of Lords in *Leigh & Sillivan Ltd v Aliakmon Shipping Co Ltd* [1986] 1 AC 785—ibid at 689a–e and 700h–701e.

[85] See Curwen (n 1). This misguided analysis probably owes much to an unnecessarily narrow interpretation of *Jarvis v Williams*, for which see text to n 77 ff.

[86] Goode, Right to Trace (*LQR*, 1976) at 363, fn 13.

[87] (1836) 4 A & E 799, 111 ER 984.

[88] [1892] 2 QB 202 (CA).

[89] [1960] AC 167 (PC).

dealing with this problem than it does to a consideration of the finer points of possessory entitlements. Denman CJ, Littledale J and Patteson J all made reference to the fact that there existed a statutory means of dealing with such an event (albeit that it was unavailable on the specific facts before the court), thereby implying that the common law should not be used to fill such gaps in statutory protection:

> The Act of Parliament directs that the books shall be given up as the vestry shall direct, to be kept for the use of the parish; and it gives the means of enforcing this by a penalty. It may be unfortunate that this remedy could not be adopted in the present case; but such remedy is all that the statute gives. Great inconvenience would follow from a different construction.[90]

Coleridge J also pointed out that the court had 'always granted a mandamus to a surveyor, commanding him to deliver up his books: I never heard that such a mandamus was refused on the ground that an action of trover was maintainable'.[91] Whilst Lord Denman CJ did also say that a 'plaintiff does not, by shewing that he has a right to obtain custody of a chattel, shew that he has a property which entitles him to maintain trover',[92] this tells us little. The main reason for this statement providing little clarity is the language used; more specifically, the word 'custody'. If His Lordship meant by 'custody' what is generally meant by lawyers today when they use that word, this explains his conclusion without any reference to the distinction between property and contractual bases, since 'custody' is something short of possession.[93] If a right to such custody is all that the claimant has, then there is no title to sue in Conversion, since what is required is the immediate right to the greater interest, possession. If, however, His Lordship was in fact referring to the concept now referred to as possession as it is now legally understood, then, with the greatest of respect, this cannot be correct, since it is axiomatic that a claimant with the right to immediate possession has title to sue in Conversion. There is nothing in this judgment to suggest that a right to immediate possession, based solely on a contractual right, is insufficient to allow a claimant to sue in Conversion.

In *Nyberg v Handelaar*, the claimant was the owner of a gold box, in which he sold a half share to a third party, under an agreement which expressly gave the claimant the right of possession of the box, until such time as it was sold. The co-owner was then given custody of the box, in order to take it to an auctioneer.

---

[90]   4 A & E 799 per Lord Denman CJ at 803, 111 ER 984 at 985.

[91]   4 A & E 799 per Lord Coleridge at 804, 111 ER 984 at 986.

[92]   n 90.

[93]   'Custody' is usually the word used, eg, to describe what an employee has over his employer's equipment, such as plant, computers, office furniture etc. See also Pollock and Wright (n 34) at 138, Clerk & Lindsell (n 6) at para 17–55 and Supreme Court Practice 1999, Vol 1 at para 24/2/8 (notes to RSC Order 24). Of course, if such 'custody' were to be held in conjunction with actual possession, the claimant would have title to sue anyone with a lesser interest, but this would be based on his actual possession, and not his 'custody'. Someone, therefore, with nothing more than a 'right to custody' has no title to sue since this is not synonymous with the right to immediate possession.

Instead of delivering it to the auctioneer, however, the co-owner lodged the box with the defendant, pledging his half share as security for a debt. The Court of Appeal had to decide whether the claimant had title to sue the defendant, and decided this question in the claimant's favour. It is not clear why Curwen chose to use this decision to defend his argument that a contractual basis for a right of possession is not sufficient to give a claimant title to sue in Conversion, since the claimant's title herein *depended* upon the agreement between his co-owner and him. As Lopes LJ made clear, 'the plaintiff could not, *in the absence of any agreement* as to possession of the box, have recovered it from the defendant' (authors' emphasis).[94] As the words in italics show, the claimant's property interest in half of the gold box would not have been sufficient to give him title to sue the defendant because the box was co-owned; the contract between the claimant and the third party was necessary to negate the defence of the absence of a requisite co-claimant. Here, a contractual basis for the right to possession was, therefore, not only sufficient but *necessary* for the claimant to be able to sue in Conversion.

In *Singh* v *Ali*,[95] the claimant had purchased a lorry from the defendant, but it remained registered with the authorities in the name of the defendant, so that a haulage permit might (fraudulently) be acquired for it. When the defendant removed the lorry from the claimant's possession without the latter's consent, the Judicial Committee of the Privy Council held that the claimant had good title to sue (in detinue). In giving the judgment of the Board, Lord Denning said of the claimant:

> He had actual possession of the lorry at the moment when the defendant seized it. Despite the illegality of the contract, the property had passed to him by the sale and delivery of the lorry ... When he commenced this action, he had the right to immediate possession. Their Lordships think that in these circumstances he had a claim in detinue ... Their Lordships would only add this: if the law were not to allow the plaintiff to recover in this case, it would leave the defendant in possession of both the lorry and the money he received for it. Their Lordships are glad to have been able to reach the conclusion that, on the facts of the present case, this is not the law.[96]

Here, the question for the court was whether property had passed to the claimant under the sales contract, despite its illegality. Unsurprisingly, given its answer in the affirmative, the court found in favour of the claimant.[97] There is nothing in the decision, however, to suggest that such a property right is essential for title to sue to be established. In fact, as is evident from Lord Denning's words above,

---

[94] [1892] 2 QB 202 at 205. The 1977 Act has, under ss 10(1)(a) and 10(1)(b), partially removed the co-ownership defence, although it still apparently applies to situations where one co-owner has not attempted to alienate the entire property in the assets, as was the case here. See Clerk & Lindsell (n 6) at paras 17–65 and 17–66.

[95] [1960] AC 167 (PC).

[96] ibid at 177–78.

[97] See also *Belvoir Finance Co Ltd v Stapleton* [1971] 1 QB 210 (CA).

there were several points militating in favour of the claimant in this case; his property under the contract, his actual possession and his right to immediate possession. His actual possession at the time of the seizure, if not trumped by any interest of the defendant, would itself have been enough, regardless of whether the property had passed to him. Whilst this argument might be met by the objection that he would not have the right to immediate possession without such property, reference need only be made to the long-standing authority of *Roberts v Wyatt*[98] in order to confirm that the right to immediate possession does not depend on either ownership or actual possession. There is nothing, therefore, in *Singh v Ali*, to rule out a superior possessory interest based on a contractual right sufficing to provide a claimant with title to sue in Conversion; the point is never discussed.

These cases do not, therefore, afford judicial support for the idea that title to sue in Conversion is dependent upon the claimant having the superior *proprietary* interest in the goods concerned.

As *Halsbury's Laws of England* states:

> It appears that a mere contractual right to possess will suffice to sue in conversion, and that a claimant's right of possession need not derive from a proprietary interest[99]

Further, The Law Reform Committee opined 'in conversion an immediate right to possession, however, arising, is sufficient'.[100]

Generally, and certainly where Curwen's arguments are concerned, it seems that the problem lies in the use of language; a superior possessory right is a property right of sorts (and is broadly covered by the less than helpful term 'special property'):[101]

> In order to maintain trover, it is necessary that the plaintiff should have either an absolute, or a special property in the goods ... So possession with an assertion of title, or even possession alone, gives the possessor such a property as will enable him to maintain this action against a wrongdoer; for possession is prima facie evidence of property.[102]

---

[98] (1810) 2 Taunt 268, 127 ER 1080.

[99] 4th edn, Vol 45 (2), 1999 reissue, at para 560.

[100] 18th Report of the LRC (1971) at para 9(1). As to detinue, the LRC took the opposite view earlier in the same paragraph, footnoting the cases of *Jarvis v Williams* and *Singh v Ali*. For the reasons advanced above, however, we would respectfully disagree. Our argument is further supported by Holdsworth, who said that detinue could 'protect proprietary *or possessory* rights against adverse claimants or mere wrongdoers, and the rights of bailors against their bailees'. (WS Holdsworth, *A History of English Law* Vol VII, 2nd edn (London, Sweet & Maxwell, 1937) at 440, authors' emphasis). See also Palmer, Bailment (n 28) at 212, fn 1.

[101] For an example of the difficulties and ambiguities associated with this term, see Lord Mersey in *The Odessa v The Woolston* [1916] 1 AC 145 (PC) at 158.

[102] Warren, *Trover and Conversion* (1936), citing *Wilbraham v Snow* (1669) 2 Wms Saund 47a, 85 ER 624.

The use of the labels 'contractual' and 'proprietary' in this context is therefore best avoided. Reference to the superior possessory right in any given situation will prevent avoidable confusion.

Equitable Rights and Conversion

Whilst, for the reasons outlined above, it ultimately does not matter whether the claimant's possessory interest has a contractual or a proprietary basis (or indeed whether the two things are mutually exclusive), it does very much matter whether the possessory right in question is legal or equitable.

In *International Factors Ltd v Rodriguez*,[103] Sir David Cairns suggested that the claimants therein had title to sue in Conversion because

> there was here something more than a contractual right. Clause 11(e) of the agreement provided both that the supplier was to hold any debt paid direct to the supplier in trust for the factor, that is, the company was to hold in trust for the plaintiffs, and immediately after receipt of a cheque ... to hand over that cheque to the company. Taking together the trust which was thereby set up and the obligation immediately on receipt to hand over the cheque to the plaintiffs, I am satisfied that the plaintiffs had here a sufficient proprietary right to sue in conversion ... it seems to me that since the fusion of law and equity that is sound law.[104]

Fortunately, these dicta have subsequently been held to have been given *per incuriam* by the Court of Appeal,[105] since the weight of authority demonstrates that equitable interests alone are *not* sufficient to establish title to sue in Conversion. Despite the fact that Sir David Cairns offered some putative authority for his position, the case to which he referred, *Healey v Healey*,[106] does not in fact support it. In that case, the claimant was a woman whose husband had assigned to trustees certain items of furniture to be used by her during her lifetime. When he withheld the assets, his wife successfully sued him in detinue. Obviously, the claimant in this case had an equitable interest in the assets which were the subject of the action, but the essential point is that this is not *all* she had. Significantly, she had also had a right to immediate possession *independent of her equitable interest*, which gave her title to sue:

> Now, the only title which it is necessary for a plaintiff to allege in order to maintain an action in detinue is a title to the immediate possession of the goods. I am of the opinion that the plaintiff has a title to the immediate possession of the chattels claimed by her,

---

[103] [1979] QB 351 (CA), already discussed under the heading What Amounts to a Sufficient Proprietary Right?, above.

[104] ibid at 357F–358A.

[105] *MCC Proceeds Inc v Lehman Bros* [1998] 4 All ER 657 (CA) at 690j–691g, 698g and 700f–h. The Court also deemed them *obiter* (text to n 84), which explains their ultimate interpretation of that decision.

[106] [1915] 1 KB 938. See also Clerk & Lindsell (n 6) at para 17–64.

because the trustees of the settlement only hold them in trust to allow them to be used by her, and it is impossible for them to be used by her unless she has an immediate right to claim possession of them from the trustees. I, therefore, hold that the plaintiff is entitled to maintain this action against her husband without joining the trustees of the settlement as parties.[107]

This perhaps explains why *Healey* was said in *International Factors* to have been 'the only decision that counsel has been able to discover of a cestui que trust being entitled to sue in conversion',[108] because in cases in which a claimant has an equitable interest without more, there will be no title to sue, no recovery and, consequently, no authority for Sir David's obiter dicta. The reason for equitable interests being an insufficient basis for title to sue in Conversion is very simple: an equitable interest is not a possessory interest per se. Equitable interests are founded on personal obligations between trustees and beneficiaries and are not, unlike legal interests, something for which possession has significance. To allow a Conversion claim based on an equitable interest alone would be to treat legal and equitable interests as if they were synonymous. This, as Worthington makes clear, is not the case

> at a fundamental structural level there is a cardinal difference between Common Law ownership and Equitable ownership. The legal owner of the painting has all the rights in the painting (bar the ability to obtain specific restoration of it from the defendant). The Equitable owner does not. Equitable ownership is derivative. The Equitable owner has in interest in the painting, but it is an interest measured by the management obligations she is owed by her trustee ... The assumption which is widely—but erroneously—made is that legal and Equitable property are the same sorts of beasts and behave in the same sorts of ways ... Equitable property is defined and circumscribed by the personal obligations owed by the legal owner to the Equitable owner.[109]

Thus, first, the main reason for not allowing Conversion claims in respect of equitable interests is the fact that Conversion is a strict liability tort: equitable relationships are based on personal obligations and, whilst these may be classified as property rights because they are protected against third parties, such protection is restricted. Equitable rights are *not* protected against third parties *without notice* of those personal obligations, since such obligations cannot be assumed unwittingly. In equity, liability for interference with the assets of others is dealt with principally by the rules on knowing receipt and dishonest assistance,[110] which, as the names suggest, are not based on strict liability. As Tettenborn has

---

[107]   [1915] 1 KB 938 at 940 per Shearman J.

[108]   [1979] QB 351(CA)at 357H–358A. Where a cestui que trust possesses assets in accordance with a trust instrument, it is the trustees who have legal possession. See *Barker v Furlong* [1891] 2 Ch 72.

[109]   S Worthington, *Equity*, 2nd edn (Oxford, Oxford University Press, 2005) at 185.

[110]   Depending on whether or not the defendant has possession of the assets; the former requires knowledge and the latter actual dishonesty. In Conversion, of course, no such distinction is made between whether a defendant is in possession of the assets or not, and there is consequently no distinction made between states of mind—see Tettenborn, Equitable Confusion (*CLJ* 1996) at 41.

suggested, it 'would be, to say the least, unfortunate were the carefully calculated scheme of equitable liability to be upset by the adventitious interposition of conversion here'.[111]

Secondly, Worthington identifies the nature of the trustee's position as being another reason why Conversion is ill-suited to the protection of equitable interests. Within the trustee/beneficiary relationship, there is a distinction to be made between capacity and authority. A trustee has legal title and so has the *capacity* to transfer this legal title to a third party, whether or not he also has the *authority* to do so, and the

> beneficiary has consented to the trustee having this capacity, even if she has not consented to his abuse of position. This does not mean that the beneficiary should have *no* rights against third parties who deal with the defaulting trustee, but it is arguable that her rights should be cut back to reflect the agreed arrangement she has with her trustee.[112]

In other words, the beneficiary should not have the benefit of strict liability protection of her rights, which is what the availability of Conversion would give her.[113] Were she to have such rights against a third party, the result would be particularly harsh where that third party is 'innocent'. In that event, the beneficiary would be able to claim the value of the asset from the third party, even if he had been a purchaser for value without notice from the trustee. This might have the doubly unjust consequence that the trustee, who was the one who behaved both wrongfully and badly (since he was the one to have assumed duties towards the claimant), would escape liability if, for instance, he were untraceable, or not worth suing.

In our view, these are probably the two strongest reasons underlying the express qualification to the Law Reform Committee's recommendation in 1971 that

> not only actual possession (or a right to immediate possession) at the material time, but also any other interest in a chattel, whether present or future, possessory or proprietary (*but not being an equitable interest*), should constitute sufficient title to sue.[114] (authors' emphasis.)

The Report couched the reason for this qualification in far broader terms, since it said of those with equitable interests alone

> they could be given a remedy in tort only at the cost of much complication and will in a proper case have a remedy against the trustees for breach of trust or be able to compel the trustees to recover the trust property on their behalf.[115]

---

[111] ibid at 41.
[112] Worthington, *Equity* (2005) at 185.
[113] See, eg, *Cooper v Willomatt* (1845) 1 CB 672, 135 ER 706.
[114] 18th Report (n 36) at para 128(5).
[115] ibid at para 34.

This is consistent with the two more specific reasons given above for requiring more than a mere equitable interest to sue in Conversion, since it highlights how the trust framework itself provides the beneficiary with an 'internal' means of protection, far better suited to the job than the 'external' action of Conversion. Of course, the protection of the beneficiary is not the only issue to be considered and, as Tettenborn explains, making Conversion available to beneficiaries without more would expose trustees to a strict liability from which they are otherwise protected by section 61 of the Trustee Act 1925.[116] This provision means that a trustee will escape liability if he has 'acted honestly and reasonably and ought fairly to be excused for the breach of trust', but is something a beneficiary could, were his equitable interest to allow him, sidestep by suing his trustee in Conversion.[117]

Conclusions

The rule about title to sue in Conversion is very simple: it attaches to the superior *possessory* right in the assets concerned. If this basic rule is borne in mind, there should be no need for any inquiry about such title to be distracted by questions which are at best peripheral and at worst confusing or irrelevant. Adherence to this rule, and an understanding of the system of relative title within the common law, is necessary in order to recognise Conversion as a means of protecting personal property which is not only perfectly coherent, but also remarkably effective in practice.

---

[116] Tettenborn, (n 78) at 42.

[117] There has been some suggestion in Australia that an equitable title would be a sufficient basis to sue in Conversion: see *Brybay Pty Ltd v Esanda Finance Corp Ltd* [2002] WASC 309, per McLure J at [18], citing *Maynegrain Pty Ltd v Compafina Bank* [1984] 1 NSWLR 258. This conflicts, however, with the contrary suggestion in *Finesky Holdings Pty Ltd v Minister for Transport for Western Australia* [2001] WASC 87 per Roberts-Smith J at [164], citing *White v Elder, Smith and Co Ltd* [1934] SASR 56 (an appeal against the *Finesky* decision was dismissed at [2002] WASCA 206, 26 WAR 368, though this point was not touched on). The latter decision represents the better view, for the reasons given in the text.

5

The Subject Matter of Conversion

Property and Possession

A S THE PREVIOUS chapter makes clear, the proprietary interest with which the tort of Conversion is concerned is that of possession. The fact of possession is, therefore, the key concept for determining the scope of Conversion; the physical characteristics of an asset are only relevant to the extent that they affect the ability of an asset to be the subject of possession. What matters is whether the relationship between the asset and the individual is susceptible to behaviour which fits the definition of a Conversion.[1]

Attempting to establish this in any given case, within the constraints of *stare decisis*, can have the effect of entrenching certain ideas within the law, so that they outlive their substantive relevance to the evolving society in which they continue to feature. For instance, even the most cursory examination of case law on Conversion will reveal that there is no authority for there being a Conversion of, say, a set of electronic accounts. To conclude on this basis alone, however, that assets of this type are not susceptible to Conversion would be to do the common law a disservice: the lack of existing authority for such a situation owes more to the nature of scientific and economic evolution than it does to conscious judicial deliberation. For instance, the issue of property in, and possession of, electronic data has only become pertinent over the last two decades. In order to preserve the coherence of the common law in such a situation, it is necessary to look to its common substantive concerns, rather than to focus only on the single dimension of its past formal results. As the preceding chapters have established, such an exercise reveals that the common substantive concerns of the courts in Conversion cases are that the asset in question is one in which property interests can vest, and which is capable of being possessed. The primary contention of this

---

[1] For which see ch 3, in particular under the heading The Three Elements of Conversion. The civil law approach to protecting property rights is generally abstract and rights-based, and consequently far less concerned with the physical nature of its subject matter than the common law has been historically. See JH Dalhuisen, *Dalhuisen on Transnational and Comparative Commercial, Financial and Trade Law*, 3rd edn (Oxford, Hart Publishing, 2007) at 557.

chapter is that, if an asset fulfils both these criteria, it is possible to convert it, regardless of whether that asset has physical similarities with the subject matter of previous Conversion cases.

The first question to ask, therefore, is whether a particular asset can properly be described as being the subject of a property right. As Baroness Hale succinctly pointed out in *OBG Ltd v Allan*, the

> essential feature of property is that it has an existence independent of a particular person: it can be bought and sold, given and received, bequeathed and inherited, pledged or seized to secure debts, acquired (in the olden days) by a husband on marrying its owner.[2]

The relationship between the concepts of ownership and possession in the common law is, however, highly complex and, as Mattei explains, 'in dealing with movable property, the distinction between ownership and possession tends to blur'.[3] In his analysis of the legal concept of property, Penner offers two theses to assist in identifying the proper objects of property rights: he refers to these as the 'Exclusion Thesis' and the 'Separability Thesis'. Broadly, the former is defined as

> the right to property is a right to exclude others from things which is grounded by the interest we have in the use of things.[4]

The latter thesis is characterised by the idea that:

> Only those 'things' in the world which are contingently associated with any particular owner may be objects of property; as a function of the nature of this contingency, in theory nothing of normative consequence beyond the fact that the ownership has changed occurs when an object of property is alienated to another.[5]

The definition of a property right which results from these two theses in combination is

> the right to determine the use or disposition of a separable thing, (ie a thing whose contingent association with any particular person is essentially impersonal and so imports nothing of normative consequence), in so far as that can be achieved or aided by others excluding themselves from it, and includes the rights to abandon it, to share it, to license it to others (either exclusively or not), and to give it to others in its entirety.[6]

In essence, these two criteria of excludability and separability, corresponding as they do to Baroness Hale's more concise dicta on the matter, would appear to

---

[2] *OBG Ltd and anor v Allan and ors* and two other cases [2007] UKHL 21, [2008] 1 AC 1 at [309].
[3] U Mattei, *Basic Principles of Property Law: A Comparative Legal and Economic Introduction* (Westport Connecticut, Greenwood Press, 2000) at 88.
[4] JE Penner, *The Idea of Property in Law* (Oxford, Oxford University Press, 2003) at 71.
[5] ibid at 111.
[6] ibid at 152.

provide an elegant means of distinguishing those things which can be the subject of property rights from those which cannot.[7]

The second question to ask, in order to establish if a particular asset can be converted, is whether it is capable of being possessed. The common law's concept of possession cannot be defined in particularly brief terms. Nevertheless, some sort of definition is required in order that we might recognise possession when we see it. It is important to note, first, that possession is a matter of fact rather than a matter of law. As such, it transcends any categorisation in terms of property and obligations. As Milsom points out, 'Our concept of property appears to have grown from factual possession and the right to get possession may have been indistinguishable from what we should call an obligation.'[8] This perhaps explains why an action which evolved to deal with wrongful disposses-sion finds itself straddling the modern and somewhat artificial boundary between the law of property and the law of obligations.[9] The factual possession to which Milsom refers would have looked very different in physical terms to many of the instances of factual possession which exist today. Nevertheless, it is possible to outline some fundamental features common to both ancient and modern phenomena.[10]

Meaningful Indicia of Possession

Such features can essentially be divided into two types, the manual and the cognitive. The first of these is perhaps the most apparent characteristic of possession, that of physical control over an asset. This covers both direct control, where the claimant has physical contact with the asset, and indirect control, where he has the means of accessing it (such as the holder of a key to the place where it is stored). The second feature is the claimant's mental state with regard

---

[7] The United States Court of Appeals (9th Circuit) has recently applied a three-stage test to determine when and where property rights exist: 'there must be an interest capable of precise definition; . . . it must be capable of exclusive possession or control; . . . the putative owner [*sic*] must have established a legitimate claim to exclusivity'. See *Kremen v Cohen* 337 F 3d 1024 (2003) at 1030. See also K Gray, 'Property in Thin Air' [1991] *Cambridge Law Journal* 252 and P Cane, *Tort Law and Economic Interests*, 2nd edn (Oxford, Oxford University Press, 1996) at 21–25.

[8] SFC Milsom, *Historical Foundations of the Common Law*, 2nd edn (London, Butterworths, 1981) at 7.

[9] ibid at 7 where Milsom admits that his exegesis of the history of the common law 'commits the fundamental anachronism of a single classification to cover its whole life: Property, Obligations and Crime. In a general way, this can be applied to any developed system and in detail it has never been applicable in England.'

[10] In DR Harris, 'The Concept of Possession in English Law', in AG Guest (ed), *Oxford Essays in Jurisprudence* (Oxford, Oxford University Press, 1961), the author identifies nine such characteristics, which he refers to as 'factors of possession'. For present purposes, however, it is submitted that the concept of possession can be analysed in more concise terms, as outlined in the text that follows. Despite the authors' conclusion on this point, we remain indebted to Harris' enlightening analysis of the concept.

to the asset in question, his '*animus possidendi*'.[11] Here, cognitive control encompasses the claimant's active intention to exclude others from it, as well as his passive awareness of the asset's existence and form. This gives us four indicia of possession: direct manual control, indirect manual control, passive cognitive control and active cognitive control.

None of these four is either necessary or sufficient in its own right, but there must be at least one manual element and at least one cognitive element present in order to establish possession in legal terms.[12] Finally, each element, or combination of elements, is subject to an important qualification; since possession is a 'functional and relative concept',[13] a claimant wishing to be deemed the legal possessor has not only to exhibit such qualities, but to do so to a greater extent than anyone else.[14] Such indicia facilitate the identification of the individual who is in legal possession of an asset[15] but, importantly, they also provide a means of identifying which goods can be the subject of possession. If it is possible for an individual to have at least one each of the cognitive and manual indicia of possession in relation to a particular asset, then that asset can be possessed in a legal sense.

In terms of the cognitive indicia of possession, an individual claiming to possess an asset would first need to show knowledge of the asset's existence and form. This knowledge might or might not then be accompanied by an intention to exclude others from that asset. The former indicium requires an individual only to demonstrate that he knows what the asset is, and that it exists. For the latter, it must be apparent that he regards it as something which should be within his control, and not subject to the authority of anyone else. Both of these requirements are arguably easy to satisfy, regardless of the nature of the asset in question. An asset does not need to have a physical presence in order for us to be aware of its existence (as the very concept of intangibility demonstrates), or for us to hold an intention towards it (to which the law relating to choses in action can testify). This is why, in order to establish legal possession, at least one indicium of manual control must also be present, in addition to the requisite cognitive state. After all, if my belief that I possess something and/or my intention to possess something were to be sufficient to establish possession, then the fact that someone else holds that same belief or intention would not affect my 'possession' in any way, notwithstanding that the asset in question could be entirely at the disposal of someone else.

---

[11]   F Pollock and RS Wright, *An Essay on Possession in the Common Law* (Oxford, Clarendon Press, 1888) at 8.

[12]   M Bridge, *Personal Property Law*, 3rd edn (Oxford, Oxford University Press, 2002) at 17. On this point, common law possession has something in common with the civil law understanding of the concept; see R Caterina, 'Concepts and Remedies in the Law of Possession' (2004) 8 *Edinburgh Law Review* 267 at 268.

[13]   Bridge, *Personal Property* (2002) at 71.

[14]   See Pollock and Wright, *Possession* (1888) at 42–45.

[15]   ibid at 44: 'there can only ever be one possession at any time, sole or shared'.

The two manual indicia of possession relate to an individual's physical control over the asset in question. In order to have direct control over an asset, an individual must have physical contact with it, and this presumes that the thing in question has a physical form. Indirect physical control, on the other hand, requires no such contact. All that must be demonstrated in order to assert indirect control is that the individual claiming possession has a means of controlling access to that asset. For either of these indicia of manual control to be possible, the asset in question must possess two particular characteristics: excludability and exhaustivity. In other words, if a thing is amenable to exclusive custody, and can be exhausted so as to deprive the claimant substantially of its value, then it can be possessed by one party to the detriment of another and can, therefore, be converted. Assets without either of these characteristics could not be subject to the extent and nature of the deprivation of rights necessary for a successful action in Conversion.[16]

Having established that an asset's amenability to possession is determinative of whether it can be subject to Conversion, we will look at several types of asset in turn, so that such a determination might be made in relation to each of them. All of the assets considered herein have already been the subject of judicial deliberation in the context of Conversion,[17] and all have thereby presented the courts with problems. This chapter aims to show that there are no convincing reasons for excluding *some* of these assets from the remit of the tort, and that property interests in them are, in most cases, as deserving of protection as those in assets of a more traditional nature. Indeed, as Mattei puts it, most 'of the general principles of efficient property law can be applied by analogy if the interpreter is creative enough to understand in which areas differences in economic nature are crucial and in which areas they are not'.[18]

Cognitive Indicia

As established above, the *cognitive* indicia of possession are not dependent upon the nature of the asset concerned, and are determined by reference to the mental state of the individual claiming possession. So, an individual wishing to demonstrate one of these indicia (either will suffice) would need to show that he intends to exclude others from it, or is at least aware of the asset's existence and form. Consequently, the cognitive indicia of possession alone are neither a sufficient nor an appropriate means of distinguishing those things which can be legally

---

[16] This characteristic distinguishes those assets which will be substantively affected by interferences from those whose substance would remain unchanged regardless of the extent of the interference. For instance, as discussed under the heading Copyright below, a copyright is not exhaustible since, no matter how many times it sustains a wrongful interference, it remains perfectly intact, and therefore no less valuable to its possessor. See also, in relation to debts, under the side-heading Intangible Property, Manual Indicia, ii. Exhaustibility.

[17] Although not all by UK courts.

[18] Mattei, *Basic Principles* (2000) at 70.

possessed from those which cannot. Where a digitized asset is concerned, for example, cognitive indicia would cover a range of relationships between an individual and the asset in question; from one which is based merely on the fact that the individual would recognise a piece of software if he happened to notice it listed on the applications menu of a shared computer,[19] to one in which an individual has no idea which digitized assets are contained on his hardware but nevertheless intends to prevent everyone else from accessing them, to one in which an individual aims actively to ensure that he is the only user able to access the contents of a particular program.[20]

Such indicia, however, are equally applicable to those assets which cannot be manually (and therefore legally) possessed. As demonstrated below,[21] information cannot be subject to legal possession, and yet it exhibits cognitive indicia of possession, in that holders of it can be aware of its nature and form, and can *intend* to exclude others from it, even if such exclusion is impossible in practical terms. Suffice it to say, therefore, that all of the assets specifically dealt with later in this chapter are clearly capable of being the subject of the cognitive indicia of possession; it is in relation to the manual indicia, however, that the position is rarely as straightforward.

Money

Money is a term so frequently used and of such importance that one is apt to overlook its inherent difficulties, and to forget that the multitude of its functions necessarily connotes a multitude of meanings in different legal situations.[22]

This is essentially the reason for there being some confusion over whether money[23] can be the subject of Conversion. The particular problem with money in this context is that, as we will explain, it amounts, in its physical form,[24] to both tangible and intangible property.[25] Banknotes and coins are clearly tangible items which have the requisite indicia of possession outlined above, but they are also, more often than not, worth more to their possessors in terms of the intangible asset they represent than they are in terms of their intrinsic value as a tangible

---

[19] Whilst this might sound like an insufficiently substantial requirement, it must be borne in mind that the cognitive indicia are not sufficient to demonstrate possession in their own right, but need to be combined with the requisite manual indicia if legal possession is to be achieved.

[20] For instance, by password protection.

[21] Under the heading Information.

[22] C Proctor, *Mann on the Legal Aspect of Money*, 6th edn (Oxford, Oxford University Press, 2005) at para 1.01.

[23] Of course, the question of what we mean by the term 'money' is by no means an easy one to answer. Somewhat circuitously, any definition will to some extent be context-dependent: for a full discussion, see ibid at paras 1.07–1.14. For the purposes of the current discussion, 'money' refers to banknotes and coins.

[24] ie when it is in the form of banknotes and coins, rather than as 'money in the bank'. When it is in the latter form, it is intangible property, as to which see under that heading below.

[25] See Proctor, *Mann* (2005) at para 1.29.

asset. The purpose for which money is held will determine its particular worth in a given situation; a collector of coins, for example, is likely to value the tangible worth of her coins over the intangible worth which they represent; she keeps them because she values *those particular* coins. Conversely, someone who possesses coins for the sole purpose of exchanging them for other assets will value their intangible worth more highly, and is unlikely, therefore, to be concerned about *which particular* coins she possesses as much as she is about their collective worth as a unit of exchange. In the former situation, the coins' use value exceeds their exchange value whereas in the latter the opposite is true.[26] An appreciation of the difference between the two is crucial in determining whether money can be converted.[27]

That said, the basic rule is a very simple one: money can be converted unless and until it passes into currency:

> The true reason is, upon account of the currency of it: it can not be recovered after it has passed in currency. So, in case of money stolen, the true owner can not recover it, after it has been paid away fairly and honestly upon a valuable and bona fide consideration: but before money has passed in currency, an action may be brought for the money itself.[28]

Whilst, therefore, money is physically held as a specifically identifiable asset, it can be converted in the way that any such asset can, but once it has been employed as a unit of exchange, and transferred in good faith and for value, Conversion is no longer available to the claimant.[29] The reason for this can be found in the common law's rules about the passing of title in relation to money. Whereas, in relation to specific and identified assets, a possessor may pass only such title as he himself has,[30] this is not the case where money is concerned; title to money is transferred as soon as it passes in currency to a good faith purchaser, as *Miller v Race* demonstrates. In that case, Lord Mansfield explained concisely why this should be so:

> A bank-note is constantly and universally, both at home and abroad, treated as money, as cash; and paid and received, as cash; and it is necessary for the purposes of commerce, that their currency should be established and secured.[31]

---

[26] For a further account of the difference between such interests, see B Rudden, 'Things as Things and Things as Wealth' (1994) 14 *Oxford Journal of Legal Studies* 81 and Cane, *Tort Law* (1996) at 8

[27] RM Goode, 'The Right to Trace and its Impact on Commercial Transactions—I', (1976) 92 *Law Quarterly Review* 360 at 382.

[28] *Miller v Race* (1758) 1 Burr 452 at 457–58, 97 ER 398 at 401 per Lord Mansfield.

[29] *cf* §935, para 2 of the German Civil Code. See also *Wookey v Poole* (1820) 4 B & Ald 1, 106 ER 839; *Higgs v Holiday* (1653) Cro Eliz 746, 78 ER 978.

[30] This is the basic rule known as *nemo dat quod non habet*, to which there are, however, certain exceptions: see M Bridge, *The Sale of Goods*, 2nd edn (Oxford, Oxford University Press, 2009) at paras 5.42–5.180 for a fuller account of these. Suffice it to say here that those exceptions are limited to specific factual situations and are nothing like as general as that which applies to the transfer of money.

[31] *Miller v Race* (1758) 1 Burr 452 at 459, 97 ER 398 at 402.

In other words, it is vital for the efficacy of commercial dealings that currency can be relied upon as a secure means of valuable exchange.[32] Moreover, the implications of putting on to every transferee a duty to inquire into the title of his transferor would be, to say the least, detrimental to the efficiency of economic activity.[33] Ultimately, the transfer of money in good faith and for value deprives the original possessor of the necessary title to sue in Conversion, since the superior possessory right passes to the transferee as a result of the exchange.[34]

This latter point also goes to explain why money which retains its primary use value, and so remains a specifically identified asset, may still be converted. So, where, for instance, a coin collector sells a particular set of coins (and receives in return money as currency), the subject matter of that sale remains capable of being converted because a seller cannot pass a better title to that collection than she herself has. Here, the coins comprising such collection are not currency, but have intrinsic worth as tangible assets, which means that the basic rule of *nemo dat* applies to them. The essential distinction between money and specific assets was also explained by Lord Mansfield in *Miller v Race*, who used a lottery ticket as an example of the latter:

> Now no two things can be more unlike to each other, than a lottery-ticket, and a bank-note. Lottery tickets are identical and specific: specific actions lie for them. They may prove extremely unequal in value: one may be a prize; another, a blank. Land is not more specific, than lottery-tickets are.[35]

Even where money is possessed by one who values its exchange value over its use value, and therefore intends to use it only as currency, it will be protected as a specific asset unless and until it passes into currency. So, where a thief takes a banknote from its possessor, or a possessor loses it and it is found by another, that possessor can sue the thief or the finder in Conversion as long as that thief or finder still has the particular note which she took or found. Since it is only a good faith transfer for value which will destroy the possessor's title to sue for money in Conversion,[36] this protection of the note as a specific asset will continue until such a transfer occurs. There are two justifications for this position. The first is

---

[32] It is also the case that, were money as currency to be treated as specific assets, an individual to whom a transfer was made temporarily (say for the purpose of a loan) could only acquit himself by returning to the transferor the exact same notes or coins that were delivered to him—see *Orton v Butler* (1822) 5 B & Ald 652, 106 ER 1329.

[33] See *Newco Rand Co v Martin* 213 SW 2d 504 (Miss Sup Ct 1948) at 509.

[34] See ch 4 for a detailed discussion of the requisite title to sue in Conversion. That is not to suggest, of course, that someone dispossessed in this way has no means of recourse in law: even once money has passed into currency, he may well have a claim in money had and received if his money can be traced into the possession of a defendant who did not receive it in good faith and for value. See *Lipkin Gorman v Karpnale Ltd* [1991] 2 AC 548; *Clarke v Shee* (1774) 1 Cowp 197, 98 ER 1041; R Goff and G Jones, *The Law of Restitution*, 7th edn (London, Sweet & Maxwell, 2007), ch 2.

[35] *Miller v Race* (1758) 1 Burr 452 at 459, 97 ER 398 at 402.

[36] Money is capable of being recovered specifically from a holder who received it in bad faith or for no consideration—*Clarke v Shee* (1774) 1 Cowp 197, 98 ER 1041; *Collins v Martin* (1797) 1 Bos & P 648, 126 ER 1113.

that it is perfectly reasonable that the law's protection of the security of transactions over the protection of property rights should only apply to bona fide purchasers. The second is that, regardless of the intentions of any possessor with regard to his money, it makes more sense for the law to presume that, until he uses it as currency, he wants the specific notes or coins in which he currently has property rights than it does for the law to presume that he is happy for anyone to interfere with his money, so long as he or she replaces it with money amounting to the same value.

Parts or Products of the Human Body

Where this particular type of subject matter is concerned, the contentious question is not whether it can be possessed, but whether it can properly be subject to property rights. After all, tangible items such as a vial of blood, or an amputated finger, obviously have the requisite manual and cognitive indicia of possession. It is not so clear, however, that such things can appropriately be regarded as being the subject of property rights.[37]

'*Dominus membrorum suorum nemo videtur*'.[38] This is the basic common law rule that no person is to be regarded as having property rights in his own limbs,[39] which owes its existence largely to policy considerations. Essentially, not having property in one's own body parts means that one cannot lawfully either intentionally destroy those parts, or enter into commercial dealings in relation to them.[40] The point has also been made, in relation to human corpses, that a recognition of 'property rights in a human body could be regarded by some as sacrilegious, and that allowing such property rights to be contended could have adverse public health effects, if it meant that burial would be delayed'.[41] Nevertheless, there has existed for over a century a questionable exception to this basic rule. It was formulated by the High Court of Australia in the grisly case of *Doodeward v Spence*,[42] in which the defendant was found by a policeman to be exhibiting for commercial purposes the preserved corpse of a two-headed stillborn baby. The policeman seized the corpse in order to bury it, and the defendant sued him successfully in detinue. The element of this case which gave rise to the common law exception was that the baby's corpse had been 'subject to

---

[37]   See also J Harris, *Property and Justice* (Oxford, Clarendon Press, 1996) ch 11.

[38]   Ulpian, *Edict*, D9 2 13 pr.

[39]   *Williams v Williams* (1882) 20 Ch D 659 and *Dobson and anor v North Tyneside Health Authority and anor* [1997] 1 WLR 596 (CA).

[40]   See also RS Magnusson, 'Proprietary Rights in Human Tissue' in N Palmer and E McKendrick (eds), *Interests in Goods*, 2nd edn (London, LLP, 1998), and Nuffield Council of Bioethics, 'Human Tissue, Ethical and Legal Issues' (London, 1995).

[41]   *Yearworth & ors v North Bristol NHS Trust* [2009] EWCA Civ 37, [2009] 2 All ER 986 at [31].

[42]   [1908] HCA 45, 6 CLR 406.

the lawful exercise of work or skill' which meant that it acquired 'some attributes differentiating it from a mere corpse awaiting burial'.[43]

The practical effects of this limited (and some would say arbitrary) exception to the general rule that body parts or products cannot be the subject of property rights were recently considered in a more modern context in *Yearworth and ors v North Bristol NHS Trust*.[44] Amongst other issues, the Court of Appeal had to decide in that case whether the claimants had property rights in their own sperm, following its removal from their bodies, sufficient to enable them to sue the defendant Trust for failing to store it so as to maintain its suitability for future reproductive use.[45] At first instance, this question had been answered in the negative by HHJ Griggs, who was influenced on this point by the effects of the Human Fertilisation and Embryology Act 1990 (HFEA 1990), which restricts some of an individual's rights over his or her human gametes after they have been removed in circumstances to which the Act applies. According to HHJ Griggs, these restrictions operate so as to prevent the provider of such gametes from being capable at common law of maintaining property rights in the same.

In explaining the Court of Appeal's contrary conclusion on this point, Lord Judge CJ said:

> A decision whether something is capable of being owned cannot be reached in a vacuum. It must be reached in context … The concept of ownership is no more than a convenient global description of different collections of rights held by persons over physical and other things. In his classic essay on 'Ownership' (Oxford Essays in Jurisprudence, OUP, 1961, Chapter V) Professor Honoré identified 11 standard incidents of ownership but stressed that not all of them had to be present for ownership to arise. He suggested that the second incident was the 'right to use' and he added, at p. 116, that: 'The right (liberty) to use at one's discretion has rightly been recognised as a cardinal feature of ownership and the fact that … certain limitations on use also fall within the standard incidents of ownership does not detract from its importance'[46]

In essence, the Court of Appeal took the view that the limits imposed by the HFEA 1990 upon the claimants' right to use their stored sperm were not sufficiently extensive to prevent their having property rights in that sperm.[47] Although the Act restricts the ability to use sperm which has been removed and stored for reproductive treatment to those licensed by the Act to do so, thereby preventing the claimants themselves from so using it, the Court gave much

---

[43]   ibid at 414.

[44]   [2009] EWCA Civ 37, [2009] 2 All ER 986.

[45]   The claimants in question were all cancer patients, who had been asked by the Trust if they wanted their sperm stored for future use, since the chemotherapy which they all needed to undergo could well have caused them to lose their natural fertility. The Trust undertook expressly to store it in such conditions as would allow them to use it for reproductive purposes in the future, and then failed to do so by allowing the liquid nitrogen in which it was stored to fall below the necessary level. None of this is, however, relevant to the property question.

[46]   [2009] EWCA Civ 37, [2009] 2 All ER 986 at [28].

[47]   [2009] EWCA Civ 37, [2009] 2 All ER 986 at [41]–[44].

weight to the *negative* control of the claimants; that is, the fact that their sperm could neither continue to be stored, nor used for any purpose, without their consent.[48] Lord Judge CJ also pointed out that, whilst those licensed to store and use the sperm undoubtedly have *duties* in relation to it, only the claimants themselves have any *rights* over it.[49] Finally, the Court of Appeal also considered it relevant that the there was a 'precise correlation between the primary, if circum-scribed, rights of the men in relation to its future use, and the consequence of the Trust's breach of duty, namely preclusion of its future use'.[50] Thus, the judgment provides a 'broader basis' on which its decision about property rights should be interpreted, indicating that it is to be preferred to the previously exceptional approach as outlined in *Doodeward*.[51]

Of course, the Court of Appeal was here considering the issue of property rights in body parts or products in the context of a negligence action. Despite the fact that its reasoning is bound to affect other areas of the common law, however, the judgment also contains an express invitation for the common law to re-evaluate the issue:

> In this jurisdiction, developments in medical science now require a re-analysis of the common law's treatment of and approach to the issue of ownership of parts or products of a living human body, whether for present purposes (viz. an action in negligence) or otherwise.[52]

Arguably, such a re-analysis is needed in the context of Conversion. Consider, for example, a situation similar to the one in *Yearworth*, but which involves a wrongful removal of the sperm from its storage.[53] As far as the claimants are concerned, this would have exactly the same effect as the Trust's failure to store it effectively; they would still be denied the use of their sperm for future reproduc-tive treatment; that is, they would still be denied their 'rights of use'. Since this is undoubtedly an interference with the claimants' property rights, there is a strong argument for their being able to recover in Conversion. As Bridge has pointed out, the classification of something as property does not need to be absolute,[54] and so something may be 'property' for some purposes and not for others. This may well be the solution where body parts and products are concerned, since there is a clear conflict between the need to prevent commercial dealings in such things and the need to protect an individual's use rights in the products of his own body from wrongful interference by another. In the light of this, it seems reasonable to argue that the property rights analysis in relation to body parts and

---

[48]   [2009] EWCA Civ 37, [2009] 2 All ER 986 at [45], (f)(ii) and (iii). In (i), the Court also stated that it thought it relevant that the claimants had by their bodies alone generated and ejaculated the sperm.

[49]   [2009] EWCA Civ 37, [2009] 2 All ER 986 at [45], (f)(iv).

[50]   [2009] EWCA Civ 37, [2009] 2 All ER 986 at [45], (f)(v).

[51]   At [2009] EWCA Civ 37, [2009] 2 All ER 986 at [45], (d) Lord Judge CJ makes it clear that the Court does not consider *Doodeward* to be a principle worthy of retention, largely because of its arbitrary nature.

[52]   [2009] EWCA Civ 37, [2009] 2 All ER 986 at [45](b).

[53]   For the approach taken by the law of theft, see under the heading The Law of Theft, below.

[54]   Bridge, Property (n 12) at 5.

products could be used to give an individual title to sue for wrongs done in relation to those parts and products, but will not, where that use is proscribed by law, act as a defence to any use of the same by those from whom they came.

Digitized Products

A genie has left the bottle and has transformed our economy and the way we lead our lives. It blurs legal categories, eliminates or greatly reduces concepts of location and distance, diversifies the marketplace . . . and fundamentally calls for new ways of understanding law and business, as well as their interaction.[55]

A digitized asset is one which exists in an electronic format, often referred to under the umbrella term 'software'. Digitized assets have a material presence and therefore alter the physical state of whichever medium on which they are held. A digitized asset, such as computer software, consists of both instructions and data. The data is the initial information to be stored, manipulated or displayed by the program. The instructions form the program itself and control the way in which the machine deals with the data. In some situations, it will be the data element of the asset which is the most valuable to its possessor, such as the information contained within a set of electronic accounts or an electronic share certificate,[56] and in others the instructions themselves, such as a bespoke computer program commissioned by a particular user.

There are several formats in which this software is stored, each with varying degrees of permanence. When stored in a relatively permanent form on a CD-ROM[57] (analogous to a pre-recorded video or DVD), each 'bit' is represented by either the presence or absence of a tiny pit in the surface of the disc. These pits determine the amount of light reflected back from that surface when the machine runs a sharply focussed light beam over it, allowing the machine to 'read' both the instructions and the data provided by the software. Sometimes, however, when software needs to be stored in a less permanent manner, so that it can be erased or overwritten at a later date, it is stored on computer hard discs and rewriteable CDs. Even here, although the information is not permanent, it has a physical presence on its storage medium, albeit that it might be a temporary one. In this format, tiny magnets are used, and their north and south poles directed towards or away from the surface of the disc, thus representing 0s and 1s for the machine to read. Obviously, the magnets can then be redirected as appropriate when the software is overwritten or erased. Thus, the storage medium on which the

---

[55] RT Nimmer, 'International Information Transactions: An Essay on Law in an Information Society' (2000) 26 *Brooklyn Journal of International Law* 5 at 47.

[56] See, eg, the business data for which the claimant was suing in *Thyroff v Nationwide Mutual Assurance* 8 NY 3d 283, 864 NE 2d 1272 (NY Ct Apps 2007).

[57] Compact Disc, Read-Only Memory.

program is loaded is physically different from that same storage medium with different software on it, and physically different again from a blank medium containing no software.

Whilst such variations in storage methods can determine the longevity of a piece of software, they do not alter the fact that, as long as such a product exists *qua software*, it does so in a corporeal form because hardware containing software is, in one way or another, a physically different entity from hardware which contains no software, regardless of whether or not this difference can be perceived by the naked eye. The corporeal nature of software is further illustrated by the fact that hardware has only a finite capacity for storing it; because software has a material presence, it takes up physical space on whichever medium on which it is stored.

Given that such 'dematerialized' assets are of increasing commercial significance in our digital age,[58] it is remarkable that the purported Conversion of this particular asset has yet to be directly considered by an English court; by the same token, it is unsurprising that this issue has received considerable judicial attention elsewhere in the common law world. Much of this attention, however, has been directed towards the question of whether digitized material is tangible or intangible, largely because tangibility has hitherto been regarded as an essential characteristic of those things which are susceptible to Conversion.[59] Although, as Kozinski J points out in *Kremen v Cohen*, the position in the United States has been somewhat different in recent times, he refers to the distinction as being one which

> tort law once drew between tangible and intangible property: Conversion was originally a remedy for the wrongful taking of another's lost goods, so it applied only to tangible property … Virtually every jurisdiction, however, has discarded this limitation to some degree … Many courts ignore or expressly reject it.[60]

Similarly, it is a contention of this work that the identification of something as tangible or not should not be dispositive of the question of whether it can be possessed. The more pertinent, and more commercially relevant, inquiry is whether such things have at least one cognitive *and* at least one manual indicium of possession.[61]

---

[58] See BW Napier, 'The Future of Information Technology Law' [1992] *CLJ* 46, particularly at 50–55 for an account of such dematerialization.

[59] See inter alia, *South Central Bell Telephone Co v Sidney J Barthelemy* 643 So 2d 1240 (La Sup Ct 1994), *City of New Orleans v Baumer Foods Inc* 532 So 2d 1381 (La Sup Ct 1988), *Comptroller of the Treasury v Equitable Trust Co* 296 Md 459, A 2d 248 (Md Ct Apps, 1983), *Chittenden Trust Co v King* 143 Vt 271, 465 A 2d 1100 (Vt Sup Ct 1983) and *Maccabees Mutual Life Ins Co v State Dep't of Treasury* 122 Mich App 660, 332 NW 2d 561 (Mich Ct Apps 1983).

[60] 337 F 3d 1024 (2003) at 1030.

[61] For reasons that one of the authors has made clear elsewhere (see S Green, 'Can a Digitized Product be the Subject of a Conversion?' [2006] *Lloyd's Maritime and Commercial Law Quarterly* 568 and S Green and D Saidov, 'Software as Goods under the Sale of Goods Act and the CISG' [2006] *Journal of Business Law* 161), software should be regarded as a corporeal asset. Hence we here deal

Manual Indicia

In order for an asset to be the subject of the manual indicia of possession, it must bear the characteristics of both excludability and exhaustibility. Digitized assets have both of these characteristics.

i. Excludability and movability

The excludability of digitized assets is demonstrated in part by the fact that they are moveable; a piece of software can, for example, be removed from one hardware device and stored instead on another. This point is sometimes over-looked or challenged in the case of digitized products, most likely because such assets can also be, and often are, copied rather than moved. The same might be said, however, of many conventional assets, such as manuals or restaurant reservation books,[62] and whilst copying might be easier in the case of digitized assets,[63] the essential distinction (for present purposes) between those things which bear excludability and those which do not is the *possibility* of deleting them from the source from which they are removed.[64] This distinction is important because, if something cannot be removed in this way, thereby limiting access and control to the remover, the exclusion element of Conversion cannot be achieved. So, if an individual gains unauthorised access to another's computer hard disc and *takes a copy* of a digitized asset, such as a database containing financial information, but leaves the original where it is, this is not a Conversion. Where, on the other hand, an unauthorised user moves the database (and in doing so deletes the original), this is a Conversion, since the owner of the database is then denied access and, therefore, loses both physical and legal possession of it.

This is exactly what happened in *National Surety Corporation v Applied Systems Inc*,[65] wherein the claimant sued two former employees in Conversion for

---

[62] with digitized assets under a separate heading from intangible property. However it is not (or should not be) necessary to establish whether or not an asset is tangible in order to determine whether it can be converted, for the reasons developed under the heading Intangible Property, below.

[62] For an entertaining modern example of their (perceived) importance see www.caterersearch.com/Articles/2007/04/05/312687/marco-pierre-white-to-sue-gordon-ramsay-over-book-theft.html.

[63] The nature of digitized assets is such that they are easily *scalable*, meaning that there is a low marginal cost involved in duplicating them, but this characteristic has no bearing whatsoever on the movability of such assets. See JA Cohen, *Intangible Assets: Valuation and Economic Benefit* (New Jersey, Wiley & Sons, 2005) at 30.

[64] This also serves to distinguish the tort of Conversion from that of trespass to assets. Arguably, a product need not be excludable in order to be susceptible to trespass under the 1977 Act, since appropriation is not an element of that tort. For a discussion of the applicability of trespass to computer software, see JN Adams, 'Trespass in a Digital Environment' [2002] 1 *Intellectual Property Quarterly* 1.

[65] 418 So 2d 847 (Ala Sup Ct 1982).

removing[66] a proprietary software package[67] from the claimant's system and using it for their own commercial purposes. Despite the fact that one of the two defendants had himself developed the programs concerned, his former employer retained the proprietary rights in them. Considering that the case was heard by the Supreme Court of Alabama over a quarter of a century ago, the judgment is remarkable for the perspicacious nature of its commercial pragmatism. The Court decided in favour of the claimants and recognised that a 'computer program, in appropriate circumstances, can be the subject of Conversion'.[68] This conclusion was based in part the court's interpretation of the following section of the Alabama Code 1975:

> The owner of personalty is entitled to possession thereof. Any unlawful deprivation of or interference with such possession is a tort for which an action lies.[69]

According to Almon J, this section makes 'no distinction between tangible and intangible personal property'.[70] This decision marks a clear departure from the idea that tangibility per se is determinative of an asset's ability to be possessed by one individual to the detriment of another. The crucial characteristic of the software programs as far as the court in *National Surety* was concerned was the fact that the former employees had been able to behave in relation to them in such a way as to deny the rightful owner the possessory benefits of its property rights. This was partly because the dispossessors had been able to *move* the assets concerned, and partly because they were able to take and maintain exclusive access to them.

ii   Excludability and exclusive access

> Possession is single and exclusive. As the Romans said, '*plures eandem rem in solidum possidere non possunt*'. This follows from the fact of possession being taken as the basis of a legal right. Physical possession is exclusive or it is nothing.[71]

Digitized assets are also amenable to exclusive access. An individual can exercise exclusive control over a digitized asset by storing it only on hardware which he possesses and from which others can be excluded by a range of means, from physical exclusion from the hardware, to the use of exclusive user accounts. Such custody is perhaps the highest degree of direct manual control that can be

---

[66]   When Applied Systems came to process some data for a customer, it 'discovered it did not have the programs or the master files with which to do so', ibid at 849.

[67]   A proprietary software package is one which is bespoke to (and has usually been commissioned by) a particular institution. Interference with such a program thereby creates problems for the dispossessed party; in addition to the obvious confidentiality issues, there is also the fact that the product cannot be replaced with a readily available substitute. Indeed, according to the testimony of a software expert in the *National Surety* case, the appropriated programs were 'unique and no software house would have these for sale': ibid at 849.

[68]   ibid at 849.

[69]   Code 1975 §6–5-20.

[70]   418 So 2d 847 (Ala Sup Ct, 1982) at 849.

[71]   Pollock and Wright (n 11) at 11.

exercised over this type of asset, because a digitized product exists as a physical attribute of the hardware on which it operates. Physical control of the hardware on which software is stored, is therefore, synonymous with physical control of the software itself, despite the fact that we cannot see or feel the presence of a program on, for instance, a computer memory stick. A broader interpretation of direct manual control such as this is not without precedent. After all, it is not only those assets which are imperceptible to the unaided senses which present difficulties in terms of their amenability to manual control. In his seminal work on the concept of possession in English law, Harris cites physical control as the first 'factor of possession' and describes it as the 'degree of physical control over the chattel which the plaintiff actually exercises, *or is immediately able to exercise*' (authors' emphasis). He states, further, that the 'plaintiff's degree of physical control should not be considered in isolation, but in relation to the greatest degree of physical control which it is possible for the particular plaintiff to exercise over the particular chattel'. The examples he offers of assets over which physical control is difficult are a 'very large chattel or a wreck at the bottom of the sea'.[72]

Arguably, a subjection to either direct or indirect manual control is easier to achieve in relation to a digitized asset than it is in relation to the wrecked ship on the seabed. For example, such an asset can be held in one's hand if it exists on a disc or chip. It would be very difficult, on the other hand, to conceive of such direct manual control being exercised over a shipwreck, and yet it is unlikely that such an asset would be considered not to be amenable to possession.

A similar argument can be made in terms of indirect manual control. An individual claiming to be in possession of a digitized product should not face any insurmountable problems in attempting to control access to it: it is far from uncommon, for example, for software programs to be password protected in order that they can be used only by those who have the requisite access information. This is analogous to the conventional scenario where an asset is locked within a contained area, with access being denied to all who do not have the relevant key. Whereas such indirect control is a straightforward matter in relation to digitized products, it is a far less simple feat to achieve where a very large asset, such as a wrecked ship, is concerned. It is, for instance, no easy task to control the area of the sea bed on which a ship lies, and yet it is well established that such an unwieldy object is something capable of being possessed. It seems,

---

[72] Harris, Possession (*Oxford Essays* 1961) at 74. The allusion here is to *The Tubantia* [1924] P 78, a case in which the claimants claimed possession of the wreck of a Dutch steamship which had sunk in 1916 in over 100 ft of water in the North Sea. They had spent two summers attempting to salvage the wreck when weather conditions permitted, only to have their operation compromised by the rival salvage efforts of the defendants, who came onto the scene at the end of that second summer. The claimants asserted possessory rights over the wreck and its contents and complained of the defendants' trespass and wrongful interference with it. The court had then to decide whether or not the claimants had possession of the *Tubantia* at the material time. Sir Henry Duke decided that they did.

therefore, reasonable to argue that objects presenting fewer logistical problems to the exercise of control should, perhaps a fortiori, be considered to exhibit excludability. Moreover, as Bridge explains, the 'size of a thing is no obstacle to its being a chose in possession: microdots and ships both fall into the category'.[73] This being the case, the minuteness of a digitized product's physical form should no more exclude it from the class of choses in possession than should the enormity of a wrecked ocean liner.

iii. Exhaustibility

Digitized assets are exhaustible in that they can be expended so as to deprive a rightful possessor of their benefit. This is illustrated by the fact that they can be deleted altogether (albeit not as easily as many assume), or moved and modified so as to render them useless or inaccessible to a dispossessed individual: 'electronic documents and records stored on a computer can ... be converted by simply pressing the delete button.'[74]

In relation to this point, it is important to distinguish between the physical manifestation of the program itself, and the idea for, and knowledge of how to create, the program, contained within the designer's brain. Whilst the two are completely separate phenomena, they seem often to have been treated, in a legal context, as if they were the same thing.[75] Moreover, this seems to be a mistake which occurs, for some reason, only in the context of digitized assets: there would appear to be no similar difficulty, for instance, in accepting that the design for, say, a particular car, is factually and legally distinct from the automobile which ultimately results from that design. Whilst this may well be due to the fact that digitized assets exhibit physical characteristics unlike those with which the law is familiar, nevertheless digitized assets are distinct from the designs from which they originate and are, as such, exhaustible. A digitized asset exists independently of any person and can therefore be exhausted, deleted or destroyed; the same cannot be said of the blueprint of, or idea for, such an asset.

Policy Implications

Should digitized assets be excluded from the ambit of Conversion, it is difficult to see how any individual's possessory and proprietary interest in such things would be consistently protected. Under these conditions, the average user who buys, for example, a computer software package, would be left in a potentially strange position in the event that someone interferes with her interest in it. This

---

[73] Bridge, Property (n 12) at 3.
[74] *Thyroff v Nationwide* 8 NY 3d 283, 864 NE 2d 1272 (NY Ct Apps 2007) at V, per Graeffo J.
[75] See inter alia the judgment of Sir Iain Glidewell in *St Albans City and District Council v International Computers Ltd* [1997] FSR 251 at 264 and the judgment of the Court of Appeals of Louisiana in *South Central Bell Telephone Co v Sidney J Barthelemy* 631 So 2d 1340 (1994) (corrected by Hall J in the Supreme Court 643 So 2d 1240 (1994) at 1246).

individual would no doubt be surprised to learn that, should someone unlawfully appropriate that program from her whilst it is stored on its moveable disc, then she would have an action in Conversion,[76] but that, should her dispossessor remove the same program from the memory of her computer, she could make no comparable claim. This is an unsatisfactory position, not least because it makes the protection of interests in assets dependent upon the manner in which their possession is acquired and maintained. In a digital age, such inconsistent legal treatment is neither justifiable nor necessary.[77]

In addition to the consistency point, there is also an argument based on considerations of commercial efficacy. This was an issue to which the court in *National Surety* gave considerable weight. Simply put, the argument of the dispossessed software owners was that, should digitized products be denied the protection of the law of personal property, the software industry would suffer. More specifically, a refusal to recognise property rights in certain assets leads to a situation in which those assets are neither produced nor employed in the most efficient manner. In that case, the court ascribed significance to the following passage:

> Improvements in software are necessary to the rapid growth of computer technology; effective protection for those improvements is, by the same token, also necessary. Programs are expensive to develop. Programmers are scarce, and thus relatively well paid, and the painstaking process of formulation, coding and testing a new program requires much valuable time. Without revenues on the use of its product by others, a company may be reluctant to invest the necessary time and money. Until now any program not of sufficient use to the developer himself to warrant the investment simply was not developed. At present, however, there is a rapidly growing interest in propri-etary programs, i.e. 'packages' developed primarily for sale. Use of program packages will enable the development of programs of a quality significantly higher than those developed and proliferated under the current system in which, by and large, each must develop every program he uses. The obvious result is duplication and wasted effort. The one essential ingredient of the package concept is a means of protecting the program, for without protection, it ceases to be a commodity. The wise man will not buy the cow when he can get the milk for nothing. The consequence for the software industry will be more expensive (in terms of development costs) but inferior software.[78]

Digitized assets are commodities in the same way as those assets which are conventionally protected by the law of property. Failing to safeguard property interests in them will have the same effects as failing to recognise property in

---

[76] At present this is more likely to be treated as a Conversion of the disc, rather than of the program itself—see *St Albans v ICL* [1997] FSR 251 at 265 per Sir Iain Glidewell. This position emphasises the inconsistency of the legal protection currently available for digital products them-selves.

[77] The issue is also of significance in the context of private international law: see N Fawcett, J Harris and M Bridge, *International Sale of Goods in the Conflict of Laws* (Oxford, Oxford University Press, 2004) at paras 10.188–10.198.

[78] D Bender, 'Trade Secret Protection of Software' (1970) 39 *George Washington Law Review* 909 at 910, as cited in *National Surety* 418 So 2d 847 (Ala Sup Ct 1982) at 850.

traditional assets, since the legal relationship between person and asset is much the same where both types of asset are concerned. As we have seen, it is the behaviour of the parties in relation to the assets in question which is, or should be, determinative of whether a Conversion has occurred. As Pollock and Wright observed:

> Facts have no importance for the lawyer unless and until they appear to be, directly or indirectly, the conditions of legal result, of rights which can be claimed and of duties which can be enforced. Rights cannot be established or enforced unless and until the existence of the requisite facts is recognised.[79]

Their point is well illustrated by the decision of the Ontario Court of Justice in *Unisys Canada Inc v Imperial Optical Company Ltd and ors*.[80] In that case, the claimant (Unisys) supplied the first defendant (Imperial) with software products under a sale and service agreement, which explicitly reserved the claimant's proprietary right in that software until the purchase price had been paid in full. In order to finance this transaction, Imperial entered into a lease agreement with the second defendant, Lease Underwriting Corporation of Canada Ltd. An appendix to the sale and service agreement between Unisys and Imperial expressly denied Lease Underwriting any rights in the products supplied. Notwithstanding this, the lease agreement between Imperial and Lease Underwriting purported to provide Imperial with an option to purchase the equipment for a price of $1 on the expiration of the term of the lease. Unisys was not a party to this option, nor did it know of, or consent to, its inclusion in the lease agreement. Ultimately, Imperial attempted to exercise its purported option to purchase, and consequently asserted a right of ownership over the software.

In deciding whether any of the defendants[81] were liable for Conversion of the computer software concerned, the court had to resolve the conceptual question of whether such an asset is capable of being converted. Hoilett J cited with approval the following excerpt from Fridman's *The Law of Torts in Canada*:

> Knowledge in some permanent form, for example, on paper or a disc used for computers, would seem to have the character of a chattel, and should be capable of being converted.[82]

Whilst his Lordship never expressly stated his approval of this viewpoint, his judgment proceeds in a manner which implicitly accepts its premise. This, combined with the remarkably small proportion of the judgment devoted to the consideration of the nature of software as an asset, illustrates that the Court did

---

[79] Pollock and Wright (n 11) at 7.
[80] (1999) 72 OTC 231.
[81] The inclusion of other defendants was necessary due partly to Imperial's bankruptcy, partly to Lease Underwriting having assigned its lease agreement with Imperial to Toronto Dominion Leasing Ltd, and partly to the several corporate forms in which Lease Underwriting had existed.
[82] GHL Fridman QC, *The Law of Torts in Canada* Vol 1 (Toronto, Carswell, 1989) at 95, cited in *Unisys Canada v Imperial Optical* (1999) 72 OTC 231 at [12].

not consider this factual issue to be problematic. In deciding in favour of the claimants, the Court focussed on the behaviour of the defendants in relation to the subject matter of the claim, and found it necessary only briefly to touch on the physical characteristics of computer software. The deciding factor in this case was that the defendants' acts had amounted 'to an absolute denial and repudiation of the plaintiff's right'.[83]

The tenor of the decision was that, if the nature of an asset allows such an action to be performed in relation to it, it can be converted. This is consonant with the analytical approach outlined above; if an asset exhibits the requisite indicia of possession, it will be susceptible to such behaviour and capable, therefore, of being converted. Concentrating on the legal rights to be protected, rather than on the subject matter of those rights, is an approach which 'transposes the physical object into a man-made representative universe where we can disengage the resource from its burdensome material constraints and concentrate on its potential'[84] as an economically productive commodity.

In *Thyroff v Nationwide*, in which the New York Court of Appeals answered in the affirmative the certified question of whether digitized assets can be converted, Graffeo J made the following point:

> [I]t is the strength of the common law to respond, albeit cautiously and intelligently, to the demands of commonsense justice in an evolving society, (Madden v Creative Servs. Inc., 84 NY 2d 738, 744 [1995]) . . . That time has arrived. The reasons for creating the merger doctrine[85] and departing from the strict common-law limitation of conversion inform our analysis. The expansion of conversion to encompass a different class of property, such as shares of stock, was motivated by 'society's growing dependence on intangibles' (Franks, Analysing the Urge to Merge: Conversion of Intangible Property and the Merger Doctrine in the Wake of Kremen v Cohen, 42 Hous. L Rev at 498). It cannot be seriously disputed that society's reliance on computers and electronic data is substantial, if not essential ... We cannot conceive of any reason in law or logic why this process of virtual creation should be treated any differently from production by pen on paper or quill on parchment. A document stored on a computer hard drive has the same value as a paper document kept in a file cabinet.[86]

In *Kremen v Cohen*,[87] the disputed property was the remarkably lucrative domain name, 'sex.com'. The claimant had registered this domain name as his in the days

---

[83]   ibid at [15], adopting words from the headnote of *Oakley v Lyster* [1931] 1 KB 148 (CA).

[84]   H de Soto, *The Mystery of Capital* (London, Black Swan, 2000) at 48.

[85]   Referred to in this book as the 'documentary exception', a situation in which an asset is so closely associated with its documentary representation that the law regards the two things as having merged. See further ch 2 under the side-headings Conversion in the Nineteenth Century, a New Legal Fiction and Conversion in the Twentieth Century, Expansion of the New Legal Fiction and ch 7 under the side-headings The Measure of Damages for Conversion, (e) Special Rules, Negotiable Instruments etc and Other Documents etc.

[86]   8 NY 3d 283, 864 NE 2d 1272 (NY Ct Apps 2007) at V.

[87]   n 7. This is the same case to which the article in the excerpt just quoted refers. See also K McCarthy, *Sex.Com* (London, Quercus, 2007) for a very detailed, if journalistic, account of the extended story behind the case.

before such electronic assets became recognised as valuable resources. Subsequently, an infamous conman managed to persuade the domain name registrar to transfer the name to him, on the basis of a forged letter purporting to be from the claimant. The conman then went on to build a multi-million dollar business in the sex industry, based largely on his exploitation of the asset that is 'sex.com'. In ultimately concluding in favour of the claimant[88] that the asset had indeed been converted by the domain name registrar, the United States Court of Appeals for the Ninth Circuit (determining and applying Californian law) recognised that a domain name is the equivalent of a collection of documents, stored in electronic form rather than on ink and paper, and, as such, is capable of being converted. Indeed, as the Court pointed out in that case:

> It would be a curious jurisprudence that turned on the existence of a paper document rather than an electronic one. Torching a company's file room would then be conversion while hacking into its mainframe and deleting its data would not.[89]

The facts of *Kremen v Cohen* demonstrate how valuable digitized assets can be, and how someone can be dispossessed of them, just as they can of any tangible asset. In essence, the basis of Kremen's claim was that the defendant domain name registrar had given away his property to a third party, thereby depriving him of it and allowing that third party to exploit Kremen's property for an enormous amount of money. The nature of the asset aside, this situation is a typical example of a Conversion and, as the Court pointed out, 'there is nothing unfair about holding a company responsible for giving away someone else's property'.[90] It makes no legal or commercial difference that the physical characteristics of the asset involved are different to those with which the law has historically been concerned, and this point really constitutes the 'bigger picture' recognised by the Court in *Kremen v Cohen* when it proclaimed that 'the common law does not stand idle while people give away the property of others'.[91]

There is much, therefore, to commend to the English courts the idea that digitized assets are susceptible to, and therefore should be protected by, the tort of Conversion. This would, of course, necessitate something of a modified approach to this long-established tort, but as we have seen in chapter two, its lengthy history has featured numerous expansions to its scope borne of judicial pragmatism, and there is much to be said in favour of the English common law now recognising its applicability to digitized assets in order to ensure that it continues in the twenty-first century effectively to perform its juridical role of protecting interests in personal property:

> Computers stimulate the process of change in the law, and it is vital that the law we develop in response is the law that we need and want. We must not just think of

---

[88]   Thereby reversing the judgment of the lower court (*Kremen v Cohen* 99 F Supp 2d 1168).
[89]   337 F 3d 1024 (2003) at 1034.
[90]   ibid at 1035.
[91]   ibid at 1036.

technology as something that simply lets us do better tasks with which we are already familiar. There is a need to grasp opportunities for fundamental reform as they arise . . . it should become a matter of course for the Law Commissions, in undertaking their work, to consider what possible contributions can be made by the developing technology.[92]

It is significant indeed that much of the material in this section, both judicial and academic, comes from the United States, and even more so that not all of it is particularly recent. It is clear that the issue of the law's recognition and protection of digitized assets is at a far more advanced stage of consideration in the United States than it is in England, and that the legal result of such consideration is something to which the English common law should look when dealing with analogous situations.

Intangible Property

> This is not a world where the labels of the past long survive. Their breakdown affects
> law in complex ways.[93]

Items of intangible property have traditionally been classed as 'choses in action'. The term 'choses in action', however, long used to describe all those things assumed to be incapable of possession (and so only capable of recognition through legal action), has, depending on one's viewpoint, either outlived its usefulness as a meaningful classification, or fallen into misuse. Essentially, it too suffers from commonly held but, as we have argued, unduly narrow assumptions as to the law's concept of possession, and has thus come to be taken to comprise all things intangible, rather than being limited to those which are incapable of being possessed. The potential for analytical confusion generated by such assumptions is apparent from the following passage from a judgment of Slesser LJ:

> [T]he general definition of chose in action will apply as being things in action, as 'when a man hath cause, or may bring an action for some duty due to him . . .. because they are things whereof a man is not possessed, but for recovery of them is driven to his action,' to quote the well known definition in Termes de la Ley, described by Bayley J. in *Hewlins v. Shippam* ((1826) 5 B. & C. 221, 229) as a book of great antiquity and accuracy. The equally well known observations on this subject made by Fry L.J. in *Colonial Bank v. Whinney* (30 Ch.D. 261, 285) and by Lord Blackburn in the same case (11 App. Cas. 426, 434) clearly show how the two conditions of chose in action and

---

[92] Napier, Future (*CLJ* 1992) at 65. It is also worth pointing out that the advent of the dematerialized economy brings with it many efficiency advantages, which are to be both welcomed and encouraged. For instance, 'An automobile, once built, can be modified only with substantial, costly and skilled effort. A computer information database, on the other hand, ordinarily carries with it the inherent capability to alter its structure or utility with relative ease'—see Nimmer, Essay (*BJIL* 2000) at 12.

[93] ibid at 15.

chose in possession are antithetical and how there is no middle term. 'Choses in possession *are tangible, movable things*': see *Williams on Personal Property*, 18th ed., p. 47. 'Choses in possession *are movable goods*, of which their owner has actual possession and enjoyment, and which he can deliver over to another upon a gift or sale': Ibid. 29. 'The term choses in action appears to have been applied to things, to recover or realise which, if wrongfully withheld, an action must have been brought; *things, in respect of which a man had no actual possession or enjoyment, but a mere right enforceable by action*': Ibid. 30. (authors' emphasis)[94]

If 'chose in action' is to survive as a meaningful legal term, it needs to be applied carefully and accurately for the avoidance of conceptual confusion, and consequent practical inconsistency. In *Murungaru v Secretary of State for the Home Department*, Lewison J appeared to acknowledge the need for such precision when he recognised that:

The classic definition of a chose in action is that of Channel J in Torkington v Magee [1922] 2 KB 427: it is a personal right of property which can only be claimed or enforced by action, and not by taking physical possession.[95]

Intangible property has tended to be regarded as a chose in action per se, since at first blush it appears to fit the description of 'a personal right not reduced to possession'.[96] It is important to note, however, in addition to the above-mentioned assumptions as to the potential scope of 'possession', that the category of 'choses in action' is one which includes a broad range of phenomena, with very different attributes and functions, whereas items of intangible property form a more specific category, sharing common characteristics. 'Intangible property' is not limited to choses in action which can be the subject of property rights; it is wider than this, in that there are some assets such as patents, which, whilst undoubtedly items of intangible property, are not classed as choses in action.[97] Though on any view there is a substantial area of overlap between choses in action and intangible property, neither is a subset of the other. Quite apart from specific statutory provisions, some intangible property is certainly capable of being possessed.

Holdsworth, writing in the *Harvard Law Review* as long ago as 1920, identified the breadth of the term 'choses in action' as the source of difficulty in the law,

---

[94] *Allgemeine Versicherungs-Gesellschaft Helvetia v Administrator of German Property* [1931] 1 KB 672 (CA) at 704.

[95] [2008] EWCA Civ 1015, [2009] INLR 180 at [44].

[96] 'Conversion of choses in action' (1941) 10 *Fordham Law Review* 415 (Note principally prepared by Lester Rubin, Member of the Board of Editors, 1940–41) at 416.

[97] See E Griew, *The Theft Acts*, 7th edn (London, Sweet & Maxwell, 1995). at para 2–18: in particular, his reference to s 30(1) Patents Act 1977 (wherein patents and applications for patents are declared not to be choses in action) and to *Attorney-General of Hong Kong v Nai-Keung* [1987] 1 WLR 1339 (HL), a case concerning export quotas which conferred the expectation of a licence to export textiles, but no enforceable right to such licences. The quotas were held to be intangible property, capable of being stolen by a dishonest director, even though they were clearly not choses in action.

the fact that all these things are classed as choses in action has left its mark upon the law; and, partly from this cause, partly by reason of the divergencies between the different classes of choses in action created from time to time by the courts and the legislature, the law upon many points connected with this subject was long, and still is, to some extent, confused, inconvenient and uncertain[98]

He concluded that:

[T]he modern English law as to choses in action can hardly be called satisfactory; and this history shows that its unsatisfactory character is due mainly to the following causes: Firstly, the enormous extension given to the term has included in this category a very large number of things of very different kinds. *Rules which were made for choses in action, when the term meant literally rights of action against some person, are obviously inapplicable to proprietary rights of an incorporeal nature;* but it is clear that these rules must be applied to these rights because they are choses in action, unless some authority—legislative or otherwise—can be produced which shows that they are subject to some other rule. Secondly, even in the case of some of the original class of choses in action, the old rule of non-assignability has been gradually modified; and in this work of gradual modification both law and equity have lent a hand. The result has been that *some of these choses in action have changed their original character, and become very much less like merely personal rights of action and very much more like rights of property.* But this process has been retarded and the whole question obscured by the distorting influence of the fear of encouraging maintenance. Owing to the disorderly state of the country in the fifteenth and early sixteenth centuries this fear rightly exercised a large effect upon this branch of the law; but unfortunately its effect lasted long after the cause for it had been removed. The result has been that the development of the law was slow, and the slowness of the modification of the original conception of a chose in action as a personal unassignable thing has caused a long continued uncertainty in the modern law. Thirdly, a further source of complication has been added by the piecemeal exceptions introduced by the legislature to the general rules applicable to choses in action in favour of some or all of them. It is sometimes difficult to ascertain the sense in which the legislature has used the term 'chose in action'—we have seen that the Bankruptcy Act affords one and, as we can see from the case of *Edwards v Picard* [1909] 2 K.B. 903, the modifications introduced by the courts have sometimes occasioned a similar difficulty. Some of these difficulties might be perhaps mitigated by a codifying Act, for which there is plenty of material. But it is probable that a branch of the law which comes at the meeting place of the law of property and the law of obligation can never be anything but difficult to formulate and apply. (authors' emphasis)[99]

Hence, the concept of a chose in action is not a helpful starting point for the present discussion, and is indeed a demonstrably inaccurate label to apply to certain forms of intangible property. Rather, the determinative quality of those assets which can be the subject of property rights is that they have an exchange

---

[98]   WS Holdsworth, 'The History of the Treatment of Choses in Action by the Common Law' (1920) 33 *Harvard LR* 997 at 999.

[99]   ibid at 1029–30.

value and can be transferred.[100] Once assets have been identified as having such qualities, analysing them by reference to the traditional dichotomy between choses in action and choses in possession is not helpful, a fortiori if that dichotomy is misunderstood by reason of a mistaken assumption as to the nature and scope of 'possession' as discussed above. Most if not all intangible assets with an exchange value and capable of transfer will, as we have contended above, be well capable of being possessed.

Whether one explains the true legal status of such intangible property by proposing what some might regard as a radical reassessment of what can constitute a chose in possession, or by discarding the traditional dichotomy between choses in action and choses in possession as one which has outlived its usefulness and relevance to modern circumstances, is perhaps of secondary importance. However, to provide protection for property rights in tangible assets but not for the same rights in intangible assets is to discriminate between situations which, though physically dissimilar, are legally similar. Such discrimination is not consistent with a coherent legal response to interference with property rights. 'Once the law recognises something as property, the law should extend a proprietary remedy to protect it.'[101] This is something which has been recognised for a relatively long time in many US states: in California, for instance, it had been judicially observed, well before the decision in *Kremen v Cohen*, that 'there is perhaps no very valid and essential reason why there might not be conversion of intangible property',[102] and that Conversion is 'a remedy for the conversion of every species of personal property'.[103]

The question of whether intangible assets can be subject to Conversion *has*, unlike the issue of digitized assets, been considered by a UK court. In *OBG Ltd v Allan*,[104] the House of Lords had before it three appeals concerning tort claims for financial loss suffered as a result of intentional acts. The first of these, *OBG*, included a claim for Conversion in respect of intangible property. The respondents to this appeal were receivers who, acting in good faith, had assumed control of the claimant companies' assets and undertakings. It transpired, however, that their purported appointment as receivers was invalid, since it had occurred under a nugatory floating charge. Consequently, the claimants brought proceedings for trespass and Conversion to their land and (tangible) assets, for unlawful interference with their contractual relations and for the Conversion of their debts and contractual rights. The latter claim is not a common one, nor did it take up a large proportion of the judgments. Such facts, however, belie the legal significance of the question. In terminating the contracts of the majority of OBG's sub-contractors and settling other outstanding contractual claims, the joint

---

[100]   See Baroness Hale in *OBG Ltd v Allan* [2007] UKHL 21, [2008] 1 AC 1 at [309]–[310].
[101]   ibid at [311].
[102]   *FMC Corp v Capital Cities/ABC Inc* 915 F 2d 300 (US Ct Apps 7th Cir 1990) at 305.
[103]   *Payne v Elliot* 54 Cal 339 at 341, 35 Am Rep 80 at 82 (Cal Sup Ct 1880(!)).
[104]   n 2.

receivers thereby assumed control of nearly 90 per cent of the claimants' total assets. It is therefore easy to see why, in an age in which a party's intangible assets routinely dwarf their tangible counterparts, the coherence of the law in this area is of increasing importance.

The question of whether intangibles can be the subject of Conversion divided the House. Lords Hoffmann, Walker and Brown answered the question in the negative, whilst Lord Nicholls and Baroness Hale were of the opinion that intangibles should no longer be excluded from the ambit of the tort. It is respectfully suggested that the majority's is an outdated approach, and one which creates unnecessary inconsistency within the law. The defendant receivers admitted trespass and Conversion in relation to the land and tangible assets of the companies over which they took control, but disputed that the same liability applied to their intangible assets. Whilst the physical distinction between OBG's tangible and intangible assets might attract attention, their respective *legal* characteristics are not so dissimilar. Although, according to Lord Brown,[105] intangible property lacks the capability of being possessed, thereby preventing it from being susceptible to Conversion, this view, with respect, is founded on a narrow and static interpretation of possession. For the reasons which follow, intangible property *can* have the necessary indicia of possession, and therefore be susceptible to acts of Conversion.

Manual Indicia

As outlined above, the relevant manual indicia applicable to a particular asset are to a certain extent dictated by the nature of the asset itself. As *OBG Ltd v Allan* illustrates, it is irrelevant, in terms of the practical effects of interfering with property interests, that manual control *looks* different, according to the type of asset concerned. It would, after all, have made little sense to require the claimants in *OBG* to show that they had manual control of their intangible property in the same manner as they did of their land and tangible assets in order to prove that they had possession of it. If a certain manner of control is the most that the party with the property rights, and the superior possessory rights, can exercise, there is no reason why a defendant need do more than this in order to be liable in Conversion. By interfering with that right of control, the defendants in *OBG* deprived the claimants of the benefit and use of their intangible property: they prevented the claimants from executing similar actions themselves, and so interfered with the claimants' interests sufficiently to attract a claim in Conversion.

As long ago as 1941, a note in the *Fordham Law Review*, concerned with the question of whether or not choses in action could be converted, included the following observation:

---

[105]　ibid at [321].

[I]t has been pointed out that many courts which deny an action in conversion for choses in action which are not evidenced by a writing do so on the notion that conversion will lie for tangible property only, thus limiting the action to situations involving physical force. The new test is: Has dominion been exercised inconsistent with the rights of the owner? Such a test applies equally well to those choses in action which are evidenced by a writing as those which are not, and today this affords a much more satisfactory standard than that based on the concept of physical force.

Certain it is that the expansion of conversion to choses in action represented by a writing and the further extension of conversion where no writing has been physically taken—all these changes conform with the shift of wealth from tangible to intangible personal property. Thus a procedural change parallels a similar one in the economic order, and is both desirable and defensible.[106]

Similar sentiments have been expressed in the UK. Napier makes the following points about the advent of widespread dematerialized commerce:

The advantages of electronic as opposed to paper documents are easy to state and readily comprehensible. In business terms, paper is expensive to use, slow to send, and often productive of time-consuming delays. The processing of information by electronic means is, on the other hand, not only cheap but also astonishingly quick. Had Puck been a salesman of EDI systems,[107] his boast of forty minutes to 'throw a girdle round the earth' would have brought him little business in today's market. But of course there are disadvantages of paperless transactions which should not be overlooked—the business community knows and trusts paper records and feels relatively secure when using them. One reason for that security is the knowledge that the rule of commercial law will provide support for the transactions there recorded. How true is that for paperless trading? The short answer is that we do not know. So far the courts have had few occasions to pronounce on the legal implications of dematerialisation. Indeed it is only now that other bodies—notably the Law Commissions—are beginning to appreciate that reforms in trading law should be presented in a form that will be compatible with the introduction of paperless transactions.[108]

As this passage suggests, the inevitable increase in the volume and commercial importance of dematerialized assets, which will not necessarily be represented in any conventional form, requires the law to keep pace with these technological developments and recognise that such assets are as worthy, and in need of protection, as conventional assets.[109] Since commerce may be conducted far more efficiently, easily and cheaply through digital means, it would be very much a case

---

[106] Rubin, Choses in action (*Fordham LR* 1941) at 432.

[107] Electronic Data Interchange (basically the technical term for data transmission by electronic means).

[108] Napier (n 58) at 52. Despite the fact that his article was written over 16 years ago, the courts have still had little to say about the legal implications of dematerialization, despite the continuing (and exponential) growth of the phenomenon in the commercial world.

[109] See also J Lipton, 'Property Offences into the 21st Century' (1999) 1 *Journal of Information, Law and Technology*; www2.warwick.ac.uk/fac/soc/law/elj/jilt/1999_1/lipton/ at 3.1.

of the tail wagging the dog, were such practices to be restricted as a result of the law's failure to protect such transactions.

i. Excludability

It remains to establish, however, exactly what constitutes manual control over intangible property. Although, as has already been made clear, the documentary exception is too narrow in its recognition of possessory relationships between individuals and assets, it does go some way towards answering this question. Where, for instance, an intangible asset is so closely identified with a particular document that the two are regarded legally as having 'merged', an exercise of dominion over that document, inconsistent with the rights of the true owner, will, in effect, be a Conversion of the asset it represents.[110] In substance, however, this exception is really just a means of identifying those assets which have the necessary element of excludability. As Lord Hoffmann points out, in cases where the misappropriation of the document 'could case actual loss to the creditor', that misappropriation will be treated as 'a Conversion of a thing equal in value to the debt which it evidenced'.[111] The reason for this is that, in such cases, the asset clearly has the characteristic of excludability because access to it is limited to the holder of the document. A document, however, is just one means of controlling access to, or symbolising, a form of intangible property and, increasingly, the function of such a document is performed by other, usually electronic, means. It is worth noting that the limited effectiveness of the documentary exception has already been recognised elsewhere in the common law world. In *Kremen v Cohen*, for example, the United States Court of Appeals for the Ninth Circuit concluded that:

> California does not follow the strict requirement in Restatement (Second) of Torts §242 (1965) that some document must actually represent the owner's intangible property right. On the contrary, California courts routinely apply the tort to intangibles without inquiring whether they are merged in a document.[112]

ii. Exhaustibility

Where intangibles are concerned, exclusive control obviously cannot amount to the physical holding of an asset, but equates instead to controlling access to the benefit of an asset in the way that the owner of any valuable thing would wish to do. Of course, there are situations in which a debtor, having made a payment to someone not entitled to it, remains liable to his creditor for the debt. Such a situation may explain why the 'documentary exception' first came into

---

[110]   See, inter alia, *Alsager v Close* (1842) 10 M & W 576, 152 ER 600; *Morison v London County and Westminster Bank* [1914] 3 KB 356 (CA); *Pierpoint v Hoyt* 260 NY 26, 182 NE 235 (NY Ct Apps 1932).
[111]   *OBG Ltd v Allan* [2007] UKHL 21, [2008] 1 AC 1 at [104].
[112]   337 F 3d 1024 (2003) at 1033.

being,[113] since payments made to the holder of a document evidencing a debt operate to satisfy that debt, regardless of whether the person in possession of the document is the rightful holder or not.

The facts of *OBG Ltd v Allan* demonstrate the deficiencies of this exception in a contemporary context; no longer is it the case that an individual requires a representation of intangible property in a documentary format in order to have control over it. As Baroness Hale acknowledged

> there are many debts and some other obligations which can now be readily assigned, attached, form part of an insolvent estate, and enjoy all the other characteristics of property, but which are not represented by a specific document.[114]

For example, where the asset in question is a debt, it is very important to the party who claims that intangible property as his own that he be recognised as the sole party to whom the debtor can reasonably consider himself indebted. So, in having the attributes and the information necessary to achieve this recognition, a party has possession of the debt in the only way such an item of property allows, for as Lord Macnaghten rehearsed in *Ward v Duncombe*, when discussing the application of the concept of possession to a debt, 'in the case of a chose in action, you must do everything towards having possession that the subject admits'.[115]

The question of whether the actions of a defendant in relation to a debt or other chose in action have constituted a sufficient interference with the claimant's possession thereof to amount to a Conversion of the same, should be regarded as a matter of fact for determination in the particular case, not as something which must be regarded as a legal impossibility or contradiction in terms, precluding any claim for the Conversion of such an asset *in limine*.

In *Marsh and two others v Keating*[116] the case before the House of Lords concerned a claimant (one Ann Keating) who had been the registered holder of a considerable amount of Bank of England reduced 3 per cent annuities stock. By use of a (purported) power of attorney on which her signature had been forged by one Henry Fauntleroy, the banking house of Marsh & Co (in which the three defendants and Fauntleroy had been the partners) sold most of her stock to a member of the Stock Exchange (one William Tarbutt), and procured the Bank to register the transfer. Owing to the numerous dealings in Bank of England reduced 3 per cent annuities stock thereafter undertaken by Tarbutt, the claimant's fraudulently transferred stock had become so 'blended and mixed with

---

[113] See ch 2 under the side-headings Conversion in the Nineteenth Century, A New Legal Fiction etc.

[114] *OBG Ltd v Allan* [2007] UKHL 21, [2008] 1 AC 1 at [310].

[115] *Ward and anor v Duncombe and ors* [1893] AC 369 at 386, the quoted passage being a citation from *Dearle v Hall* (1828) 3 Russ 1 at 23, 38 ER 475 at 483 per Sir Thomas Plumer MR.

[116] (1834) 1 Bing (NC) 199, 131 ER 1094 (HL), a case which seems to have come on for its first effective hearing, albeit as a notional appeal, before the House by virtue of directions of the Lord Chancellor which are set out in the report.

other stocks standing in the [Bank of England's] ledgers in the said W. B. Tarbutt's name ... that it was not possible to distinguish the account to the credit of which [her stock] stood'. In answer to the claimant's case for money had and received (the proceeds of the sale to Tarbutt), the defendants contended that the claimant 'was still the proprietor of the ... stock. She could not be deprived of her property in the stock by the wrongful acts of other persons, without her knowledge or consent ... [her] rights were therefore untouched, and her property in the stock was not divested'.[117]

Park J, delivering the opinion of the judges which the House accepted in affirming the formal decisions in favour of the claimant in the courts below, opined that even if that contention were

> true to its full extent ... still, under the circumstances ... we are of opinion that the Plaintiff below is at liberty to abandon and give up all claim to her former stock so standing in her name, and to sue for the money produced by the sale of such stock as for her own money ... It is unnecessary to enlarge upon the extreme difficulty, or, more properly, impracticability, under which [the plaintiff] would be placed, if, as matters now remain, she should elect either to receive the dividends or to sell her stock ... she would be met with a difficulty, insuperable in fact: although the stock may, in contemplation of law, still be vested in her ... we think her at liberty to give up the pursuit of the stock itself, and to have recourse to the price paid for it

If the practical value of Keating's rights to her stock had been so badly affected by the events which had in fact occurred, despite the position in legal theory being that her underlying chose in action represented by the lost stock subsisted, unaffected by these events, there would appear to be no good reason why a claim for Conversion of that stock should not equally have succeeded on such facts.[118]

The defendants in *OBG Ltd v Allan* certainly did 'everything towards having possession that the subject admit[ted]' when, acting as purported receivers, they brought about the settlement of debts to which they were not entitled. Since such settled debts no longer exist as items of property, the receivers thereby deprived the claimants of their property rights in those assets.[119] If the destruction of a tangible asset can amount to a Conversion, it is only reasonable to argue that the complete extinction of an intangible piece of property should attract the same legal redress.

In *OBG Ltd v Allan*, Lord Brown stated that he viewed the proposed extension of Conversion to intangible property as

---

[117]   ibid at 202, 1095 and 210, 1098.

[118]   ibid at 214–15, 1100.

[119]   Although the liquidator added his signature to the settlement agreement, he did so under great pressure and with all the relevant information being withheld from him. The trial judge, HHJ Maddocks, therefore held (in his unreported judgment of 18 February 2004 at [74]; see also that of 9 March 2004 at [5]–[6]) that the liquidators were not in a position to renegotiate the settlement which the receivers had reached. Hence there was no question of estoppel, acquiescence or ratification (see [2007] UKHL 21, [2008] 1 AC 1 at [212] and [240] per Lord Nicholls), and no break in the chain of causation from the receivers' acts.

no less that the proposed severance of any link whatever between the tort of conversion and the wrongful taking of physical possession of property (whether a chattel or a document) having a real and ascertainable value ... to my mind there remains a logical distinction between the wrongful taking of a document of this character and the wrongful assertion of a right to a chose in action which properly belongs to someone else. One (the document) has a determinable value as at the date of its seizure. The other ... does not.[120]

With respect, however, it is not the value of the document which is important to a claimant in a case alleging the Conversion of intangible property, but the value of the asset which it represents. The determinable value to which his Lordship refers is the value of the asset itself at the time of the purported Conversion. The existence of the document is, as far as the valuation of the asset is concerned, of no consequence.[121] Moreover,

an analysis of ... choses in action will disclose that their value may be ascertained within fairly definite limits ... Stocks, commercial paper, debts, contracts, accounts and judgments are rights and representations of rights that may be determined and are generally liquidated in amount.[122]

Since the document is regarded as the physical embodiment of the intangible property itself, it is hard to see why the value of the former is any more determinable than that of the latter.

The facts of *OBG Ltd v Allan* well illustrate why Conversion should apply to interferences with intangible assets, both conceptually and practically. Not only does the situation therein show how one party can deal with intangible assets in a way which is inconsistent with the true owner's interest in them, but it also illustrates how, if such an interference with property rights is not addressed by Conversion, the law provides no protection for what can amount to a considerable proportion of a party's total assets. Any continued exclusion of intangible assets from the ambit of Conversion looks, in the contemporary commercial environment, like a steadfast refusal to acknowledge a fundamental shift in the nature of economic activity. It is not easy to identify the reason for such a refusal, particularly as the law 'has the happy faculty of expanding to meet new needs',[123] should this be necessary. The protection of intangible property is, it is submitted, just such a new need, representing as it does a large, and increasing, proportion of assets in today's economy.

Is there currently a statutory obstacle to such a development in English law? In *OBG Ltd v Allan*, Lord Hoffmann highlights the fact that section 14(1) of the Torts (Interference with Goods) Act 1977 defines 'goods' as including 'all things personal other than things in action and money'.[124] Lord Walker and Lord Brown

---

[120]   *OBG Ltd v Allan* [2007] UKHL 21, [2008] 1 AC 1 at [321].
[121]   See ch 7, text to fns 120–25.
[122]   Rubin (n 96) at 425.
[123]   ibid at 430. See also ch 6, text to and citations in fn 118.
[124]   *OBG Ltd v Allan* [2007] UKHL 21, [2008] 1 AC 1 at [100].

both make more general references to the Act,[125] resulting in a majority decision that, since Parliament made no allowances therein for intangibles to be the subject matter of a wrongful interference, the common law should not presume to take such a step. With respect, this is something of a non sequitur. It has to be emphasised that the 1977 Act was *not* a codification of the common law position.[126] This being the case, and considering that the Act came into being more than 30 years ago, there is much to be said for not allowing it to stifle the common law's ability to meet the exigencies of a new and ever-changing world. As Lord Nicholls succinctly suggests in the same case:

> Parliament cannot be taken to have intended to preclude the courts from developing the common law tort of conversion if this becomes necessary to achieve justice.[127]

A salutary lesson on this point could be learned from The Supreme Court of Errors of Connecticut which, as long ago as 1874, delivered a prescient judgment on the matter of an alleged Conversion (trover) of shares of manufacturing stock. The decision is a triumph of reason over technical formality, and characterised by the pragmatism evinced by the following passage:

> A majority of the court however are of opinion that at the present time, when the action of trover is diverted from its original object of recovering the value of goods lost by the plaintiff and found by the defendant, and all the allegations with respect to such loss and finding are merely formal and unmeaning, there is no good reason for keeping up a distinction that arose wholly from that original peculiarity of the action, and therefore hold that trover will lie for shares of stock as well as for other kinds of personal property. There is really no difference in any important respect between this and other kinds of personal property. A man purchases a share of stock and pays one hundred dollars for it. He afterwards purchases a horse, and pays the same price. The one was bought in the market as readily as the other and can be sold and delivered as readily. The one can be pledged as collateral security as easily as the other; as easily attached to secure a debt; and its value as easily estimated. The one enriches a man as much as the other, and fills as important a place in the inventory of his estate. It is considered personal property of as substantial value as the other, both in law and in the transactions of men.[128]

---

[125]   At [271] and [321] respectively.
[126]   And consequently, according to *Clerk & Lindsell on Torts*, 19th edn (London, Sweet & Maxwell, 2006) at para 17–33, s 14(1) of the 1977 Act 'does not affect the common law position on what kinds of property are amenable to conversion'.
[127]   *OBG Ltd v Allan* [2007] UKHL 21, [2008] 1 AC 1 at [235].
[128]   *Ayres v French* 41 Conn 142 at 149–50, 1874 WL 1571 at 1574, per Park CJ. See also *Kuhn v McAllister*, 1875 WL 380 (Utah Terr Sup Ct); *Budd v Multnomah Street Ry* 12 Or 271, 53 Am Rep 355 (Or Sup Ct 1885); *Story v Gammell*, 94 NW 982 (Neb Sup Ct 1903); *Arkansas Anthracite Coal Co v Stokes* 2 F (2d) 511 (CCA 8th Cir 1924); *Shipley v Meadowbrook Club* 126 A 2d 288 at 292 (Md Ct Apps 1956); all of which state that choses in action can be the subject of Conversion. To like effect re intangibles, see further *Payne v Elliot* 54 Cal 339 at 341, 35 Am Rep 80 at 82 (Cal Sup Ct 1880); *Arnold v Hamilton Investment Co* 38 A 2d 118 (NJ Sup Ct 1944), affirmed 40 A 2d 649 (NJ Ct Apps 1945); *Freeman v Corbin* 391 So 2d 731 (D Fla App, 1980) at 732–33; *Schafer v RMS Realty* 138 Ohio App 3d 244 at 285, 741 NE 2d 155 at 184 (2000); *Taylor v Powertel* 551 SE 2d 765 at 769 (Ga Ct Apps 2001).

Whilst these sentiments are similar to those voiced by Baroness Hale in *OBG Ltd v Allan*, hers was a minority opinion, and this is not an argument to which much credence was given by those in the majority. This is unfortunate, since it appears to be the most reasonable and pragmatic way to approach the issue. There are, in our view, no convincing reasons, either conceptual or of policy, for excluding many forms of intangible personal property from the ambit of the legal protection afforded to tangible property. Such exclusion is symptomatic of a stagnant common law, ill-equipped to deal with the reality of modern day commercial practice. The susceptibility of intangible property to Conversion is something which has long been recognised in other jurisdictions, and a decision of the English common law to follow suit was long overdue. It must now fall to the Law Commission to take up this cause.

Copyright

As the foregoing argument is based upon the premise that the applicability of Conversion to any given asset depends upon the particular physical characteristics of that asset, rather than on its generic legal classification, it does not follow that *all* forms of intangible property can be subject to Conversion.[129] The essence of the position expounded here is that intangible property ought not automatically to be denied the protection of Conversion without regard being had to its particular physical properties. For instance, copyright, a very important form of intangible property, is not an appropriate subject for Conversion because it does not exhibit exhaustivity.

Copyright is not exhaustible because, if the holder of a copyright has it infringed, she has not had that right taken from her and transferred to the infringer. On the contrary, the right stays with her and is what enables her to take the appropriate legal action.[130] Since it is not exhaustible in this way, copyright cannot be appropriated from one party by another so that the former party is excluded from exercising her rights in relation to her property. No matter how many times someone interferes with another's copyright, that right does not diminish or lose its value for the holder; on the contrary, it benefits its holder anew with each infringement of it.[131] Copyright itself, therefore, as an item of personal property, cannot be converted.

---

[129] An argument for extending Conversion to intangible property with far fewer limits than those suggested here can be found in Val D Ricks, 'The Conversion of Intangible Property: Bursting the Ancient Trover Bottle with New Wine' (1991) 4 *Brigham Young University Law Review* 1681.

[130] Such an action will be a direct statutory one under the Copyright, Designs and Patents Act 1988 and not one for Conversion.

[131] Although see *Pacific Software Technology Ltd v Perry Group Ltd* [2004] NZLR 164 for a decision which held that the copyright therein had indeed been converted. With respect, the result in this case is difficult to accept, and the same result could have been reached on the basis of an infringement of copyright, without any reference being made to Conversion. It was also based, in part, upon

This issue could be somewhat confused, however, by the practice, adopted elsewhere in the Commonwealth, of statutes dealing with copyright infringement explicitly to allow for the granting of 'Conversion damages' for certain infringements.[132] In England, however, since the passing of the Copyright, Designs and Patents Act 1988 there is no longer any *explicit* reference to 'Conversion damages' for such infringements. Rather, section 96(2) of that Act states that:

> In an action for infringement of copyright all such relief by way of damages, injunctions, accounts or otherwise is available to the plaintiff as is available in respect of the infringement of any other property right.[133]

The recommendation of the Whitford Report, which preceded the enactment of the Copyright, Designs and Patents Act 1988,[134] was that 'Conversion damages' should be abolished because they were anomalous (in that they were not available in other fields dealing with intellectual and industrial property), and may have been 'out of all proportion to the injury suffered'.[135] The threat of this latter consequence is arguably ever-increasing, since technological advances mean that huge numbers of infringing copies can now be produced reasonably easily and quickly, thereby exposing a defendant to extensive damages as a result of a single breach of copyright.[136]

Nevertheless, whenever such damages are granted, they are not awarded in order to remedy the Conversion of a copyright itself since, for the reasons outlined above, this is not possible. Where 'Conversion damages' are available, they operate so as to treat the holder of the copyright *as if* he has property rights over all the infringing copies made as a result of the copyright infringement. It is these infringing copies that the law treats as having been converted, rather than the copyright itself. Such a position is clear from the wording of, for example, the relevant provision in the Australian Act:

Hammond J's interpretation of s 120(2) Copyright Act 1994 (NZ), according to which 'all the remedies that are available for "property" are available to the copyright owner', at [102].

    132   See, eg, s 166 Copyright Act 1968 (Aus) and s 120(2), Copyright Act 1994 (NZ).

    133   Contrast s 18 of the Copyright Act 1956 which provided expressly for Conversion damages.

    134   Report of the Committee to consider the Law on Copyright and Designs, 'Copyright and Designs Law' (Cmnd 6732, 1977).

    135   ibid at para 702. Although it is interesting that, at para 700, the Committee notes how, despite the vociferous calls they had received to abolish such damages, the Bank of England was strongly in favour of retaining them since it felt they provided the only real financial threat against the infringement of copyright in bank notes, and allowed the bank to ask for delivery up of infringing copies of bank notes, as well as the plates used to make them.

    136   Particularly given that the measure of such damages would generally be the market value of each copy produced. See Lord Scarman in *Infabrics Ltd and ors v Jaytex Ltd* [1982] AC 1 at 26. Not only could this measure of damages lead to excessive liability for a defendant, but its statutory existence amounted to something of an anomaly in European terms—see HL Vol 489 cols 1475–540 at 1485 (12 November 1987). See also D Bainbridge, *Intellectual Property*, 6th edn (London, Longman, 2007) at 168 for the argument that, although s 96(2) of the new Act does not explicitly *exclude* the availability of Conversion damages, a judge asked for them is likely to question why Parliament did not choose specifically to include them in the new statute.

Subject to this Act, the owner of the copyright in a work or other subject-matter is entitled in respect of any infringing copy, or of any plate used or intended to be used for making infringing copies, to the rights and remedies, by way of an action for conversion or detention, to which he or she would be entitled if he or she were the owner of the copy or plate and had been the owner of the copy or plate since the time when it was made.[137]

Not only is copyright itself, in a factual sense, not susceptible to the treatment necessary to amount to a Conversion, but, in a legal sense, there is no need for such a right to be protected by Conversion, since its protection is the explicit concern of statute.

Information

In terms of the law of property, information is perplexing. Whilst often very valuable to those who have access to it, it does not lend itself well to the mechanisms usually employed to protect things of value. Attempting to ascertain whether information is susceptible to Conversion, using the criteria outlined in this chapter, demonstrates the practical legal difficulties presented by the concept of information in this particular context.

Unlike the types of asset so far discussed, it is by no means generally accepted that information *simpliciter* can be the subject of property rights.[138] It would be reasonable to conclude, on the basis of the criteria outlined above for determining whether something can be the subject of a property right,[139] that since, where information is concerned, 'the transferor retains the information that was transmitted, which denies one of the features of a property right, namely its exclusivity',[140] that information does not exhibit excludability, thereby precluding it from being amenable to the exercise of a property right.[141] Correspondingly, it is also the case that, because information cannot practically be separated from any person who once possessed it, it lacks the 'essential feature of property' identified by Baroness Hale, namely that it must have 'an existence independent of a particular person'.[142]

---

[137] s 116(1) Copyright Act 1968 (Aus) (as amended). For its application, see *Polygram Pty Ltd and ors v Golden Editions Pty Ltd and anor* [1997] FCA 686, 76 FCR 565 and *Sony Entertainment (Australia) Ltd v Smith* [2005] FCA 228, 215 ALR 788. For the application of a very similar provision (s 120(2)) in the Copyright Act 1994 (NZ)) see *Pacific Software v Perry* [2004] 1 NZLR 164.

[138] An extensive analysis of the issue can be found in, inter alia, P Kohler and N Palmer, 'Information as Property', in N Palmer and E McKendrick (eds), *Interests in Goods*, 2nd edn (London, LLP, 1998) and Penner, *Idea of Property* (2003), chs 4–6. See also, however, E Weinrib, 'Information and Property' (1988) 38 *University of Toronto Law Journal* 117 for the opposing viewpoint.

[139] See text to n 7.

[140] Bridge, Property (n 12) at 6.

[141] See n 7.

[142] *OBG Ltd v Allan* [2007] UKHL 21, [2008] 1 AC 1 at [309]. See also Penner's separability criterion, text to n 5. This is not to suggest, however, that the point is a settled one; under a

Where information is concerned, it is not in any event clear whether a proprietary classification would add anything to its legal protection. As Kohler and Palmer point out, since 'most Commonwealth legal systems already possess a developed law of confidentiality', it would be reasonable to argue that the idiosyncracies of information as an asset would be better protected through this bespoke branch of the law, which is also less likely than a proprietary classification to stifle creative freedom.[143] The same authors also suggest that the notion of 'property' is over-used in the common law, and that such a classification can in some cases have counter-productive effects in terms of the assets to which it is assigned; the 'property label', they convincingly argue, 'is a conclusion not a premise'.[144]

Even were information appropriately to be classified as 'property', this would, of course, not be determinative of whether it can be the subject of Conversion. As has already been established, only those assets which can be possessed can be converted, and it is by no means clear that information can be possessed.

Manual Indicia

It is important to distinguish at this stage between information itself, and any physical embodiment of it, such as a paper or digitized record, which might exist. This section is concerned with the intangible entity which is information itself.[145] As a purely intangible entity, information is not truly moveable because, in practical terms, it is not possible to remove it from its original source (a human intellect) whether or not it has been transferred (by communication).

i. Excludability

For the same reasons, it is not possible to maintain exclusive access to information once it has been transferred. Prior to any transfer, exclusive access to

---

Hohfeldian interpretation, for instance, 'property' refers to the legal relationship between persons in relation to things, thereby leaving room for the argument that the physical characteristics of the objects of such rights are irrelevant for classification purposes. See, eg, WN Hohfeld, 'Some Fundamental Legal Conceptions as Applied in Judicial Reasoning' (1913) 23 *Yale LJ* 16. This touches on the considerable jurisprudential debate as to the nature of property, which is of a scale which places it outside the realistic scope of this chapter. See, eg, J Bentham (JH Burns and HLA Hart (eds)), *An Introduction to the Principles of Morals and Legislation* (London, Athlone Press, 1970) at 211; Penner (n 4) at 1–2; W Swadling, 'Unjust Delivery' in A Burrows and A Rodger (eds), *Mapping the Law: Essays in Memory of Peter Birks* (Oxford, Oxford University Press, 2006) at 279–80; J Tarrant, 'Property Rights to Stolen Money' (2005) 32 *University of Western Australia Law Review* 234 at 236.

[143] Kohler and Palmer, Information (*Interests in Goods* 1998) at 3–4, and see Law Commission 'Breach of Confidence' (Law Com No 110 Cmnd 8388, 1981).

[144] ibid, *passim* but particularly at 3 and 20. See also Bridge, Property (n 12) at 5.

[145] There has in the past been some conceptual confusion over this issue, with digitized products being regarded as synonymous with information. The argument that there is no practical basis for this equation, and that the two are undoubtedly distinct, is presented in detail in Green, Digitized Product (*LMCLQ* 2006) at 573–76.

information can of course exist if the individual in possession of it chooses not to relay it, but something lacking transferability in this way can hardly be regarded as property. As Latham CJ pointed out in the High Court of Australia:

> Knowledge is valuable, but knowledge is neither real nor personal property. A man with a richly stored mind is not for that reason a man of property ... It is only in a loose metaphorical sense that any knowledge as such can be said to be property. Either all knowledge is property, so that the teaching of, for example, mathematics, involves a transfer of property, or only some knowledge is property. If only some knowledge is property then it must be possible to state a criterion which will distinguish between that knowledge which is property and that knowledge which is not property. The only criterion which has been suggested is the secrecy of the knowledge—it is said that the fact that knowledge is secret in some way creates a proprietary right in that knowledge. I confess myself completely unable to appreciate this proposition as a legal statement. It is obvious that a monopoly of knowledge may be valuable, whether it be knowledge of a place where a person has discovered gold or knowledge of a method or process of making a machine or a chemical product, or of a means of deciphering cryptograms. But is such property knowledge only so long as it is secret? Does it cease to be property when it is communicated to one other person or to two other persons or to two hundred other persons? The value of secret knowledge as such depends upon the ability to keep it secret and to use it and the possibility of persuading other people to pay for being let into the secret. These facts, however, do not show that the knowledge is property in any legal sense.[146]

This passage addresses a major problem presented by the nature, and commercial use of, information. In most cases, the value of information lies in its confidential nature so that, once such confidentiality has been lost, the information itself loses its value. This means that, although the rightful possessor of such information might well still be in possession of it following its dissemination, its value will be negated. It is by no means obvious, therefore, that Conversion, as a possessory remedy, would be of any real benefit to a party whose information has been devalued in this way.[147]

ii. Exhaustibility

Furthermore, information differs from the other types of asset described above in that it is not exhaustible, which is really a corollary of its lack of moveability and lack of excludability. Since pure information is an asset which cannot be moved, and from which previous owners cannot be excluded, it cannot be extinguished as against anyone who has ever possessed it. Therefore, since the essence of Conversion lies in a dispossessor's ability to appropriate an asset and to prevent the dispossessed party from having access to it, it is not easy to see how pure

---

[146]   *Federal Commissioner of Taxation v United Aircraft Corporation* [1943] HCA 50, 68 CLR 525 at 535.

[147]   See Kohler and Palmer (n 138) at 11.

information could ever be susceptible to such behaviour.[148] If information could be converted, for instance, would that mean that the defendant would be liable anew for each day on which he continued mentally to retain it?[149] It would seem, then, that information, despite potentially being a highly valuable asset, is not an appropriate subject either of property rights or of legal possession, and that it cannot, therefore, be converted.[150] Given the existence of the specific action of breach of confidence in English law,[151] this is not too troubling a conclusion to reach, since the valuable characteristics of information can most appropriately be protected by means other than the wrongful interference torts.

The Law of Theft

It is remarkable, given the approach of the civil branch of the common law to the protection of interests in non-traditional and intangible property, that the criminal law has, for the last four decades, adopted a far more expansive attitude to the protection of the same. There would be little merit in arguing for the civil and criminal law approaches to interferences with property to match, not least because of the different underlying objectives of each branch of the law; after all, the 'refusal to equate conversion in crime and tort is right and inevitable'.[152] Nevertheless, whilst equation would undoubtedly be a step too far, there are elements of the offence of theft which could usefully be employed by the tort of Conversion. The Theft Act 1968 is an interesting statute in this respect, since it marks the emergence of an energised law of theft, explicitly adapted in several ways for the economic realities of the day.

Its form is based on the Eighth Report of the Criminal Law Revision Committee, entitled *Theft and Related Offences*.[153] This report, the main objective of which was to reform the criminal law's response to dishonest appropriation, was the genesis of the offence of theft as we know it today, which subsumed the common law offences that had existed previously. It clearly sets out the reasons of the Committee for so doing. In terms of relevance to the current discussion,

---

[148]   See under the heading The Law of Theft, below, for the criminal law's treatment of property.

[149]   Kohler and Palmer (n 138) at 20.

[150]   Although see Cane (n 7) at 25 for the argument that confidential information could 'be treated as property for the purpose of the law of tort' and the US case of *Benaquista v Hardesty and Associates* 20 Pa D & C 2d 227 (1959), wherein it was held that an idea which has 'taken definite form in the mind of its creator' (at 229) can be converted.

[151]   For more on which see, inter alia, H Carty, 'An analysis of the modern action for breach of commercial confidence: when is protection merited?' (2008) 4 *Intellectual Property Quarterly* 416; M Conaglen, 'Thinking about proprietary remedies for breach of confidence' (2008) 1 *Intellectual Property Quarterly* 82; R Flannigan, 'The (fiduciary) duty of fidelity' (2008) 124 *LQR* 274; and J O'Sullivan, 'Intentional Economic Torts in the House of Lords' [2007] *CLJ* 503.

[152]   Griew, *Theft* (1995) at para 2–61.

[153]   The 8th Report (Theft and Related Offences) of the Criminal Law Revision Committee (1966), Cmnd 2977.

paragraph 33 is particularly illuminating. In referring to the previous offences, to be replaced by the single offence of theft, the Committee stated

> the important element of them all is undoubtedly the dishonest appropriation of another person's property—the treating of 'teum' as 'meum'; and we think it not only logical, but right in principle, to make this the central element of the offence.[154]

This explains why choses in action are, by virtue of section 4(1) of the 1968 Act, *expressly* included within the category of personal property which can be the subject of a theft: '"Property" includes money and all other property, real or personal, including things in action and other intangible property'.

This explicit inclusion of intangibles sets theft apart from the old offence of larceny, which applied only to those assets which could be physically carried away. Essentially, this limited the scope of larceny to tangible assets, and the Committee clearly did not want such a limitation to survive the transition of the offence into the updated crime of theft. One of the limitations which did survive, however, was that, in order to commit theft, a defendant must be shown to have stolen some particular piece of property; that is, 'something which can be the subject of "possession or control" or of a "proprietary right or interest"'.[155] This limitation requires, in effect, the subject matter of theft to exhibit those indicia of possession identified above as determinative of which assets can be converted. The justification for the requirement is the same in both cases: there needs to be exclusive possession or control in the first place, or there is no pre-existing right with which the defendant can interfere. The most significant exclusion from those things which can be the subject of theft is information. In *Oxford v Moss*,[156] a case in which a student took an exam paper, and read its contents before returning it, the court held that confidential information is not property capable of being stolen and that, since the student had returned the tangible paper itself, there had been no theft.[157] This is consistent with the conclusions reached above about the Conversion of information. Whilst the problem in criminal law is expressed as being that the defendant is unable permanently to deprive his victim of the information, the problem for the civil law action is that information lacks the quality of excludability which would render it susceptible to Conversion.

---

[154] ibid at para 33.
[155] Griew (n 97) at para 2–26.
[156] (1979) 68 Cr App R 183.
[157] But see Weinrib, Information (*UTLJ* 1988) for a discussion of two conflicting Canadian cases, *R v Stewart* (1983) 149 DLR (3d) 583 (Ont CA) (in which it was found that property could be the subject of a theft) and *R v Offley* (1986) 45 Alta LR (2d) 23 (Alta CA) (in which the opposite conclusion was reached). Weinrib's article argues in support of the former approach.

The Importance of Effective Protection of Property Interests

The first reason why the tort of Conversion should cover digitized material and appropriate types of intangible property is that the law should be consistent in its treatment of property interests, and that it is arbitrary to distinguish, as the law currently does, between legally identical rights on the basis of the physical characteristics of their subject matter. This is something which has already been recognised elsewhere in the common law world, and it is difficult to see why the English common law is apparently so reluctant to ensure that its approach is correspondingly responsive to social, technological and economic progress.

The second reason is perhaps of greater practical significance. If personal property interests in certain assets are not effectively protected, those assets will not function as live and productive economic commodities. In the view of one commentator, for instance

> where the commercial value of an entity, whether tangible or intangible, has been brought about by the expenditure of time, effort, labour or money, the person who created that commercial value has a proprietary right to its commercial exploitation.[158]

In order for assets to be both produced and employed in the most productive way possible, property interests in them must receive the full recognition and protection of the law.[159]

This idea has recently received empirical support from the work of the economist, Hernando de Soto.[160] The principal conclusion of his work was that western nations owe their vastly superior ability to generate wealth to their formal legal systems of property. In contrast, although developing nations are not poor in terms of their resources, their inability to exploit them to anything like their maximum potential, and so more effectively to compete with 'First World' economies, is due to their lack of such open and comprehensive property systems.

---

[158] D Libling, 'The Concept of Property: Property in Intangibles' (1978) 94 *LQR* 103 at 119, as cited in Cane (n 7) at 24.

[159] See also A Ogus, *Costs and Cautionary Tales: Economic Insights for the Law* (Oxford, Hart Publishing, 2006) ch 2; H Demsetz, 'Towards a Theory of Property Rights' (1967) 57 *American Economic Review (Papers and Proceedings)* 347; L Anderson and PJ Hill, 'The Evolution of Property Rights: A Study of the American West' (1975) 18 *Journal of Law and Economics* 163.

[160] de Soto *Capital* (2000) at 49.

6

Conversion and the Economic Torts

The Need to Examine their Relationship

THERE IS A closer relationship between Conversion and the economic torts than is always appreciated. It is a product of the respective roles they play in affording legal protection to proprietary and economic interests. Little attention has until recently been paid, however, to how they relate to one another.[1] In order to ascertain how the law of tort affords such protection, whether it does so with logic and consistency, and what developments may be required to improve it, an exploration and explanation of this relationship is necessary. To that end, we must start by establishing its juridical background.

Background—The Framework of Tortious Liability

The search for 'general principles of liability' based on types of conduct is at best a waste of time, and at worst a potential source of serious confusion; and the broader the principle, the more is this so. Tort law is a complex interaction between protected interests, sanctioned conduct, and sanctions; and although there are what might be called 'principles of tort liability', by and large, they are not very 'general'. More importantly, they cannot be stated solely in terms of the sorts of conduct which will attract tort liability. Each principle must refer, as well, to some interest protected by tort law and some sanction provided by tort law.[2]

---

[1] Some recent comment has touched on this, provoked by the juxtaposition of claims in Conversion and economic tort in *OBG Ltd and anor v Allan and ors* [2005] EWCA Civ 106, [2005] QB 762, and (with two other cases) [2007] UKHL 21, [2008] 1 AC 1. See, eg, H Carty, 'The Need for Clarity in the Economic Torts' (2005) 16 *King's College Law Journal* 165 (commenting on the Court of Appeal judgments) and J O'Sullivan, 'Intentional Economic Torts in the House of Lords' [2007] *CLJ* 503, P Watts, 'Self-appointed agents—liability in tort' (2007) 123 *Law Quarterly Review* 519, and S Douglas, 'Converting Contractual Rights' [2008] *Lloyd's Maritime and Commercial Law Quarterly* 129 (commenting on the speeches in the House of Lords).

[2] P Cane, 'Mens Rea in Tort Law' (2000) 20 *Oxford Journal of Legal Studies* 533 at 552, a passage endorsed by Lord Hoffmann in *OBG Ltd v Allan* [2007] UKHL 21, [2008] 1 AC 1 at [32].

Many if not all of the torts which exist in English law serve to protect legally recognised interests.[3] The gist of such torts is the infringement of the claimant's relevant interest. Lord Scott has recently said that:

> The [main] function of the civil law of tort ... is to identify and protect the rights that every person is entitled to assert against, and require to be respected by, others.[4]

One important category of rights which the law of tort, and in particular the torts of trespass and Conversion, protects, is proprietary rights.[5] The gist of such torts is the infringement of the proprietary right in question. Whether and on what basis the ambit of Conversion should be extended so as to protect such rights in respect of appropriate types of intangible property, including in particular contractual rights, is a matter which we have already considered in chapter five.[6] However the economic torts, and most particularly the *Lumley v Gye* tort of inducing or procuring breach of contract, have a role in the protection of contractual rights, whether or not Conversion is, or should be, also available.

There is a broad hierarchy of the interests protected by the law of tort. The first and most important such interest is that of bodily integrity, with which may be grouped other interests in an individual's person. As Hale LJ has put it:

> The right to bodily integrity is the first and most important of the interests protected by the law of tort ... Included within that right are two others. One is the right to physical autonomy: to make one's own choices about what will happen to one's own body. Another is the right not to be subjected to bodily injury or harm. These interests are regarded as so important that redress is given against both intentional and negligent interference with them. In contrast, economic interests come very much lower in the list, and for obvious reasons:
>
> 'in a competitive economic society the conduct of one person is always liable to have economic consequences for another and, in principle, economic activity does not have to have regard to the interests of others and is justifiable by the actor having regard to his own interests alone': see *Perrett v Collins* [1998] 2 Lloyd's Rep 255, 260.
>
> The object of much commercial activity is deliberately to harm the economic interests of competitors: only in very special situations, therefore, does the law recognise a liability to compensate those whose economic interests have been damaged.[7]

---

[3] The scope of this work neither requires nor allows a diversion into the murky waters of the continuing debate as to whether all torts are properly or best understood as 'interest torts', whether the gist of some torts should be understood as the defendant's conduct rather than the infringement of the claimant's interest and/or the claimant's resultant loss, and so forth. A thought provoking starting point for enquiry into the same is afforded by Robert Stevens' recent work *Torts and Rights* (Oxford, Oxford University Press, 2007).

[4] *Ashley v Chief Constable of Sussex Police* [2008] UKHL 25 [2008] 1 AC 962 at [18].

[5] See, eg, *Clerk & Lindsell on Torts*, 19th edn (London, Sweet & Maxwell, 2006) at paras 1–20 and 1–32 to 1–35.

[6] See ch 5 under the heading Intangible Property.

[7] *Parkinson v St James and Seacroft University Hospital NHS Trust* [2001] EWCA Civ 530, [2002] QB 266 at [56].

The second category in the broad hierarchy is property interests. As Weir has argued, 'if anything can be discovered which can be called "property" or a "right", even if it is not a thing in fact or a right in general law, it tends to be more strongly protected'.[8] The law of tort protects interests in the possession of property, including—as we have seen in the context of Conversion[9]—the immediate right to possession, and interests in its enjoyment,[10] as well as its physical integrity.[11]

Lower down come non-proprietary general economic interests. The law will protect a claimant from interference with the same where the defendant has in one way or another assumed an obligation or responsibility for protecting the claimant's economic interests or expectations.[12] Otherwise it generally limits the imposition of liability to cases founded on conduct which is regarded as highly reprehensible, such as deceit or the intentional infliction of harm, or against which the law regards a higher level of protection as necessary, such as conspiracy. The amorphous nature of non-proprietary general economic interests[13] may be regarded as explaining, and perhaps justifying, a comparatively restrictive approach to the imposition of tortious liability for interference with the same.

The means by which the law recognises the relative importance of the interest being protected include the applicability (or otherwise) of strict liability or any mental element, and of actionability without loss, and the recoverability (or not) of purely economic loss. Rix LJ has commented, in the context of the *Lumley v Gye* tort, on the desirability of some flexibility in their application:

> For these purposes [the balancing demands of moral constraint and economic freedom] the concepts of knowledge and intention, direct participation, the causative relevance of unlawful means, and the possibilities of justification, are presumably sufficiently flexible to enable the principles of the tort to produce the right result. Where in specific areas policy makes its own specific demands, statute law is present to lend a hand.[14]

Inevitably, there are tensions at the boundaries between various categories of protected interest, and questions as to exactly where those boundaries lie, and which interests should attract the more stringent forms of protection. For example, should C be entitled to recover in tort against D for economic loss it has

---

[8]   T Weir, *A Casebook on Tort*, 10th edn (London, Sweet & Maxwell, 2004) at 572.

[9]   See ch 4 under the heading Relativity of Title.

[10]   See under the side-heading Property Torts, Nuisance, below.

[11]   See under the side-heading Property Torts, Trespass to Goods, below.

[12]   See, eg, *Hedley Byrne & Co Ltd v Heller & Partners Ltd* [1964] AC 465 (providing a credit reference to the claimant), *White and anor v Jones and anor* [1995] 2 AC 207 (agreeing to prepare a will under which the claimant was to benefit), and *Spring v Guardian Assurance plc and ors* [1995] 2 AC 296 (providing an industry required reference about a former agent/employee).

[13]   For example, the so-called 'right to trade', as to which see SF Deakin and JY Randall, 'Rethinking the Economic Torts', (2009) 72 *Modern Law Review* 519 under the side-heading The rationale of the economic torts (528 ff, especially at 529).

[14]   *Stocznia Gdanska SA v Latvian Shipping Co, Latreefer Inc and ors* [2002] EWCA Civ 889, [2002] 2 Lloyd's Rep 436 at [131].

suffered by reason of some impact on C's contract with A which was caused by D having physically damaged A's tangible asset? Elements from both higher and lower parts of the hierarchy are present in such a case. We discuss below the rationale of the cases by which the common law has said no.[15]

Another controversial area is where D has in some way interfered with C's contract with A, so as to cause C loss. C's contractual rights may be regarded as a 'species of property which deserve special protection'.[16] However to what extent should C's claim be categorised as proprietary, and her contractual rights be afforded the same level of protection as her tangible property? It is generally—though not universally[17]—accepted that C should at least have a cause of action under the tort widely known by the name of the leading case *Lumley v Gye*,[18] if the interference has taken the form of procuring or inducing A to break his contract, and C can demonstrate that D actually, subjectively appreciated and intended that a breach of contract be brought about.[19] However should that be C's only recourse, even in cases where D's conduct has deprived her of the whole value of her rights? Why should the protection afforded to C's interests in her intangible property by the law of tort be so much more restricted than that afforded to her interests in her tangible property?

The Place of Contractual Rights and Other Intangible Property

It is, we suggest, clearly appropriate that the common law should afford proper protection to intangible as well as tangible property. We have discussed the reasons why this is so in chapter five, in the context of Conversion.[20] In essence, it reflects the commercial realities of the twenty-first century. As Honoré puts it, the distinction between corporeals and incorporeals is 'so unimportant that we ought always to speak of owning rights over material objects, never of owning the objects themselves'.[21] 'Possessions', in respect of which Article 1 of the First Protocol to the European Convention on Human Rights and Fundamental Freedoms affords protection, may include intangibles, such as choses in action and other rights and interests which constitute assets, and the mere fact (where it

---

[15]   See under the side-heading Comparison of *Lumley v Gye* and Conversion, The Right to Claim, below.

[16]   Lord Hoffmann in *OBG Ltd v Allan* [2007] UKHL 21, [2008] 1 AC 1 at [32].

[17]   See, eg, D Howarth, 'Against Lumley v Gye' (2005) 68 *MLR* 195, and R Cunnington, 'Contract Rights as Property Rights' in A Robertson (ed), *The Law of Obligations: Connections and Boundaries* (London, UCL Press, 2004) at 172–75.

[18]   (1853) 2 E & B 216, 118 ER 749.

[19]   *OBG Ltd v Allan* [2007] UKHL 21, [2008] 1 AC 1, especially at [39]–[44] per Lord Hoffmann and [168]–[172] and [191]–[192] per Lord Nicholls.

[20]   See ch 5 under the heading Intangible Property.

[21]   T Honoré, 'Ownership' in AG Guest (ed), *Oxford Essays in Jurisprudence* (Oxford, Oxford University Press, 1961), at 131.

is so) that such rights are contractual does not disqualify them from counting as property or possessions.[22] The distinction between corporeal and incorporeal property is not decisive for the purposes of the meaning of 'possessions' in Article 1. As Lord Nicholls said in *Wilson v First County Trust (No 2)*: 'Possessions' in article 1 is apt to embrace contractual rights as much as personal rights. Contractual rights may be more valuable and enduring than proprietary rights.[23]

Examples of intangible rights which have been treated as possessions for the purposes of Article 1 include shares in a limited company,[24] 'economic interests connected with the running of [a business]',[25] the right to payment under a final and binding arbitration award,[26] the contractual entitlement of Danish GPs under a collective agreement to indexation of their remuneration,[27] and a right to compensation in tort.[28] This list accords with our views, outlined in chapter five, as to what counts, or should count, as possession for contemporary legal purposes, since each item on it has the requisite indicia of possession.[29]

Accordingly, Carnwath LJ's instincts when first confronted by the facts of *OBG Ltd v Allan*—where complete control over a mixture of real property and tangible and intangible assets had been taken in one fell swoop by (purported) administrative receivers, acting without any true legal authority—were entirely appropriate:

> My initial instinct at the beginning of the case was that the receivers should be strictly liable for all the consequences of their unlawful appropriation of the business, by analogy with the long-established principles applied to unlawful receiverships under the law of trespass and conversion ... The Canadian cases ... seemed to point in that direction.[30]

---

[22] *Murungaru v Secretary of State for the Home Department* [2008] EWCA Civ 1015, [2009] INLR 180 at [29]–[30] per Sedley LJ, [42] per Jacob LJ and [43]–[58] per Lewison J, citing *Gasus Dosier v Netherlands* (1995) 20 EHRR 403 (E Ct HR), at [53]: 'The Court recalls that the notion "possessions" (in French: biens) in Article 1 of Protocol No. 1 has an autonomous meaning which is certainly not limited to ownership of physical goods: certain other rights and interests constituting assets can also be regarded as "property rights" and thus as "possessions" for the purposes of this provision.'

[23] [2003] UKHL 40, [2004] 1 AC 816 at [39]. Cunnington, Contract Rights (*Obligations* 2004) offers a critical discussion of some of the issues raised by the treatment of contractual rights as property.

[24] *Bramelid and Malmström v Sweden* (1982) 5 EHRR 249 (E Comm HR).

[25] *Tre Traktorer Aktiebolag v Sweden* (1989) 13 EHRR 309 (E Ct HR), at [53].

[26] *Stran Greek Refineries and Stratis Andreadis v Greece* (1994) 19 EHRR 293 (E Ct HR), at [58]–[62]. In consequence, a law passed to declare void the arbitration agreement and annul the award was a contravention of article 1 of the First Protocol, there being no legitimate public interest to justify the intervention of parliament. 'Just satisfaction' in the amount of the award plus interest was ordered.

[27] *Association of General Practitioners v Denmark* (1989) 62 DR 226 (E Comm HR).

[28] *Pressos Compania Naviera SA v Belgium* (1995) 21 EHRR 301 (E Ct HR), at [29]–[32].

[29] See ch 5 generally, but particularly under the side-heading Intangible Property, Manual Indicia.

[30] [2005] EWCA Civ 106, [2005] QB 762 at [115].

The practical common sense of the approach in the Canadian unlawful receivership cases to which Carnwath LJ referred,[31] which drew no distinction between the tangible and intangible assets seized by unlawfully appointed 'receivers', is nonetheless such despite the fact that the many judges involved in those cases found it unnecessary to give separate consideration to the real assets, the other corporeal assets and the incorporeal assets over which the respective (purported) receivers had asserted dominion.[32] The issues of categorisation between tangibles and intangibles, or choses in possession and choses in action, should not be allowed to become an obstacle to the incremental development of the common law—cases should decide labels, not vice versa.

Principle and policy also point in the same direction. The public interest in the promotion of competitive economic activity does not generally outweigh the principle *pacta sunt servanda* which underpins the law of contract;[33] on the contrary, the latter principle is accepted as an essential foundation to a functioning market economy. As Epstein has put it:

> contracts move resources to more valued uses, so that both parties to the agreement are better off under the agreement than without it. Duress, misrepresentation and undue influence become relevant to identify those conditions in which the general proposition may not hold because one party has been prevented by the other from soundly assessing the desirability of his agreement.[34]

A contractual right is fundamentally different from, and merits substantially greater protection than, a general economic interest such as the expectation of future trade (which was all the claimants had to protect in the classic economic torts cases of *Mogul Steamship Co Ltd v McGregor, Gow & Co and others*[35] and *Quinn v Leathem*[36]). The victim of an unauthorised interference with his contractual rights should not be 'forced' by the law to 'waive the tort' and adopt the

---

[31]   *Kavcar Investments v Aetna Financial Services* (1989) 62 DLR (4th) 277 (Ont CA), affirming (1986) 36 ACWS (2d) 330, Hollingworth J; *McLachlan v Canadian Imperial Bank of Commerce* (1989) 35 BCLR 100, 57 DLR (4th) 687 (BCCA), affirming (1987) 13 BCLR (2d) 300, Gould J; *Bradshaw Construction v Bank of Nova Scotia* [1993] 1 WWR 596 (BCCA), especially [58] and [88]–[90]; *Royal Bank v Got* [1999] 3 SCR 408 (Sup Ct Can), affirming (1997) 196 AR 241 (Alta CA), affirming (1994) 17 Alta LR (3d) 23, McDonald J. See also *Lister v Dunlop Canada Ltd* [liability] [1982] 1 SCR 726 (Sup Ct Can), reversing (1979) 27 OR 2d 168 (Ont CA) and restoring (1978) 19 OR (2d) 380, Rutherford J; [damages] *sub nomine Lister v Dayton Tire Canada Ltd* (1985) 52 OR (2d) 88 (Ont CA).

[32]   As did the Privy Council in *Gulf Insurance Ltd v Central Bank of Trinidad and Tobago* [2005] UKPC 10, 66 WIR 297 (an appeal from the Court of Appeal of Trinidad and Tobago, concerning the unlawful taking of the assets and undertaking of a Bank): see at [50], [53] and [54].

[33]   The common law doctrine of unreasonable restraint of trade limits the application of the principle to its logical extreme, but does not call the principle itself into question.

[34]   R Epstein, 'A Common Law for Labor Relations: a Critique of New Deal Labor Legislation' (1983) 92 *Yale LJ* 1357 at 1381.

[35]   (1889) 23 QBD 598 (CA), [1892] AC 25 (no liability).

[36]   [1901] AC 495 (liability found, distinguishing *Allen v Flood and anor* [1898] AC 1, only because of the element of unjustified conspiracy, coupled with an intention to injure). See also Cunnington (n 17) for a discussion of what sorts of protection the law should afford to contractual rights.

interferer as his agent, thereby limiting his rights of redress to breach of duty remedies, such as negligence or its equitable equivalents.[37]

Peter Cane, in his book *Tort Law and Economic Interests*, says in relation to the general considerations applicable to the law's treatment of intangible property:

> Once we move away from the paradigms of property—land, chattels—to deal with intangible property, we enter the area of what we might call 'property in a metaphorical sense'. The metaphor resides, first, in the obvious fact that intangible property does not possess all the characteristics of the paradigms of property; it cannot, for example, be physically possessed or occupied. But the metaphor extends further than this in two directions. First, in relation to any particular intangible asset, it is possible to ask whether the law does, or ought to, treat it as property; or, in other words, as capable of being the subject of proprietary rights and interests. Secondly, if the law does treat a particular intangible asset as property, it does not automatically follow that the asset will have all the legal characteristics of the paradigms of property: the law may accord to it some, but not other, protections which attach to the paradigms of property. Of course, the fact that a particular intangible asset does not enjoy the legal status of property or does not receive the full protection accorded to the paradigms of property does not mean that, pro tanto, it is without legal protection. Property is only one of the concepts which the law uses as a basis for legal protection of intangible (and tangible) assets; others are contract and wrongful infliction of economic loss. One of the merits of saying that intangible assets are property in only a metaphorical sense is that it emphasizes the choice involved in deciding to accord legal protection to an intangible asset by classifying it as property.[38]

Thus, on Cane's approach, it is a matter of legal policy whether non-paradigm (that is incorporeal) property receives like legal protection to paradigm (that is corporeal) property, and if not to what extent such protection should differ. As we will see, a decade or so later, the alternative bases for protection which Cane identified were scaled back by the House of Lords in *OBG Ltd v Allan*, leaving a choice starker than that which would have appeared available at the time he wrote. In that context, a short review of the legal protection currently afforded by the relevant property torts and the economic torts is called for.

Property Torts

Trespass to Goods

As we saw in chapter two, the action for trespass is of ancient origin, though in its early days it required a plea of *vi et armis* to enable it to be brought in the royal courts. Though the ancient name trespass *de bonis asportatis* speaks of a physical

---

[37] A point explored by Mance LJ in his dissenting judgment in *OBG Ltd v Allan* in the Court of Appeal [2005] EWCA Civ 106, [2005] QB 762 at [95].
[38] 2nd edn (Oxford, Oxford University Press, 1996) at 59.

carrying away of the subject goods, trespass to goods extends beyond that to encompass not only physical damage to the fabric of the goods, but also a mere unauthorised touching thereof. The common element is direct, physical interference,[39] almost however minor,[40] by a deliberate (in the sense of non-accidental) act committed without express or implied authority, and whether or not any damage is caused.[41] Given that the interference must be physical and direct, this is not a promising cause of action for the protection of incorporeal property.

Conversion

The elements of Conversion have already been reviewed in detail in chapters three to five, and the remedies available will be considered in chapter seven. It is therefore sufficient, for present purposes, to note that in Conversion liability is, for all practical purposes, strict,[42] that remedies may—depending on the circumstances—be obtained against subsequent holders of the converted asset, and not just the initial dispossessor (both common features of torts protecting property interests), and that the measure of damages commonly available is by reference to the value of the asset converted, rather than the loss suffered by the particular claimant (again, something consistent with the protection of property interests).

Nuisance

Whilst nuisance is in one sense of little relevance, in that its essence is 'a tort to land. Or to be more accurate . . . a tort directed against the plaintiff's enjoyment of rights over land',[43] its ambit is noteworthy in the present context for it protects against the disturbance of a claimant not only in his exercise or enjoyment of his ownership or occupation of land itself, but also in his exercise or enjoyment of an incorporeal hereditament such as an easement or profit à prendre.[44] To qualify for protection under the law of nuisance, that incorporeal right must be one used

---

[39]   Contrast, eg, locking a room in which the claimant has his goods, which is not a trespass to them: *Hartley v Moxham* (1842) 3 QB 701, 114 ER 675.

[40]   See *Clerk & Lindsell on Torts* (2006) at para 17–123; note also the dicta in *Bushel v Miller* (1718) 1 Str 128, 93 ER 428, CHS Fifoot, *History & Sources of the Common Law* (London, Stevens & Sons, 1949) at 121, discussed in ch 3, text to fns 93–94, indicating that a minor touching which clearly did not suffice for Conversion was nevertheless arguably sufficient to constitute a trespass.

[41]   This was the view expressed in the 18th Report (Conversion and Detinue) of the Law Reform Committee (1971), Cmnd 4774 at para 17, and is described as 'the better position' in Clerk & Lindsell (n 5) at para 17–123, citing (in fn 55) Salmond & Heuston, Street and Winfield & Jolowicz. It is consistent with the well-established position in trespass to land.

[42]   *MCC Proceeds Inc v Lehman Bros International (Europe)* [1998] 4 All ER 675 (CA), at 685j per Mummery LJ.

[43]   FH Newark, 'The Boundaries of Nuisance' (1949) 65 *LQR* 480 at 482, cited with approval by Lord Goff in *Hunter and ors v Canary Wharf Ltd* [1997] AC 655 at 687G–H.

[44]   See, eg, Clerk & Lindsell (n 5) at paras 20–01 and 20–49.

or enjoyed in connection with land—hence the oxymoron 'incorporeal hereditament'. Accordingly nuisance affords an example of a tort protecting both the corporeal and incorporeal species of the same basic category of property, real property.

Kennaway v Thompson and another illustrates the former. The claimant's use and enjoyment of her house and garden was grossly interfered with by increasingly noisy and increasingly frequent racing of motor boats by the Cotswold Motor Boat Racing Club on immediately adjacent water, which, the trial judge held, 'at times is quite intolerable and wholly unreasonable'.[45] The representatives of the club were held liable in nuisance, and the Court of Appeal granted an injunction against them.

An example of the latter is afforded by *Fitzgerald v Firbank*,[46] where the claimants (the representatives of a 40-member angling association known as the True Waltonian Society) had been granted by Lord Ebury 'the exclusive right of fishing in [a specified] part of the River Colne' which 'only extend[ed] to fair rod and line angling at proper seasons, and to netting for the sole purpose of procuring fish-baits' for a 15-year term. This right was held to be a profit à prendre, and hence a species of incorporeal hereditament.[47] The defendant railway contractor, which had been working certain gravel-pits, pumped out quantities of water loaded with mud into the Chess, a tributary of the Colne. This dirty water passed along a great part of the Colne over which the claimants' right was enjoyed, with the effects of making the water too opaque for the fish to see the bait, driving away the fish, and damaging the spawning-beds. Though Lindley LJ was unaware of any precedent arising from a right of fishing, he held that the claimants had 'an action on the case for nuisance at common law for such an interference with his right as is proved in this case'.[48]

We have discussed the parallels between Conversion and nuisance in chapter three,[49] and detect no good reason why Conversion should not be similarly developed so as to protect both the corporeal and incorporeal species of personal property.

Economic Torts

Following the fundamental reconsideration of the economic torts by the House of Lords in *OBG Ltd v Allan*, there are now two principal economic torts, and

---

[45] [1981] QB 88 (CA) at 91G-H quoting Mais J.
[46] [1897] 2 Ch 96 (CA).
[47] Per Lindley LJ at 101; see also per Lopes LJ at 102.
[48] Per Lindley LJ at 102; see also per Rigby LJ at 104.
[49] Under the heading Conversion in the Context of the Property Torts.

probably still a separate tort of intimidation (*Rookes v Barnard and others*[50]), together with those involving an element of conspiracy.

Lumley v Gye—Procuring or Inducing a Breach of Contract

> Lumley v Gye [was 'founded on a different principle of liability than the intentional harm tort'. It] treats contractual rights as a species of property which deserve special protection, not only by giving a right of action against the party who breaks his contract but by imposing secondary liability on a person who procures him to do so.[51]

The gist of this interest based tort is the breach of the claimant's contractual rights. Though it is almost universally treated as one of the 'economic torts', unlike the others it directly performs a role in protecting contractual rights. As Rix LJ has put it, its 'philosophical basis appears to be that contracts should be kept rather than broken'.[52] Nevertheless, its requirement for an actual, subjective appreciation and intention on the defendant's part that a breach of contract be brought about introduces a distinct fault element to liability unlike anything seen in the property torts.

It is important in the present context to note that another tort, that of interference with contractual relations, has now been suppressed as heretical. This was not a tort invented and deployed only by the 'usual suspect', Lord Denning.[53] Those who also participated in its development included Lords Macnaghten,[54] Jenkins,[55] Diplock,[56] Griffiths,[57] and Donaldson.[58] The willingness of these, among other, distinguished judges to find tortious liability for interferences with the contractual rights of others which did not bring about any breach of contract, surely evidences a widespread judicial recognition that such

---

[50] [1964] AC 1129. See Deakin and Randall, Rethinking (*MLR* 2009) under the side-heading Interferences, The interference should not have to be independently actionable (544 ff).

[51] Per Lord Hoffmann in *OBG Ltd v Allan* [2007] UKHL 21, [2008] 1 AC 1 at [32].

[52] *Stocznia v Latco* [2002] EWCA Civ 889, [2002] 2 Lloyd's Rep 436 at [130]. Consistently with this underlying philosophy, it is not tortious to induce a breach of a contract which is voidable at the instance of the party so procured. In *Proform Sports Management v Proactive Sports Management* [2007] 1 All ER 542 an agency contract made with the footballer Wayne Rooney when aged just 15 was held not to fall within the class of minors' contracts which are analogous to contracts of apprenticeship, education and service, and therefore to be voidable at his instance (see judgment of HHJ Hodge QC at [36]–[41]). There could therefore be no liability for inducing Rooney to break it, as he enjoyed the legal right to avoid it in any event (ibid at [33]).

[53] Most notably, in *Torquay Hotel Co Ltd v Cousins and ors* [1969] 2 Ch 106, especially at 138D–E.

[54] In *Quinn v Leathem* [1901] AC 495 at 510, a 'well-known passage' nevertheless dismissed by Lord Hoffmann in *OBG Ltd v Allan* [2007] UKHL 21, [2008] 1 AC 1 at [16] as 'capable of giving rise to confusion'.

[55] As Jenkins LJ in *DC Thomson Co Ltd v Deakin and ors* [1952] Ch 646, especially at 693 and 695.

[56] In *Merkur Island Shipping Corporation v Laughton and ors* [1983] 2 AC 570, especially at 606H–608F.

[57] As Griffiths LJ in *Dimbleby & Sons Ltd v National Union of Journalists* [1984] 1 WLR 67 (CA) at 73D–E and 74D–E (decision affirmed at 427 ibid (HL)).

[58] As Sir John Donaldson MR ibid at 78B–G.

rights are important, and do merit greater legal protection than that afforded to lesser interests such as general economic interests.

Causing Loss by Unlawful Means

Whilst the gist of this tort may be said to be the loss suffered by the claimant, the essential requirements for liability are wrongful interference with the actions of a third party in which the claimant has an economic interest, coupled with an actual, subjective intention on the defendant's part that loss be thereby caused to the claimant.[59] Controversially, the acts against the third party only count as 'unlawful means' if they are independently actionable by that third party (or would have been so had loss resulted).[60] However liability does not depend on the existence of contractual relations between the claimant and the third party.[61] Thus in substance, this tort appears to be conduct based, although there is much force in Neyers' recent conclusion that this tort 'is radically under-theorised and … could benefit tremendously from more intense examination'.[62]

Lawful and Unlawful Means Conspiracies

An unlawful means conspiracy comprises combination in the course of which unlawful means are used, causing loss to the claimant. In common with the tort of causing loss by unlawful means, it requires an intention to cause that loss.[63] However, in contrast with that tort, the House of Lords has recently decided in *Revenue and Customs Commissioners v Total Network SL*[64] that the unlawful means do *not* have to satisfy the controversial independent actionability requirement mentioned above, rejecting, in the process, the idea that unlawful means conspiracy was an instance of accessorial liability. According to Lord Mance, this tort, and the tort of causing loss by unlawful means, are 'different in their nature', so that 'the requirements of justice may require their development on somewhat different bases'.[65] Whilst its ambit includes combinations which cause damage to

---

[59] *OBG Ltd v Allan* [2007] UKHL 21, [2008] 1 AC 1 per Lord Hoffmann at [47].

[60] ibid at [49]. Baroness Hale and Lord Brown agreed (at [302]–[303] and [319]–[320] respectively), Lord Nicholls dissented (at [149]–[162]) and Lord Walker suggested that 'neither [view] is likely to be the last word on this difficult and important area of the law' (at [269]). Contrast the position subsequently established by the House of Lords in respect of cases of unlawful means conspiracy, for which see text to nn 64–66.

[61] ibid, at [8].

[62] JW Neyers, 'Rights-based justifications for the tort of unlawful interference with economic relations' (2008) 28 *Legal Studies* 215 at 233. A revised conceptual basis for the economic torts is proposed by Deakin and Randall (n 13).

[63] *Lonrho plc v Fayed and ors* [1992] 1 AC 448.

[64] [2008] UKHL 19, [2008] 1 AC 1174.

[65] At [123].

the claimant by intimidatory threats to breach contracts, and by the procurement of breaches of contract,[66] it is by no means limited to cases of such interference with the claimant's contractual rights.

The gist of the tort of lawful means conspiracy, also known as conspiracy to injure,[67] is unjustified combination leading to economic pressure or harm. Its distinctive feature is that it can be made out even if no unlawful means have been used, and no interference with a pre-existing contractual or other legal right has taken place, which has been acknowledged as rendering it anomalous.[68] Thus there is the most stringent mental element, the requirement of malice, or in modern language a predominant purpose of injuring the claimant,[69] and this has in practice operated to keep an otherwise potentially far-reaching tort within narrow bounds.

Conclusion

Of the various economic torts, the one whose role is closest to that of Conversion is *Lumley v Gye*. Nevertheless there are major differences between the two, particularly after the strict and limiting approach to the mental element of the *Lumley v Gye* tort taken by the House of Lords in *OBG Ltd v Allan*, which are best highlighted by a short but structured comparison.

Comparison of *Lumley v Gye* and Conversion

The Gist of these Torts

The gist of the *Lumley v Gye* tort is the infringement of the claimant's contractual right. The gist of a Conversion, as we have seen in chapter three, is the infringement of the claimant's (superior) possessory interest. Hence there is here an obvious similarity between them, in that infringement of a legal right is in both cases the gist of the tort.

---

[66]   Clerk & Lindsell (n 5) at para 25–121.

[67]   Which has its origins in *Quinn v Leathem* [1901] AC 495.

[68]   See *Lonrho Ltd and anor v Shell Petroleum Co Ltd and anor (No 2)* [1982] AC 173 per Lord Diplock at 188E–189H and *OBG Ltd v Allan* [2007] UKHL 21, [2008] 1 AC 1 per Lord Hoffmann at [15].

[69]   See *Crofter Hand Woven Harris Tweed Co Ltd and ors v Veitch and anor* [1942] AC 435 especially per Viscount Maugham at 452 and Lord Wright at 468–70, and *Lonrho v Fayed* [1992] 1 AC 448 per Lord Bridge at 463–68.

The Nature of the Interference Required

In *Lumley v Gye*, the requisite interference is generally referred to as procuring or inducing a breach of contract. Thus, in its simplest form, this occurs 'where the intervenor ... speaks, writes or publishes words or does other acts which communicate pressure or persuasion to the mind or person of one of the contracting parties themselves'.[70] However it is well established that 'dealings by the third party with the contract breaker which to the knowledge of the third party are inconsistent with the contract between the contract breaker and the person wronged'[71] will also suffice as such.[72] One example of such dealings is the provision of funding without which the breach of contract cannot proceed. Thus in *Mainstream Properties v Young*, Norris J (as he now is) at first instance held:

> I have found that [the contract breakers'] only real hope of funding lay with [the defendant] ... The provision of funds to facilitate an apparent breach of contract (which could not otherwise proceed) is a sufficient interference.[73]

Hence Carty, notwithstanding her scepticism as to this rule, is driven to accept that in *Mainstream* the defendant funder's participation in the breach of contract 'was clearly causative'.[74]

As the law stands, the key to assessing whether any given interference suffices for liability is to apply the House of Lords' repeatedly expressed view in *OBG Ltd v Allan*[75] that the nature of liability under *Lumley v Gye* is that of an accessory to the primary liability of the contract breaker.[76]

To constitute Conversion, we have seen that the interference must be one by which the defendant has infringed the claimant's (superior) possessory interest in, and himself exercised possessory rights over, the subject asset; nothing further is required.[77] In *Howard Perry & Co v British Railways*,[78] the defendant held

---

[70]   Slade J in *Greig v Insole* [1978] 1 WLR 302 at 334A (describing 'direct interference').

[71]   Neill LJ in *Middlebrook Mushrooms v TGWU* [1993] ICR 612 at 618.

[72]   See also *Thomson v Deakin* [1952] Ch 646 at 694 per Jenkins LJ, *Law Debenture Trust Corp plc v Ural Caspian Oil Corp Ltd* [1993] 1 WLR 138 at 151 per Hoffmann J (decision reversed at [1995] Ch 152 (CA)), and Clerk & Lindsell (n 5) at paras 25–49 to 25–50.

[73]   15 July 2004, unreported at [116]. This finding was not questioned in either the Court of Appeal ([2005] EWCA Civ 861 [2005] IRLR 964) or the House of Lords *sub nomine OBG Ltd v Allan* (n 1).

[74]   H Carty, 'OBG Ltd v Allan: the House of Lords shapes the economic torts and explores commercial confidences and image rights' (2007) 15 *Torts LJ* 283.

[75]   See per Lord Hoffmann at [3], [5], [6], [8], [9], [16], [20], [21], [29], [32], [36], [37], [67], [69] and [86], per Lord Nicholls at [172], [178] and [194], and per Lord Brown at [320]; the term 'secondary liability' is used by Lord Hoffmann at [32] and [44,] Lord Nicholls at [172] ('this tort is an example of civil liability which is secondary in the sense that it is secondary, or supplemental, to that of the third party who committed a breach of his contract') and Lord Brown at [320].

[76]   This view is not without its critics: see Deakin and Randall (n 13) under the side-heading Interferences, The economic torts are not based on a theory of 'accessorial' or secondary liability (542 ff).

[77]   See ch 3 under the headings The Importance of Possession and The Three Elements of Conversion.

[78]   *Howard E Perry & Co Ltd v British Railways Board* [1980] 1 WLR 1375.

consignments of the claimant's steel at various of its depots, but—in order to avoid antagonising NUR men who were 'blacking' steel in support of a steelworkers' strike—refused either to deliver them up or to allow their collection. However, it did not in any way challenge the claimant's right to possession, nor set up any rival right in itself or any other party. Sir Robert Megarry V-C was able to state that 'looking at the matter as one of first principle, … this is a clear case of conversion'.[79] Though not cited in the *Howard Perry* case, the opening words of Holt CJ's judgment in *Baldwin v Cole* would have afforded apposite support for this conclusion: 'The very denial of goods to him that has a right to demand them is an actual conversion, and not only evidence of it'.[80] Samuel's questioning of the Vice-Chancellor's conclusion, on the grounds that, although the defendant had interfered with the claimant's right to possession, 'the law of actions clearly distinguished interference with possession (detinue and trespass) from interference with title (conversion)',[81] is with respect misconceived, for the reasons already explained in chapter three.[82] Samuel's suggestion[83] that the *Howard Perry* case could be considered as one of economic tort, more specifically that now known as causing loss by unlawful means, cannot stand with the subsequent restrictive redefinition of that tort by the House of Lords in *OBG Ltd v Allan*.

Thus, on the one hand, *Lumley v Gye*[84] cannot offer an alternative means of meeting the need we have identified for Conversion to be developed so as to include within its ambit (in appropriate circumstances) incorporeal as well as corporeal assets,[85] but, on the other, such a development of Conversion would by no means wholly supercede *Lumley v Gye*, for reasons developed below.[86]

The Right to Claim

In *Lumley v Gye*, the claimant must show that it has suffered loss by reason of a breach of its contract with a third party brought about by the defendant.

In Conversion, as we have seen in chapter four, the right to sue depends simply on establishing a possessory interest in the subject asset which is superior to any

---

[79]   ibid, at 1380C–D.

[80]   (1704) 6 Mod 212, 87 ER 964.

[81]   G Samuel, 'Wrongful Interference with Goods' (1982) 31 *International & Commercial Law Quarterly* 357 at 380–81.

[82]   See ch 3 under the headings Interests Protected, The Relationship Between the Wrongful Interference Torts and The Importance of Possession.

[83]   ibid, at 382.

[84]   Following its narrow re-definition, coupled with the suppression of the tort of Interference with Contractual Relations, in *OBG Ltd v Allan* (n 1). See under the side-heading *Lumley v Gye*—Procuring or Inducing a Breach of Contract, above.

[85]   See under the heading The Place of Contractual Rights and Other Intangible Property, above, and also ch 5 under the headings Intangible Property and The Importance of Effective Protection of Property Interests.

[86]   Under the side-heading The Permissible Subject Matter of a Claim.

possessory interest of the defendant's. As to the need for a possessory interest, an analogy may be drawn with the right to sue in negligence for loss caused by damage to an asset. Only a party with a possessory right in the asset may bring such a claim; someone with only a contractual right to the use of the services of an asset for the purposes of profit may not do so.

Thus in *Candlewood Corpn v Mitsui Ltd*,[87] whilst the first claimant, a bare-boat charterer of the negligently damaged Ibaraki Maru (thereby entitled to the possession thereof for the duration of the demise), was able to recover the costs of repair and the reduction in the hire payable to it under a time sub-charter for the period the vessel was out of service because under repair, the second claimant, the time sub-charterer, could not recover damages for its lost profit for the period of the repair, nor for the wasted hire (at the reduced rate) it had to pay for that period. Lord Fraser, giving the judgment of the Board of the Privy Council, stated the common law rule thus:

> a time charterer is not entitled to recover for pecuniary loss caused by damage by a third party to the chartered vessel. The reason is that a time charterer has no proprietary or possessory right in the chartered vessel: his only right in relation to the vessel is contractual

and went on to explain that the rule in relation to time charters was but one example of a more general principle in respect of damage to assets.[88]

In the absence of either any proprietary or possessory right in the damaged asset,[89] or some special additional factor to support liability, such as the defendant having accepted a responsibility to protect the second claimant from such loss, or a high level of fault in the defendant's conduct such as having acted with the actual, subjective intention of causing loss to the claimant, *Candlewood Corpn v Mitsui Ltd* was simply a claim in the tort of negligence, for pure economic loss, and failed accordingly.

It may be noted that a development of the law of Conversion so as to encompass incorporeal property, and in particular appropriate contractual rights, would not alter the outcome of such a case. The negligent crew of the Mineral Transporter, responsible for the collision in which the Ibaraki Maru was damaged, in no way infringed the first claimant's possessory interest in its bare-boat charter, nor exercised any possessory rights over it; therefore a 'strict liability' claim in Conversion would not be available, and any claim would have to be pursued in negligence (as it in fact was). Any claim by the second claimant in Conversion would fail both for like reasons, namely want of any infringement of its possessory interest in its time sub-charter, and of any exercise of possessory rights over the same by the defendant, and for the same reason its claim in

---

[87] *Candlewood Navigation Corpn Ltd v Mitsui OSK Lines Ltd and anor* [1986] AC 1 (PC).
[88] See also *Leigh & Sillivan Ltd v Aliakmon Shipping Co Ltd* [1986] AC 785 (HL).
[89] A contractual right to possession would suffice: see ch 4 under the heading What Amounts to a Sufficient Proprietary Right?

negligence in fact did, namely want of any possessory interest. Any claim in *Lumley v Gye* would fail for (it seems probable) want of any breach of either of the charter-parties, and in any event for want of an actual, subjective appreciation and intention that a breach be brought about.

Thus, in respect of the right to claim, there is a quite distinct approach (whether or not the same result would be reached) between Conversion and *Lumley v Gye*, and this would remain so following a development of the law of Conversion so as to encompass incorporeal property, and in particular those contractual rights which endow their holder with a possessory interest.

The Permissible Subject Matter of a Claim

A claim in *Lumley v Gye* is dependent, or parasitic, on a breach of the claimant's contract with a third party. The procuring or inducing defendant is held liable for bringing about an infringement of the claimant's contractual right(s). As we have seen, this is because the law regards such rights as a species of property worthy of special protection.[90]

In chapter five we saw that any corporeal asset may be the subject of a claim in Conversion, and argued for a development of the law in England, following other common law jurisdictions, to bring within the scope of Conversion those incorporeal assets in which a possessory interest is capable of subsisting. Although such a development would mean that both Conversion and *Lumley v Gye* could, depending on the nature and circumstances of the infringement, potentially have a role to play in the protection of contractual rights, the two would by no means be interchangeable, and would not provide alternative means of dealing with the same issues. Hence the importance of Conversion being extended to embrace incorporeals for which we have argued, however the practical operation of the *Lumley v Gye* tort may develop after *OBG Ltd v Allan*.

The potential for debate at the margins of these torts is well illustrated by a case from the United States where, as we have seen, Conversion of contractual rights is a recognised cause of action in many jurisdictions. In *Plunkett-Jarrell Grocery Co et al v Terry*[91] a country merchant disappeared without apparent explanation for some two months (when found, he claimed to have suffered an attack of amnesia). During his absence certain of his creditors entered into an agreement with two persons[92] under which the latter agreed to take over and operate his store and all of its assets, retaining all profits for payment of the creditors. The jury found in favour of the merchant's case, holding that the creditors had thereby, though their two agents, converted his entire stock of merchandise, equipment, notes and accounts. The creditors appealed against that

---

[90]   Text to n 16 above.
[91]   263 SW 2d 229 (Ark Sup Ct 1954).
[92]   In fact, Mr Terry's wife and daughter!

part of the award of damages[93] which represented his 'open' or 'book' accounts, which the jury had been directed to quantify as 'the fair market value of the accounts owing [to the] plaintiff by store customers'.[94] They contended that there could be no action for trover or Conversion of such an account, citing authority that

> the term 'accounts', as here used, means a demand or claim or rights of action. It is a mere incorporeal right to a certain sum, or to the collection of a debt. In this sense, it has no tangible entity and will not support an action of trover[95]

The majority of the Supreme Court of Arkansas observed that such statements emanated from old cases based on the common law forms of actions, which had long since been abolished. Giving its judgment, McFaddin J acknowledged that from old definitions of trover

> it is easy to see why the old common-law cases would hold that trover could not be maintained as the proper action for damages for conversion of open accounts; because open accounts were not 'personal chattels', and trover could be maintained only for 'goods or personal chattels'. An account receivable was intangible, and not susceptible of that possession essential for manual delivery or manual seizure. An account receivable was personal property, but not a 'personal chattel'.[96]

Nevertheless, the majority went on to point out, 'an account receivable is property and the owner possesses a property right in it'.[97] Having observed that the burden of establishing a Conversion of his book accounts lay on Mr Terry, and referred to authority that changing the lock on the door of a building could amount to a Conversion of assets inside,[98] McFaddin J continued

> the account book ... listed the accounts due Terry from various debtors totalling between $8,000 and $9,000 ... When the only evidence Terry has as to the names of his debtors and the items due him by such debtors was taken from him, certainly there was a dominion exercised over the property of Terry. When the book was taken in the case at bar, it had the same effect as changing the locks on the store had ...When Terry's book containing his accounts was taken, he was effectively denied the ability to establish his claims against his debtors just as thoroughly as if promissory notes executed to him by his debtors had been taken from him. Whether the conversion be considered actual or constructive, there was nevertheless a conversion of his book accounts.[99]

---

93   The sum awarded under this head by the jury was $4,500.
94   The direction as to quantification was upheld as correct at 263 SW 2d 229 (1954), at 234 (para [5]).
95   *Knox v Moskins Stores* 241 Ala 346, 2 So 2d 449 (1941).
96   263 SW 2d 229 (1954) at 232.
97   ibid.
98   *Thomas v Westbrook* 206 Ark 841 (1944) at 843 citing *Jones v Stone* 78 NH 504 (1917).
99   263 SW 2d 229 (1954), at 233–34 ([2, 3]).

It should be noted that the case was neither argued nor decided on the basis of a fictional valuation of the account book over which the creditors' agents took control.[100]

The proximity between Conversion, when applied to incorporeal property, and the economic torts, is demonstrated by the following passage from one of the three dissenting judges, George Rose Smith J:

> It has long been the rule that choses in action such as an open account cannot be the subject of conversion, but of course this does not mean that the injured person is without a remedy. 'Obligations not merged in a document are not the subject of an action to recover damages [for conversion] under the rules stated in §§223 to 241; although interference with or appropriation of such obligations may make liable an actor under some other rule of law.' Rest., Torts, §242. Ever since the decision in Lumley v Gye … it has been recognized that one who wrongfully interferes with another's contract is liable in tort. I have no difficulty in extending this principle to the wrongful taking of a merchant's account book, but I see no need for distorting the definition of conversion in order to reach the same conclusion.[101]

The creditors' appeal against the award of damages[102] representing the claimant merchant's 'open' or 'book' accounts was dismissed, four of the seven judges[103] upholding this award on the basis of Conversion.[104]

In England, the suppression of the tort of wrongful interference with contractual relations coupled with the conservative re-definition of *Lumley v Gye* effected by the House of Lords in *OBG Ltd v Allan* now precludes the application of George Rose Smith J's approach in *Plunkett-Jarrell Grocery v Terry*. This, in our view, adds weight to the case for a development of Conversion so as to encompass appropriate types of intangible property.

The Mental Element Required

In *OBG Ltd v Allan* the House of Lords has recently laid down a strict requirement of actual, subjective appreciation[105] and intention by the defendant that a

---

[100] As to the relevant fiction, which has not been extended in England to mere documentary evidence of the existence of an underlying liability, see ch 2 under the side-headings Conversion in the Nineteenth Century, a New Legal Fiction—the Conversion of Choses in Action Evidenced by Converted Documents and Conversion in the Twentieth Century, Expansion of the New Legal Fiction. It should be noted that the creditors' agents appear to have collected just over $4,500 of his debts during his absence: see the majority judgment ibid at 234 ([5], fn 9), and per George Rose Smith J (dissenting) at 235–36.

[101]   ibid, at 235.

[102]   See n 93.

[103]   McFaddin, J Seaborn Holt, Milwee and Ward JJ.

[104]   Two of the three dissentients, Griffin Smith CJ and Robinson J, founded their dissents on the absence of sufficient evidence of Conversion on the facts; George Rose Smith J founded his on what he regarded as the claimant's failure to prove that he had suffered damage in the sum found by the jury.

[105]   In both fact and law.

breach of contract will and should be brought about as a necessary element to establishing liability in *Lumley v Gye*. Lord Hoffmann, giving the leading judgment, held that

> to be liable for inducing breach of contract, you must know that you are inducing a breach of contract. It is not enough to know that you are procuring an act which, as a matter of law or construction of the contract, is a breach. You must actually realise that it will have this effect. Nor does it matter that you ought reasonably to have done so.[106]

This imposes an extremely high evidential burden on would-be claimants. The House rejected arguments, founded particularly on the Earl of Halsbury LC's much quoted dictum in *South Wales Miners' Federation v Glamorgan Coal Company*[107] that it is 'a principle of the law, applicable even to the criminal law, that people are presumed to intend the reasonable consequences of their acts', and on the judgment of Slade J in the *World Series Cricket* case,[108] that the mental element in *Lumley v Gye* should be judged at least in part objectively, similarly to that in, for example, passing off.[109] Lord Halsbury's dictum had for a century been treated as important for proof of the necessary intention in the context of this tort, and Sedley LJ had quite recently observed that

> the combination of the doctrine that people are initially presumed to intend the ordinary consequences of their acts with the principles that intention to injure does not have to be a dominant motive and that bad faith is not needed, makes the tort of interference with contractual relations relatively easy to assert.[110]

Although none of the five speeches in *OBG Ltd v Allan* expressly commented on this principle or its future significance in the context of economic torts,[111] it seems unlikely that it will continue to be of any practical importance now that actual, subjective appreciation and intention is undoubtedly required.[112]

By contrast, Conversion is in essence a strict liability tort. We have seen in chapter two the leading authorities from the nineteenth century which put this position beyond doubt.[113] Some writers have labelled torts including Conversion

---

[106] At [39], citing *British Industrial Plastics Ltd v Ferguson* [1940] 1 All ER 479 (HL); see also at [42]–[43].

[107] *South Wales Miners' Federation and ors v Glamorgan Coal Company Ltd and ors* [1905] AC 239 at 244.

[108] *Greig and ors v Insole and ors* [1978] 1 WLR 302, especially at 337H–338A and 344C-D.

[109] For which see Clerk & Lindsell (n 5) at paras 1–54 and 27–17.

[110] *R Cruickshank Ltd v Chief Constable of Kent* [2002] EWCA Civ 1840, [2002] Po LR 379 at [51].

[111] Despite these and a number of further authorities concerning the application of this principle having been cited in argument.

[112] For a critique of this method as a desirable means of containing the potential scope of liability in *Lumley v Gye* see Deakin and Randall (n 13) under the side-headings Interests, The continuing problem of inferring mental states (538 ff), and Interferences, Intention is neither necessary nor sufficient for there to be a relevant 'interference' (541 ff). For a contrasting argument that the House of Lords should have been yet more stringent in its formulation of the requirement as to intention in *Lumley v Gye*, see Carty, OBG (*Torts LJ* 2007).

[113] Under the side-heading Conversion in the Nineteenth Century, Affirmation of Strict Liability.

as 'the intentional torts', but the term is potentially confusing and best avoided, for the label refers only to intentional conduct in the sense of deliberate or non-accidental conduct.[114]

Thus the nature of the required mental element is an important distinguishing factor between *Lumley v Gye* and Conversion. We would suggest that the lesser requirement of acting intentionally only in the sense of deliberately rather than accidentally, familiar in the context of most torts protecting proprietary interests, is appropriate to the protection of intangible as well as tangible assets, for the reasons already developed in chapter five.[115] As with the nature of the required interference, this is something which *Lumley v Gye* cannot now offer, and can only come through a development/expansion of Conversion.

The Remedies Available

In both *Lumley v Gye* and Conversion, the basic remedy is an award of compensatory damages. The nature of the fact situations which give rise to claims in *Lumley v Gye* is such that injunctions *quia timet*, or to restrain continuing wrongs, generally as interim orders, are more commonly appropriate in respect of that tort than Conversion. On the other hand, as we shall see in the next chapter, the statutory[116] expansion of the remedies available for Conversion, so as to include relief of the sort previously available at common law for detinue, and for delivery up on an interlocutory basis, means that on occasion specific remedies are available for Conversion. Nevertheless, in the generality of cases damages are the common form of relief in both torts.

Conclusions

Whilst English law recognised a tort of interference with contractual relations, the economic torts offered the prospect of somewhat broader protection for contractual rights.[117] However following the suppression of that tort as heretical, as part of the House of Lords' conservative re-alignment of the economic torts in *OBG Ltd v Allan*, with the accompanying severance and restrictive re-definition of the two principal economic torts which remain, *Lumley v Gye* can now afford only limited legal protection to contractual rights.

The tort of causing loss by unlawful means operates to protect general economic and trade interests. As the latter are lesser interests in the hierarchy of

---

[114]   See *Kuwait Airways Corpn v Iraqi Airways Co (Nos 4 & 5)* [2002] UKHL 19, [2002] 2 AC 883 at [39] per Lord Nicholls; Clerk & Lindsell (n 5) at para 1–54. See also ch 3, text to fns 121–22.

[115]   See ch 5 under the heading Intangible Property.

[116]   Torts (Interference with Goods) Act 1977, ss 3 and 4.

[117]   As demonstrated by the judgments of HHJ Maddocks (at first instance) and Mance LJ (in the Court of Appeal) in *OBG Ltd v Allan* (n 1) itself.

those protected by the law of tort, and of ill-defined ambit, there is some logic to the protection it affords them being dependent on a high level of fault, whether or not it is wise for that to have been so directly linked to the infringer's actual, subjective mental processes.

Thus there is now little prospect of the economic torts fulfilling the role of affording proper protection to proprietary interests in intangibles, at least for the foreseeable future.

However it is anomalous that incorporeal property such as contractual rights, though clearly established as being a species of property, and as capable of falling within the category of 'possessions' in European human rights law, should effectively be equated with general economic and trade interests, and similarly attract only very limited protection. It makes little commercial or economic sense in the twenty-first century for incorporeal property to remain relegated to a markedly lower legal status than its corporeal counterpart.

Properly applied, however, Conversion could rectify this and, for the reasons set out above and in chapter five, this is a role which it is well equipped to take on, and has successfully taken on in other common law jurisdictions, most notably in North America. Principle and policy support the proposition that the law of tort ought to accord all proprietary interests equivalent protection, and it makes sense that one tort should take a leading role in that regard. The law of tort is supposed to develop incrementally as and when circumstances fall for judicial consideration which in the courts' judgement require it.[118] While it is to be regretted that only two members of the panel which decided *OBG Ltd v Allan* were willing to sanction such an incremental development of Conversion, we must now follow Baroness Hale in looking to the Law Commission to consider the matter further and hopefully lay the ground for such a development.

---

[118] See, eg, *JD v East Berkshire Community Health NHS Trust* and 2 other cases [2005] UKHL 23, [2005] 2 AC 373 at [50] per Lord Bingham (dissenting in the result) and *Kleinwort Benson Ltd v Lincoln City Council* and 3 other cases [1999] 2 AC 349 at 377D-H per Lord Goff.

7

Damages and Other Remedies

Introduction

U NTIL STATUTORY INTERVENTION in 1978,[1] an award of damages
was the sole common law remedy for Conversion,[2] and to this day it
remains by far the most important in practice. However awards of
damages for Conversion can often give rise to theoretical, as well as practical,
difficulties. Though their resolution can prove controversial, the genesis of many
is clear: it is in the working out of the remedy that many of the difficulties which
flow from Conversion's hybrid jurisprudential nature discussed in chapter three
manifest themselves. The statutory addition of remedies for the abolished tort of
detinue,[3] which at common law had been quite distinct from those for Conversion,[4] without making express consequential provision for the resolution of
important differences,[5] has only exacerbated matters.

The first aspect of the hybrid is the proprietary role of Conversion, as 'the main
vehicle of English law for the protection of proprietary rights,'[6] *aliter* 'the
principal means whereby English law protects the ownership of goods'.[7] Yet, in
contrast to the protection of real property, where a free-standing action of
ejectment emerged to sit alongside the tort of trespass to land, the common law
developed no truly proprietary cause of action, to sit alongside Conversion and

---

[1]   By the coming into force of s 3 of The Torts (Wrongful Interference with Goods) Act 1977 ('the
1977 Act'), the enactment of which was at least partly prompted by the abolition of detinue in s 2.

[2]   See per Diplock LJ in *General & Finance Facilities Ltd v Cooks Cars (Romford) Ltd* [1963] 1
WLR 644 (CA) at 649. Equity, however, would grant claimant owners of articles of personal property
which were physically unique, or not readily available in the market, (discretionary) orders for
delivery up against defendants in possession of the same; prior to the Common Law Procedure Act
1854, such orders were only made in Chancery—see ch 2, text to fn 187 ff.

[3]   See s 3 of the 1977 Act.

[4]   As explained by Diplock LJ in *General & Finance v Cooks Cars* (n 2) at 649–51.

[5]   In particular, as to the date at which loss is to be assessed (commented on by Neill and Nicholls
LJJ in *IBL Ltd v Coussens* [1991] 2 All ER 133 (CA) at 138j and 143j–144a respectively).

[6]   The 18th Report (Conversion and Detinue) of the Law Reform Committee (1971), Cmnd 4774
at para 15.

[7]   *Kuwait Airways Corp v Iraqi Airways Co and anor (Nos 4 and 5)* [2002] UKHL 19, [2002] 2 AC
886 per Lord Nicholls at [77]. See also at [130] per Lord Hoffmann: 'The primary purpose of
conversion is to protect the proprietary or possessory interest in the chattel'.

trespass to goods, in protection of personal property.[8] It was in this context, albeit arguably as something of a second best,[9] that particular and strict rules were adopted with regard to damages for Conversion, justified by reference to the proprietary nature and role of the tort. Most fundamentally, the principle of strict liability for Conversion is 'deeply ingrained in the common law [having] survived since at least the days of Lord Mansfield in *Cooper v Chitty* (1756)'.[10]

The second aspect of the hybrid is the tortious classification of Conversion: in common with other torts it is a wrong (a defendant's breach of a duty imposed on him by the law), for which the aim and purpose of the law is to provide just compensation. Yet, whilst that is the one fundamental legal function performed by most torts, and in particular the paradigm[11] torts such as negligence, Conversion also has the distinct but equally fundamental function of protecting proprietary rights.

Hence it should come as no surprise that the law with regard to the assessment of damages for Conversion has not always conformed to the 'givens' of compensatory damages awarded for the paradigm torts. Conversely, if one appraises the law as to the proprietary aspect by reference to that concerning damages in tort, apparent anomalies should be expected to emerge.[12] In the relatively recent and still leading case of *Kuwait Airways*, Lord Nicholls asserted that:

> Despite its proprietary base, this tort does not stand apart and command awards of damages measured by some special and artificial standard of its own. The fundamental object of an award of damages in respect of this tort, as with all wrongs, is to award just compensation for loss suffered.[13]

It is unsurprising, in light of this dictum, that subsequent judges have been led to think that 'developments in the law relating to the assessment of damages for conversion have rendered any argument based on a strict proprietary view of the nature of the cause of action unsustainable'.[14] It must, however, remain important as a matter of principle that the proprietary function of the tort continues to have an influential effect on how awards of damages are structured and quantified, for the reasons given by Lord Hoffmann in the same case.[15]

---

[8] A point well made in N Curwen, 'The Remedy in Conversion: Confusing Property and Obligation' (2006) 26 *Legal Studies* 570 at 576.

[9] See, eg, the argument of Curwen (ibid) for the statutory restoration of detinue to provide a true proprietary action guaranteeing the recovery of wrongfully detained goods, or more fundamentally the argument of Weir in T Weir, *A Casebook on Tort*, 10th edn (London, Sweet & Maxwell, 2004) at 483–87.

[10] (1 Burr 20, 97 ER 166): Lord Nicholls in *Kuwait Airways* (n 7) at [80]. See also P Cane, 'Causing Conversion' (2002) 118 *Law Quarterly Review* 544 at 544.

[11] At least to a contemporary lawyer.

[12] See, eg, A Tettenborn, 'Damages in Conversion—The Exception or the Anomaly?' [1993] *Cambridge Law Journal* 128.

[13] n 7, at [67].

[14] *Uzinterimpex JSC v Standard Bank plc* [2008] EWCA Civ 819, [2008] 2 Lloyd's Rep 456 at [64] per Moore-Bick LJ.

[15] n 7 at [130].

Judicial efforts to assimilate, so far as practicable, the approach to damages in Conversion with that in other torts, are nothing new, and go back at least to the judgment of Thesiger LJ in *Hiort v London & North Western Railway Co.*[16] However they face the inevitable difficulty identified above, implicitly acknowledged by the opening words of Lord Nicholls' dictum, that in the tort of Conversion there is a second fundamental object sitting alongside that on which he focussed, namely the vindication of the claimant's proprietary rights in the subject asset. 'But for' that second object, the awards of damages to claimants who in reality have suffered no loss, such as the claimants in *Solloway v McLaughlin* and *BBMB Ltd v Eda Holdings Ltd* (both discussed below[17]), or who sue in tort for damage to goods which they have nevertheless been able to sell on at an unaffected price,[18] would be hard indeed to justify.

That being so, are such difficulties, or 'anomalies', bound to remain a feature of the law of Conversion for the future, as they have been for many years past? A radical argument advanced by Weir, and backed by impeccable theoretical logic, is that a rational legal system should treat proprietary claims and claims in tort separately.[19] However hundreds of years of English legal history stand in its way, and for better or worse the common law has developed Conversion as a tort. Unlike the proverbial Irishman who, when asked for directions, responded that he would not have started from here, we must seek to address the law on damages for Conversion as it has developed to this day, for all its anomalies and inherent tensions.

Whether the bold aim of Lord Nicholls and his judicial forebears[20] is capable of being achieved without bringing about fundamental disruption to the delicate web of common law rules woven over many centuries which, taken as a whole, comprises the English law of personal property, depends in part upon a consideration of the detail of the various established rules which make up the law as to the measure of damages for Conversion. However the answer will also depend upon the level of abstraction at which the courts apply Lord Nicholls' dictum in future cases of Conversion. If his dictum is taken at a high level of abstraction, affording overarching guidance as to how the various rules should be applied in particular cases, and what result should be aimed for, it can be welcomed. If,

---

[16]   *Hiort and anor v The London and North-Western Railway Company* (1879) LR 4 Ex D 188 at 199. See also the judgments of Taylor and Owen JJ and of Menzies J in the High Court of Australia in *Butler v Egg & Pulp Marketing Board* [1966] HCA 38, 114 CLR 185 at 191 and 192 respectively; of Brandon LJ in *Brandeis Goldschmidt & Co Ltd v Western Transport Ltd* [1981] QB 864 (CA), albeit a detinue case, at 870 and 872; and of Neill LJ in *IBL Ltd v Coussens* [1991] 2 All ER 133 (CA) at 139b–d and j.

[17]   See text to nn 66–67 ff and 68–71 ff respectively.

[18]   See *The Sanix Ace* [1987] 1 Lloyd's Rep 465 Hobhouse J, especially at 468 l/h col.

[19]   T Weir, Tort, (n 9) at 483–87.

[20]   See text to nn 13 and 16.

however, it becomes adopted as a justification for discarding those rules whole-sale, in favour of the simple application of any given trial judge's sense of what seems just in the particular case, such disruption is likely to result

As for the effect of the statutory addition of detinue remedies, the leading case remains *IBL Ltd v Coussens*[21] in which the (deputy) Master apparently granted relief in the form provided for in section 3(2)(a) of the 1977 Act[22] (specific delivery without an alternative of paying the value in lieu, plus consequential damages—'form (a)'); the (deputy) Judge granted relief in the form provided for in section 3(2)(b) (specific delivery with the alternative, at the defendant's election, of paying 'damages by reference to the value' in lieu, plus in either case consequential damages—'form (b)'); and the Court of Appeal made orders varying the sums to be inserted into the latter, form (b) order. (The third form of relief under section 3 is a simple order for damages—'form (c)'.) Unfortunately the analysis of this case is bedevilled by a number of procedural difficulties: the Master appears to have granted relief in form (a), which is only available at the discretion of the Court,[23] notwithstanding that the claimant's summons before him did not seek it, even in the alternative;[24] the Judge, who substituted relief in form (b), though purporting to dismiss an appeal by the defendant, did not appreciate the important distinctions between the two, and gave no sufficient consideration to how the damages should be assessed;[25] and the Court of Appeal, only two of whose members gave reasons for their decision,[26] made the order it did despite the (claimant) appellant, who had a statutory right to elect between orders in forms (b) or (c),[27] apparently indicating a preference for relief in form (c)![28] Further, notwithstanding the statutory scheme under section 3(2), only Nicholls LJ made direct reference to the need for a separate assessment of consequential damages to be included in the (varied) form (b) order directed by the Court of Appeal,[29] though Neill LJ drew attention to the fact that neither of the form (a) and form (b) orders made below had included any provision in respect of consequential damages.[30]

Finally, and at the risk of stating the obvious, it will be appreciated that the very nature of Conversion is such that the resultant loss will most probably be economic loss, reflecting the monetary value of the converted asset(s), together

---

[21] n 5.

[22] n 1.

[23] See s 3(3)(b) ibid.

[24] See at 144j per Nicholls LJ.

[25] Per Neill LJ at 138g–h.

[26] Butler-Sloss LJ did not: see at 145b–c.

[27] See s 3(3)(b). *Quaere* whether, if the point had been considered, the claimant might have been held bound by any election made in the court below, in particular given the form of its summons (for which see at 144j in the judgment of Nicholls LJ).

[28] See per Neill LJ at 135d: 'IBL do not now seek the return of the two cars'. Contrast however the words of Nicholls LJ at 144b–c.

[29] At 145b.

[30] At 138e.

with any resultant consequential loss. Unlike torts such as negligence, where the scope of the duty imposed by the law on the defendant may or may not extend to protecting the claimant from economic loss, the fact that the loss to be recovered for a Conversion will most probably be 'pure economic loss' presents no relevant legal obstacle to its recovery.[31]

The Measure of Damages for Conversion

(a) The Basic Rule

The fundamental object of an award of damages for Conversion, as with all torts, is to award just compensation for the loss suffered by the claimant, having regard to the particular circumstances of the case.[32] However it must be recognised that the general rule that the claimant recovers the loss he has actually suffered, no more and no less, often has to be departed from.[33] Put another way, what amounts to 'just compensation' in the overall factual and legal context can often be less than straightforward. The basic or prima facie rule in Conversion is that the measure of damages will be the market value of the converted asset.[34] It should be noted that damages are not limited to the value of the claimant's interest in the converted asset. Thus, for example, a pawn-broker's claim for Conversion of assets held by him in the course of such a business is not limited to the amount he has advanced against them plus interest. He is entitled to recover the full value of the converted assets, though 'he will be liable to hand over the surplus to the respective owners of the goods'.[35]

However depending on the circumstances (for example, where there has been market movement between the Conversion and its discovery, or perhaps even judgment, or where return of the original asset has been tendered and accepted)

---

[31]   See ch 3, text to fn 75.

[32]   *Kuwait Airways* [2002] UKHL 19, [2002] 2 AC 886 per Lord Nicholls at [67] (quoted in the text to n 13); *Uzinterimpex v Standard Bank* [2008] EWCA Civ 819, [2008] 2 Lloyd's Rep 456 at [67] per Moore-Bick LJ.

[33]   *Strand Electric and Engineering Co Ltd v Brisford Entertainments Ltd* [1952] 2 QB 246 (CA) per Denning LJ at 253.

[34]   *Clerk & Lindsell on Torts*, 19th edn (London, Sweet & Maxwell, 2006) at para 17–89; *Kuwait Airways* (n 7) per Lord Nicholls at [67]; *Kuliarchar Sweater Industries Ltd v Frans Maas (UK) Ltd* [2000] EWHC 194 (Comm) Langley J.

[35]   *Swire v Leach* (1865) 18 CB (NS) 479, 141 ER 531 especially at 492, 536 per Erle CJ. See also *The Winkfield* [1902] P 42 CA at 60–61 where Collins MR said that 'as the [claimant] bailee has to account for the thing bailed, so he must account for that which has become its equivalent and now represents it. What he has received above his own interest he has received to the use of his bailor ... The liability by the bailee to account is ... well established'. See ch 4, text to fn 53.

some other measure may be appropriate. Additional damage may have been suffered consequential on the Conversion, and (as has now been recognised by statute[36]) that too is recoverable.[37]

(b) Time of Valuation

It was well established at common law that the prima facie date at which the converted asset is to be valued is the date of Conversion.[38] By contrast, in detinue damages were assessed at the date of judgment.[39]

The position has been considerably complicated by the statutory abolition of detinue, coupled with the insertion of its remedies into the surviving tort of Conversion. As Neill LJ put it in *IBL Ltd v Coussens*

> when making an award of damages under s 3 of the 1977 Act the court is faced with a number of competing considerations. These considerations include: (a) the fact that the tort of detinue has been abolished (b) the fact that the remedies now available for the tort of conversion (hitherto a purely personal action) have in effect extended the scope of the tort so that a proprietary claim can be asserted (c) the general rule that where goods have been irreversibly converted their value is assessed at the date of conversion (d) the former general rule that in detinue the value of the goods detained was assessed at the date of judgment (e) the fact that after conversion the value of goods may fall instead of rise.[40]

One can therefore sympathise with his conclusion that, given also the several different remedies available under section 3 of the 1977 Act

> it is not possible, or indeed appropriate, to attempt to lay down any rule which is intended to be of universal application as to the date by reference to which the value of goods is to be assessed. The method of valuation and the date of valuation will depend on the circumstances.[41]

Although, therefore, there is no 'rule of universal application', many writers remain of the view, we would suggest rightly, that the established common law

---

[36] By inclusion of express reference to the same in ss 3(2)(a) and (b) of the 1977 Act.

[37] See under the side-heading (g) Consequential Loss below.

[38] See, eg, per Diplock LJ in *General & Finance v Cooks Cars* [1963] 1 WLR 644 (CA) at 649; 18th Report of the LRC (1971) at para 88; *Industria Azucarera Nacional SA v Empresa Exportado de Azucar, The Playa Larga and The Marble Islands* [1983] 2 Lloyd's Rep 171 (CA) at 181 r/h col; *Chubb Cash Ltd v John Crilley & Son* [1983] 1 WLR 599 (CA) at 601B–C and 604B; *Clerk & Lindsell on Torts* (2006) at para 17–89 fn 8.

[39] Per Diplock LJ in *General & Finance v Cooks Cars* [1963] 1 WLR 644 (CA) at 650.

[40] [1991] 2 All ER 133 (CA) at 139f–g.

[41] ibid at 139j. See also *Halsbury's Laws of England*, 4th edn, vol 45(2), 1999 reissue, at paras 615–20 and *Uzinterimpex v Standard Bank* [2008] EWCA Civ 819, [2008] 2 Lloyd's Rep 456 at [64]–[67] per Moore-Bick LJ.

rules remain relevant, and indeed commonly applicable.[42] In particular, the prima facie date and basis for assessing damages in Conversion remains valid as such after *IBL*.[43]

A clear example of the practical application of the prima facie rule is afforded by *Chubb Cash v John Crilley*.[44] On 30 July 1979 the Defendants, bailiffs who were engaged in the execution of a warrant, seized from the debtor's premises, and six weeks later sold at public auction, a cash register which was in fact owned by the claimant company, but which had been let to the debtor pursuant to a finance agreement under which the claimant retained title until the final instalment was paid. The amount outstanding under the finance agreement at the date of Conversion was £1,232. However, the claimant had previously assigned the right to receive payments under the finance agreement, and, by reason of default on the debtor's part in paying an instalment (possibly following the Conversion), was bound under the terms of the assignment to pay the assignee the sum of £951, in which sum the trial judge assessed its damages. The Court of Appeal substituted an award of £178, being the sum for which the register was sold at auction. The auction house in question regularly sold such registers, and attracted a good attendance at its auctions. Thus, Fox LJ reasoned

> the market having been tested at such an auction as I have mentioned, on September 11, the proper inference is that the value on July 30 was the same as that fetched at the auction because we have no evidence of any change in the market between the two dates[45] and we have no evidence of any change in the condition of the article between the two dates.[46]

The claimant company's assertion that it could itself have obtained far more for the register, by what amounted to a special realisation, was rejected, in the absence of clear and independent evidence in support.[47]

Where the claimant acts to purchase a replacement asset within a reasonable time of the Conversion, or does not immediately find out that the Conversion has occurred, and the market value of the asset has increased in the meantime, his aggregate recovery is likely (via whichever exact theoretical route) to include the amount of such increase.[48]

---

[42]   See, eg, Clerk & Lindsell (n 34) at para 17–89 (especially final sentence); H McGregor, *McGregor on Damages*, 17th edn (London, Sweet & Maxwell, 2003) at paras 33–011 and 33–013.

[43]   See, eg, *Kuwait Airways* [2002] UKHL 19, [2002] 2 AC 886 at [67] per Lord Nicholls; *Kuliarchar v Frans Maas* (n 34); *Malkins Nominees Ltd v Societe Financiere Mirelis SA and ors* [2004] EWHC 2631 (Ch) per Laddie J at [34].

[44]   n 38.

[45]   Contrast the presence of just such evidence in *Sachs v Miklos*, discussed in text to nn 205–206.

[46]   At 602H. For a recent case in which the realisable price of converted assets, rather than their cost of manufacture, was (in the absence of other evidence of 'market value') held to be recoverable, see *Sony Computer Entertainment Ltd v Cinram Logistics UK Ltd* [2008] EWCA Civ 955, [2008] 2 CLC 441 especially at [49]–[50] per Rix LJ.

[47]   See at 602F–G and 602H–603A (Fox LJ) and 604G (Bush J).

[48]   *The Playa Larga* (n 38); *IBL Ltd v Coussens* [1991] 2 All ER 133 (CA) at 139g–h per Neill LJ.

A departure from the date of Conversion in favour of the date of judgment is most likely to be justified in cases of Conversion by temporary deprivation, reflecting its origins in detinue.[49]

Rising Market Value

The general principle in such cases is that the benefit of any increase in the value of a converted asset between the date of Conversion and the date of judgment should be to the credit of the claimant rather than the defendant.

At common law such loss has been treated as consequential loss,[50] although ultimately a single sum has been awarded comprising both value at the date of Conversion and any consequential damage.[51] One consequence of it being so treated has been that a claimant has more to prove in order to establish causation in respect of the lost increase in value[52] than in respect of his prima facie loss.

However in recent times, and possibly prompted by an (albeit unspoken) appreciation of the potential for unintended and problematic consequences of the scheme of section 3(2)(b) of the 1977 Act, judges have attempted to short-circuit the process by applying to Conversion the approach, more familiar in respect of the generality of tortious damages, that the Court is free to select whatever date for assessment of a claimant's loss is most apt to provide just compensation for the claimant, and thus in cases of rising value between Conversion and judgment to arrive at a single figure based on a valuation of the asset(s) in question at the latter date.

In *IBL Ltd v Coussens*[53] the claimant company's ex-Chairman converted (by refusal of a demand for their return) the Aston Martin and Rolls Royce motor cars which had thitherto been provided for his use. Their value at the date of their Conversion had apparently been £62,000,[54] but had allegedly increased markedly prior to the date of judgment.[55] The Court of Appeal, in varying an order in form (b) which had given £62,000 as the figure which the defendant could elect to pay as an alternative to delivery up, ordered an assessment of

---

[49] See discussion under side-heading (f) Where the Goods are Returned—'Temporary Deprivation', below.

[50] See *Munro v Willett* [1949] 1 KB 295 at 298–9 per Lynskey J, citing with approval *Salmond's Law of Torts*, 10th edn (London, Sweet & Maxwell, 1945); 18th Report (n 6) at para 88; *The Playa Larga* [1983] 2 Lloyd's LR 171 (CA) at 181 r/h col.

[51] See per Diplock LJ in *General & Finance v Cooks Cars* [1963] 1 WLR 644 (CA) at 649. However the wording of s 3(2) of the 1977 Act necessitates an adjustment as to the form of award, at least under s 3(2)(b): see the discussion of *IBL Ltd v Coussens* in the text to nn 53–62.

[52] See the discussion as to Causation under that heading, below.

[53] n 5.

[54] The figure at which the claimant company had offered to sell them to him at the time.

[55] The detailed facts are more complicated, in that the Rolls Royce had been returned before the judgment, but most of the alleged increase in value was attributable to the Aston Martin.

damages which, subject to questions of causation and mitigation,[56] was 'likely'[57] to result in an assessment by reference to the cars' value at the date of judgment.

At first blush this would appear to be a heterodox decision, where an orthodox approach (awarding damages in respect of the post-Conversion increase in value as consequential loss[58]) could equally have been adopted to achieve the desired effect. Given that the claimant was, however, *sub silentio* treated as having elected for the alternative form of remedy under section 3(2)(b) of the 1977 Act[59] rather than damages *simpliciter* under section 3(2)(c) (the point was not expressly addressed in either of the reasoned judgments), the orthodox approach would have produced a practical problem. Where relief is given in form (b), the alternative for the defendant is between 'delivery of the goods' and 'paying damages by reference to [their] value', and consequential damages are payable in addition 'in either alternative'. Given that any consequential damages generally fall to be assessed at the same time, however, their assessment has to be compatible with *whichever* of the primary alternatives (delivery up, or payment of damages by reference to value) with which the defendant chooses to comply.

It is therefore suggested that the decision in *IBL Ltd v Coussens* should in this respect be regarded as a necessary consequence of the enactment of section 3 of the 1977 Act,[60] and as one specific to a case where *both* the value of the converted asset has increased between the Conversion and judgment, *and* the claimant has elected under section 3(3)(b) of the 1977 Act for the alternative remedy under section 3(2)(b) rather than damages *simpliciter* under section 3(2)(c).[61] For that pragmatic reason, it is further suggested that henceforth, at least in any award made in form (b), the post-Conversion increase in value aspect of 'consequential loss' ought to be included within the (presumably single, composite figure in respect of) 'damages by reference to value of the goods', rather than the (again presumably single, composite) figure in respect of 'any consequential damages'.[62]

Delay in bringing and/or prosecuting a claim may operate to limit the extent to which the courts are willing, via whichever theoretical route, to give a claimant the benefit of a post-Conversion rise in the value of the subject asset.[63]

---

[56]   Nicholls LJ saw nothing in the mitigation point (see at 144c–f), but Neill LJ indicated that it should remain open at the assessment (see at 140a–b).

[57]   Per Neill LJ at 140b.

[58]   See text to nn 50–52.

[59]   This is necessarily implicit in the making of an order under s 3(2)(b), given the terms of s 3(3)(b) of the 1977 Act. See also text to n 27.

[60]   Which in turn was driven by the abolition of detinue in the same Act.

[61]   Which further suggests, perhaps regrettably, that Bush J's *dictum* in *Chubb Cash v John Crilley* [1983] 1 WLR 599 (CA) at 604A–B that 'The Wrongful Interference of Goods Act 1977 abolished the tort of detinue, but it did not interfere with the common law rules relating to damages for conversion with which we are at present concerned' has not in practice proved wholly correct.

[62]   See further under side-heading (g) Consequential Loss, below.

[63]   See further ibid, and also under the heading The Duty to Mitigate, below.

Falling Market Value

Here, the application of the prima facie rule will ordinarily ensure that the loss resulting from such fall is born by the wrongdoer. This measure is unaffected if the claimant is a mere bailee, though he may hold that part of the damages recovered which exceeds his own loss on trust for his bailor.[64]

Two decisions of the Privy Council demonstrate that a defendant guilty of Conversion will not escape full liability to pay damages based on value at the time of Conversion by subsequently purchasing a like replacement for the claimant at a lower cost.[65] In *Solloway v McLaughlin*[66] the claimant McLaughlin had given instructions to the first defendant, a company of Ontario stock brokers ('Solloway') and two of its directors, to purchase 7,000 shares in Sudbury, a mining company, in mid-October 1929. Their then market price was $7.00. He deposited 3,500 shares in Sudbury, which he already held, as 'margin'. Sudbury's price fell, and in response to the defendant's call for further 'margin' he deposited an additional 10,500 such shares together with some cash. In mid January 1930 he closed his account with the defendant company, paying the sum ostensibly due and receiving 21,000 shares in Sudbury. It later transpired that, as part of a fraudulent system of business,[67] the original instruction to purchase had never been implemented, and most (11,800) of the 14,000 shares deposited as 'margin' had been sold by the defendants without any authority. Hence the vast majority of the 21,000 shares 'returned' to McLaughlin had just been bought in by the defendants at their then market price of $2.90 to $3.40. So far as the claim in Conversion (that in respect of the 11,800 shares) was concerned, the Privy Council (varying the decision of the Supreme Court of Canada in this respect) held the defendants liable to pay damages based on their value at the time of their Conversion (the unauthorised sale). The effect of applying the prima facie rule in such circumstances was, of course, to strip the defendant company of the profit it would otherwise have made from its own wrong. Quite apart from the relative antiquity of the case, in these circumstances the ordinary rules as to the measure of loss in Conversion render resort to modern juristic concepts such as unjust enrichment unnecessary to achieve this end.

More recently, this decision was applied in *BBMB Ltd v Eda Holdings Ltd* (on appeal from the Court of Appeal of Hong Kong),[68] where the defendant stock brokers, with whom a certificate representing 10,886,885 valuable shares was deposited as security in September 1981, converted the same the following

---

[64] See, eg, *Trailways Transport Ltd v Thomas* [1996] 2 NZLR 443 at 445–46, applying *The Winkfield* (n 35).

[65] See also *Rhodes v Moules* [1895] 1 Ch 236 at 254, for the Court of Appeal's rejection of the defendant's submission that he should be given the opportunity to 'replace' converted shares in De Beers at a lesser cost than damages calculated in accordance with the prima facie rule.

[66] *Solloway Mills & Co and ors v McLaughlin* [1938] AC 247 (PC).

[67] Which involved other clients' affairs too, as Solloway were 'short' c.100,000 shares in Sudbury.

[68] *BBMB Finance (Hong Kong) Ltd v Eda Holdings Ltd and ors* [1990] 1 WLR 409 (PC).

month by an unauthorised disposal at their then market price of $HK5.75 per share. The following May the brokers purchased a replacement holding[69] at the then market value of $HK2.40 per share, re-crediting the claimant's account with it, and subsequently denied liability to pay damages equivalent to $HK3.35 per share, arguing that the claimant had received what it was entitled to, namely a holding of 10,886,885 shares in the relevant company, and had therefore suffered no loss. The defendant brokers' appeal was rejected. The Privy Council applied the general rule that where assets are irreversibly converted and not returned,[70] the measure of damage is their market value at the date of Conversion.

As Tettenborn has pointed out, it can hardly be the case that a defendant who does not replace the converted asset should be in a better position than one who does.[71] Hence the decision in *BBMB* demonstrates a fortiori that a post-Conversion but pre-judgment fall in the market value of a converted asset cannot be relied on by a defendant as reducing the measure of the claimant's recoverable loss. This approach is in marked contrast to the so-called '*Bwllfa* principle',[72] under which a court making an assessment of damages is entitled to take account of events which have occurred up to the date of hearing, rather than speculate about what might have happened in the interim. This principle has recently been upheld in the context of damages for breach of contract by a bare majority of the House of Lords in *Golden Strait Corporation v Nippon Yusen Kubishka Kaisha*.[73] In Conversion, where the market has fallen between the accrual of the cause of action and the assessment of damages, as a matter of legal policy judicial blinkers must be applied, and the loss assessed at the former date. Where, however, a claim is proprietary, and the loss for which the claimant is being compensated is the loss of an interest in an asset, the fact that the defendant has subsequently proffered a similar asset does not negate the fact that the claimant has lost his property, but merely calls for credit to be given, should the claimant accept it.[74]

(c) Absence of a Market

The absence of any market in which the subject asset can be purchased or (as the case may be) sold makes it necessary for other methods of valuing the same to be

---

[69]   Being 14,125,911 shares, allowing for two bonus issues which had been made since the date of the original Conversion.

[70]   In contrast to 'temporary deprivation' of possession, even if for a significant period (eg in *Brandeis Ltd v Western Transport Ltd* (n 16) 9 months).

[71]   A Tettenborn, 'Conversion Damages Clarified' (1991) 141 *NLJ* 452.

[72]   *Bwllfa and Merthyr Dare Steam Collieries (1891) Ltd v Pontypridd Waterworks Company* [1903] AC 426.

[73]   [2007] UKHL 12, [2007] 2 AC 353.

[74]   The position where the market value has, between the Conversion and judgment, first risen and then fallen is briefly discussed in Clerk & Lindsell (n 34) at para 17–92.

used. This may involve taking the price of acquisition (whether of the converted asset itself[75] or of a replacement[76]), or the price at which the asset would (but for the Conversion) have been sold.

In *J & E Hall Ltd v Barclay*[77] the subject assets were a pair of experimental davits and associated testing apparatus. They had been of no commercial use for some years due to a slump in the shipping market, but when that market started picking up and the claimant required them once more, it transpired that the defendants had sold them as scrap in the meantime. Greer LJ looked at the position from the point of view of the claimant, requiring his assets for commercial use:

> [I]f he cannot get them in the market, what is his position? He must do that which is analogous to getting them in the market, namely, he must go to the only people from whom he can get goods to put him in the same position as he would have been in if his davits had never been taken away from him, that is to say, he must go to the manufacturer and see for what price the manufacturer will supply him with similar goods.[78]

Scott LJ put the position in broader terms:

> [T]he selling value of the property converted at the time of the conversion … is a convenient measure of value where the article is of a kind for which there is a current market price, but, where there is no market, in my view it would be doing injustice to the owner of the article converted if a hard-and-fast rule were applied that, unless he could prove a market selling price, he could get nothing.[79]

The cost of a replacement may, in an appropriate case, include the cost of transporting the same to the location from which the asset was converted, and of installing it there. In a Western Australian case concerning the alleged Conversion of certain mining equipment from a site in the remote Murchison goldfields,[80] it was held that if the claimant had intended to use the complete plant of which the allegedly converted equipment formed a necessary part on that remote site, it would have been entitled to recover such costs.[81] Equally, however, if (as the judge held) the claimant in truth has no use for the converted asset, then it could not recover any more than its realisable value at the place from which it was

---

[75] *Ewbank v Nutting and anor* (1849) 7 CB 797 at 809–11, 137 ER 316 at 321–22 (a case where there may well have been a market in the subject asset (salt), but no evidence as to the same was adduced save for the claimant's purchase invoice).

[76] *Chubb Cash v John Crilley* [1983] 1 WLR 599 at 604C–D per Bush J.

[77] [1937] 3 All ER 620 (CA).

[78] ibid at 624B–D.

[79] ibid at 627A–B.

[80] North of Meekatharra, WA: *Brybay Pty Ltd and ors v Esanda Finance Corporation Ltd* [2002] WASC 309, McLure J.

[81] ibid at [237].

converted.[82] As *Clerk & Lindsell* puts it, 'generally speaking goods in the course of trade should be valued at the place of conversion'.[83]

In *France v Gaudet*[84] the claimant had contracted to buy from the defendant 100 cases of champagne of a particular brand and quality which was not (otherwise) available on the market, at a price of 14s per case. He promptly secured a highly profitable contract for their resale to the captain of a vessel shortly to sail from London, at 24s per case. However the defendant then converted the same by wrongfully withholding them from the claimant, the purchaser's ship sailed, and the profitable resale was lost. The claimant recovered his full loss of 10s per case (£50). As Mellor J (who had delivered the judgment of the court) himself subsequently explained the decision, absent any market (and hence any market price) the evidence of the claimant's own sale was the best evidence of the value of the champagne: 'Champagne of a similar quality was said not to be procurable in the market. There was, therefore, no other test of the value of the goods.'[85] Cases where the loss of a profitable resale has been sought *as such* often give rise to issues of foreseeability and remoteness, which are dealt with under that side-heading below.[86]

In less common commercial situations, the court is often left in a position where it simply has to 'do the best it can' on the available evidence to arrive at a proper value for the converted asset. For example, in *Fairfax Gerrard Holdings v Capital Bank*[87] HHJ Mackie QC quantified damages for the Conversion[88] of a specialised industrial printing machine imported from China by taking the price paid by the defendant bank (which was to hire the machine to the end user to whose specification it had been ordered) and then discounting the same by almost 25 per cent 'to reflect the realities of realising the value of a very particular machine delivered for one customer bearing the [importer's] brand name'.[89]

---

[82] ibid, at [238]–[240].

[83] n 34, at para 17–93.

[84] (1871) LR 6 QB 199.

[85] *Horne and anor v Midland Railway Company* (1873) LR 8 CP 131 at 132 per Mellor J *arguendo*. See also *Stroud v Austin & Co* (1883) Cab & E 119 (QB), and Maugham LJ's explanation of both cases in *The Arpad* [1934] P 189 (CA) at 230–31 and 234–35.

[86] For an example of such a case, where there was no issue on foreseeability or remoteness, see *Sony v Cinram* (n 46); see also text to n 212.

[87] *Fairfax Gerrard Holdings Ltd and ors v Capital Bank plc* [2006] EWHC 3439 (Comm), [2007] 1 Lloyd's Rep 171; reversed on other grounds at [2007] EWCA Civ 1226, [2008] 1 Lloyd's Rep 297.

[88] By the granting of a finance lease over the same (to a hirer to whom it was then delivered)—see ibid at [34].

[89] ibid at [41].

(d) Presumptions as to Value

In the classic case of *Armory v Delamirie*[90] Pratt CJ applied the maxim *omnia praesumuntur contra spoliatorem* and directed the jury that in assessing damages they should, unless the defendant produced the missing stone and showed that it was not 'of the finest water', take the value of the best jewel that would fit the (empty) socket in the ring they returned to the chimney-sweep's boy. However in modern times this presumption is no longer applied with eighteenth century vigour. It is now limited to circumstances where it is consistent with the rest of the facts,[91] where there is an evidential vacuum,[92] or where 'there is insoluble doubt' between any two possible assessments.[93]

A more modern approach to assessing damages in Conversion for non-delivery of lost jewels is well illustrated by the judgment of Field J in *Colbeck v Diamanta*.[94] There the judge found that application of the presumption in *Armory v Delamirie* would not be appropriate, because assuming that the lost jewels were of the finest quality would be inconsistent with the evidence as to what the claimant had originally paid for the subject jewels. He went on to accept evidence from the claimant's expert which extrapolated the likely colour and clarity of the jewels from those prices.[95]

(e) Special Rules

Assets Severed from Land

Where assets are brought into existence as such by being severed from land, for example by unlawful mining for minerals, the injured land-owner may elect between claims based on trespass to his land, and claims based on Conversion of

---

[90] (1722) 1 Str 505, 93 ER 664, JH Baker and SFC Milsom, *Sources of English Legal History* (London, Butterworths, 1986) 547, AKR Kiralfy, *A Source Book of English Law* (London, Sweet & Maxwell, 1957) 153, already discussed in ch 2, text to fn 100 ff and ch 4, text to fns 10–11.

[91] See *Malhotra v Dhawan* [1997] 8 Med LR 319 at 322 r/h col per Morritt LJ.

[92] *Williamson v Phillips, Son & Neale*, QBD 29 July 1998 (unreported, Lawtel AC0007208). There Hidden J accepted the defendant's submission that 'where the court had acceptable evidence upon which it was satisfied that a given proposition was proved in favour of the wrongdoer, there was no room for [the *Armory v Delamirie*] presumption', and continued 'the law, like nature, abhors a vacuum . . . in *Armory*, where there was a vacuum, in that there was no evidence at all as to what the stone was, the law filled that vacuum by the use of the maxim *omnia praesumuntur contra spoliatorem*. Here, however, there is no lack of evidence' (transcript pp 89–90).

[93] *Seager v Copydex Ltd (No 2)* [1969] 1 WLR 809 (CA) at 815B per Winn LJ; see also *Malhotra v Dhawan* (n 91) at 322 r/h col per Morritt LJ.

[94] *Colbeck v Diamanta (UK) Ltd and anor* [2002] EWHC 616 (QB).

[95] ibid at [24]–[26].

the severed asset.[96] Damages awarded on the latter basis are assessed by reference to the value of the severed minerals, rather than the damage to the claimant's land.[97]

In computing that value, however, a particular rule has developed with regard to what allowances are to be made against their gross realisable price in respect of the costs incurred in their 'production'. The costs of hauling them below ground and raising them to the surface will be allowed, because the Conversion occurs immediately upon their severance from the land, and that takes place at the bottom of the mine, not at the surface. However, contrary to the early cases,[98] the costs of hewing and getting them (that is the process leading to the severance itself) came to be allowed to those defendants who undertook that work under a bona fide claim to, and belief that they had, title to the same.[99] As a matter of pure principle this rule seems hard to justify, and Lord Hatherley LC could not 'say that this doctrine is very satisfactory';[100] but the injustice to the 'innocent' defendant,[101] giving rise to something of a windfall for the claimant, seems to have led to its emergence.

Improvements

At common law, reflecting the *nemo dat quod non habet* principle, the victim of a Conversion was entitled to take back the converted asset without making any payment in respect of improvements effected to it whilst out of his possession. This rule was not limited to improvements effected by the converter, for a third party to whom the asset was delivered for repair could only exercise the usual repairer's lien in answer to the true owner's claim for delivery up if his possession

---

[96]   In principle, the remedy of recaption could be exercised on the latter basis, under the principle that an owner may claim a chattel wherever he finds it; hence the owner (by then of both the land and the severed mineral) can claim the mineral at (say) the entrance to the quarry or mine: see *Martin v Porter* (1839) 5 M & W 351 at 354, 151 ER 149 at 150 per Lord Abinger CB; *Jegon v Vivian* (1871) LR 6 Ch App 742 at 760 per Lord Hatherley LC; *Bilambil-Terranora Pty Ltd v Tweed Shire Council* [1980] 1 NSWLR 465 (NSWCA) at [114] per Mahoney JA (as to which see further at n 267).

[97]   *Martin v Porter* (ibid); *Clarke v Holford* (1848) 2 Car & K 540 at 543–44, 175 ER 224 at 225–26 per Rolfe B (concerning fixtures severed and taken from a dwelling); *Bilambil-Terranora P/L v Tweed SC* (ibid) per Reynolds and Mahoney JJA, discussed in *Finesky Holdings Pty Ltd v Minister for Transport (WA)* [2002] WASCA 206, 26 WAR 368 at [50]–[58] per Stytler J.

[98]   See, eg, *Martin v Porter* (n 96), for a fuller analysis of which, see DM Gordon, 'Anomalies in the Law of Conversion' (1955) 71 *LQR* 346, especially at 350–51.

[99]   *Wood v Morewood* (1841) 3 QB 440n at 441, 114 ER 575n at 576, Parke B; *Jegon v Vivian* (n 96); *Bilambil-Terranora P/L v Tweed SC* [1980] 1 NSWLR 465 at [38], [48] and [53] per Reynolds JA and [93]–[95] and [99]–[109] per Mahony JA. For criticism of this rule see Gordon, (ibid).

[100]   *Jegon v Vivian* (n 96) at 761.

[101]   *Pace* P Matthews, 'Freedom, Unrequested Improvements, and Lord Denning' [1981] *CLJ* 340.

was lawful when the lien first attached; this in turn depended on whether the delivery to the repairer was effected with the owner's express or implied authority.[102]

Greenwood v Bennett[103] tested the common law position one stage further. What if the repairs had been effected by an innocent purchaser of the converted asset, before selling it on to another? Such facts, as Weir put it, 'lie at a clover-leaf, where the motorways of law and equity, property and obligation, become a maze'.[104] The case was resolved unanimously on the basis that the order obtained by the true owner was equitable in nature, and that, applying established principles,[105] such orders should only be made on terms that the claimant gave the repairer/improver a fair and just allowance. Absent that equitable jurisdiction, however, only Lord Denning MR considered that the repairer would have a cause of action (in restitution) to recover recompense for his work.[106] Cairns LJ expressly disagreed on this point, opining that 'If the car had, before any proceedings were brought, reached the hands of [the true owner], it is difficult to see that [the repairer] could have had any claim against him'.[107]

It is noteworthy that in *Munro v Willmott*,[108] a somewhat simpler case concerning a car repaired for good motives, but without either the true owner's authority or any belief that the repairer had good title, Lynskey J made a point of stating that, on the one hand, he was not awarding the claimant the current value of her car, which the defendant had much improved at considerable cost to himself, nor, on the other hand, awarding the defendant payment for what he had done as such. Rather, he took account of the defendant's work and expenditure as a means of enabling him to arrive at (or back-calculate) what the claimant's car would have been worth absent the improvements brought about by the defendant.[109] Properly understood, this illustrates how the prima facie rule that damages in Conversion are assessed at the date of Conversion, not judgment, can assist in alleviating the potential difficulties generated by post-Conversion improvements.[110]

The common law position has been supplemented by a number of specific provisions in the 1977 Act, which, at least at first blush, make the law in this area

---

[102] *Bowmaker Ltd v Wycombe Motors Ltd* [1946] KB 505 (DC); *Tappenden v Artus and anor* [1964] 2 QB 185 (CA) at 195–96 per Diplock LJ (giving the judgment of the Court); and see also 18th Report (n 6) at para 89.

[103] *Greenwood v Bennett & ors* [1973] QB 195 (CA).

[104] T Weir 'Doing Good by Mistake—Restitution and Remedies' [1973] *CLJ* 23.

[105] In particular, a dictum of Lord Macnaghten in *Peruvian Guano Co v Dreyfus Brothers & Co* [1892] AC 166 at 176.

[106] *Greenwood v Bennett* (n 103) at 202C–F.

[107] ibid at 203B–C.

[108] [1949] 1 KB 295.

[109] ibid at 299.

[110] As to which see also *Greenwood v Bennett* (n 103) at 201B–C per Lord Denning MR. Note however that in detinue the prima facie rule was that damages were assessed at the date of the judgment, giving rise to an unfortunate anomaly in the present context.

a good deal more just.[111] In proceedings for wrongful interference[112] against anyone who has improved the subject asset in the mistaken but honest belief that he had good title to it, she is to be given an allowance to the extent that the asset's value is attributable to her improvement of it; the same applies where the proceedings are against a purchaser in good faith from an improver.[113] Further, where in such a case an order is made for specific delivery of the asset, the court may impose a condition that such an allowance be made by the claimant.[114]

However, as we have already noted,[115] the 1977 Act is not a codifying statute, and, therefore, save where the Act otherwise provides, the common law position remains unaltered. Thus, for example, an effective 'self-help' recaption of converted assets, without involving the courts, is unaffected by the above provisions, and it remains highly questionable whether an innocent improver would then have any free-standing cause of action in restitution against the true owner in (resumed) possession.[116]

Title Deeds

Historically, a claimant suing for Conversion of title deeds was prima facie entitled to recover the value of the subject land.[117] As *Clerk & Lindsell* points out, however, in modern times it is 'extremely unlikely that loss of title deeds will cause loss of the land they represent: and in this case the traditional measure of damages is obviously inappropriate'.[118] We mention this old rule only because it may give some insight into the thinking underlying the so-called 'documentary exception', to which we now come.

Negotiable Instruments, Securities and Like Documents

As Lord Hoffmann summarised the position in *OBG Ltd v Allan*, there is a

> line of authority, which in England goes back to the beginning of the 19th century or earlier, by which a person who misappropriates a document which constitutes or evidences title to a debt can be liable in conversion for the face value of the document . . . in cases in which the title to the debt was evidenced by a negotiable instrument, or even in some cases where it was not negotiable, the wrongful misappropriation of the document could cause actual loss to the true creditor, who might not be

---

[111]   For a well reasoned argument to the contrary see Matthews, Freedom (*CLJ* 1981) at 340. For a critique of the provisions of s 6 see V Sacks' Note on the 1977 Act in (1978) 41 *MLR* 713 at 713–17.

[112]   As defined in s 1, the 1977 Act.

[113]   The 1977 Act, ss 6(1) and (2).

[114]   ibid s 3(7).

[115]   See ch 2, text to fn 232 and ch 5, text to fn 126; see also n 249 below.

[116]   Though she may, of course, have contractual or restitutionary rights against others (and see s 6(3) of the 1977 Act). For criticisms of Lord Denning MR's minority view in *Greenwood v Bennett* (text to n 106) see T Weir, Doing Good (*CLJ* 1973) at 26–27 and Matthews (n 101).

[117]   Clerk & Lindsell (n 34) para 17–100, citing dicta of Alderson B in *Loosemore v Radford* (1842) 9 M & W 657 at 659, 152 ER 277 at 278 and of Parke B in the detinue case of *Williams v Archer* (1847) CB 318 at 327–29, 136 ER 899 at 903–904 (giving the judgment of the Court).

[118]   n 34, at para 17–100; see also at para 17–36.

able to recover the debt. That left a gap in the law. The judges filled it by treating the misappropriation as a conversion of a chattel equal in value to the debt which it evidenced.[119]

Thus, to take the best known example, the prima facie measure of damages for a converted cheque is its face value, that is its value as a chose in action rather than as a small, rectangular piece of paper.[120] As Lord Nicholls observed in the same case, the same common law which had originally established trover, the predecessor of Conversion, by way of a legal fiction, hereby 'resorted to another legal fiction ... [as now] is openly recognised'.[121]

Other Documents of Some Evidential Status

As would be expected, the reach of this useful tool gradually expanded. Now it is not confined to documents of title and negotiable instruments. It includes insurance policies, guarantees, share certificates and much else. In Clerk & Lindsell the principle is said to extend to 'any document which is specially prepared in the ordinary course of business as evidence of a debt or obligation'[122]

As early as 1900, in *Bavins Jnr & Sims v London & South Western Bank Ltd* the Court of Appeal suggested that the damages payable for Conversion of a document which was not a cheque, but mere documentary evidence of a chose in action (an acknowledgement of debt coupled with an informal instruction for payment to the debtor's bank), may nevertheless extend to the value of the chose in action.[123] *Clerk & Lindsell*, which also identifies bills of lading and trading stamps[124] as categories of document to which this fiction has been applied, states that it is not clear to what further categories this 'face value' measure of loss may apply, citing as examples of such uncertainty 'book tokens, credit cards, tickets of various sorts'.[125]

---

[119] [2007] UKHL 21, [2008] 1 AC 1 at [102] and [104]. The leading cases include *Morison v London, County and Westminster Bank Ltd* [1914] 3 KB 356 (CA); *AL Underwood Ltd v Bank of Liverpool and Martins* [1924] 1 KB 775 (CA); and *Lloyds Bank Ltd v The Chartered Bank of India, Australia and China* [1929] 1 KB 40 (CA).

[120] See Clerk & Lindsell (n 34) paras 17–35 and 17–99. In some circumstances credit may be given for payments subsequently made by the converter to the claimant: see *Hunter BNZ Finance Ltd v Australia and New Zealand Banking Group Ltd* [1990] VR 41 at 48 (though on the facts of that case, the claim to credit failed).

[121] [2007] UKHL 21, [2008] 1 AC 1 at [225] and [227], citing Pill LJ and Potter LJ in *Smith v Lloyds TSB Group plc* [2001] QB 541 at 551 and 557, and Mance LJ in the court below [2005] EWCA Civ 106, [2005] QB 762 at [76].

[122] ibid per Lord Nicholls at [226], citing Clerk & Lindsell (n 34) at para 17–35; see also per Baroness Hale at [310].

[123] [1900] 1 QB 270 at 275 per AL Smith LJ, 276 per Collins LJ, and 278 per Vaughan Williams LJ.

[124] For which see *Building and Civil Engineering Holidays Scheme Management Ltd v Post Office* [1966] 1 QB 247 (CA).

[125] n 34 at para 17–99, especially fn 59.

Claimant with a Limited Interest

The basic common law rule is that a claimant who can establish actual possession will recover the full value of the converted asset from a converter with no interest in it, regardless of whether the claimant has a limited proprietary interest in the same, for example by reason of having entered into a bailment of the same (whether as bailor or bailee).[126] Thus in *Swire v Leach*[127] a pawnbroker recovered the full value of pawned goods held in his possession, and upon which distress was unlawfully levied, rather than just the value of his interest in them. This reflects the principle discussed in chapter four that the interest protected by Conversion is that of the superior right to possession.[128]

Where a bailee recovers damages in Conversion in excess of his interest in the subject asset, as between himself and the bailor he has an obligation to account in respect of the same, just as he would have had in respect of the bailed asset itself.[129] However once a bailee has made full recovery of its value, that bars any subsequent claim which the bailor might otherwise have made,[130] and vice versa.[131]

The common law has admitted various exceptions to the basic rule. Perhaps the most commercially relevant in modern times relates to goods on hire-purchase, where the proprietary interest of the claimant (be it the finance company or the hirer) will be limited. In the cases of *Wickham Holdings Ltd v Brooke House Motors Ltd*[132] and *Belvoir Finance Co Ltd v Stapleton*[133] the claimant finance companies' recovery against hirers who had sold the hired assets without authority was limited to what they had in fact lost, being the amount of the unpaid hire instalments. The principle[134] was explained by Fox LJ in *Chubb Cash v John Crilley* thus:

> In both cases the measure of damages permitted was held to be the actual loss to the plaintiffs which, on the facts, was the amount still owing under the hire-purchase agreement at the date of conversion ... The object of the court in those decisions was not to give the plaintiff more than the value of the chattel at the date of the conversion, but less. The court regarded it as unjust that, if the hire-purchase owner had only a limited interest in the goods (i.e., the outstanding instalments), he should recover their

---

[126]   *The Winkfield* [1902] P 42 (CA) per Collins MR at 54–55, and see also at 60: 'the root principle of the whole discussion is that, as against a wrong-doer, possession is title'; *The Jag Shakti* [1986] AC 337 (PC) at 345.

[127]   (1865) 18 CB (NS) 479, 141 ER 531.

[128]   See ch 4 generally, but especially under the headings Relativity of Title, Legal Possession and The Significance of Legal Possession.

[129]   *The Winkfield* [1902] P 42 (CA) per Collins MR at 60–61; *Hepburn v A Tomlinson (Hauliers) Ltd* [1966] AC 451 at 468 per Lord Reid and 480 per Lord Pearce.

[130]   *The Winkfield* (ibid) per Collins MR at 61.

[131]   *O'Sullivan v Williams* [1992] 3 All ER 385. See also ch 4, text to fn 52 and ch 2, fn 104.

[132]   [1967] 1 WLR 295 (CA). See also the older case of *Whiteley Ltd v Hilt* [1918] 2 KB 808 (CA).

[133]   [1971] 1 QB 210 (CA), where the HP contracts in question were illegal.

[134]   Which has been followed since the *Kuwait Airways* case (n 7) as unaffected by it: see *VFS Financial Services (UK) Ltd v Euro Auctions (UK) Ltd and ors* [2007] EWHC 1492 (QB) at [93]–[108] and [134].

full value. The damage, therefore, was limited to the actual amount of the loss, that is to say the amount still outstanding under the hire-purchase agreement.[135]

Hence in the *Chubb Cash* case itself,[136] the claimant finance company was not able to recover the amount outstanding under the finance agreement, because there the market value of the asset was less.[137]

As to the theoretical basis for the approach in these hire purchase cases, in *VFS Financial Services v Euro Auctions* HHJ Richard Seymour QC, having cited paragraphs [63] to [67] of Lord Nicholls' speech in *Kuwait Airways*,[138] opined that

> in the light of the more general formulation of the basis of assessment of damages in the case of conversion set out in the passage from Lord Nicholls's speech which I have quoted, it is probably technically more correct hereafter to consider the decision in *Wickham Holdings Ltd v Brooke House Motors Ltd* not, as has hitherto been the case in most academic writings, as laying down a principle applicable to the assessment of damages in all cases of a claim in conversion by a finance company which has let the goods converted on hire purchase, but as an example of a situation of common occurrence in which the application of the general formulation of Lord Nicholls will lead to the same conclusion as that reached by the Court of Appeal in *Wickham Holdings Ltd v Brooke House Motors Ltd.*[139]

A similar principle was applied by the High Court of Australia in *Butler and ors v The Egg and Egg Pulp Marketing Board.*[140] There the Board, which had the benefit of a statutory vesting in it of title to the converted eggs, would as a condition thereof (if the eggs had been submitted to it, as they should) have been bound to account to the producers for a proportion of their net proceeds of sale (a condition at least broadly equivalent to a limitation on its title). The net profit which the Board would have made on selling the eggs represented its actual loss,

---

[135] [1983] 1 WLR 599 (CA) at 601B–E; see also at 602A–B: 'The Wickham case and the Belvoir case are quite different as they are concerned solely with the problem which arises where the hire-purchase company seek to recover in respect of the conversion an amount which is more than the amount still outstanding under the hire-purchase agreement, which the court in those cases thought to be unfair ... Their purpose was to limit the damages.'

[136] For a discussion of which see text to n 44 ff. Note that this was a claim against a third party, not against the hirer or his agent.

[137] Cf *Millar v Candy* (1981) 58 FLR 145 where the Full Court of the Federal Court of Australia held that a claimant, who was the hirer and bailee of a car destroyed by the defendant's negligence, could not recover damages representing the sum he was liable to pay under the finance agreement insofar as it exceeded the market value of the car at the date of its destruction. In principle an award would have been made to compensate the claimant for the loss of certain rights under the finance agreement which terminated upon the car's destruction (the right to acquire ownership, rather than return the car, at the end of the hire period, and the right to pay by instalments over time rather than an immediate lump sum), though on the facts no such loss was proved and quantified. It is submitted that this result would have been the same had the cause of action been Conversion.

[138] For part of [67], see text to n 13.

[139] [2007] EWHC 1492 (QB) at [102].

[140] [1966] HCA 38, 114 CLR 185, cited with approval in *Kuwait Airways* [2002] UKHL 19, [2002] 2 AC 886 by Lord Nicholls at [66].

and therefore the limit of its recovery (the value of the eggs when converted would have been a materially higher sum).

The common law concerning claimants with a limited interest has in some respects been modified by provisions of the 1977 Act. So far as assets in which more than one party has an interest are concerned, provided the identity of the interested parties is known, the procedural position is greatly eased by sections 7 and 8, the operation of which we have discussed in chapter four.[141]

(f) Where the Goods are Returned—'Temporary Deprivation'

As long ago as 1860, Bramwell B asserted that 'where a defendant, after having been guilty of an act of conversion, delivers the goods back to the plaintiff, the actual damage sustained, and not the value, is the measure of damages'.[142] Notwithstanding the antiquity of this dictum, and the distinction of its author, it and its subsequent application have given rise to doctrinal problems in the law of Conversion. A more principled approach need not be a less pragmatic or less just one. A simple and reasonably modern example is afforded by the New Zealand case of *Aitken Agencies Ltd v Richardson*. The defendant took the claimant's van for a joyride, and crashed it. The van was 'fairly severely damaged', and in due course recovered from the police station by the claimant, who then had it repaired at a cost of about £247. No evidence of value as such, at either the time of Conversion or the time of restoration, was adduced. McGregor J nevertheless held that the evidence submitted as to the cost of repair afforded prima facie evidence of the depreciation in value, and therefore awarded that sum *as a measure of the reduction in value.* He also awarded the cost of hiring an alternative vehicle in the meantime as consequential loss.[143]

This decision is consistent with the decision of the Privy Council in *Solloway v McLaughlin*.[144] Where a claimant has received from the defendant the 'return' of what turns out to be the equivalent of his (previously converted) asset, rather than the asset itself, the 'only effect' of the fact that he had received and accepted from the wrongdoer the equivalent asset recently bought in (not knowing of the earlier Conversion) was that 'he must give credit for the value of what he has received at the time he received it, and the damages are reduced by this amount'.[145]

The most problematic modern case is *Brandeis Ltd v Western Transport Ltd.*[146] The claimant sued for wrongful detention of certain copper—which it had

---

[141] Under the side-heading What is Actual Possession, *Jus Tertii*.

[142] *Chinery v Viall* (1860) 5 H&N 288 at 295, 157 ER 1192 at 1195.

[143] [1967] NZLR 65, especially at 67.

[144] Discussed in text to n 66 ff.

[145] *Solloway v McLaughlin* [1938] AC 247 (PC) at 258 per Lord Atkin; see also *Uzinterimpex JSC v Standard Bank plc* [2008] EWCA Civ 819, [2008] 2 Lloyd's Rep 456 per Moore-Bick LJ at [63]. *Cf Trailways Transport Ltd v Thomas*, text to n 154 ff.

[146] [1981] QB 864 (CA).

purchased to have refined and then use as a raw material in the manufacture of cathodes—for a period of some nine months, during which (a) the market price of copper had fallen and (b) the claimant was paying interest on the bank overdraft facilities by which it funded such purchases. The claimant called no evidence as to what would have happened to the copper had it not been wrongfully detained, and eschewed any basis of quantifying its losses other than (a) and (b) above; the Court of Appeal awarded it nominal damages only. In a case note Tettenborn pointed out that it seems hard to reconcile this with the decision in *The Mediana*,[147] and argued that in such a case the claimant should recover damages calculated as notional interest on the capital tied up in its withheld property.[148]

The Privy Council in *BBMB Ltd v Eda Holdings Ltd*[149] explained the *Brandeis* decision as being dependent on the fact that the defendant had retained the assets in question all along, with the consequence that the claim was in substance merely one for temporary deprivation of possession and use of property. The asset returned to the claimant was one and the same as that which it had entrusted to the defendant. With regard to such cases, Lord Templeman stated: '*in conversion or in detinue* ... the appropriate measure of damages may be assessed by reference to the value at the date when the plaintiff demanded the return of the property[150] or the date when the plaintiff was prevented from reselling the property'[151] (authors' emphasis).[152] He went on to contrast cases 'when the property is irreversibly converted and the plaintiff loses that property. The plaintiff loses the value of the property at the date of conversion and the general rule is that the measure of damages is the value thus lost.'[153]

In *Trailways Transport Ltd v Thomas* in the New Zealand High Court, Tompkins J suggested that this part of the reasoning in *BBMB* is not easy to follow, and that it is difficult to see why the return of an identical replacement asset should be treated differently from the return of the asset itself.[154] With respect, we would suggest that there are clear policy reasons why that should be so, as is amply illustrated by the facts of both *Solloway v McLaughlin* and *BBMB*.[155] However Tompkins J's decision on the facts of the *Trailways Transport* case, where the subject refrigerated containers were returned to the claimant bailee some three and a half years after their Conversion, does not appear open to criticism. He awarded damages on the basis of the containers' value at the date of their Conversion, reduced by their (much lesser) value when returned. His decision is

---

[147] Discussed in text to n 171 ff.
[148] A Tettenborn, 'Loss, Damage and Wrongful Detention' (1982) 132 *NLJ* 154.
[149] [1990] 1 WLR 409.
[150] Citing *Williams v Archer* (1847) 5 CB 318, 136 ER 899 (a detinue claim).
[151] Citing *Barrow v Arnaud* (1846) 8 QB 595, 115 ER 1000 (an action on the case).
[152] *BBMB Ltd v Eda Holdings Ltd* (n 149) at 412G–H.
[153] ibid at 413D–E.
[154] [1996] 2 NZLR 443 at 448.
[155] Already discussed at text to n 66 ff.

in marked contrast to that in *Brandeis v Western Transport,* but consistent with that in *Aitken Agencies Ltd v Richardson* (albeit not cited to him). It would appear to follow a sound and principled approach to the quantification of damages in a successful Conversion claim, in that the primary measure of loss is taken as the value of the converted asset at the time of its Conversion, and the credit against that sum required to be given by a claimant who has later accepted back the converted asset is quantified by reference to its value at the time of its return.

The underlying difficulty which the courts seem from time to time to have felt is that the facts of some cases of Conversion instinctively feel more like a claim for temporary detention (even before the 1977 Act most cases of detinue could equally have been pleaded as a Conversion[156]), and in such circumstances they appear to have felt a concern, which we would suggest to be misplaced,[157] that application of the conventional measure of damages for Conversion would produce an unfair or unjust result, or—reverting to the words of Bramwell B—an award which does not accord with 'the actual damage sustained' by the claimant. This thinking emerges from the following statement in the same paragraph of his judgment in *Chinery v Viall* from which we quoted at the commencement of this section:

> [T]he principle deducible from the authorities being that a man cannot by merely changing the form of action entitle himself to recover damages greater than the amount to which he is in law entitled, according to the true facts of the case and the real nature of the transaction.

Where does this leave the *Brandeis* decision? We would suggest that it is of questionable authority with regard to claims in Conversion, and that the approach in the *Aitken Agencies* and *Trailways Transport* cases should, at least generally, be preferred. Notwithstanding that *Brandeis* did not reach the Court of Appeal until March 1981, it was a claim in the (abolished) tort of detinue: the relevant detention occurred in August/September 1976, proceedings were commenced on 15 September of that year, and the goods were returned on or about 27 May 1977, all well before the 1977 Act came into force on 1 January 1978.

The approach adopted in the New Zealand cases is true to the principle that a successful claimant in a Conversion case should be compensated for the infringement of her property rights as such, rather than for what she happens to have lost by reason of being deprived of them, whether temporarily or permanently. A claimant is entitled to the use and possession of her property to do with as she will. An enquiry into her intentions at the time of the Conversion (or subsequently), is not to the point. The position was starkly and compellingly put by the Earl of Halsbury LC in *The Mediana*: 'Supposing a person took away a chair out of my room and kept it for twelve months, could anybody say you had a right to

---

[156] See 18th Report (n 6) at paras 7 and 10.
[157] See, eg, *Aitken Agencies Ltd v Richardson* (n 143).

diminish the damages by shewing that I did not usually sit in that chair, or that there were plenty of other chairs in the room?'[158]

Furthermore, a particular curiosity arises from the approach adopted in *Brandeis*. It would seem to follow from that approach, that in a case where an asset has been converted, and its value has then fallen, an astute claimant should decline any subsequent offer of its return, and instead exercise its statutory right of election under section 3(3)(b) of the 1977 Act in favour of damages *simpliciter* (under section 3(2)(c)) rather than delivery with the alternative of paying damages by reference to value (under section 3(2)(b)). Whether the claimant's duty to mitigate his losses could be relied on as *obliging* him to accept a tendered return of his (previously converted) asset from the converter or his agent would seem far from certain. The better view, we would suggest, is that the claimant should be free to elect whether to accept back the converted asset, though there would be room for a *de minimis* exception where the asset was withheld from the claimant for only a very short, and commercially insignificant, time. This would, after all, recognise that, by depriving the claimant of his possessory rights, a defendant has thereby deprived him of the opportunity to dispose of that asset as and when he chose to do so (which may, for example, have been before a fall in the market).

(g) Consequential Loss

[A]lthough damages for conversion normally consist in the value of the goods at the date of conversion, consequential damages are always recoverable if not too remote.[159]

Post-Conversion Increases in Value

As mentioned above, an increase in value in the subject asset between the date of the Conversion and the date of judgment should in principle be to the credit of the claimant, not the defendant, and at common law such increase has been treated as consequential loss. Apart from the resultant question as to causation, which is considered under that heading below, other limits to the principle have developed. The increase must not have been due to any act of the defendant.[160] It will not be recoverable if and so far as attributable to undue delay on the part of the claimant in seeking to recover his property.[161] Further, given the practical difficulty following from the formulation of section 3(2)(b) of the 1977 Act,[162] any award in form (b) should include this aspect of the 'consequential loss' within

---

[158] *The Mediana* [1900] AC 113 at 117. This sentence forms part of a longer citation which appears at text to n 173.

[159] *Hillesden Securities Ltd v Ryjack Ltd and anor* [1983] 1 WLR 959 at 963E–F per Parker J.

[160] *Munro v Willett* [1949] 1 KB 295 at 298–99 per Lynskey J; see also 18th Report (n 6) at para 88.

[161] *Sachs v Miklos* [1948] 2 KB 23 per Goddard LCJ at 41. See also *Graham v Voigt* [1989] ACTSC 5, 89 ACTR 11 Kelly J (discussed in text to n 177); Clerk & Lindsell (n 34) at para 17–91.

[162] As explained in text to nn 58–62.

the (presumably single, composite) figure in respect of 'damages by reference to value of the goods', rather than the (again presumably single, composite) figure in respect of 'any consequential damages'.

User Damages

A particular head of damage, generally referred to as 'user damages', is recoverable where the subject asset was profit-earning in the hands of the claimant, classically by virtue of ordinarily being let out for hire as part of the claimant's business, and was in fact applied by the defendant for his own purposes during the period of deprivation. In the leading case of *Strand Electric v Brisford*, a claim in detinue, Denning LJ put the justification for this rule with customary clarity:

> If the wrongdoer had asked the owner for permission to use the goods, the owner would be entitled to ask for a reasonable remuneration as the price of his permission. The wrongdoer cannot be better off because he did not ask permission.[163]

Interestingly, given the proprietary aspect to Conversion discussed above, the nearest analogy was said to be a claim for mesne profits.[164] The notional hiring charge runs up to the date when the goods are returned, or are irreversibly converted as the case may be.[165]

Strand Electric v Brisford was applied to a claim in Conversion by Parker J in *Hillesden Securities Ltd v Ryjack Ltd*.[166] There a Rolls Royce motor car was purportedly sold, by the original lessee under a leasing agreement, to the defendants. Over two years later it was returned to the claimant (the lessor's assignee), after the commencement of the trial but before judgment. The claimant recovered damages calculated as the agreed reasonable weekly hire charge for the entire period between its Conversion and its return.

The facts of *Kuwait Airways* could have given rise to consideration of this head of loss at the highest appellate level, so far as concerned those aircraft referred to as 'the Iran Six'. However no such claim was pleaded or formulated, and understandably the House of Lords declined to allow it to be argued there for the first time.[167]

In the Queensland case of *Meredith & anor v Eggins*,[168] where the subject of the Conversion was a fishing vessel, there was a claim for loss of business profits in addition to the value of the vessel itself. The claimant was deprived of the immediate right to its possession by the defendant from its initial Conversion in or about November 2002 until its destruction in Cyclone Larry in March 2006.

---

[163] [1952] 2 QB 246 (CA) at 254. See further as to this case under the heading Causation, below.
[164] Per Denning LJ ibid at 252.
[165] ibid, at 253, 255, 257–58.
[166] [1983] 1 WLR 959.
[167] *Kuwait Airways* [2002] UKHL 19, [2002] 2 AC 886 at [87]–[90].
[168] [2006] QDC 164.

However the judge held that it would only have been economic to use the vessel for fishing from January 2003 to July 2004. He held that:

> The plaintiff's claim for loss of profits is in the nature of a claim for damages for the loss of a chance to use the vessel to generate income from fishing. Such a claim is allowed in an action for damages for conversion ... The vessel was clearly a "profit-earning chattel".[169]

An uncertain question to which this case gives rise is whether the claimants might have made a greater recovery had they simply sought a reasonable hire charge or similar in respect of the vessel. Damages so quantified may be awarded even in cases where the claimant did not in fact intend to hire out the subject asset at all, and are in that sense nominal.[170] In *The Mediana* the respondents were the owners of a lightship, the *Comet*, which was damaged by the appellants' negligence.[171] Rather than hire a replacement vessel commercially, they used in its place another vessel, the *Orion*, which they already had lying idle. The appellants submitted that the respondents were not thereby put to any additional expense.

Lord Brampton summarised the position thus:

> They might have used a hired vessel had they so pleased, in which case the liability for the hire would have been clear. But the respondents prudently, having a vessel suited for the purpose lying idle, thought it right in their discretion to use her instead of hiring perhaps a less efficient substitute for the *Comet*. The services of the *Orion*, however, were valuable, and why should the appellants claim to have them gratuitously, including the wages of the men who might have been employed on board her?[172]

The Earl of Halsbury LC rejected the appellants' argument thus:

> [T]he broad proposition seems to me to be that by a wrongful act of the defendants the plaintiffs were deprived of their vessel. When I say deprived of their vessel, I will not use the phrase 'the use of the vessel.' What right has a wrongdoer to consider what use you are going to make of your vessel? More than one case has been put to illustrate this: for example, the owner of a horse, or of a chair. Supposing a person took away a chair out of my room and kept it for twelve months, could anybody say you had a right to diminish the damages by shewing that I did not usually sit in that chair, or that there were plenty of other chairs in the room? ... the broad principle seems to me to be quite independent of the particular use the plaintiffs were going to make of the thing that was taken[173]

---

[169]   ibid, written judgment at 5 (CF Wall QC). This claim was discounted for contingencies by 10%.

[170]   Which term 'does not mean small damages': see per the Earl of Halsbury LC in *The Mediana* [1900] AC 113 at 116.

[171]   The Earl of Lord Halsbury LC expressly noted that the claim was not one in trover or detinue, but observed that 'the principle upon which damages are to be assessed does not depend upon the form of action at all' (ibid at 118).

[172]   ibid at 123.

[173]   ibid at 117. See also ch 3 under the heading The Three Elements of Conversion.

Given the labels applied to the only types of damages included within the forms of order provided for by sections 3(2)(a) and (b) of the 1977 Act,[174] it would appear that any element of user damages ought to be included within the figure for 'consequential damages' in an Order made in form (a) or form (b).

Costs of Mitigation, and Loss of Business and/or Profits

In *Kuwait Airways*, when hostilities in the first Gulf War ceased, the claimant airline had found itself without most of its fleet. The need to hire substitute aircraft for both passengers and cargo, and losses of business and profits until substitute capacity was found, were 'eminently to be expected'. Hence the claimant was entitled to recover as consequential losses sums representing the reasonable costs of such hire, and making good any such loss of profits.[175]

In accordance with general principle, it is of course important to ensure that any award for loss of business or profits does not give rise to a double recovery when taken together with the basis on which the converted asset has been valued.[176]

Miscellaneous

Consequential losses may, of course, take a myriad of forms. *Graham v Voigt* was a claim in Conversion brought by an (almost) life-long stamp collector. Kelly J, sitting in the Supreme Court of the Australian Capital Territory, accepted his evidence that he had collected Australian and Antarctic stamps for 45 years, assisted by gifts from the headmistress of his junior school of parts of her collection, and from his mother of at least two first day covers of every issue from 1940 to 1985. As an older man, he had been working towards a final objective of assembling a complete collection of mint and used copies of every Australian stamp since Federation, with a view to giving it to his daughter to carry it on. His formal collection comprised nine albums, eight so full of Australian stamps as to be bulging, and a ninth containing Antarctic stamps. When he realised he would not recover most of his stamps from the defendant, he was not interested in starting again, because there was no way in which he could get back to what he had had. He was so disgusted and depressed by the loss that his interest in philately had ended. In addition to recovering the value of his collection, the claimant was awarded sums by way of special damages (discounted for eight months' delay in commencing proceedings, and other delay not attributable to the defendant) representing the increase in its value between the date of valuation and the date of judgment, and by way of general damages for the loss of his hobby.[177]

---

[174] As to which see the text to nn 21–30 and 58–62.
[175] [2002] UKHL 19, [2002] 2 AC 886 at [95] per Lord Nicholls.
[176] See, eg, *The Llanover* [1947] P 80.
[177] [1989] ACTSC 5, 89 ACTR 11.

Foreseeability and Remoteness

Kuwait Airways has established[178] that, as against defendants who act in good faith, only consequential loss of a type 'which can be expected to arise from the wrongful conduct', that is satisfies the familiar, more restrictive tortious foreseeability test, is recoverable; however as against persons who knowingly commit Conversion, and thus are acting dishonestly, any loss which 'directly and naturally' flows from the wrongful act, that is satisfies the less restrictive remoteness test applied in deceit, is recoverable.[179]

Though the moral case for such a split rule is obvious, the theoretical basis for two different tests within one tort, none of the elements of which is or involves dishonesty or acting in bad faith, is, with respect, open to considerable question. It may be that Lord Nicholls was unduly influenced by his apparent sympathy for a 'radical reappraisal of the tort of conversion' introducing dishonesty as the test for recovery of loss (as opposed to an account of benefits), which he felt unable to consider at any length in the absence of any argument in its favour from either side on the appeal before the House.[180] In any event, in most cases it is the familiar, more restrictive tortious foreseeability test which will continue to apply.

Whilst the existence of that test is familiar enough, its application on any given set of facts may be far from easy. In *The Arpad*[181] the Court of Appeal was divided as to the recoverable measure of damages in contract and Conversion (which all three judges found to be the same, at least on the facts before them[182]). In August 1930, when the price of wheat was apparently high, the claimant merchants entered into a contract to buy 1,000 tons of Romanian wheat (to a very fine sample) at 36s (less 2.5 per cent) per quarter, for shipment in September/October ex Galatz on the *Arpad*. They almost immediately entered into contracts of resale (to the same sample) at 36s 6d. The *Arpad* arrived in Hull in January 1931, and made a short delivery by 47 tons for which its owners were liable in Conversion (as well as contract). Although the price of wheat generally had fallen markedly over the intervening five months, there was no (buyers') market at Hull in wheat to the contractual sample/specification, due to its special quality, so the claimant was unable to replace the 47 tons, and pro tanto lost the benefit of its contracts of resale. The judges differed as to the consequence of there being no market, from which a market value as at January 1931 (the time of the Conversion) could be ascertained.

---

[178]   Albeit, strictly, in obiter dicta.

[179]   [2002] UKHL 19, [2002] 2 AC 886 at [100]–[104] per Lord Nicholls, with whom Lord Hoffmann (at [125]) and Lord Hope (at [169]) expressly agreed.

[180]   See ibid at [79].

[181]   [1934] P 189.

[182]   Though Scrutton LJ thought the principle that they were necessarily the same 'not ... strictly accurate': ibid at 201.

The majority's reasoning for calculating the merchants' loss by reference to an estimated value as at January 1931 of 23s 6d per quarter was, in essence, as expressed by Greer LJ

> it seems to me unreasonable to hold that a shipowner contracting with the shipper on the terms of a bill of lading should be held liable to pay damages occasioned to an unknown assignee of the bill of lading [the sub-buyer], measured by the loss sustained by reason of the latter's inability to comply with a contract made two months before the shipment by such unknown assignee ... [absent a] market, the value must be otherwise ascertained, and the price at which the holder of the bill of lading [the claimant] has in fact sold them five months before is not very satisfactory evidence of their value at the time of the breach. In the case of a claim by a purchaser against a vendor of goods as to which a market price is unascertainable, the price at which the buyer has resold the goods may be accepted as evidence of their value. But the Court is not bound to accept such evidence as conclusive if the value can be otherwise ascertained. On the facts proved in the present case it is clear that the price fixed by the August contracts cannot be relied on as any evidence of the value of the goods at the date of breach.[183]

Scrutton LJ, dissenting, would have upheld the decisions below calculating the merchants' loss by reference to the contractual price on the sub-sale, 36s 6d per quarter:

> In the cases of claims in tort, damages are constantly given for consequences of which the defendant had no notice. You negligently run down a shabby-looking man in the street, and he turns out to be a millionaire engaged in a very profitable business which the accident disables him from carrying on; or you negligently and ignorantly injure the favourite for the Derby whereby he cannot run. You have to pay damages resulting from the circumstances of which you have no notice. You have to pay the actual loss to the man or his goods at the time of the tort, which is fixed by the circumstances at the time of the demand ... the damages in conversion should be the value to the purchaser or goods owner at the time of the conversion. If there is a market in which he can buy, this will fix the value; if there is no market, it may be determined by the goods owners' contract with a solvent purchaser, for that is what he has in fact lost by the conversion.[184]

Sixty five years later, in *Saleslease Ltd v Davis*,[185] the Court of Appeal was again divided on the application of the foreseeability requirement to a claim for Conversion damages. The defendant's former tenant left certain MoT testing equipment which belonged to the claimant[186] at the defendant's premises. The claimant found another customer, a Mr Gyles, to lease the equipment, on what were in fact (unknown to the defendant) uniquely advantageous terms which there was no prospect of the claimant securing from anyone else. The defendant then converted the same by imposing unjustified conditions on agreeing to the

---

[183] ibid at 209–10.
[184] ibid at 202–203 and 205.
[185] [1999] 1 WLR 1664 (CA).
[186] The former tenant had leased the same from the claimant.

claimant's demand for delivery up, which the claimant did not accept, and in consequence the claimant lost the benefit of the advantageous new lease. Waller LJ summarised the position, as the majority saw it,[187] thus:

> [T]he plaintiffs had the opportunity of a deal with Mr. Gyles by chance, and that was the only deal available to them which could have produced a value of £13,194. Second, the value otherwise was £5,000 for which the plaintiffs would, and ultimately did, sell the equipment. Third ... the ordinary expectation of the defendant who was retaining the equipment would be (1) that retention might lead to a difference between what the plaintiffs could dispose of the goods for as between the date of original detention and the date when the goods were handed back, or conceivably (2) might lead to a loss of hire (if the goods could have been hired out) during the period of detention ... The question to my mind is whether the defendant could reasonably have anticipated that the loss on the Campbell contract would be fully mitigated by a further lease if the equipment was returned when demanded, but could not be mitigated other than by a sale if there was a delay in return. That raises various questions. What knowledge did the defendant have of any of the features relating to Mr. Gyles? At what date did he have that knowledge? Should he have anticipated the consequences of not returning the equipment on demand? If so, when? If he should have anticipated the consequences, and be liable for them, how should damages be assessed? ... There was nothing to put the defendant on notice that the plaintiffs could not in the ordinary course of things lease the equipment to one of any number of customers once they obtained its return, or, putting the matter the other way, there was nothing to put the defendant on notice that the only assignee available was Mr. Gyles, and that a delay in handing the equipment back would have any effect other than to delay the ability of the plaintiffs to enter into a new lease ... In my view accordingly it could not be said that the defendant should have reasonably anticipated that, if the equipment was not handed back immediately on demand, the only possibility of entering into a leasing contract would be lost.[188]

The essence of Schiemann LJ's trenchant dissent appears from the following passage:

> I accept that he had not been told that there probably would be difficulty, at the time when he might ultimately decide or be compelled to release the goods, in finding another proposed assignee prepared to pay that sum. I accept that the *name* of the proposed assignee had not been revealed to the defendant. I accept that he had not been told that the value of the goods for resale would be likely to be less than the value to the plaintiffs of the proposed assignment. [The majority] ... attribute crucial significance to these three factors. They seem to me of no significance. What matters in my judgment is ... that the defendant was informed that there was a proposed assignee (who might even be in a position to sue the plaintiffs) and of the loss [in the region of £12,500] attributable to any inability to assign.[189]

---

187 See also Butler-Sloss LJ's concurring judgment ibid at 1678A–B.
188 ibid, at 1669B–E and 1701B–G.
189 ibid, at 1674F–H.

Thus, the type of loss being financial loss on any view, the majority considered the foreseeability requirement to be satisfied only if the defendant was on notice of the factual mechanism by which the loss in question stood to be suffered, whereas Schiemann LJ considered it satisfied if the defendant was put on notice of its approximate amount or extent. The effect of the majority decision is to impose a stricter foreseeability requirement on the victim of a Conversion than is imposed on the victim of negligence; the latter requires the defendant only to foresee the *nature* or *type* of damage from which the claimant suffers (in this case, financial loss),[190] and, once this has been deemed to be reasonably foreseeable, the exact manner in which the loss came about, and its extent, are irrelevant.[191] Whilst this might at first appear counter-intuitive, it may be argued that a more stringent foreseeability requirement in respect of consequential loss is justified by the strict liability nature of Conversion.

A further 'vexed question' which arose in argument, but which Waller LJ found it unnecessary to decide, and preferred to express no view on, was whether, once return of a converted asset has been demanded, the claimants can subsequently put the defendant on notice of special features so as to render him liable in respect of the same insofar as his detention of the asset continues thereafter.[192]

Causation of Consequential Loss

Issues in relation to causation in the context of consequential loss are dealt with under the general heading 'Causation', which follows.

Causation

In *Kuwait Airways*, Lord Nicholls treated causation, or more fully whether the wrongful conduct causally contributed to the loss, as the first aspect of a two-fold inquiry of general applicability in the law of tort (the second being the extent of the loss so caused for which the defendant ought to be held liable, in other words remoteness).[193]

In practical terms, where the relief sought in a straightforward case is damages, there is little a claimant need prove to recover the prima facie measure of loss in Conversion: sufficient causation to support such recovery is inherent in making out the cause of action, that is proving ownership or other proprietary interest

---

[190] See Clerk & Lindsell (n 34) at para 2–107. For an example of a Conversion claim where the type of liability to which the claimant became subject by reason of the Conversion was held not to be foreseeable by the relevant defendants (carriers) see *Sandeman Coprimar SA v Transitos y Transportes Integrales SL and ors* [2003] EWCA Civ 113, [2003] QB 1270 at [28] and [31].

[191] See Clerk & Lindsell (n 34) at paras 2–107 to 2–151.

[192] *Saleslease Ltd v Davis* [1999] 1 WLR 1664 at 1701G–H.

[193] [2002] UKHL 19, [2002] 2 AC 886 at [69]. For a perceptive criticism of Lord Nicholls' approach to the question of causation in this speech, see R Stevens, *Torts and Rights* (Oxford, Oxford University Press, 2007) at 63–65.

sufficient to make out the requisite possessory right in the assets in question,[194] and an act constituting a Conversion.[195] As Lord Hoffmann has put it, 'The liability [in conversion] is strict. Thus the causal questions are answered by reference to the nature of the liability.'[196] Cane puts the same underlying point a little differently:

> Conversion consists of depriving a person of their goods *and thereby* of the value of the goods. It makes no sense to ask whether depriving a person of goods caused loss consisting of that deprivation … the real explanation of why causation is irrelevant to loss of value claims for conversion is that the gist of such a claim is interference with the plaintiff's property interest in the converted chattel(s).[197]

However in less straightforward cases, including claims to recover other heads of damage, or where a less usual measure of the primary loss is sought, it is helpful to bear in mind Lord Nicholls' recognition that the apparent application of a simple 'but for' test may in practice involve the court in making a value judgment on responsibility.[198] In doing so, the court must have regard to the purpose, or more strictly we would suggest the twin purposes, sought to be achieved by the tort of Conversion, as applied to the particular circumstances of the individual case. Those purposes are the vindication of the claimant's proprietary rights in the subject asset, with indeed possible proprietary consequences flowing from the very payment of damages,[199] as well as the general purpose of the law of tort, the affording of just compensation for wrongs. As Lord Hoffmann put it, again in the *Kuwait Airways* case, 'One is never simply liable, one is always liable for something'.[200] So, in order for the causal inquiry to be properly conducted, one must first establish what constitutes the damage to which the claimant is attempting to link the Conversion.

A clear value judgment on responsibility was made by the Privy Council in rejecting the defendants' submissions of 'no loss' in the cases *Solloway v McLaughlin* and *BBMB Ltd v Eda Holdings Ltd* (both discussed above[201]). In such cases the defendant will, really as a matter of legal policy to vindicate the claimant's rights of ownership,[202] be held to have caused the claimant loss the moment the Conversion first occurs, regardless of whether the claimant would

---

[194] See ch 4 *passim* and ch 3 under the heading The Gist of Conversion.

[195] Subject to the possible effect of an (accepted) return of the converted asset to the claimant, as to which see under the side-heading The Measure of Damages for Conversion, (f) Where the Goods are Returned—'Temporary Deprivation', above.

[196] *Kuwait Airways* (n 7) at [129].

[197] Cane, Conversion (LQR 2002) at 549.

[198] ibid, at [70].

[199] See discussion under the heading Extinction of Title below.

[200] *Kuwait Airways* (n 7) at [128].

[201] Text to nn 66–67 ff and 68–71 respectively.

[202] Lord Atkin, giving the opinion of the Board in *Solloway v McLoughlin* [1938] AC 247 (PC), put it thus (at 259): 'fraudulent brokers have often sounder judgment than their clients as to the future course of markets … no injustice is done if the principal benefits, as he occasionally may, by the superior astuteness of an unjust steward in carrying out a fraud'.

otherwise have retained the asset as the market fell. Hence a claimant does not have to prove that he would have sold the asset in question immediately (or at all), and thereby avoided loss on the falling market, in order sufficiently to prove causation to support recovery of the value of his asset at the date of Conversion; equally it will not avail a defendant to establish by evidence that the claimant would not have done so, and would have held on to the asset in any event.[203]

By contrast, when it comes to consequential losses, a claimant *does* have to prove how he would have acted but for the Conversion in order to prove causation, and equally a defendant can undermine the claim against him by adducing such evidence. Hence when it comes to recovery of any increase in value after the initial Conversion, provided it is dealt with under the heading of consequential losses, as we have suggested it properly should be, causation in respect of that head of loss does have to be distinctly proved in the normal way.[204]

In *Sachs v Miklos*[205] the assets in question were items of furniture, which had been the subject of a (war time) gratuitous bailment. The defendant bailee had twice written to the claimant bailor, asking him (as she recalled) to take his furniture back and informing him of her intention otherwise to sell it at public auction. No finding as to the content of those letters, or whether they had been received by the bailor, had been made by the trial judge, and the case was remitted for that purpose. Goddard LCJ made it abundantly clear that had the claimant bailor received such letters, then the loss represented by the increase in value (which occurred after the auction sale, but before the claimant's initial demand for the return of his furniture) should be treated as flowing not from the Conversion, but from his own (in)action;[206] in other words, the claimant's (in)action would have constituted a break in the chain of causation.

In *IBL Ltd v Coussens*[207] the claimant's appeal was directed to obtaining an order that its damages be assessed at the date of judgment rather than the date of Conversion. The Court of Appeal indicated that a proper assessment of damages would require findings of fact to be made as to whether, if the subject cars had not been converted, or had promptly been returned when demanded, the claimant would have kept them or disposed of them.[208] On the footing that the post-Conversion increase in value was being treated as a distinct head of (consequential) loss, the need for such classic causation questions to be addressed accords with principle.

---

[203]   See the argument advanced by Radcliffe KC for the appellant in *Solloway v McLoughlin* (ibid) at 253–54, and its rejection in the opinion of the Board delivered by Lord Atkin at 259.

[204]   In addition to the examples which follow in the main text, see also *The Playa Larga* [1983] 2 Lloyd's Rep 171 (CA) at 181 r/h col–182 l/h col, and *Kuwait Airways* (n 7) at [130] per Lord Hoffmann.

[205]   [1948] 2 KB 23 (CA).

[206]   ibid, especially at 40–41. An alternative analysis of failure to mitigate was also suggested, as to which see text to n 224.

[207]   [1991] 2 All ER 133 (CA).

[208]   See ibid per Neill LJ at 140a and Nicholls LJ at 144g–h.

In *Chubb Cash v John Crilley*[209] Bush J, having recognised that in addition to the prima facie measure of damage the claimant 'may recover any additional damage he may suffer which is not too remote', found that the claimant's claim to a higher measure of damages in that case failed on causation grounds: 'This damage does not in this case flow from the conversion but flows from the failure of the debtor to perform his obligations under the agreement.'[210]

Where a claimant is unable to fulfill her contract for sale of the subject assets due to a Conversion thereof, the loss caused by the defendant's Conversion, and therefore recoverable by her, is the loss of the value of those assets, which in such a case will be taken as prima facie being their price under the unfulfilled contract.[211] Should the defendant wish to argue that no such loss has been suffered, because the 'lost' profit has been recouped on a substitute sale, the burden of proving that lies on him; it is not for the claimant seller to prove a negative, namely that she has not so recouped her profit.[212]

User damages under the principle in *Strand Electric v Brisford* discussed above[213] may be regarded as an exception to the need to prove causation in the usual way, for the claimant owner may recover them 'even though [he] has in fact suffered no loss'.[214] Since this measure of damages is in reality no more than a pragmatic approach to arriving at a value to be attributed to having the use, or at least the availability of use, of another's asset, one should not, for the reasons already stated, expect there to be a causation test attached.[215]

Extinction of Title

At common law, it became established that an award of damages for Conversion, assessed so as to give the claimant full compensation for her interest in the subject asset, had the effect of extinguishing the claimant's title thereto; this could be relied on not only by the defendant converter but by a successor in title.[216]

---

[209]   [1983] 1 WLR 599 (CA).

[210]   ibid at 604C–D. For a stimulating contemporary discussion of the law's approach to causation generally see L Hoffmann, 'Causation' (2005) 121 *LQR* 592.

[211]   Assuming there are no problems with remoteness or lack of knowledge on the defendant's part, as to which see under the side-heading The Measure of Damages for Conversion, (g) Consequential Loss, Foreseeability/Remoteness, above.

[212]   *Sony v Cinram* [2008] EWCA Civ 955, [2008] 2 CLC 441 at [49] per Rix LJ.

[213]   See under the side-heading The Measure of Damages for Conversion, (g) Consequential Loss, User Damages, above.

[214]   [1952] 2 QB 246 per Denning LJ at 254, a remark reinforced by his later observation ibid that 'I am here concerned with the cases where the owner has in fact suffered no loss, or less loss than is represented by a hiring charge.' Cf *The Mediana* (text to n 171–73); contrast on the facts the failure of the claim for damages based on wrongful user of property in *Finesky Holdings Pty Ltd v Minister for Transport for Western Australia* [2002] WASCA 206, 26 WAR 368 at [50]–[59].

[215]   See text to nn 194–97.

[216]   See, eg, *Cooper v Shepherd* (1846) 3 CB 266, 136 ER 107.

It is important to note that it was not the entering of such a judgment in itself, but only the actual payment of the full amount so awarded, which so operated. As Willes J put it:

> The only way the judgment in trover can have the effect of vesting the property in the defendant is, by treating the judgment as being (that which in truth it ordinarily is) an assessment of the value of the goods, and treating the satisfaction of the damages as payment of the price as upon a sale of the goods, according to the maxim in Jenk. 4th Cent. Case 88 ... there is a series of decisions shewing that a mere recovery, without satisfaction, has not the effect of changing the property.[217]

The title thereby acquired by the defendant converter (or his successors in title) has been said to be obtained by estoppel,[218] and the principle operates whether the underlying judgment had been simply for damages, or had given the defendant the alternative of delivering up the asset or paying damages in lieu.[219]

The Law Reform Committee recommended retention of this rule,[220] and the same was duly enacted (in respect of all the wrongful interference torts) as section 5 of the 1977 Act. A well advised defendant ordered, or given the alternative, of paying compensation to the claimant for the whole amount of her interest in a converted asset will seek to ensure that the court order expressly records that the sum awarded has been assessed on the basis set out in section 5(1).[221] The Committee's further recommendation that part satisfaction of a judgment should not operate to extinguish title, but should be taken into account in assessing the claimant's loss in any further proceedings between the parties, was not enacted. This, however, was already the position under the existing law in any event, as the Committee's report expressly acknowledged.

In one sense the extinction of title rule can be said to be a unique feature of the tort of Conversion (and the other wrongful interference torts), but an analogy may be drawn with a refusal of injunctive relief coupled with an award of damages under the jurisdiction derived from Lord Cairns' Act[222] in substitution for an injunction in support of real property rights. In such cases the practical effect of such a decision is to award the claimant a 'once and for all' payment in substitution for an injunction, compensating him for the future wrongs which will thereby go unrestrained, and thus to authorise the continuance of what technically remains an unlawful state of affairs. The doctrine of res judicata will

---

[217] *Brinsmead v Harrison* (1871) LR 6 CP 584 at 588–89. See also *Morris and anor v Robinson* (1824) 3 B & C 196, 107 ER 706.

[218] *Ellis v John Stenning & Son* [1932] 2 Ch 81 at 96 per Luxmoore J.

[219] ibid at 97.

[220] 18th Report (n 6) at para 96.

[221] ie 'on the footing that the claimant is being compensated for the whole of his interest in the goods', or (if applicable) the equivalent words in s 5(4).

[222] The Chancery Amendment Act 1858 (21 and 22 Vict c27).

operate to prevent the claimant and his successors in title from thereafter bringing any proceedings in respect of further wrongs, for which the claimant has ex hypothesi been fully compensated.[223]

The Duty to Mitigate

The duty to mitigate loss consequent upon a Conversion may take a variety of forms, depending on the circumstances.

In *Sachs v Miklos* an alternative analysis to that mentioned under 'Causation' above was indicated by Goddard LCJ, albeit briefly, namely that the claimant owner's failure to act by removing the furniture in response to the bailee's (alleged) letters, or by making his claim straightaway, would have constituted a breach of his duty to mitigate.[224]

In some circumstances, the duty to mitigate may oblige the innocent party to go into the market and buy in replacements for the converted assets; where that is appropriate, the innocent party will be allowed a reasonable time to take those steps. In *The Playa Larga*[225] the Chilean purchaser whose sugar was converted by the Cuban vendor's action in sailing its ship, still largely laden with the same, out of Valparaiso on the evening of the *coup d'état* in which General Pinochet's military junta ousted the Allende government, was (in the context of a rising market) allowed a period equating to a month or so before it ought reasonably to have 'covered itself' by purchasing replacement sugar.

However on the very different facts of *IBL Ltd v Coussens*,[226] given that the claimant was not in the business of buying and selling cars, and that the sums concerned were not insubstantial, Nicholls LJ did not consider that the claimant's duty reasonably to mitigate required it to go into the market and buy replacements, even though there was nothing unique about the two vehicles (save for a personalised number plate).[227]

More recently, in *Uzinterimpex v Standard Bank*[228] the converted asset was cotton, which was held unsold in warehouses in various ports in Europe and the Middle East for a protracted period[229] pending resolution of a dispute as to title. The defendant, which was ultimately held liable for Conversion of the cotton on and after 17 April 2000, had on 9 August 2000 proposed its sale on terms that the

---

[223] *Jaggard v Sawyer and anor* [1995] 1 WLR 269 (CA) at 280H–281A per Sir Thomas Bingham MR and 285F–286B per Millett LJ.

[224] [1948] 2 KB 23 (CA), at 40.

[225] [1983] 2 Lloyd's Rep 171 (CA).

[226] [1991] 2 All ER 133 (CA).

[227] See ibid at 144c–f.

[228] [2007] EWHC 1151 (Comm), [2007] 2 Lloyd's Rep 187 David Steel J, and (on appeal) [2008] EWCA Civ 819, [2008] 2 Lloyd's Rep 456.

[229] After the discharge by consent on 17 April 2000 of an interlocutory injunction which had restrained dealing with the same: see [2008] EWCA Civ 819, [2008] 2 Lloyd's Rep 456 at [8] per Moore-Bick LJ.

proceeds be paid into a joint account pending resolution of the dispute. This proposal, which the trial judge held to be 'the obvious way forward to avoid further losses', was rebuffed for some eight or nine months, and in the event never implemented. In the meantime the cotton was at risk of deterioration, together with exposure to market fluctuations, and storage charges continued to accrue throughout. Whilst allowing the innocent claimant 'some latitude', he accepted the defendant's submission that the resultant decline in the cotton's value, and other losses (in particular, storage charges), sustained after mid-September 2000 were caused by unreasonable want of mitigation on the claimant's part, and therefore irrecoverable by it.[230]

The Court of Appeal dismissed the claimant's appeal.[231] In what is now the leading case on the point, it rejected a direct challenge to the applicability of any duty to mitigate in a case of Conversion, put on the basis that a claimant is under no duty to co-operate with a defendant in the disposal of its own property, and is entitled to maintain a demand for its return, and that a defendant fails to comply with such a demand at its peril.[232]

In a thoughtful judgment, which was effectively that of the Court, Moore-Bick LJ tested the claimant's argument by reference to a number of principles. He accepted that mitigation

> can be viewed [in terms of causation], but I am not sure that to do so adds greatly to one's understanding of the principles. If one analyses a failure to mitigate in terms of a new event which breaks the chain of causation between the wrongful act and the subsequent loss, it is necessary to recognise that the way in which the test of a new supervening cause has traditionally been formulated must be adapted or applied so as to take into account the relatively undemanding level of the duty to mitigate which the law imposes on the victim of a wrongful act.[233]

He also accepted that

> a person whose property has been stolen is not bound *in the exercise of his duty to mitigate* to accept an offer from the thief to pay him the value of the property, since such an offer does not mitigate the loss; it merely involves an acknowledgment of the thief's liability and an offer to pay damages accordingly. Even in a case where the claimant seeks an order for delivery up of the property, it does no more than offer an alternative remedy of the same monetary value. The claimant is not bound to choose between these two remedies because to do so would not reduce his loss, though ... he might well incur liability for the costs of any proceedings if the outcome was not more advantageous than that which he had been offered.[234]

[230] See [2007] EWHC 1151 (Comm), [2007] 2 Lloyd's Rep 187 per David Steel J at [162]–[167].
[231] [2008] EWCA Civ 819, [2008] 2 Lloyd's Rep 456.
[232] ibid, per Moore-Bick LJ at [48].
[233] ibid, per Moore-Bick LJ at [56].
[234] ibid, per Moore-Bick LJ at [61].

Whilst recognising that to 'say that a person whose goods have been wrongfully seized by another is not obliged to negotiate with the person who has taken them ... has some attraction', Moore-Bick LJ took the view that this was

> only because in many cases it will be unreasonable to expect him to do so. That is particularly true if one takes as an example the person whose property is stolen by a thief. Is he obliged to negotiate with the thief to purchase its return? Probably not, because it would be offensive to ordinary notions of morality to expect him to do so, but, if he had the chance to recapture his property without risk to himself, he might reasonably be expected to take it.[235]

When it came to reviewing David Steel J's conclusions on reasonableness, he found that:

> In the end the judge had to decide whether [the claimant's] objections based on practical considerations ... were strong enough, taken in conjunction with [its] other objections, to justify its refusal to accede to the disposal of the goods. He came to the clear conclusion that they were not, and I am not persuaded that on the evidence before him his decision was wrong.[236]

Accordingly it is now clear that the duty to avoid or minimise loss flowing from a wrongful act, which has obvious attractions in terms of economic efficiency and which Moore-Bick LJ characterised as 'an important principle of the common law', arises when assets are converted just as it does when other legal wrongs are committed.[237] However the fact that this point was susceptible of substantial debate reflects, once again, the complexities which flow from the hybrid nature of Conversion.

As with the law of damages generally, costs reasonably incurred by a claimant in performing his obligation to mitigate his loss are themselves recoverable.[238] In *Kuwait Airways* Lord Hoffmann made it clear that he regarded the costs incurred in paying a ransom to gain the release of the surviving aircraft referred to as 'the Iran Six' (Iraq Airways Company had sent them to Iran for safe-keeping), and in repairing them, as 'part of the damage or expenditure incurred in mitigation of the damage to the proprietary interest', that is not as consequential loss.[239] As Cane spells out, that means that it is properly to be classified as part of the loss of value claim.[240]

---

[235] ibid, per Moore-Bick LJ at [55].
[236] ibid, per Moore-Bick LJ at [53].
[237] ibid, per Moore-Bick LJ at [69].
[238] *McGregor on Damages* (2003) at paras 7–083 to 7–088.
[239] [2002] UKHL 19, [2002] 2 AC 886 at [130]. Stevens agrees—see his *Torts and Rights* (2007) at 66.
[240] Cane, LQR (n 10) at 549 (though he considered the proposition questionable so far as it applied to the costs of repair—ibid).

Contributory Negligence

Prior to the 1977 Act there was some doubt as to whether contributory negligence was available as a partial defence to a claim in Conversion.[241] The 'classic example' given by Moore-Bick LJ in *Uzinterimpex v Standard Bank* is that of 'the person who carelessly leaves his bicycle unlocked, thereby enabling a thief to steal it'.[242] The Law Reform Committee recommended that it should not in general be so,[243] and section 11 of the 1977 Act duly so provided. A limited exception to section 11 is afforded to bankers, so as to preserve a partial defence of contributory negligence by the drawer in actions within section 4 of the Cheques Act 1957 where they are unable to establish a complete absence of negligence, and hence rely on the statutory defence afforded by the latter section.[244]

Though the Committee's reasoning appears sound overall, the availability of contributory negligence as a partial defence to other causes of action, which may overlap with Conversion in not uncommon factual circumstances, does mean that somewhat odd results can follow. As *Clerk & Lindsell* points out,[245] a car owner who lends his car to a friend who is obviously drunk, and who then destroys it in a crash, will have his damages reduced if he sues in negligence or breach of bailment, but not if he frames his claim under section 2(2) of the 1977 Act (so-called statutory Conversion).

Other Remedies

[H]istorically the cause of action in conversion was a claim in personam which gave rise to a money judgment only, and although the remedies for conversion now include an order for specific delivery, it would be unusual for the court to make such an order in respect of goods whose only value is as a commercial commodity. Even a successful claim in detinue would not necessarily lead to a judgment for delivery up of the goods. In general the law provides a monetary remedy in the form of damages, except in those cases where the nature of the property in issue renders that inadequate.[246]

We have seen in chapter two, going back to Blackstone's *Commentaries*, why providing an *in rem* remedy for the restoration of assets to those entitled to possession of the same was not regarded as generally important, or perhaps desirable, even in detinue; and how limited in practice the jurisdiction to order specific delivery was, even after its statutory extension from the Court of

---

[241]   See Clerk & Lindsell (n 34) at para 17–121 fn 42; 18th Report (n 6) at paras 79–80.

[242]   [2008] EWCA Civ 819, [2008] 2 Lloyd's Rep 456 at [58].

[243]   18th Report (n 6) at paras 81–82.

[244]   s 47, Banking Act 1979.

[245]   n 34, at para 17–121 fn 44.

[246]   *Uzinterimpex JSC v Standard Bank plc* [2008] EWCA Civ 819, [2008] 2 Lloyd's Rep 456 at [68] per Moore-Bick LJ.

Chancery to the courts of common law.[247] Since 1978, the primary jurisdiction to grant such remedies has been that conferred by sections 3 and 4 of the 1977 Act.

(a) Final Orders for Delivery Up: Section 3(1)(a) of the 1977 Act

Section 3 of the 1977 Act applies to 'proceedings ... against a person who is in possession or in control of goods'. These words have been held apt to describe proceedings where the defendants are in such possession or control when the proceedings are launched, whether or not they remain so when judgment is entered.[248] Curiously, however, it would appear that section 3 is of no application to proceedings against a defendant converter who had ceased to have possession or control of the subject asset even before proceedings were commenced. In such circumstances the pre-existing common law position with regard to remedies must presumably continue to apply.[249]

Where, as is far from unknown, there is a factual dispute as to whether the defendants have ever had such possession or control, the court will have to resolve it. Given the significance of this issue for what statutory relief is available, it is desirable that its resolution be expressly recorded in the court order. Even so, in the event of persistent non-compliance with an order in form (a), subsequent proceedings for contempt of court have to be approached with care, for, if possession or control continues to be disputed by the defendant, the court will then have to resolve that issue again, this time by reference to the higher (criminal) standard of proof which is applicable to contempt proceedings. In such circumstances the court may prefer to exercise its statutory discretion under section 3(4) to revoke the form (a) order, and substitute a monetary order; for these purposes the resolution of the question of whether the court is satisfied that a form (a) order 'has not been complied with' may properly be resolved on the balance of probabilities.

Where it is accepted, or found by the court, that the defendants, though in possession or control of the subject asset when the proceedings commenced, ceased to be so prior to judgment, the obvious practical impediment to awarding specific relief can be taken into account by virtue of the discretion inherent in the final words of section 3(1) 'so far as appropriate'.[250]

As was noted above,[251] relief in form (a)—specific delivery without an alternative of paying the value in lieu, plus consequential damages—is only available

---

[247] Ch 2, text to nn 80–85 and nn 187–88.

[248] *Hillesden Securities Ltd v Ryjack Ltd* [1983] 1 WLR 959 at 963A–B.

[249] Despite the presence of express qualifying provisions in s 3(8); as noted above, the 1977 Act is not a codifying statute (as the Law Reform Committee concluded it should not be: see 18th Report (n 6) at para 128(4)).

[250] *Hillesden Securities Ltd v Ryjack Ltd* [1983] 1 WLR 959 at 963C.

[251] Text to n 23, citing s 3(3)(b) of the 1977 Act.

at the discretion of the court. Conditions may be imposed.[252] Further, preserving the common law position that a part owner cannot sue for Conversion (because he does not alone have an immediate right to possession) but is limited to a claim for damages under the tort of reversionary injury,[253] the provisions of section 3 have been modified by Civil Procedure Rules 40.14 so as to limit the relief available in respect of claims by part owners to damages only, save where they are proceeding with the written authority of every other part owner.

In practice, the discretion to grant relief by way of an order for specific delivery in form (a) continues to be exercised very sparingly, as its equitable and (from 1854) common law predecessors were. As Sir Robert Megarry summarised the position:

> A principle on which the court has long acted is not to order delivery of goods which are ordinary articles of commerce with no special value or interest, whether to the plaintiff or others, when damages will fully compensate: see *Whiteley Ltd. v. Hilt* [1918] 2 K.B. 808, 819, *per* Sir Charles Swinfen Eady M.R.; and see also *General and Finance Facilities Ltd. v. Cooks Cars (Romford) Ltd.* [1963] 1 W.L.R. 644, 649, 650, *per* Diplock L.J. If a plaintiff can easily replace the goods detained by purchasing their equivalent on the market, then the payment of damages out of which the price of the equivalent may be paid is adequate compensation to the wronged plaintiff, and there is little or no point in making an order for the delivery of the goods. Far better to let the plaintiff fend for himself with the defendant's money.[254]

An example of a case where, had the matter proceeded to trial, it seems clear that an order in form (a) would have been obtained is afforded by *Defence Secretary v Guardian Newspapers*, which concerned a memorandum from the Secretary of State to the Prime Minister marked 'Secret. UK eyes only', with a very restricted high level circulation, which was leaked to *The Guardian*; sight of the leaked copy was sought in order to identify the civil servant responsible in the interests of national security.[255] In that case, as with perhaps most of those where exercise of the discretion to grant a form (a) order is a realistic possibility, the matter was brought on as an urgent interlocutory application. Accordingly cases where an order for specific delivery has been sought under section 4 may be looked to for guidance on the exercise of this discretion.

---

[252] ibid, s 3(6).

[253] See Clerk & Lindsell (n 34) at para 17–138.

[254] *Howard E Perry & Co Ltd v British Railways Board* [1980] 1 WLR 1375 at 1382H–83B.

[255] *Secretary of State for Defence and anor v Guardian Newspapers Ltd* [1984] Ch 156 (CA) especially at 169A–C and 172B per Slade LJ; see also ibid at 165C–166B per Sir John Donaldson MR, and 167G–168D per Griffiths LJ; and [1985] AC 339 at 349C–E and 356A–B per Lord Diplock, 370A–B and 371D–F per Lord Roskill (Lord Bridge agreed with Griffiths LJ and Lords Diplock and Roskill).

(b) Alternative Final Orders at the Defendant's Election: Section 3(1)(b)

The Act gives claimants the right to choose between a form (b) order, and an order simply for damages (form (c)).[256] A form (b) order was previously a common form of order at common law in detinue claims.[257] The key feature of a form (b) order is that, once made, it confers on the *defendant* the right to elect between returning the subject asset at any time before execution of judgment, and paying damages in respect of its value;[258] the form of order should specify the latter figure. In either case the obligation to pay such consequential damages, if any, as are assessed is cumulative, not alternative.[259]

It will be noted that the application of this classic detinue remedy to Conversion cases, coupled with the extinction of title principle already discussed, has the effect of allowing the wrongdoer the choice of whether to expropriate the victim's property, albeit at a value set by a court.[260]

(c) Interlocutory Orders for Delivery Up: Section 4

This section confers jurisdiction on the court to make an interlocutory order on an application in accordance with rules of court[261] 'for the delivery up of any goods which are or may become the subject matter of subsequent proceedings'. The leading case (and, according to *Clerk & Lindsell*, the first) is that of *Howard Perry & Co v British Railways*, aspects of which we have already discussed.[262] The Vice-Chancellor's reasons for taking the unusual course of making an order for specific delivery up of commercial goods, and doing so on an interlocutory basis, are best understood by reference to key passages from his characteristically full judgment:

> In normal times, the steel here in dispute might indeed be in this category; but these times are not normal, and at present steel is obtainable on the market only with great difficulty, if at all. If the equivalent of what is detained is unobtainable, how can it be said that damages are an adequate remedy? ... Damages would be a poor consolation if the failure of supplies forces a trader to lay off staff and disappoint his customers (whose affections may be transferred to others) and ultimately impels him towards insolvency ... In any case, I think that what matters is the adequacy of damages in place of the thing that ought to have been delivered ...

---

[256] The 1977 Act, s 3(3)(b).

[257] 18th Report (n 6) para 82; *General & Finance v Cooks Cars* [1963] 1 WLR 644 at 650 per Diplock LJ.

[258] ibid, s 3(2)(b) and 3(5).

[259] As to the procedural position with regard to quantifying the two heads of damage for a form (b) order, see the discussion of *IBL Ltd v Coussens* at text to nn 53–62.

[260] See further Curwen, (n 8) at 570–75.

[261] See CPR Pt 25, especially at 25.1(1)(e).

[262] [1980] 1 WLR 1375, discussed in ch 6 at text to fn 78 ff.

In my judgment, the exercise of the court's discretion calls for a balancing of the considerations on each side. In this case I think that the plaintiffs have a strong case for their claim to be permitted to collect their own steel, and I think that the defendants' case for the court not to make the order is weak ...

The evidence is that the tube division [of Brasway Ltd of Brierley Hill, which manufactures electrically welded steel tubes, and obtains most of its steel from the plaintiffs] can obtain no steel elsewhere, and if it receives no further supplies it will have to lay off 120 employees almost at once. The two main manufacturers that the division supplies have stated that if the division fails to supply them, they will cease to place orders with the company, in which case the division would probably have to close, and 120 jobs would be lost. [Nearly 100 workers at Brasway who have signed a petition] not surprisingly state that they cannot see why their jobs should be put at risk because the plaintiffs are unable to obtain their own material ... it seems quite plain to me that on the evidence and the law I ought to make the order sought by the plaintiffs.[263]

(d) Recaption

This is the traditional name for exercise of the classic self-help remedy of (at least peaceably) retaking possession of one's own assets from the unlawful possession of another, after they have been converted. The Law Reform Committee looked at some of the issues to which it gives rise, including to what extent, if at all, force may be used, or the premises of others may be entered, to this end; it concluded that the law in these respects was 'far from clear' and 'should be clarified'.[264] In the event, however, the 1977 Act did not touch upon this difficult area.

Beyond the obvious attraction of a self-executing remedy which (at least initially) need not involve lawyers or the courts, and the associated expense, recaption has potential economic advantages in its own right. It outflanks the jurisdiction of the courts to require allowance to be given for improvements made by mistaken but honest converters when calculating damages (under section 6 of the 1977 Act, or at common law), and to impose conditions (to that end or otherwise) on orders for specific delivery (under section 3(6) and (7), or in equity). It will be recalled from discussion earlier in this chapter that, in this context, 'improvements' is a term of wide import, and would include (in cases of unlawful mining) not only the costs of hewing and getting the minerals (recovery of which through the courts depends on proof that the work was undertaken under a bona fide claim to, and belief that they had, title to the same) but also those of hauling them below ground and raising them to the surface (which are normally allowed as a matter of course).[265] Only if Lord Denning MR's minority view in *Greenwood v Bennett*, that an innocent improver in any event has a

---

[263] ibid at 1383B–85F. Another, more recent example of such an order being made in a commercial context is afforded by *Pendragon plc and ors v Walon Ltd and anor* [2005] EWHC 1082 (QB), HHJ Grenfell.
[264] 18th Report (n 6) paras 116–26, especially 121.
[265] See text to nn 97–101.

free-standing cause of action (in restitution) to recover recompense for his work,[266] were to be vindicated would the victim of a Conversion who had effectively exercised his right of recaption have to pay for the same.[267]

Of course, it is inherent in seeking to exercise such a self-help remedy that the (thitherto) innocent party exposes himself to the risk that for some reason, including—in this field of property rights and generally strict liability—one which may not be known to him and of which he may have no means of knowledge, his right to do so has already been lost; if that is so, he will inadvertently render himself liable for Conversion to the party whose possession he has disturbed. Compare the case of *White v Garden*.[268] Garden had sold two quantities of iron to a rogue named Parker, who had paid partly for the first, and wholly for the second, by bills of exchange. Both consignments were delivered to Parker's order, without Garden first checking the authenticity of the bills. Parker in turn sold, and caused to be delivered, both quantities to White, who (it transpired) was a bona fide purchaser who had bought from Parker through a broker at a fair market price. When it turned out that the bills of exchange were fake, Garden seized back part of the second consignment which was still at White's wharf. White then successfully sued Garden in trover—Garden's right to avoid his relevant (second) sale for Parker's fraud had been lost when Parker sold and delivered the subject iron to White, so Garden's (subsequent) seizure from White was unlawful.

Adding a further twist, in *Uzinterimpex v Standard Bank* Moore-Bick LJ has made the thought-provoking suggestion that, in some circumstances, a claimant's duty to mitigate his loss may *require* him to take a chance to recapture his converted assets which presents itself, provided it does not involve any risk to himself.[269]

(e) 'Waiver of Tort'

For completeness, it should be noted that one response available to a victim of Conversion is to 'waive the tort' and follow the asset and its proceeds in order to obtain what some would describe as a restitutionary remedy. A simple example is afforded by the Conversion of a banknote, which is then used to purchase a winning lottery ticket. As Swadling explains 'the victim can, by "waiving the tort", recover (in restitution for wrongs) the amount of his winnings or the proceeds of

---

[266] [1973] QB 195 (CA) at 202C–F; see text to n 106.

[267] *Pace* an obiter dictum of Mahoney JA in *Bilambil-Terranora P/L v Tweed SC* [1980] 1 NSWLR 465 (NSWCA) at [114], which assumes (without explaining why) that a sale of unlawfully mined minerals by the rightful owner following a reception 'before sale, eg at the entrance to the quarry' would be 'subject to its obligation to make proper allowances to the defendant' [ie the converter].

[268] (1851) 10 CB 919, 138 ER 364 (Ct CP), cited in W Swadling, 'Rescission, Property, and the Common Law' (2005) 121 *LQR* 123.

[269] *Uzinterimpex v Standard Bank* [2008] EWCA Civ 819, [2008] 2 Lloyd's Rep 456 at [55].

sale'.[270] This is a waiver only in a limited sense—it is an election to take a gain-based, rather than a loss-based, recovery, not an election to be treated as if no tort has been committed.[271]

There is continuing controversy as to whether a victim of Conversion can maintain a common law strict liability claim in unjust enrichment. Birks favoured that view.[272] Swadling, however, has persuasively argued that, where title does not pass to the defendant following a Conversion, for example a pickpocket's physical acquisition of his victim's wallet, a prerequisite of a successful unjust enrichment claim is *ex hypothesi* absent.[273] Whilst this debate is beyond the reasonable scope of this book, we would commend to the interested reader Swadling's emphasis on the need properly to analyse such cases in terms of what proprietary interest has passed and exactly how; on how we should consider the matter by reference to 'rights in respect of things' rather than simply 'things'; and his recognition that 'there is an unfortunate ambiguity in the word "property"', and identification of the advantage of conducting the analysis by reference to the term 'title' rather than other, less contextually satisfactory, terms such as 'property', 'ownership' and so forth.[274]

(f) An Equitable Claim to Converted Assets and their Proceeds of Sale?

Tarrant[275] has drawn attention to two early twentieth century decisions of the High Court of Australia, *Black v S Freedman & Co*[276] and *Creak v James Moore & Sons*,[277] said to support a doctrine whereby the victim of a theft per se acquires an equitable interest in stolen money, stolen assets and the proceeds of sale of the latter. Suffice it to say that it seems most unlikely that this, without refinement, represents the position in English law. It is hard to improve on the summary of the basic position in the latter given by Sir Peter Millett (as he then was) in the *Law Quarterly Review*:

> The only restriction on the ability of equity to follow assets is the requirement that there must be some breach of trust or other fiduciary obligation which permits the assistance of equity to be invoked. The requirement has been widely condemned by

---

[270] W Swadling, 'Ignorance and unjust enrichment: the problem of title' (2008) 28 *Oxford Journal of Legal Studies* 627 at 627.

[271] ibid at 627–28, citing *United Australia Bank Ltd v Barclays Bank Ltd* [1941] AC 1 at 18 per Viscount Simon LC. See, however, P Birks, *Unjust Enrichment*, 2nd edn (Oxford, Oxford University Press, 2005) at 15 and 83.

[272] ibid at 15.

[273] Swadling, Ignorance (*OJLS*, 2008) at 628 and *passim*.

[274] ibid at 638–41.

[275] J Tarrant, 'Theft Principle in Private Law' (2006) 80 *Australian Law Journal* 531.

[276] *Black and anor v S Freedman & Co Ltd* [1910] HCA 58, 12 CLR 105.

[277] *Creak v James Moore & Sons Pty Ltd* [1912] HCA 67, 15 CLR 426.

academic writers, but the law was settled in England by *Re Diplock*.[278] The doctrine can be reconsidered only by the House of Lords ...

> The requirement is, in fact, less restrictive of equity's ability to intervene than is often supposed. In the first place, it is not necessary that the fund to be traced should have been the subject of fiduciary obligations before it got into the wrong hands; it is sufficient that the payment to the defendant itself gave rise to a fiduciary relationship: *Chase Manhattan Bank N.A. v. Israel-British Bank (London) Ltd*[279]...
>
> In the second place, the requirement is readily satisfied in most cases of commercial fraud, since the embezzlement of a company's funds almost inevitably involves a breach of fiduciary duty on the party of one of the company's employees or agents ...
>
> The only situation in practice in which it may be impossible to invoke the assistance of equity is where the money has been stolen by a thief. In England, at least, it would be heretical to regard a thief as a fiduciary or a simple theft as giving rise to a *constructive* trust. It is otherwise in the United States of America and, possibly, in Australia.[280]

However Sir Peter went on to point out that:

> There is no reason in principle why equity should not intervene in such a case on the basis of a resulting trust. Theft does not deprive the true owner of his legal title; and *a fortiori* it does not deprive him of his equitable title. It has never been a requirement of the equitable tracing claim that the legal and equitable titles should be divided. The requirement that the loss must have arisen from a breach of fiduciary duty is difficult to understand and impossible to defend." [n: Despite the authority of *Re Diplock*, it is difficult to believe that an English court would in fact deny a tracing remedy against a thief: see Goff and Jones, *Law of Restitution* (3rd ed.), at pp. 71–72.]

It is noteworthy that this resulting trust analysis has since found favour in New South Wales, as a preferred explanation for the *Black* decision.[281] This places potential equitable tracing claims against a defendant converter on a more conventional footing. So far as subsequent recipients are concerned, there are well established principles of equitable liability for knowing receipt, and of the defence of being 'equity's darling', in English law.[282] Having identified the potential for equitable claims to arise out of some factual situations which also disclose a Conversion, there is no need for a work concerning the latter to stray further into the territory of equity.

---

[278] [1948] Ch 465.

[279] [1981] Ch 105.

[280] P Millett, 'Tracing the Proceeds of Fraud' (1991) 107 *LQR* 71 at 75–76 (authors' emphasis).

[281] *Robb Evans of Robb Evans & Associates v European Bank Ltd* [2004] NSWCA 82, 61 NSWLR 75 per Spigelman CJ at [112] and [116], speaking of a 'presumed or resulting trust'.

[282] Often referred to as the first limb of *Barnes v Addy* ((1874) LR 9 Ch App 244). See DJ Hayton (ed), *Underhill & Hayton, Law Relating to Trusts and Trustees*, 17th edn (London, Butterworths, 2006) at article 100(4), paras 100.52–100.86; *Westdeutsche Landesbank Girozentrale v Islington London Borough Council* [1996] AC 669 per Lord Browne-Wilkinson at 705C–6C and 707B–9G; *Bank of Credit and Commerce International (Overseas) Ltd v Akindele* [2001] Ch 437 (CA); *Dubai Aluminium Co Ltd v Salaam and ors* [2002] UKHL 48, [2003] 2 AC 366 at [87] per Lord Millett; *Robb Evans v European Bank* (ibid) per Spigelman CJ at [160].

Conclusions

The issues which result from the hybrid nature of Conversion are particularly apparent in the context of its remedies. The intuitive difficulties associated with holding 'innocent' defendants liable in tort has, for instance, led to a notable judicial suggestion that there should be a dual response to wrongful interference with assets, with a more lenient approach being taken where fault is not a factor,[283] and to an incipient tendency to attach little weight to the proprietary role of Conversion when assessing damages.[284]

It would be a matter for concern were such developments to lead to a dilution of the strict liability standard which Conversion has historically employed. Strict liability is not a creature unknown to the law of torts, and we would suggest that the difficulties with Conversion's strict liability standard are rooted in generic reservations about that standard per se, rather than being related to its place within the law of tort, a fortiori torts whose role is the protection of proprietary interests. Since strict liability has an undoubted purpose to serve, and a valuable role to play within the law,[285] such reservations should not be allowed to negate its effects without good reason.

As we have made clear elsewhere, the imposition of a particular liability standard merely determines where the burden of responsibility for actions should fall;[286] a negligence standard exhorts us all to be careful in whatever we do; a strict liability standard, on the other hand, tells us that if we cause something to happen, we will be held responsible for it. Since we are all potential causes of such events, as well as potential 'victims' of the same, the imposition of a strict liability standard has the effect of putting the responsibility for ensuring a particular outcome on one party rather than the other. Where the protection of property interests is concerned, strict liability means that this burden falls on the potential interferer rather than the rightful possessor. Any dilution of this standard has the effect of blurring what is otherwise a clear and definitive guideline for behaviour: one deals with personal property at one's peril.[287] Such a clear rule gives anyone dealing with property the strongest incentive to investigate title as fully as possible. Quite apart from matters of principle with regard to proprietary rights, logistically this seems the most pragmatic approach, for it would be far less practicable, in the absence of a scheme of registration of title to personal property, to expect a possessor of assets to ensure that everyone knows

---

[283] See text to nn 178–80.

[284] See text to nn 13 and 14; contrast text to n 15.

[285] See P Cane, *The Anatomy of Tort Law* (Oxford, Hart Publishing, 1997) at 45–49 and T Honoré, *Responsibility and Luck*, (Oxford, Hart Publishing, 2002) at 23–32.

[286] See ch 3 under the side-heading The Requisite Conduct of the Defendant, Intention, Innocent Converters.

[287] See ch 2, text to fn 234 and ch 3, text to nn 133–34.

at all times which personal property belongs to him. Particularly given Conversion's ultimate aim of protecting property interests, therefore, there are strong grounds, even in the context of its tortious aspect, for it to attract strict liability.

Such is the position with regard to liability. The same does not necessarily apply, however, to the extent of damages for which a defendant in Conversion should be held liable, and there may be something to be said for not allowing *all* of the loss resulting from a Conversion to fall on a morally innocent defendant. As advocated by Lord Nicholls in *Kuwait Airways*, employing a 'softer', or less stringent, remoteness test in situations in which the defendant has not been at fault might be one way in which the otherwise arguably harsh effects of Conversion could be modified.[288]

Similarly, there is nothing fundamentally objectionable in the statutory provisions which provide for allowance for 'improvements' etcetera having to be given, when quantifying remedies in Conversion, to defendants who have acted in good faith.

The fact that the primary purpose of Conversion is to protect property interests provides the clearest justification for most of the other rules outlined above. As pointed out in chapter three, the gist of Conversion is the deprivation of a claimant's possessory rights in an asset.[289] Since these rights include the ability to keep, use and dispose of her assets, it seems right to presume *against the interferer* that the rightful possessor might have exercised any of these rights at any time, thereby perhaps hiring them out on the most preferential terms, or selling them before a fall in the market. There is no discernible reason why someone who has had her property rights interfered with should have the burden of displacing the contrary presumption, which would operate in favour of a wrongful interferer.

In practical terms at least, there would seem to be little advantage to be gained from engaging in what could only, given the inherently hybrid nature of Conversion, be a semantic debate as to whether the remedies for Conversion are tortious rather than proprietary or vice versa. Whilst damages in tort generally look to what the claimant has lost rather than to what she is owed, proprietary claims certainly do not exclude loss as a measure, and may give rise to the recovery of consequential loss.[290]

On a different point, it seems clear that the law has yet properly to deal with the consequences of the no doubt well-intended, but in the event perhaps somewhat unhelpful, annexation of classic detinue remedies onto the cause of

---

[288] Clerk & Lindsell (n 34) at para 2–112 notes this somewhat radical development with no apparent reservation.

[289] See ch 3 under the heading The Gist of Conversion.

[290] It was, for example accepted in *OBG Ltd v Allan* that any loss which as a matter of fact resulted from trespass to a company's land committed by invalidly appointed receivers would be recoverable as consequential loss, thereby explaining at least some of the Canadian receivership cases there cited—see [2005] EWCA Civ 106, [2005] QB 762 at [39] and [55] per Peter Gibson LJ and [77] and [92] per Mance LJ.

action for Conversion. The difficulties and absence of clarity encountered to date have been amply illustrated in our discussion of *IBL Ltd v Coussens*.[291]

---

[291] See text to nn 21–30 and 53–62.

8

Conclusion

I N THIS BOOK we have analysed the key elements of Conversion, with a view to providing both a clarification of its operation and functions, and suggestions as to how it should be developed, particularly in order to keep pace with social and technological advances. The work has turned out to be something of a defence of Conversion, although this was certainly not our intention at the outset. Although Conversion, in its current state, is not without aspects in need of reform, the analysis in this book leads us to the conclusion that it is, at a fundamental level, an action well suited to its purpose. The fact that Conversion is a creature peculiar to common law is something which could be, and has been,[1] taken to suggest that the common law is somehow deficient in this regard. We conclude that, on the contrary, the protection offered by the common law to property interests is as comprehensive as that provided by comparable systems. In order to understand this, however, it is essential to recognise that Conversion plays only one role within a set of actions for wrongful interference which, in combination, form an effective means of protecting personal property interests.[2] It is perhaps the dearth of scholarship relating to this system of title to personal property and its protection which represents the true deficiency,[3] in that an insufficient understanding of Conversion, and the context of the property torts within which it operates, appears substantially to contribute to the impression that it is not 'fit for purpose'.

It was one of the principal objectives of this book to provide a working definition of Conversion; one that could be applied to factual situations as yet unfamiliar to a court, in order that it might identify the presence or absence of a

---

[1] T Weir, *A Casebook on Tort*, 10th edn (London, Sweet & Maxwell, 2004) at 483–87, N Curwen, 'The Remedy in Conversion: Confusing Property and Obligation' (2006) 26 *Legal Studies* 570 at 570 and AKR Kiralfy, 'The Problem of a Law of Property in Goods' (1949) 12 *Modern Law Review* 424.

[2] Or at least, they do in formal terms. Of course, there are gaps in this protection, owing to a measure of misinterpretation of the rules relating to those actions; these are outlined primarily in ch 5 and below.

[3] See P Birks, 'Personal Property: Proprietary Rights and Remedies' (2000) 11 *King's College Law Journal* 1 at 2.

Conversion, even in situations which it is not yet possible to anticipate.[4] In chapter three, such a definition was given: we outlined three elements requisite for the tort:

1 the claimant must have had the superior possessory right in the asset;
2 the defendant's action must have deprived the claimant of the full benefit of that possessory right; and
3 the defendant must have assumed that possessory right.

Where, and only where, *all* of these elements are present, will there be a Conversion; there are no additional requirements. Conversion is thus, as we have argued, a far simpler concept than is often perceived. A general recognition of this point will, we hope, mean that Conversion will no longer be 'the forgotten tort'[5] and that, as a consequence, its development will be more coherent and more likely to ensure that it remains relevant and effective in a contemporary context.

This work has not only demonstrated that Conversion is generally fit for the purpose to which it is directed, but has also highlighted several issues pertaining to it which have yet to be fully resolved.

The first of these relates not directly to Conversion, but to the manner in which it has been interpreted and applied. As was made clear in chapter five, it is essential for the enduring worth of the action that it be applied in such a way as to ensure that it fulfils its role as the common law's primary means of protecting personal property. In order for this to happen, the subject matter of the tort must not be unduly restricted on out-dated grounds. Currently, judicial decisions about what can and cannot be subject to a Conversion are made on the assumption, derived from the long history of the common law, and of this tort in particular, that it applies only to assets susceptible of being lost and found; these in turn are generally equated to 'goods' by virtue of the use and definition of that term in the Torts (Interference with Goods) Act 1977, notwithstanding that it was *not* a codifying statute. Section 14(1) of the 1977 Act defines 'goods' as 'all things personal other than things in action and money'. Both of these sources, however, were formulated in such a way, and at such a time, as to preclude any consideration of many of the types of asset which have come to feature prominently in the contemporary economic environment. The time has come for these rules to be revised so that the protection of the common law is no longer denied to a substantial proportion of the valuable assets of individuals and businesses alike. The recent House of Lords decision in *OBG Ltd v Allan*[6] suggests, however, that such revision is unlikely to be achieved by judicial means. It would seem, therefore, that Baroness Hale's suggestion in that case that the cause now be taken

---

[4] Such as those involving technology as yet undeveloped.
[5] WL Prosser, 'The Nature of Conversion' (1957) 42 *Cornell Law Quarterly* 168 at 168.
[6] *OBG Ltd and anor v Allan and ors* and two other cases [2007] UKHL 21, [2008] AC 1. See ch 5 for a full discussion of the judgment and its underlying issues.

up by the Law Commission[7] is a sensible one, and one with which, having considered the issue at length, we would wholeheartedly agree. Statutory reform, if carefully implemented, could ensure that the historical baggage which seems to have hindered Conversion's judicial development for so long, could finally be discarded.

Another contention of this work has been that, where Conversion is concerned, the term 'goods' should be replaced by the broader, and therefore more contextually accurate, term 'assets'. As pointed out in the introductory chapter, the latter term is more conducive to an approach which does not automatically exclude from the scope of Conversion those assets which, whilst they might be intangible, are nonetheless susceptible to possession. A more sophisticated and contemporary, but nevertheless entirely principled, approach to the ambit of Conversion, has already been offered by the Ohio Court of Appeals, which suggested that 'the correct approach is to analyze the particular type of intangible asset, to see if allowing a conversion claim makes sense'.[8] As chapter six has already argued, the protection of intangible property should, and must, be achieved through the medium of Conversion since the economic torts are not appropriate for filling the gaps in the protection of such property caused by an out-dated and misguided approach to what the law can properly recognise as being the subject matter of a Conversion.

Many of the other issues relating to Conversion stem, it would seem, from its hybrid nature, and the difficulties presented in some contexts by there being no clear means of identifying it either as a tort or as a property claim.[9] On the one hand, it could be argued that the precise classification of such a claim is irrelevant; that the label applied to a cause of action is not important as long as the purpose of that claim is served. In general terms, this may be true, but, as the following paragraphs show, it will sometimes be important to provide an answer to the classification question. Our view, formed as result of our analysis in this book, is that the hybrid nature of Conversion is something which should be both acknowledged and accepted, since both aspects of the action are important to its overall juristic function. Consequently, we do not see anything undesirable or problematic in Conversion being classified as a tort for some purposes, and as a property claim for others.

One such classification issue relates to the remedies currently available for Conversion. At the moment, any *in specie* recovery of assets is dependent upon either the discretion of the court (under a form (a) order), or the election of the defendant (under a form (b) order), rather than being something which the claimant in a successful Conversion action can expect as of right.[10] Since *in specie*

---

[7]   ibid at [316].

[8]   *Shafer v RMS Realty* 138 Ohio App 3d 244 (2000) at 285.

[9]   Both elements of which are discussed in ch 5.

[10]   See s 3 of the Torts (Interference with Goods) Act 1977 and ch 7 under the heading Other Remedies.

recovery will usually be awarded where it is appropriate, given the unique nature of the specific assets, or their particular intrinsic worth to the claimant, at least in the circumstances prevailing at the time,[11] it might be argued that the discretionary approach is all that is required properly to safeguard possessors' rights. After all, where such assets hold no such significance for their possessor, and so can be replaced, the claimant will lose nothing by being awarded their market value in damages. Whilst any *in specie* recovery remains discretionary and not automatic, however, there are implications for any claimant in the event of the tortfeasor's insolvency, since a claim for damages alone ranks only as a personal claim, and therefore lower in priority than a proprietary claim, which is what a claimant would have, had she been awarded *in specie* recovery. Consequently, the effects of this discretionary remedy would appear to be potentially arbitrary in this particular context, and difficult to justify.

Despite, therefore, chapter three's argument that the remedies available for Conversion are in fact broader than those provided by the *vindicatio*,[12] this is not achieved without there being some inconsistency in protection, albeit only in the narrow context of the tortfeasor's insolvency. This resulted from the 1977 Act's elision of the torts of detinue and Conversion and the consequent merger of their respective remedies under the latter action, as explained in chapter seven. Before this, *in specie* recovery was only available for detinue and never for Conversion, thereby precluding the possibility of inconsistent treatment for claimants bringing the same action. That is not to suggest, however, that the possibility of *in specie* recovery should be removed from the list of possible remedies available for Conversion, but merely that some thought should be given to how to avoid the potential inconsistencies which currently exist. One suggestion, which would, of course, need to be achieved by legislative means, would be to recognise the proprietary basis of Conversion claims by establishing that all awards made under this head are to be given priority in the event of insolvency. Whilst we acknowledge that there has to be a balance struck between the interests of different creditors in insolvency situations and that, consequently, the prioritising of one claim means the potential reduction in the real value of another, every award made for Conversion is made in recognition of a property interest; interests which are already given precedence in such situations. The equal treatment of damages and *in specie* awards would not, therefore, be at odds with the current principles of distribution in the event of insolvency, but would rid personal property law of an inconsistency the existence of which is difficult to justify.

The classification question is also an important one for the purposes of private international law, in which the choice of law rules which are to be applied to a

---

[11] See, eg, *Whiteley Ltd v Hilt* [1918] 2 KB 808 (CA) and *Howard E Perry & Co Ltd v British Railways Board* [1980] 1 WLR 1375.

[12] The action with which Conversion is often unfavourably compared; see ch 3, under the heading *Relationship to Vindicatio*.

claim will depend on whether that claim is viewed as tortious or proprietary.[13] It is Dickinson's conclusion that Conversion should for these purposes be regarded as a claim in tort, because the

> essence of the claimant's action ... is not to vindicate his proprietary entitlement, which may not be in doubt, but instead to establish the defendant's responsibility for the consequences of his own conduct in dealing with the claimant's property[14]

In choice of law terms, it is the nature of *the obligation* which is material,[15] and so the fact that the standard remedy in Conversion is damages, rather than delivery up of the asset concerned, is of no relevance to the classification question in this context.[16] Rather, the available remedy is something which is determined by the applicable law once it has been identified,[17] and so to allow the nature of the remedy to play any role in the choice of law equation would be to put the cart before the horse. Notwithstanding our conclusions on the issues above, therefore, this would seem to be the better view for the purposes of classification within private international law. Another reason for this conclusion is that the rules about title to sue in Conversion give precedence to possessory rights over proprietary rights, which caused Goode to declare that Conversion is '*possessory*, not *proprietary*, in character' (his emphasis).[18] As the reader will appreciate from the discussion in chapters three and especially four, Conversion, in its current discrete state, resembles a tort in that it is only available to the individual with the immediate possessory right to an asset, and not to anyone with a superior proprietary, but lesser possessory, interest. It is concerned, in other words, with what one has lost, rather than with what one is owed. Anyone with a superior proprietary interest, such as a bailor where the term of the bailment has not yet expired,[19] must sue for reversionary injury, currently an action separate from Conversion. Moreover, Conversion is available not just against anyone who still

---

[13] See A Dickinson, *The Rome II Regulation: The Law Applicable to Non-Contractual Obligations*, (Oxford, Oxford University Press, 2008) at paras 3.92–3.95 and L Collins et al (eds), *Dicey, Morris & Collins: The Conflict of Laws*, 14th edn, 2nd supp (London, Sweet & Maxwell, 2008) at para S35–177.

[14] Dickinson, *Rome II* (2008) at para 3.94. The consequence of such a classification is, of course, that such claims fall within the Rome II Regulation. See, however, J Fawcett and JM Carruthers (eds), *Cheshire, North and Fawcett, Private International Law*, 14th edn (Oxford, Oxford University Press, 2008) at 794 for the opposing view.

[15] Art 1(1) Rome II Regulation.

[16] For an analogous argument in respect of constructive trusts, see Collins, *Dicey, Morris & Collins* (2008) at para S34–044.

[17] Art 15(c) of the Rome II Regulation.

[18] RM Goode, 'The Right to Trace in Commercial Transactions—I' (1976) 92 *Law Quarterly Review* 360 at 364.

[19] See ch 3 generally, and particularly under the side-heading The Relationship between the Wrongful Interference Torts, Reversionary Injury.

has possession of the converted asset, but against anyone who ever has interfered with a claimant's possessory rights over it.[20]

Another problem linked to the classification of Conversion has been identified by Battersby,[21] and it arose as a result of the Law Commission's Consultation Paper on 'The Illegality Defence in Tort'.[22] In that paper, the Commission expressed the provisional conclusion that the illegality defence should have the same effect, whether a tort relates to the claimant's person or to his property. As Battersby points out, however, such a solution is not as simple as it sounds:

> It is one thing to say, for example, that a claimant who suffers injury while carrying out a crime on the defendant's premises should be precluded from recovering compensation from the defendant; there the effect of the illegality is purely negative in barring a claim. It is quite another thing to say that illegality should bar a possessor's claim to recover property, for there the effect of barring the claimant's remedy is to improve the defendant's proprietary rights; ie the effect of the illegality is both negative and positive. The truth is that English law is to some extent mistaken in classifying conversion as a tort; it is mainly used as an action for the vindication of proprietary rights, and could be correctly viewed as belonging to the law of property rather than to the law of torts.[23]

Whilst we do not, for the reasons outlined above, agree with Battersby's assertion that English law is 'mistaken' in regarding a claim in Conversion as a tort, we do concur with his view that, since Conversion has proprietary effects, these should be reflected in its treatment. There is no need, therefore, for it to be treated in the same way as those torts which do not have proprietary implications. This in itself should not be problematic; the diversity of interests protected by the law of torts as a whole means that it is far from unusual (or particularly difficult) to apply different rules to different torts.[24]

Whilst our approach might seem inconsistent, in substance it is not. Essentially, it results in a classification of the Conversion *claim* as a tort, but of the Conversion *remedy* as proprietary, thereby acknowledging that Conversion is tortious in its cause and proprietary in its effects. This means that Conversion's hybrid nature is explicitly recognised and accommodated by both branches of the law to which it relates. Hopefully this will make it, in practical terms, a more effective action and, in theoretical terms, a legal concept more fully understood and accepted in both its tortious and its proprietary contexts/roles. Any intuitive difficulty with accepting such a dual classification is likely to be attributable to nothing more than its being something with which lawyers are not currently familiar. To allow the evolution of the law, however, to be influenced by such

[20] See also ch 3 under the side-heading The Requisite Conduct of the Defendant, Actions of the Defendant: Use and Possession.

[21] G Battersby, 'Acquiring Title by Theft' (2002) 65 *MLR* 603.

[22] Law Commission, 'The Illegality Defence in Tort' (Law Com Consultation Paper No 160, 2001).

[23] Battersby, Title by Theft (*MLR* 2002) at fn 39.

[24] Consider, eg, the non-availability of recovery for personal injury in private nuisance claims, despite this being an almost paradigmatic claim in negligence; or the fact that the remoteness rule for intentional torts is less restrictive than that for torts where intention is not a requisite element.

reservations, rather than by current exigencies, would be to relive the mistakes of the past, and to allow established form once more to haunt present substance.[25]

To complicate the issue further, the wrongful interference actions *in combination* look more proprietary than tortious, as they protect both immediate possessory interests and superior proprietary interests (the latter in the form of reversionary injury). Moreover, since liability is of course strict in this context, there would appear to be little to tell the wrongful interference actions *in toto* apart from proprietary actions. Were, therefore, the actions of trespass, reversionary injury and Conversion to be amalgamated, there might then be an argument for classifying them *jointly* as proprietary actions, at least in those circumstances in which the issue is material.[26]

Indeed, any revision of Conversion would not be complete without a simultaneous consideration of the other wrongful interference torts. In 1977, Parliament decided against the amalgamation of all of these torts under one umbrella action of 'wrongful interference with moveables', a course of action which had been suggested by the Law Reform Committee.[27] Arguably, there was good reason for its rejection of such a move, particularly since section 1 of the 1977 Act makes reference not only to Conversion and trespass, but also to negligence and 'any other tort so far as it results in damage to goods or to an interest in goods'. Clearly, negligence liability is a completely different creature to the strict liability torts of Conversion and trespass, and there would appear to be nothing to be gained from treating Conversion and 'any other tort so far as it results in damage to goods'[28] as if they were substantively similar actions.[29] There is, however, less of an immediately obvious response to the question of whether trespass to goods and reversionary injury should be subsumed within an expanded wrongful interference action (whether or not it ultimately be labelled 'Conversion').[30] Nevertheless, as we have made clear, the substance of Conversion, with its ability to protect possessory interests over superior proprietary interests where appropriate, must be retained. This, in its entirety, is a discussion clearly beyond the parameters of the current book, but, were the Law Commission or Parliament to revisit the wrongful interference torts, as we hope they will, this would certainly be a pertinent issue for their attention.

---

[25]   See ch 2, text to fn 207.

[26]   See also Curwen, Remedy (*LS* 2006) for the argument that detinue should be revived, and used as a dedicated proprietary action, whilst Conversion should be retained as a tort. In this context it should be remembered that detinue still exists as a separate action in several other common law jurisdictions, eg New South Wales.

[27]   The 18th Report (Conversion and Detinue) of the Law Reform Committee (1971), Cmnd 4774 at paras 27–30.

[28]   S 1(1), Torts (Interference with Goods) Act 1977.

[29]   See text to n 24.

[30]   Our conclusion that Conversion is, in its current form, fit for purpose, was not intended to preclude a consideration of whether its function might be expanded in order to encompass a broader remit of personal property protection; one means of achieving such an expansion which we consider worthy of consideration would be the creation of such a composite tort.

Ultimately, Conversion is a useful and important legal tool. At its current stage of development, however, there are certainly aspects of it which would benefit from rigorous and well-informed re-evaluation. We hope that this book will mark the beginning of that process.

Bibliography

Adams, JN, 'Trespass in a Digital Environment' [2002] *Intellectual Property Quarterly* 1

Ames, JB, 'The History of Trover' (1897) 11 *Harvard Law Review* 277 and 374

Anderson, L, and Hill, PJ, 'The Evolution of Property Rights: A Study of the American West' (1975) 18 *Journal of Law and Economics* 163

Anon, *The Law of Actions on the Case for Torts and Wrongs* (London, R Gosling, 1720)

Bainbridge, D, *Intellectual Property,* 6th edn (London, Longman, 2007)

Baker, JH, *An Introduction to English Legal History,* 4th edn (London, Butterworths, 2002)

—— and Milsom, SFC, *Sources of English Legal History* (London, Butterworths, 1986)

Balkin, RP and Davis, JLR, *Law of Torts,* 3rd edn (Sydney, Butterworths, 2004)

Battersby, G, 'Acquiring Title by Theft' (2002) 65 *Modern Law Review* 603

Bell, A, 'The Place of Bailment in the Modern Law of Obligations', ch 19 in NE Palmer and E McKendrick (eds), *Interests in Goods,* 2nd edn (London, LLP, 1998)

Bell, J, Boyron S, and Whittaker, S, *Principles of French Law,* 2nd edn (Oxford, Oxford University Press, 2007)

Bellewe, R, *Abridgment* (London, R Robinson, 1585)

Bender, D, 'Trade Secret Protection of Software' (1970) 39 *George Washington Law Review* 909

Benson, P, 'The Basis for Excluding Liability for Economic Loss in Tort Law' in D Owen (ed) *Philosophical Foundations of Tort Law* (Oxford, Oxford University Press, 1995)

Bentham, J, (Burns, JH, and Hart, HLA (eds)), *An Introduction to the Principles of Morals and Legislation* (London, Athlone Press, 1970)

Bentley, DJ, 'A New-Found Haliday: The Eighteenth Report of the Law Reform Committee (Conversion and Detinue)' (1972) 35 *Modern Law Review* 170

Birks, P, 'Personal Property: Proprietary Rights and Remedies' (2000) 11 *Kings College Law Journal* 1

——, *Unjust Enrichment,* 2nd edn (Oxford, Oxford University Press, 2005)

Blackstone, W, *Commentaries, Vol III Private Wrongs* (Oxford, Clarendon Press, 1768; reprinted Chicago, University of Chicago Press, 2001)

Bracton, *Treatise on the Law of England*

Bridge, MG, *Personal Property Law,* 3rd edn (Oxford, Oxford University Press, 2002)

——, *The International Sale of Goods: Law and Practice,* 2nd edn (Oxford, Oxford University Press, 2007)

——, *The Sale of Goods,* 2nd edn (Oxford, Oxford University Press, 2009)

Brooke, R, *Abridgement* (London, R Tottell, 1586)

Buckland, W, *Elementary Principles of the Roman Private Law* (Cambridge, Cambridge University Press, 1912)

Cane, P, 'Causing Conversion' (2002) 118 *Law Quarterly Review* 544

——, 'Mens Rea in Tort Law' (2000) 20 *Oxford Journal of Legal Studies* 533

————, *The Anatomy of Tort Law* (Oxford, Hart Publishing, 1997)

————, *Tort Law and Economic Interests*, 2nd edn (Oxford, Oxford University Press, 1996)

Carey Miller, DL, *Corporeal Moveables in Scots Law*, 2nd edn (Edinburgh, W Green, 2005)

Carty, H, 'An analysis of the modern action for breach of commercial confidence: when is protection merited?' (2008) 4 *Intellectual Property Quarterly* 416

————, 'OBG Ltd v Allan: the House of Lords shapes the economic torts and explores commercial confidences and image rights' (2007) 15 *Torts Law Journal* 283

————, 'The Need for Clarity in the Economic Torts' (2005) 16 *King's College Law Journal* 165

Caterina, R, 'Concepts and Remedies in the Law of Possession' (2004) 8 *Edinburgh Law Review* 267

Clerk & Lindsell on Torts, 16th edn (London, Sweet & Maxwell, 1989)

————, 19th edn (London, Sweet & Maxwell, 2006)

Cohen, JA, *Intangible Assets: Valuation and Economic Benefit* (New Jersey, Wiley & Sons, 2005)

Coke, E, *Book of Entries* (London, Societie of Stationers, 1614)

Conaglen, M, 'Thinking about proprietary remedies for breach of confidence' (2008) 1 *Intellectual Property Quarterly* 82

Cunnington, R, 'Contract Rights as Property Rights' in A Robertson (ed) *The Law of Obligations: Connections and Boundaries* (London, UCL Press, 2004)

Curwen, N, 'Title to Sue in Conversion' [2004] *Conveyancer and Property Lawyer* 308

————, 'The remedy in conversion: confusing property and obligation' (2006) 26 *Legal Studies* 570

Dalhuisen, JH, *Dalhuisen on Transnational and Comparative Commercial, Financial and Trade Law*, 3rd edn (Oxford, Hart Publishing, 2007)

Deakin, SF and Randall, JY, 'Rethinking the Economic Torts' (2009) 72 *Modern Law Review* 519

Demsetz, H, 'Towards a Theory of Property Rights' (1967) 57 *American Economic Review (Papers and Proceedings)* 347

Collins, L, et al (eds), *Dicey, Morris & Collins: The Conflict of Laws*, 14th edn, 2nd supp (London, Sweet & Maxwell, 2008)

Dickinson, A, *The Rome II Regulation: The Law Applicable to Non-Contractual Obligations*, (Oxford, Oxford University Press, 2008)

Douglas, S, 'Converting Contractual Rights' [2008] *Lloyd's Maritime and Commercial Law Quarterly* 129

————, 'The Abolition of Detinue' [2008] *Conveyancer and Property Lawyer* 30

Epstein, R, 'A Common Law for Labor Relations: a Critique of New Deal Labor Legislation' (1983) 92 *Yale Law Journal* 1357

Faust Jr, J, 'Distinction between Conversion and Trespass to Chattels' (1958) 37 *Oregon Law Review* 256

Fawcett, J and Carruthers, JM (eds), *Cheshire, North and Fawcett, Private International Law*, 14th edn (Oxford, Oxford University Press, 2008)

Fawcett, N, Harris, J, and Bridge, M, *International Sale of Goods in the Conflict of Laws* (Oxford, Oxford University Press, 2004)

Fifoot, CHS, *History & Sources of the Common Law* (London, Stevens & Sons, 1949)

Flannigan, R, 'The (fiduciary) duty of fidelity' (2008) 124 *Law Quarterly Review* 274

Fridman, GHL, QC, *The Law of Torts in Canada* Vol 1 (Toronto, Carswell, 1989)

Goff, R and Jones, G, *The Law of Restitution*, 7th edn (London, Sweet & Maxwell, 2007)

Goode, RM, 'The Right to Trace and its Impact on Commercial Transactions—I' (1976) 92 *Law Quarterly Review* 360

Gordon, DM, 'Anomalies in the Law of Conversion' (1955) 71 *Law Quarterly Review* 346

Gordley, J, *Foundations of Private Law: Property, Tort and Unjust Enrichment* (Oxford, Oxford University Press, 2008)

Gray, K, 'Property in Thin Air' [1991] *Cambridge Law Journal* 252

Green, S, 'Can A Digitized Product be the Subject of a Conversion?' [2006] *Lloyd's Maritime and Commercial Law Quarterly* 568

———, 'To Have and to Hold? Conversion and Intangible Property' (2008) 71 *Modern Law Review* 114

——— and Saidov, D, 'Software as Goods under the Sale of Goods Act and the CISG' [2006] *Journal of Business Law* 161

Griew, E, *The Theft Acts*, 7th edn (London, Sweet & Maxwell, 1995)

Halsbury's Laws of England, 4th edn Vol 45(2), 1999 reissue

Harding, CSP and Rowell, MS, 'Protection of Property versus Protection of Commercial Transactions in French and English Law' (1977) 26 *International & Commercial Law Quarterly* 354

Harris, DR, 'The Concept of Possession in English Law' in AG Guest (ed), *Oxford Essays in Jurisprudence* (Oxford, Oxford University Press, 1961)

Harris, J, *Property and Justice* (Oxford, Clarendon Press, 1996)

Hoffmann, L, 'Causation' (2005) 121 *Law Quarterly Review* 592

Hohfeld, WN, 'Some Fundamental Legal Conceptions as Applied in Judicial Reasoning' (1913) 23 *Yale Law Journal* 16

Holdsworth, WS, *A History of English Law Vol 1*, 7th edn eds AL Goodhart and HG Hanbury (London, Sweet & Maxwell, 1956)

———, *A History of English Law Vol VII*, 2nd edn (London, Sweet & Maxwell, 1937)

———, 'The History of the Treatment of Choses in Action by the Common Law' (1920) 33 *Harvard Law Review* 997

Honoré, T, 'Ownership' in AG Guest (ed), *Oxford Essays in Jurisprudence* (Oxford, Oxford University Press, 1961)

———, *Responsibility and Luck* (Oxford, Hart Publishing, 2002)

Howarth, D, 'Against Lumley v Gye' (2005) 68 *Modern Law Review* 195

Ibbetson, DJ, *A Historical Introduction to the Law of Obligations* (Oxford, Oxford University Press, 1999)

Kiralfy, AKR, *A Source Book of English Law* (London, Sweet & Maxwell, 1957)

———, *The Action on the Case* (London, Sweet & Maxwell, 1951)

———, 'The Problem of a Law of Property in Goods' (1949) 12 *Modern Law Review* 424

Kohler, P and Palmer, N, 'Information as Property', in N Palmer and E McKendrick (eds), *Interests in Goods*, 2nd edn (London, LLP, 1998)

Libling, D, 'The Concept of Property: Property in Intangibles' (1978) 94 *Law Quarterly Review* 103

Lipton, J, 'Property Offences into the 21st Century' (1999) 1 *Journal of Information, Law and Technology*; www2.warwick.ac.uk/fac/soc/law/elj/jilt/1999_1/lipton/

Magnusson, RS, 'Proprietary Rights in Human Tissue' in N Palmer and E McKendrick (eds), *Interests in Goods*, 2nd edn (London, LLP, 1998)

Markesinis, BS, and Hunberath, H, *The German Law of Torts: A Comparative Treatise*, 4th edn (Oxford, Hart Publishing, 2002)

Mattei, U, *Basic Principles of Property Law: A Comparative Legal and Economic Introduction* (Westport Connecticut, Greenwood Press, 2000)

Matthews, P, 'Freedom, Unrequested Improvements, and Lord Denning' [1981] *Cambridge Law Journal* 340

McCarthy, K, *Sex.Com* (London, Quercus, 2007)

McGregor, H, *McGregor on Damages*, 17th edn (London, Sweet & Maxwell, 2003)

Meisel, F, 'Return is No Conversion' [2004] *Conveyancer and Property Lawyer* 145

Millett, P, 'Tracing the Proceeds of Fraud' (1991) 107 *Law Quarterly Review* 71

Milsom, SFC, *Historical Foundations of the Common Law*, 2nd edn (London, Butterworths, 1981)

Napier, BW, 'The Future of Information Technology Law' [1992] *Cambridge Law Journal* 46

Newark, FH, 'The Boundaries of Nuisance' (1949) 65 *Law Quarterly Review* 480

Neyers, JW, 'Rights-based justifications for the tort of unlawful interference with economic relations' (2008) 28 *Legal Studies* 215

Nicholas, B, *An Introduction to Roman Law* (Oxford, Oxford University Press, 1962)

Nimmer, RT, 'International Information Transactions: An Essay on Law in an Information Society' (2000) 26 *Brooklyn Journal of International Law* 5

Nuffield Council of Bioethics, 'Human Tissue, Ethical and Legal Issues' (London, 1995)

Ogus, A, *Costs and Cautionary Tales: Economic Insights for the Law* (Oxford, Hart Publishing, 2006)

O'Sullivan, J, 'Intentional Economic Torts in the House of Lords' [2007] *Cambridge Law Journal* 503

Palmer, NE, 'The Application of the Torts (Interference with Goods) Act 1977 to Actions in Bailment' (1978) 41 *Modern Law Review* 629

——, 'The Vindication of Commercial Security over Commodities: Equitable Pledges and Conversion' [1986] *Lloyd's Maritime and Commercial Law Quarterly* 218

——, *Bailment*, 2nd edn (London, Sweet & Maxwell, 1991)

Penner, JE, *The Idea of Property in Law* (Oxford, Oxford University Press, 2003)

Pollock, F, *A First Book of Jurisprudence for Students of the Common Law* (London, Macmillan, 1896 (reprinted 1923))

——, *The Law of Torts*, 1st edn (London, Stevens & Sons, 1887)

—— and FW Maitland, *The History of English Law Vol 2*, 2nd edn (Cambridge, Cambridge University Press, 1898, reissued 1968)

—— and RS Wright, *An Essay on Possession in the Common Law* (Oxford, Clarendon Press, 1888)

Proctor, C, *Mann on the Legal Aspect of Money*, 6th edn (Oxford, Oxford University Press, 2005)

Prosser, WL, 'The Nature of Conversion' (1957) 42 *Cornell Law Quarterly* 168

Rastell, W, *Collection of Entries* (London, R Tottell, 1566)

Ricks, Val D, 'The Conversion of Intangible Property: Bursting the Ancient Trover Bottle with New Wine' (1991) 4 *Brigham Young University Law Review* 1681

Rodger, A, 'Spuilzie in the Modern World' [1970] *Scots Law Times (News)* 33

Rubin L, et al, 'Conversion of choses in action' (1941) 10 *Fordham Law Review* 415

Rudden, B, 'Things as Things and Things as Wealth' (1994) 14 *Oxford Journal of Legal Studies* 81

V Sacks' Note on the Torts (Interference with Goods) Act 1977 in (1978) 41 *Modern Law Review* 713

Salmond, JW, 'Observations on Trover and Conversion' (1905) 21 *Law Quarterly Review* 43

——, *The Law of Torts* (London, Stevens & Haynes, 1907)

——, *The Law of Torts*, 7th edn (London, Sweet & Maxwell, 1927)

——, *Salmond's Law of Torts*, 10th edn (London, Sweet & Maxwell, 1945)

Heuston, RVF, and Buckley, RA, (eds), *Salmond and Heuston on Torts*, 21st edn (London, Sweet & Maxwell, 1996)

Samuel, G, 'Wrongful Interference with Goods' (1982) 31 *International & Commercial Law Quarterly* 357

An Index and Paraphrase of Printed Year Book Reports, 1268–1535 (ed DJ Seipp) at www.bu.edu/law/seipp/

Simpson, AWB, 'The Introduction of the Action on Case for Conversion' (1959) 75 *Law Quarterly Review* 364

Soto, H de, *The Mystery of Capital* (London, Black Swan, 2000)

Steven, A, 'By the book: enrichment by interference' (2007) 11 *Edinburgh Law Review* 114

Stevens, R, *Torts and Rights* (Oxford, Oxford University Press, 2007)

Swadling, W, 'Ignorance and unjust enrichment: the problem of title' (2008) 28 *Oxford Journal of Legal Studies* 627

——, 'Rescission, Property, and the Common Law' (2005) 121 *Law Quarterly Review* 123

——, 'Unjust Delivery' in A Burrows and A Rodger (eds), *Mapping the Law: Essays in Memory of Peter Birks* (Oxford, Oxford University Press, 2006)

Tarrant, J, 'Property Rights to Stolen Money' (2005) 32 *University of Western Australia Law Review* 234

——, 'Theft Principle in Private Law' (2006) 80 *Australian Law Journal* 531

Tettenborn, A, 'Loss, Damage and Wrongful Detention' (1982) 132 *New Law Journal* 154

——, 'Conversion Damages Clarified' (1991) 141 *New Law Journal* 452

——, 'Conversion, Tort and Restitution' in N Palmer and E McKendrick (eds) *Interests in Goods*, 2nd edn (London, LLP, 1998)

——, 'Damages in Conversion—The Exception or the Anomaly?' [1993] *Cambridge Law Journal* 128

——, *Reversionary Damage to Chattels* [1994] *Cambridge Law Journal* 326

——, 'Trust Property and Conversion: An Equitable Confusion' [1996] *Cambridge Law Journal* 36

Thornely, JWA, 'New Torts for Old or Old Torts Refurbished?' [1977] *Cambridge Law Journal* 248

Ulpian, *Edict*

Hayton, DJ (ed), *Underhill & Hayton, Law Relating to Trusts and Trustees*, 17th edn (London, Butterworths, 2006)

Walker, DM, *Delict*, 2nd edn (Edinburgh, W Green, 1981)

——, *Principles of Scottish Private Law*, 4th edn (Oxford, Oxford University Press, 1988)

Warren, HD, *An Essay on Trover and Conversion* (Cambridge Mass., Harvard Law Review Association, 1936)

Watts, P, 'Self-appointed agents—liability in tort' (2007) 123 *Law Quarterly Review* 519

Weinrib, E, 'Information and Property' (1988) 38 *University of Toronto Law Journal* 117

Weir, T, *A Casebook on Tort*, 10th edn (London, Sweet & Maxwell, 2004)

——, 'Doing Good by Mistake—Restitution and Remedies' [1973] *Cambridge Law Journal* 23

——, *Tort Law* (Oxford, Oxford University Press, 2002)

Williams on Saunders, 6th edn ed E Vaughan Williams (London, W Benning & Co, 1845)

Worthington, S, *Equity*, 2nd edn (Oxford, Oxford University Press, 2006)

Index

Introductory Note

References such as '138–9' indicate (not necessarily continuous) discussion of a topic across a range of pages. Wherever possible in the case of topics with many references, these have either been divided into sub-topics or only the most significant discussions of the topic are listed. Because the entire volume is about 'Conversion', the use of this term (and certain others occurring throughout the work) as an entry point has been minimised. Information will be found under the corresponding detailed topics.

231